Multinationals and Global Capitalism

Multinationals and Global Capitalism

From the Nineteenth to the Twenty-first Century

Geoffrey Jones

OXFORD

UNIVERSITY PRESS

OXFORD
UNIVERSITY PRESS

Great Clarendon Street, Oxford OX2 6DP

Oxford University Press is a department of the University of Oxford.
It furthers the University's objective of excellence in research, scholarship,
and education by publishing worldwide in

Oxford New York

Auckland Cape Town Dar es Salaam Hong Kong Karachi Kuala Lumpur
Madrid Melbourne Mexico City Nairobi New Delhi Shanghai Taipei Toronto

With offices in

Argentina Austria Brazil Chile Czech Republic France Greece
Guatemala Hungary Italy Japan South Korea Poland Portugal
Singapore Switzerland Thailand Turkey Ukraine Vietnam

Published in the United States
by Oxford University Press Inc., New York

British Library Cataloguing in Publication Data
Data available

Library of Congress Cataloging in Publication Data
Data available

ISBN 0–19–927209–3
ISBN 0–19–927210–7 (pbk.)

1 3 5 7 9 10 8 6 4 2

Typeset by Kolam Information Services Pvt Ltd, Pondicherry, India
Printed in Great Britain
on acid-free paper by
Antony Rowe Ltd,
Chippenham, Wiltshire

■ PREFACE

This book examines the role of entrepreneurs and firms in the creation of the global economy over the last two centuries. It is a radically revised edition of my *The Evolution of International Business*, published in 1996, which has remained the only history of the development and impact of multinationals worldwide. There have been tumultuous political and economic changes over the past decade. When *Evolution* was first published, globalization was not the topic of everyday conversation and concern which it has become more recently. This new book reflects the many changes that have occurred over the last decade, as well as a proliferation of new research, which it aims to make accessible to a wider audience.

The text has been written with the specific intent of making the latest research in business history and international business available to non-specialists, and students taking a range of courses in business, management, economics and the social sciences more generally. The Appendices at the end of the book include a listing of the world's fifty largest non-financial multinationals at the beginning of the twenty-first century, a glossary of key terms – which are emboldened where first mentioned in the text – and a time line of decisive events in the evolution of global capitalism over the last two centuries. The brief case studies are intended to provide real world examples of central issues and leading firms, complementing and breaking up the text.

I have discussed the ideas and research in this book with colleagues in many different countries. I would like to acknowledge a number of special debts. Mira Wilkins remains my constant adviser and source of inspiration on all aspects of the history of multinationals, as well as a wonderful friend. David Merrett has once again read my text, and provided wise and critical guidance at just the right moment. Fabienne Fortanier greatly improved the arguments in the book. I have always learned much from discussions with Jean-François Hennart, Keetie E. Sluyterman, and Ken'ichi Yasumuro.

I would like to thank my former academic colleagues in business history and international business at the University of Reading, including Tony Corley, Mark Casson, John H. Dunning, Teresa Lopes, and Denise Tsang, for sharing their research and insights on the history and theory of multinational enterprise. At the Harvard Business School, where I moved permanently in 2002, Laura Alfaro, Pankaj Ghemawat, Jeff Fear, Tarun Khanna, Tom McCraw, and Richard Tedlow have been important influences on my thinking, as have several classes of MBA students. Alfred D. Chandler Jr has always been an inspiration.

Linda Kelly-Hayes worked hard on getting the manuscript ready for publication. I should thank Rattana and Dylan most of all for surviving the experience of living with an author.

Geoffrey Jones
June 2004
Cambridge, Mass.

■ CONTENTS

■ LIST OF FIGURES

■ LIST OF TABLES

LIST OF BOXES

PART I

Frameworks

1 Concepts

1.1 Business and globalization

This book is concerned with the role of multinationals in the creation of global capitalism over the past two centuries. Multinationals are firms that operate in more than one country. The central premise of this book is that they should be seen as one of the primary drivers of the flows of investment, trade, and knowledge across national borders, which are at the heart of the globalization process. It follows that it is essential to understand the historical evolution of multinationals in order to understand the nature and dynamics of globalization.

The book is organized in five parts. Part I provides a theoretical and historical context for understanding the role of multinationals in global capitalism. Part II shows how multinationals saw and exploited opportunities to create value by operating across borders in natural resources, manufacturing, and services. Part III shows how these firms learned to build organizations that functioned in multiple environments. Part IV examines the policy environment faced by multinationals which has shaped their growth and strategies. Part V reviews the historical evidence on the economic, social and political impact of multinationals.

1.2 Globalization debates

Globalization remains a highly contested subject. Countries and regions have become linked by complex flows of trade and investment. As a result, globalization has become part of the reality of the daily life of people in a way unimaginable even two decades ago. Both a blue-collar worker in Michigan and an IT software engineer in California now work in an environment where their jobs might be 'outsourced' overnight to another continent. The growth of globalization has resulted in unprecedented contacts between **cultures**, but it has not yet diminished clashes between them. The terrorist attack on September 11, 2001 demonstrated that globalization was far from a guarantor of peace and harmony.

The phenomenon of globalization has attracted a vast literature. There are many definitions. The geographer Harvey (1989) sees it as the 'compression' of time and space. The sociologist Guillén (2001) defined it as 'a process leading to greater independence and mutual awareness (reflexivity) among economic, political, and social units in the world, and among actors in general'. The economists Bordo, Taylor, and Williamson (2001) identify its most important characteristic as the between-country integration of commodity, labor, and capital markets. The management scholar Kogut (1997) regards globalization as 'the process of increasing integration in world civilization'.

There are at least three major debates concerning this 'process of increasing integration'. The first concerns the origins and extent of globalization. There is almost universal agreement that the process has a history, but there are different views whether it should be traced back to the decades after World War II, or to the nineteenth century, or to the first circumnavigation of the Earth in the sixteenth century, or the Ancient World (Moore and Lewis 1999). Nor is there a consensus on the extent of globalization today. Some see the world becoming 'borderless' (Ohmae 1990). Others regard such claims as premature, if not fallacious (Wade 1996; Ghemawat 2001).

Secondly, there are debates about the causes of globalization. It has sometimes been treated as primarily determined by the development of new technologies in communication and transportation. Yet governments and firms have been at least as important as actors (Kogut 1997). This raises the issue of the 'inevitability' of globalization. Historically, the 'integration' of world civilizations has not been a linear process. Some historians see the collapse of the international economy in the interwar years as demonstrating how today's global economy could also be reversed (James 2001).

Thirdly, there are many debates about the consequences of globalization. Although some have seen globalization as a force for convergence between countries, it is generally accepted that there is more inequality between countries now than 100 years ago. Is globalization promoting the convergence or divergence of incomes between countries and within countries? Globalization has been seen as eroding the sovereignty of nation states (Strange 1996; Kobrin 1997). Others regard such claims as highly exaggerated (Fligstein 2001). Sociologists debate whether mass consumerism is homogenizing cultures of the world. Is a global culture in the making? (Guillén 2001)

This book examines the role of multinationals in globalization. From this perspective it provides new insights into the origins, causes, and impact of this process. The remainder of Chapter 1 reviews the theoretical and conceptual literature on multinationals. This will provide a set of tools to explain the historical process, and a set of hypotheses to be tested by the historical evidence.

1.3 Concepts of the multinational enterprise

Although firms began investing across borders on a substantial scale in the nineteenth century, the term 'multinational enterprise' only appeared in the second half of the twentieth century. In 1958 the French economist Maurice Byé coined the expression 'multi-territorial firm' (Dunning 1993). In 1960 David E. Lilienthal, one-time head of the Tennessee Valley Authority in the United States, delivered a paper on the problems of US corporations with overseas operations, which he defined as 'multinational corporations' (Fieldhouse 1986). Subsequently a number of other terms have been used to describe them (see Box 1.1).

Box 1.1 Defining multinationals

A multinational is a firm that controls operations or income-generating assets in more than one country. Multinationals are owned in their **home economy** and invest in **host economies**. It has sometimes been suggested that multinationality requires operations in a minimum number of countries, usually five or six, or that a firm active across borders should be a certain size before it can be called a multinational, but there are enormous problems with such restrictive conditions. Since the 1970s the United Nations has used the term *transnational* to describe the same phenomenon. Firms with particularly extensive international operations have sometimes been described as *global*.

A firm whose sole international involvement is the exporting of goods or services from its home base is not a multinational. A multinational engages in one of two types of foreign investment. **Portfolio investment** involves the acquisition of foreign securities by individuals or institutions without any control over the management of the foreign entity. **Foreign direct investment** (FDI) involves management control. Multinationals engage in FDI because they own and control assets in foreign countries. They may do this either through acquiring an existing firm or by making a **greenfield investment** involving the establishment of a completely new operation.

The most straightforward example of multinational investment occurs when a company establishes a wholly owned subsidiary in a foreign country. However, there are a range of intermediate and alternative contractual modes available between wholly owned foreign subsidiaries and exporting, involving both equity and non-equity arrangements. Firms may share ownership in a **joint venture**. Nonequity arrangements include **licensing**, which involves a contract between independent firms to transfer technologies, rights or resources; **franchising**, when a company grants another company the right to do business in a certain way over a certain period of time in a specified place; **cartels**, which are agreements between independent firms to maintain prices or limit output, and **strategic alliances**, which are arrangements between firms to share facilities or cooperate in new product development.

(*Source*: Caves 1996.)

In 1800, only a small number of business enterprises owned and managed assets in more than one country, although many were engaged in international trade. Two hundred years later there were at least 60 000 multinationals worldwide, controlling more than 800 000 affiliates. There were a small number of corporate giants with businesses spanning the globe, but most multinationals employed fewer than 250 people.

Crossing borders raises major strategic and organizational issues for firms. This is because they encounter alien policies, cultures, languages and laws. As a result, foreign firms experience the 'liability of foreignness' (Zaheer 1995). The scale of this 'liability' rests on the distance between the home economy of a multinational and the host economy. Distance increases costs and risks. Ghemawat (2001) identified four dimensions of distance: political; geographical; economic; and cultural. Political distance includes the multiple barriers to foreign trade and investment flows which governments have traditionally maintained. Geographical distance includes not only the physical distance between countries, but also a country's transportation and infrastructure. Economic distance includes the income differences between countries, as well as differences in supply chains and distribution channels. Cultural distance includes differences in language, religious and ethical beliefs, and social norms. Cultures may differ in their levels of 'trust' (Casson 1991a). These differences affect the nature of markets in different countries, and shape the organization of firms and the behavior of managers (see Box 1.2).

The most usual quantitative measure of multinationals is FDI. However, there are serious methodological limitations with this measure (see Box 1.3). Moreover, the use of a financial measure provides a poor proxy for the total package of resources which multinationals transfer. It does not capture the dimensions of cross-border flows of knowledge or entrepreneurship. It says little about the quality of the investment.

Box 1.2 The impact of national culture on business

Cultures differ between countries. These differences impact business in multiple ways. National cultures are a set of values, expectations and behaviors that are learned, shared, and transmitted from one generation to another. They are typically associated with nation states, but countries such as India, Canada and Belgium contain multiple linguistic and cultural groups. All members of a national culture do not act in an identical fashion. National cultures overlap with regional cultures and firm cultures. Personality, economic status, social context, and other factors also determine the behavior of individuals. Cultural values may shift over time with economic conditions, technological shifts, and political interference, but as such values are typically transmitted through child-rearing practices, these shifts are rarely rapid.

The most extensive empirical research aimed at identifying national cultural differences and their impact on business is the research of Geerte Hofstede (1980). On the basis of over 100 000 answers to a questionnaire of IBM's worldwide workforce in 1967 and 1973, Hofstede identified four dimensions of culture which differed between countries: readiness to tolerate inequality (Power Distance); tolerance for uncertainty (Uncertainty Avoidance); relationships between the individual and the collective (Individualism); and attitudes towards gender roles (Masculinity). A subsequent study (Hofstede and Bond 1988) identified a fifth dimension involving short-term versus long-term orientation. Cultural values tended to be clustered.

Individualism was a characteristic of English-speaking and most other Western societies, while collectivism prevailed in most developing countries. Uncertainty avoidance was higher in German-speaking countries and in Japan than in English-speaking countries. Long-term orientation was found mostly in east Asian countries.

Hofstede and other cross-cultural theorists argue that culture has a pervasive influence on how firms are organized, business strategies, negotiations and human resource management. Cultural differences might explain national differences in the organization of firms, such as levels of hierarchy, and concluded that 'organizations are culture bound'. They suggest that different methods of motivation need to be used in different cultures. Individual incentives work well in individualist cultures, but in more collectivist cultures group incentives or paternalistic policies may motivate better.

(*Source*: Graham 2001; Hofstede 1996.)

> **Box 1.3 Foreign Direct Investment as a measure of multinationals**
>
> FDI is conventionally used as a proxy to quantify multinational investment, but it is very problematic. It is hard to define 'control'. There is no consensus on the minimum equity stake deemed necessary for 'control' of a foreign company to exist. In the US and France an investment is regarded as FDI if at least 10 percent of the equity is owned. In Germany and Britain the figure is 20 percent. There are drawbacks with measures of the *flows* and *stocks* of FDI. Measures of flows do not include direct investment financed from sources that do not pass through the country of the original investor, including capital markets in the host countries. Stock data is usually based on the historical value of an investment and not updated at market prices. Given that countries have varied widely in the timing of their direct investments, this introduces major distortions into international comparisons of FDI stocks.
>
> (*Source:* Bellak 1997; Stephan and Pfaffmann 2001/02.)

1.4 Multinationals in theory

1.4.1 Ownership and location advantages

The explanation for the existence of multinationals might seem obvious, in the sense that firms in the capitalist system seek profits, and investing in foreign countries could be seen as a logical way of making more money than staying in one country. However, there are a great many puzzles which need explaining. Not all firms in the world are multinational. Some industries are dominated by multinationals, others are not. While some countries own many multinationals and/or attract many foreign multinationals, other countries neither possess nor attract many multinationals.

Economic theorists were slow to seek explanations for the existence and characteristics of multinationals. A major difficulty was that the assumptions of mainstream neoclassical economic theory had the consequence of making all the issues raised by multinationals appear unimportant. The Heckscher–Ohlin theory, which sought to explain how a country's comparative advantage determined its trade, assumed atomistic competition, which meant that the issue of ownership did not matter, and that all technology was public, which meant that proprietary technology was also not an issue. As a result, the phenomenon of foreign firms moving technology and other assets between countries and controlling them across borders could not be identified as a matter requiring analysis. Mainstream economic theorists treated multinationals simply as arbitrageurs of capital, moving equity from countries where returns were low to those where it was higher (Dunning, Cantwell, and Corley 1986).

From the 1960s a series of theories sought to explain multinationals. These reflect the state of business and the intellectual climate of the time. Each approach retains some validity as a way of looking at the issue. The first major conceptual breakthrough came in a Ph.D. thesis at the Massachusetts Institute of Technology completed by Stephen Hymer in 1960. This thesis, which was entitled 'The International Operation of National Firms', asserted that FDI involved the transfer of a whole package of resources and not simply finance. This insight was the basis for much subsequent theoretical developments (Dunning 1993).

Beginning with the Hymer thesis, an underlying assumption of most theories of the multinational was that a firm required an 'advantage' over local firms in order to overcome the 'liability of foreignness'. In foreign markets, local firms were assumed to possess superior knowledge about the markets, resources, legal and political system, language, and culture. Foreign firms appeared to have no incentive to locate in such a market, or ability to survive in it, without an advantage.

This reasoning led to the view that a foreign firm required ownership (or competitive) advantages over its local rivals. There were many possible sources of advantage to foreign firms, including access to superior technology, information, knowledge, and know-how has been extremely important. The most tangible component of the technological advantage is access to new products and processes. This access might be protected by patents which prevent competitors copying or acquiring the technology. When technologies are standardized, the ability to differentiate products can be a significant source of advantage for a multinational. As a result, branding and product differentiation strategies can be an important source of advantage.

A second ownership advantage lies in superior management and organization techniques. These can arise from superior organizational structures compared to local rivals, or superior management techniques, such as better marketing skills or accounting methods. Advantages might also be derived from better trained or educated managers. Managerial and technological advantages are closely related and interdependent. The ability of a firm to innovate and generate new technology is critically dependent on its organization (Teece 1998).

A third source of ownership advantage can be found in access to finance. Multinationals might have access to cheaper capital than local competitors. This might arise from privileged access to capital markets which may not be so accessible to firms from certain countries, or from the large size of a multinational which enables it to borrow cheaply. In some countries where close relationships exist between banks and industrial companies, the latter might have privileged access to funding. Conversely, capital constraints can force divestments or otherwise have a major impact on the choice of contractual arrangements for international business operations (Casson 1987).

Further ownership advantages might be derived from the size of a firm. Multinationals, which are also large firms, possess an important source of market power because of **economies of scale**. The main advantages are derived from the centralization of research, marketing, finance, and other management functions that will not be available to smaller local competitors. According to a theory proposed by Knickerbocker (1973), multinational strategies can be understood in terms of the rivalry of oligopolistic firms which follow one another into new foreign markets as a defensive strategy.

Firms derive ownership advantages from privileged access to raw materials. This may arise from control over production of the material, or over processing, or over the final markets for raw materials. The availability of a mineral or other raw material in the home economy can generate ownership advantages for firms of that nationality, because they develop product-specific capabilities and knowledge which can be utilized elsewhere.

Firms can possess any number of these, or other, ownership advantages when they operate in a foreign market. The type of ownership advantage which may stimulate a foreign investment will differ considerably between products and industries. Within manufacturing, superior technology and innovative capacity are especially important in the case of production goods. Product differentiation will often be more important for consumer goods. Ownership advantages can be generated internally within the firm, or acquired by licensing a technology from a foreign competitor, or by buying an entire foreign firm.

Multinationals also derive ownership advantages from being multinational and from the ability to coordinate separate value-added activities across national boundaries. Multinationality can enhance operational flexibility by offering wider opportunities for global sources of input. It can provide more favored access to international markets. It can provide the ability to diversify or reduce risks. Ownership advantages derived from the possession of intangible assets and those derived from the common governance of geographically dispersed assets are conceptually different.

The existence of ownership advantages alone does not provide a convincing explanation for multinationals. A firm could exploit these advantages through exporting from its home country rather than engaging in FDI. To explain the choice of FDI over the alternative of exporting, a number of locational factors were identified. Locational factors within the host economy can be used to explain where they locate, and why a company should undertake FDI in a foreign country rather than exploit its ownership advantage by exporting.

Among the most important locational factors are **tariff** and nontariff barriers to trade. Insofar as exporting and local production represent two alternative ways of servicing a foreign market, measures that make exporting difficult will encourage local production, although a firm also has the option of withdrawing completely from supplying to a foreign country. Public policy impacts the locational decisions of multinationals in a variety of other ways. Governments can seek to attract foreign companies by offering subsidies, or else discourage them by restricting or prohibiting foreign participation in local industries. Government spending on physical infrastructure and educational facilities can make a country an attractive location for foreign investors. A government that is unable to provide a legal framework which offers security to foreign investors will contribute to the existence of a high-risk environment to which only risky or speculative investments will probably be attracted.

The nature of the host country market is often an important locational factor. The size and income level of a market, its growth and stage of development are important considerations. Firms can often have a better appreciation of the idiosyncrasies of a particular market if they manufacture in it rather than export to it. On the other hand, the adaptation of products to cater for differences in tastes may only be economic if the host country market is sufficiently large. Sometimes a particular host country may be an attractive location less for itself because of its membership of a wider free trade area or regional economic bloc. Another important locational factor can be differences in labor costs. In products in which labor costs form a significant proportion of total production costs, there might be incentive to transfer production to lower wage economies.

The spatial distribution of resource endowments is a critical locational factor for multinationals engaged in the exploitation of natural resources. In the case of nonrenewable resources such as mining and petroleum, there is a fundamental difference from manufacturing or service industries because the location of mines or oil wells is determined by geology. The distribution of minerals and petroleum around the world is fortuitous and asymmetric with respect to final markets. Business enterprises which seek to exploit a particular mineral can sometimes choose between host economies, but the choice can only be between countries which possess the resource. In some services, the spatial distribution of created resource endowments can be a critical locational determinant. In international banking, banks are drawn to the agglomerations of human skills and informational infrastructures found in international financial centers.

During recent decades the fact that most multinational investment takes the form of cross-investment between rich, developed countries has prompted a revaluation of the relative importance of ownership and locational advantages. Cantwell (1989) showed that multinationals were attracted to the technological capabilities of host countries. It was, from this perspective, the pull of location-specific country capabilities that attracted multinationals, rather than the desire to exploit an advantage.

1.4.2 Internalization and the boundaries of firms

Transactions costs theory provides a different perspective on the reasons for the growth of multinationals. Coase (1937) argued that firms and markets represent alternative methods of organizing production. The market is costly and inefficient for undertaking certain types of transactions. The transactions costs of the market include the cost of discovering relevant prices and in arranging contracts for each market transaction. The existence of such costs means that whenever transactions can be organized and carried out at a lower cost within the firm than through the market, they will be internalized and undertaken by the firm itself. Firms will internalize transactions until the marginal cost of doing so exceeds the marginal revenue.

This theory was extended and refined by Williamson (1975, 1981, 1985). He suggested that transactions costs could be examined systematically in relation to three factors. These are bounded rationality, opportunism, and asset-specificity. Bounded rationality refers to the impossibility of anyone knowing all possible information, which means that people invariably make less than fully rational decisions. Opportunism refers to the tendency of some people to cheat or misrepresent. Asset-specificity reflects the extent to which types of transaction, in order to be carried out, necessitate investments in material and **intangible assets** (such as knowledge) which are dedicated to particular uses, and how much their value will be diminished if used in alternative ways. If it is difficult to measure the value of goods and services, and if the opportunities for bargaining and dishonesty are therefore high, there is an incentive to replace the market by hierarchy. The combination of bounded rationality, opportunism and asset-specificity produces the strongest incentive to internalize a transaction rather than to use contracts in the market.

As applied to multinationals by McManus (1972), Buckley and Casson (1976), Hennart (1982), and others, this approach proposes that cross-border transactions in intermediate goods, in goods where intangible assets such as patents, brands, and tacit know-how are essential competitive advantages, and in goods that require display and after-sales service in foreign markets, will be undertaken through hierarchy rather than market exchange. The market for know-how, for example, suffers from the problem of information asymmetry. Buyers and sellers do not have perfect knowledge of what is being sold. The patent system allows the owner of know-how a monopoly in its use, and a mechanism for enforcement, enabling the disclosure of know-how to potential buyers without the risk of losing property rights. However it is hard to write tacit knowledge into patents, and the enforcement of patent rights is imperfect in many countries. The market for know-how will as a result be internalized within a multinational (Hennart 2001).

The primary analytical concern in this approach is not to understand the advantages held by multinationals over local rivals, but the ways in which cross-border transactions are organized within the same firms, rather than through arm's-length trade between independent firms. Casson (1986) distinguished between internationalization theory, which provided an explanation of how market failure led to the creation of firms, and the concept of ownership advantage, which he considered determined the performance of firms once that division has been made.

The eclectic paradigm incorporates both the advantage and internalization approaches, and serves as an organizing framework to understand the drivers of international production (Box 1.4).

Buckley and Casson (1998) see the concerns of the eclectic paradigm, and much of the theoretical literature, as conditioned by the circumstances of the era of stable and fast Western economic growth between the 1950s and the oil price shock of 1973–74. The primary concern was the selection of the most appropriate mode of entry. In the more turbulent conditions in recent decades, the volatility of the environment for international business and the need to develop flexibility in resource allocation to cope with it have moved up the research agenda. The historical experience of multinationals provides compelling insights on corporate responses to multiple shocks and transitions seen in the global economy over past centuries.

1.4.3 Knowledge-based theories of the firm

An alternative or complementary theory of the multinational was informed by evolutionary and resource-based theories of the firm. In the evolutionary theories of technological innovation, firms do not dip freely into some general stock or pool of 'prevailing' technological knowledge. Instead, firms produce things in ways that are differentiated technically from the production and methods of other firms, and they make innovations largely on the basis of in-house technology. The search process of identical firms to improve and diversify their technology involves them building on their existing technological base and on their existing markets (Nelson and Winter 1982; Dosi 1988).

These theories stress the role of the dynamic capability of individual firms. These capabilities have three components. The first is the strategy of the firm, or how it defines and rationalizes its objectives and how it intends to pursue them. The second is the structure of the firm, or how it is organized and governed. The third is how the strategy and structure mold organizational capabilities. Nelson and Winter propose that well-working firms can be understood in terms of a hierarchy of organizational routines.

Box 1.4 The eclectic paradigm of international production

The eclectic paradigm maintains that firms will engage in international production if they possess ownership advantages in a particular foreign market; if the enterprise perceives it to be in its best interest to add value to these ownership advantages rather than sell them to foreign firms—internationalization advantages; and if locational advantages make it more profitable to exploit its assets in a particular foreign location rather than at home.

The *ownership-specific advantages* of an enterprise of one nationality over those of another can be derived from:

(a) Possession of intangible assets. Product innovations, organizational and marketing systems, innovatory capacity, organization of work, noncodifiable knowledge; human capital; marketing, finance, know-how.
(b) Advantages of common governance, including operational flexibility by offering wider opportunities for arbitraging, production shifting, and global sourcing of inputs. More favored access to and/or better knowledge about international markets. Ability to take advantage of geographic differences in factor endowments, government intervention, markets, etc. Ability to diversify or reduce risks. Ability to learn from societal differences in organizational and managerial processes and systems. Balancing economies of integration need to respond to differences in country-specific resources and consumer demands.

Internationalization incentive advantages:

(a) Avoid search and negotiating costs.
(b) Avoid costs of moral hazard and adverse selection, and to protect reputation of internalizing firm.
(c) Avoid costs of broken contracts and ensuing litigation.

Location-specific advantages are derived from:

(a) spatial distribution of natural and created resources endowments and markets;
(b) international transport and communication costs;
(c) investment incentives and disincentives;
(d) artificial barriers to trade in goods and services;
(e) cross-country ideological, language, cultural, business, political differences.

(*Source:* Adapted from Dunning 1993.)

At any time the practiced routines that are built into an organization define the range of things the organization can do. In industries where technological innovation is important, a firm needs a set of core capabilities in R & D, and the extent of these will limit the extent of innovation a firm can undertake. Corporate competence is found in the tacit capability of a firm that results from a process of continued and collective learning. It is embodied in the firm's localized skills and organizational routines. This aspect of technology—unlike brand names or patents which can be copied or purchased—is strictly specific to a firm (Nelson 1991).

The resource-based theory of the firm emphasizes that there are stable and systematic differences between firms in the ways they controlled resources, and suggest that differences in firm resource endowments cause performance difficulties. The origins of the theory might be traced back to the classic theory of the growth of firms by Penrose (1959), but its modern manifestations emerged in the 1980s (Wernerfelt 1984). The firm's assets considered most important to yield competitive advantage were increasingly identified as knowledge. Knowledge and competence was seen as embedded in distinctive routines and practices. Much of this knowledge is tacit and not easily transferable, and can become the basis for the competitive advantage of firms (Winter 1987; Nonaka and Hirotaka 1995).

These approaches provide a basis for the view, articulated by Kogut and Zander (1993), that multinationals specialize in the transfer of knowledge that is difficult to understand and codify. As such they do not arise out of the failure of markets, but out of their superior efficiency as an organizational vehicle to transfer knowledge across borders. The role of opportunistic behavior is downgraded in this approach. The critical assumption is that knowledge transmission is not costless. Firms define a community in which there exists a body of knowledge regarding how to cooperate and communicate. Through repeated interactions, individuals and groups within firms develop a common understanding by which to transfer knowledge from ideas into production and markets. The choice of wholly owned subsidiaries as opposed to licensing or joint ventures can be seen as depending on the level of complexity, the degree of codifiability, and the extent of teachability of the knowledge.

Knowledge-based theories deepen insights into the nature of the ownership advantages held by multinationals. They also caution against assuming that there is an archetypal 'multinational'. Rather each firm is distinguished from another by its distinctive capabilities.

1.4.4 Entrepreneurship

The term entrepreneurship was coined in the eighteenth century by the economist Richard Cantillion. He believed that the primary role of the entrepreneur was to bear risk. Subsequently, definitions evolved in different and sometimes contradictory ways. Neoclassical economics conceived of entrepreneurs in a restricted fashion. A state of equilibrium is assumed in which transactors' plans are fully reconciled by the prices prevailing in equity and management markets. The emphasis on the final state rather than the process of getting there diverts attention from the distinctive contribution of the entrepreneur, for it is self-evident that equilibrium is constantly disrupted by unforeseen changes in the environment. These unforeseen changes are frequently the result of innovation by an entrepreneur, which proceeds to disturb the environment of other entrepreneurs.

A number of economists have attempted to model entrepreneurship in a more dynamic fashion than in mainstream economic theory. Knight (1921) suggested that entrepreneurship was associated with uncertainty bearing. Uncertainty was distinguished in this model from risks to which some possible outcome can be ascribed and insured against. Kirzner (1973, 1979) suggested that entrepreneurs are persons who are alert to hitherto-unexploited possibilities for exchange. In contrast to Knight, entrepreneurship is distinguished from ownership, and entrepreneurial rewards are derived solely from the possession of the knowledge that opportunities exist which no one has spotted before. For Kirzner, entrepreneurship is associated with disequilibria, and concerns the process by which the economy moves towards equilibrium.

In the model of Schumpeter (1943), the entrepreneur is an extraordinary person who brings about extraordinary events. The entrepreneurial figure is an innovator who disturbs and disrupts markets, technologies and organizational methods. Entrepreneurs constantly destabilize the world by innovation rather than, as in Kirzner's model, take the best advantage of the existing situation. Schumpeter argued that the growth of large corporations was in the process of rendering the entrepreneur obsolescent, because innovation would become routinized. Kirzner, on the other hand, regards large corporations not as alternatives to entrepreneurship, but as magnets attracting entrepreneurial talent, and as institutions which permit a more effective use of entrepreneurial alertness.

For Casson, an entrepreneur specializes in taking judgmental decisions about the coordination of scarce resources. A key feature of the model is the importance of judgment and not the ownership of resources per se. Unlike Schumpeter and Kirzner, the entrepreneur in this model is not the force behind change so much as a person who makes difficult judgments in a changing world. An entrepreneur synthesizes information through diverse sources and exploits it. Casson (1982) used this model to explain the growth process of a typical horizontal foreign direct investor. An entrepreneur gaining information on an overseas market through varying channels, and on the basis of this information, might decide to export. A sales subsidiary would give the exporting firm access to further information, which might provide the basis for a decision to set up a factory. This would provide detailed information on factor costs, which can be compared with other information from other factories, and enable over time the rationalization of international production (Casson 1985).

Powerful insights into the nature of entrepreneurship are also found in the business administration literature. Sahlman et al. (1999) propose a distinctive Harvard Business School definition, which treats entrepreneurship as an approach to management involving 'the pursuit of opportunity without regard to resources currently controlled'. In this approach, a distinction is made between the entrepreneur as a seeker of opportunity and an administrator, who is a guardian of existing resources. Entrepreneurship can be found in long-established businesses as much as start-ups.

Entrepreneurship appears to be profoundly influenced by location and geography. Entrepreneurial ideas do not arise evenly around the world, but appear to cluster in certain places at certain times (Porter 2000). Access to entrepreneurial ability can be seen as a critical ownership advantage for a multinational. It may explain why certain countries are far more important than others as homes for multinationals.

■ SUMMARY

When entrepreneurs and managers cross borders they encounter a range of costs and challenges arising from political, geographical, economic, and cultural distance between their home environment and the countries they invest in. There are a number of approaches to explaining why firms should nevertheless seek to engage in multinational investment despite the 'liability of foreignness'. They may hold an ownership advantage over a local firm. Locational factors in the host economy might either attract foreign firms or prevent them from servicing the market by exports. It might be more efficient to organize international transactions within a firm rather than use markets for certain transactions because of the costs of opportunism, bounded rationality, and asset-specificity. Multinational investment might be the most efficient means of transferring the tacit knowledge that is embedded in the routines of individual firms.

The history of multinationals can confront these insights with evidence of 'what really happened' over the past centuries. What does history show about the principal drivers of the spread of the boundaries of the firm across national borders? How were entrepreneurs able to build hierarchies that were superior to markets as channels of knowledge transfer? What is the evidence that they were really able to do this? How large was the 'liability of foreignness', and has it diminished over time? What exactly have been the consequences of firms transferring knowledge and other resources across borders? What kind of knowledge have they transferred? How, if at all, have all these things changed over time? What is new today, and what has a long history?

2 | Multinationals and globalization

2.1 Antecedents

Flows of people, trade, and capital across political borders have occurred for thousands of years. According to Moore and Lewis (1999), international trade began to develop in the Near East around 3500 BC. They identify the first 'multinationals' appearing in the Old Assyrian kingdom shortly after 2000 BC. Family-owned firms headquartered in the capital of Ashur opened branches in other political jurisdictions spread over what became the modern states of Syria and Iraq. Between 1000 and 500 BC ancient Phoenician merchants, especially those located on the island of Tyre, which is located off the coast of today's Lebanon, created firms which traded in silver from Spain, tin from Britain, ivory from Africa and textiles from all over the Mediterranean.

Over following centuries empires rose and fell, and trade routes were opened and closed. The integration of world civilization was never a continuous process, but one in which there have been numerous shocks and discontinuities, as well as periodic back-lashes. Between 50 BC and AD 500 the Roman Empire controlled the Mediterranean region, which was linked by roads, harbors and a common currency. For nearly 1500 years from before the beginning of the Christian era, trade routes known as the Silk Route joined Europe, the Middle East and China. From the sixth century Islam spread outwards from Arabia into Asia, Africa and the Iberian peninsula. This provided a political and ideological basis for the growth of trading connections and flows of knowledge. Islamic cities in Spain, such as Cordoba, flourished as clusters of knowledge at a time when much of Europe was technologically stagnant. During the fifteenth century Chinese ships reached the Arabian Gulf and east Africa, but soon afterwards political developments shifted China in a more inward direction.

The Voyages of Discovery of Spanish and Portuguese explorers to the New World and Asia in the fifteenth and sixteenth centuries saw transfers of technology—and deadly diseases—on a new scale. Entire American civilizations, including the Aztecs and the Incas, were destroyed by European armies and germs. At the end of the fifteenth century Portuguese explorers discovered the water route between Europe and Asia via the Cape of Good Hope, transforming the possibilities for trade between the two continents.

Although merchants were trading between different political sovereignties for centuries, a strong case can be made that the use of the word 'multinational' is anachronistic before the modern idea of the nation state took hold. Political scientists traditionally identify the origin of the modern system of nation states to the Peace of Westphalia, which ended the Thirty Years War in Europe in 1648. This replaced the European medieval structure of overlapping feudal hierarchies by the division of geographical space into exclusively defined jurisdictions within borders. The distinguishing feature of the multinational enterprise was that it operated in several of these clearly defined jurisdictions.

As the process of European colonization also got underway from the seventeenth century, state-sponsored trading companies were created to support colonial trading systems. The English, Dutch and Danish East India Companies, the Hudson's Bay Company, the Royal African Company, and similar firms were given monopoly trading rights by their respective governments. They became large-scale business organizations which some have seen as 'proto-multinationals' (see Box 2.1). In India, China, and the Middle East, they traded with local merchants who organized and financed the production of such commodities as pepper (Marshall 2002). As a result, they functioned as powerful drivers of regional integration.

European merchants were also traders in human beings. The commodities being developed in the New World such as sugar, tobacco, cotton and metals required large quantities of labor. This was found in the form of slaves from West Africa. The Royal African Company, chartered in Britain in 1672 and dissolved in 1752, exchanged European products for African commodities such as pepper and ivory and for slaves, which were transported to the West Indies. The proceeds in bullion were then sent back to Britain (Carlos and Kruse 1996). Between the sixteenth and the nineteenth centuries, at least 10 million Africans were transported to the Americas. Although slavery had been a feature of most human societies, capitalism resulted in an extraordinary expansion in its size and geographical scope.

Box 2.1 The English East India Company as a proto-multinational

In 1600 Queen Elizabeth I of England awarded a charter giving a body formed by a group of London merchants a monopoly over trade with the 'East Indies'. The merchants were initially concerned to secure spices such as pepper for the European market. Along with the rival Dutch East India Company formed in the Netherlands in 1602, the English East India Company came to dominate trade between Asia and Europe during the seventeenth and eighteenth centuries.

The Company was organized as a joint stock company headed by a Court of Directors. By the middle of the eighteenth century it employed 350 head office administrative staff which supervised a large managerial hierarchy which in turn supervised the trade between Europe and Asia. It functioned as a **vertically integrated** firm that undertook a full range of activities from the procurement of commodities in Asia to their wholesaling in Europe. The Company diversified into silk spinning factories in India.

In 1765 the Company obtained revenue collection rights in the province of Bengal from the ruling Mughal Empire in India. Thus began a process whereby it attained growing political power in India. In 1813 a new charter legalized the entry of private traders into the East Indian trade. Twenty years later the Company ceased trading and became concerned entirely with the colonial administration of India. The Company was liquidated in 1858 following the assumption of direct responsibility for India by the British Crown.

(*Source*: Chaudhuri 1978; Carlos and Nicholas 1988; Bowen, Lincoln, and Rigby 2002.)

By the eighteenth century, therefore, the 'integration of civilizations' had been in progress for millennia. Europe, Asia, Africa and the Americas were joined by strong trade links. There was a 'global' market in some products, including wine (Hancock 2002). There was a flourishing Atlantic economy. By then London had replaced Amsterdam as the world's largest international service center. However, distance remained a formidable obstacle to the closer integration of national markets. Transport costs were still very high. World trade probably grew at only a little over 1 percent per annum between 1500 and 1800. There seems to have been little or no price convergence between continents. Moreover, periodic wars between the European nations constantly disrupted integration (Findlay and O'Rourke 2003).

2.2 Creating the first global economy

During the nineteenth century the process of globalization accelerated on an unprecedented scale. From the 1820s international trade grew around 3.5 percent per annum for the rest of the century. The Industrial Revolution, which had begun in Britain and made it the world's largest manufacturing country by 1800, drove this growth. British exports of manufactured textiles poured into the markets of the world, dislocating the handicraft industries of China and India, formerly the world's largest manufacturers. The British industry was wholly dependent on imported cotton which created a huge demand for this commodity. During the first half of the nineteenth century modern industrialization was diffused to neighboring European countries and across the Atlantic to the United States. These newly industrialized regions sought markets for their products, and also raw materials for their industries, and foodstuffs for their rapidly expanding populations.

Exogenous circumstances favored the growth of trade. The end of the prolonged period of warfare between 1790 and the defeat of Napoleon in 1815 was followed by a century of relative world peace, despite major regional conflicts including the American Civil War (1861–65), during which half a million soldiers died. Transport costs fell sharply as steamships and railroads transformed the speed and cost of travel. International trade was further stimulated by a shift towards liberal economic policies, as monopolies were abandoned. By mid-century, tariffs had fallen to low levels. Subsequently the United States led a worldwide trend back towards protectionism. Nevertheless, by the late nineteenth century international trade was still growing much faster than world output. Overall, commodity price gaps between continents were cut by four-fifths between 1820 and 1914, primarily because of declining transport costs (O'Rourke and Williamson 1999).

There was a rapid increase in cross-border flows of capital, which accelerated from the late nineteenth century. There were few restrictions on capital movements, while the widespread adoption of the **Gold Standard**—which fixed the value of national currencies to the price of gold—sharply reduced foreign exchange risks. By 1880 quite a few countries were on the Gold Standard, and by 1900 there were a large number. Between 1820 and 1913 there was an estimated 60 percent progress from complete segmentation towards market integration in global capital markets (Obstfeld and Taylor 2003). Britain stood at the center of this monetary system. The country was by far the largest capital exporter. London functioned as the global international financial center. Sterling, fully convertible into gold, was the world's hardest currency. The Bank of England, Britain's quasi-central bank, oversaw the functioning of the Gold Standard. By participating in the international monetary system based on fixed exchange rates and balanced budgets, national governments accepted severe constraints on their domestic policies. In this respect, political 'distance' shrank remarkably in the first global economy.

There was unprecedented mobility of labor. Over the course of the nineteenth century 60 million Europeans emigrated to the Americas. There was also mass emigration of Russians to the empty lands of Siberia, and Chinese to Southeast Asia and California. By 1900, 14 percent of the population of the United States, which had grown from around five million in 1800 to reach 76 million, were foreign-born. There were few restrictions on immigration. Passports were unnecessary for international travel. Work visas did not exist. Falling steerage costs made emigration feasible for an unprecedented share of the world's population. Overall, in the Atlantic economy, the income gaps between rich and poor countries converged. Real wage dispersion declined by over a quarter between 1870 and 1910 (Hatton and Williamson 1998).

The forced movement of people as slaves finally ended. However, slavery as an institution continued in the United States until the 1860s and in Brazil till 1888. There was also the growth of cross-border movements of 'indentured' labor from regions of Asia to work as laborers in plantations in the Caribbean, Africa, and elsewhere, and on the many infrastructure projects undertaken at this time. Between the 1830s and World War I around four million Indians, Malays, Chinese, and others were sent around the world in this capacity. In many cases, they were so restricted as to become virtual slaves, and few returned to their home countries (Bayley 2004).

The incorporation of outlying regions into the emergent global economy was driven by imperialism (Cain and Hopkins 2002). Although the British Empire lost its North American colonies following the Declaration of Independence in 1776 and the formation of the United States, the borders of the British Empire spread over large parts of Asia and Africa during the nineteenth century. By 1913 Britain, whose population was 45 million, had a worldwide empire of 400 million inhabitants. France, Belgium, Portugal, and Germany also occupied substantial parts of Africa, while France's Asian colonies included the modern states of Vietnam, Laos, and Cambodia. In southeast Asia, the Dutch East Indies (Indonesia) was a colonial possession of the Netherlands. The United States occupied Cuba and the Philippine Islands following a war with Spain, their former colonial ruler, at the end of the nineteenth century. Japan, which had closed its borders to foreigners in the sixteenth century, was forced to open them following the arrival of an American naval force in 1853. By 1914 Japan, which had undergone rapid modernization and economic growth, had occupied neighboring Korea and Taiwan. Imperialism involved the forcible removal of barriers to cross-border flows of capital, trade, and knowledge.

2.2.1 The growth of multinationals

The webs of the first global economy were built by firms and entrepreneurs. As shown earlier, this was not new, but there was a new scale and durability to the business structures which began to be created in the nineteenth century. For millennia, when merchants and bankers despatched representatives across borders they employed family members, as the concept of 'professional managers' did not exist, while the problem of distance ruled out close monitoring of representatives abroad. The only option was to use people who could be 'trusted' not to act opportunistically. This greatly constrained the size of any organization. Typically such family members would in time become assimilated in their new countries, or else return home. The exceptional case of business enterprises which sustained cross-border businesses over long periods, such as the chartered trading companies, were typically supported by governments.

From the 1820s business enterprises began to make cross-border investments which were sustained without the benefit of monopoly rights. These were sometimes in a mine in a neighboring European country. They were often in colonies. During the 1830s British merchants and bankers began forming specialist 'overseas' banks to introduce banking into the Australian, Canadian, and West Indies colonies. Later entrepreneurs began to erect factories across borders. These were not large investments, but their real significance was that they were sustained. They continued to be managed from their home economies. Firms such as the German-owned electrical company Siemens and US-owned Singer Sewing Machines, which established their first overseas plants in the 1850s and 1860s respectively, were among the first manufacturing multinationals in history (see Chapter 4).

From the 1880s the numbers and scale of multinationals grew rapidly. They drove the rapid increase in international trade as they discovered and exploited natural resources and food supplies over much of the world. By 1914 multinational manufacturing was also undertaken in a wide range of manufactured products, including chemicals, pharmaceuticals, electricals, machinery, motor cars, tires, branded food products, and cigarettes. While entrepreneurs had made one-off cross-border transfers of knowledge in the past, the more sustained investments meant that there was a continuous flow of knowledge and other resources across borders within the boundaries of firms. Figure 2.1 portrays in an illustrative fashion the role of business enterprises in cross-border integration.

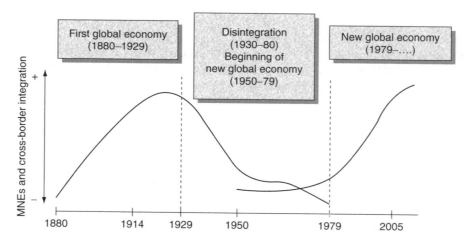

Fig. 2.1 Waves of globalization.
Source: the author.

It is not easy to quantify the amount of FDI between the late nineteenth century and 1914. There was an enormous amount of foreign investment in the world, but there remains great uncertainty about its composition. The total world stock of foreign investment by 1914 has usually been estimated at between $40 billion and $45 billion, but even the size of the capital exports from the world's largest creditor nation—the United Kingdom—remains uncertain (Platt 1980; 1986; Feinstein 1990). It was long believed that almost 90 percent of total capital flows were portfolio. J.H. Dunning's historical estimates of world FDI stock—which, although made over two decades ago, remain the only estimates of the global figure—suggest that by 1913 around one-third of total world foreign investment, or some $14 582 million, took the form of FDI (Dunning 1983; 1988a; 1992). Table 2.1 compares this sum to world output, suggesting that multinationals might have already reached an importance in the global economy, which was only achieved again in the 1990s.

In 1914 Western Europe as a region, and Britain as a single country, were the dominant sources of world FDI. The United States accounted for most of the remainder. FDI was widely dispersed around the globe. Latin America and Asia were especially important as host economies, even though the largest individual host countries seem to have been the United States and Canada. Possibly one-half of world FDI was invested in natural resources, and a further one-third in services, especially financing, insuring, transporting commodities, and foodstuffs. Multinational manufacturing was overwhelmingly located in the industrial economies of Western Europe and North America.

A central challenge in understanding the scope of multinational business at this time is posed by the diversity of organizational forms employed by entrepreneurs as they sought to take advantage of the opportunities of the rapidly globalizing world economy. Firms such as Siemens and Singer began by undertaking value-added activities in their home market, and then expanded abroad. The managerial and technological competences developed at home helped these firms sustain their investments abroad. This was the kind of firm and growth trajectory which economic theorists in the 1960s considered as the standard model of multinationals (see Chapter 1).

In fact, firms employed diverse organizational forms when they crossed borders. Many ventures were formed to undertake business activities exclusively or mainly abroad without prior domestic business. These have been termed **free-standing companies** (see Box 2.3).

The 'clustering' of free-standing companies was characteristic of the network forms of organization widely employed in the first global economy. British trading companies and merchant houses in Asia, Latin America, and Africa formed **business groups** linking nominally independent free-standing firms using both equity and nonequity modes. Many other European companies collaborated when they crossed borders, either in business groups or other types of network or alliance (see later chapters, especially Chapter 7).

1913	1960	1980	1990	1997
9.0	4.4	4.8	8.5	11.8

Table 2.1 World FDI as a percentage of world output, 1913–97 (%).

Source: World Investment Reports 1994, 1997, 1999.

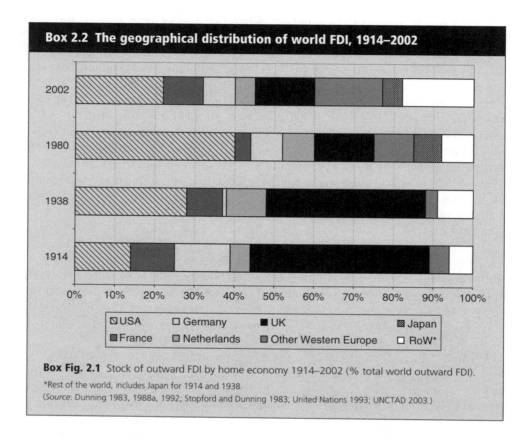

Box 2.2 The geographical distribution of world FDI, 1914–2002

Box Fig. 2.1 Stock of outward FDI by home economy 1914–2002 (% total world outward FDI).

*Rest of the world, includes Japan for 1914 and 1938
(*Source*: Dunning 1983, 1988a, 1992; Stopford and Dunning 1983; United Nations 1993; UNCTAD 2003.)

There are further complexities in interpreting the significance of FDI in the world economy because of the large percentage of investment located in colonial empires. In so far that the essence of multinational enterprise is crossing political borders, it is not evident that colonial investment is a form of FDI. The counter-argument is that metropolitan enterprises investing in colonial territories still faced different cultural, labor, and geographical conditions than in their home countries. Doing business in Saigon or Jakarta remained different from Paris or Amsterdam, whatever the borders of empire. Nor were colonial administrations necessarily supportive of expatriate firms. In the British Empire, there was often a distant relationship between individual administrators and expatriate business (see Chapter 8).

Parallel definitional issues arise when firms invested literally just over national borders. This was a common occurrence before 1914. Swiss chemical firms established factories in Germany within walking distance of the Swiss border. Early US investments in Canada were sometimes just over the border (Schröter 1993b; Wilkins 1988a). These investments might be more accurately described as 'multiregional' than 'multinational'. If both colonial and multiregional investments were excluded from current estimates of FDI in 1914, its overall importance in the world economy would decline sharply.

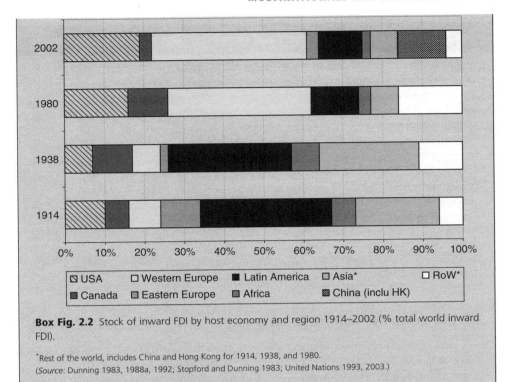

Box Fig. 2.2 Stock of inward FDI by host economy and region 1914–2002 (% total world inward FDI).

*Rest of the world, includes China and Hong Kong for 1914, 1938, and 1980.
(*Source*: Dunning 1983, 1988a, 1992; Stopford and Dunning 1983; United Nations 1993, 2003.)

Box 2.3 Free-standing companies and the first global economy

During the nineteenth century thousands of British, and hundreds of Dutch and other European, companies were formed exclusively to operate internationally with no prior domestic business. The period between 1870 and 1914 saw particularly rapid levels of firm creation. They were international venture capitalists, exploiting the numerous opportunities of the booming world economy and of expanding imperial frontiers.

Typically, free-standing companies were legally incorporated in their home economy. They would have a small head office where a part-time board of directors met, supported by a handful of other clerical staff. They usually specialized on a single commodity, product or service, often in a single overseas country. They were predominantly located in the natural resource and service sectors, and occasionally in processing. Most free-standing companies invested in developing, including colonial, countries, although many British free-standing firms were formed to conduct business in the United States. Three-fourths of the 200 Dutch free-standing companies active in 1914 operated in the Dutch colony of Indonesia, then known as the Dutch East Indies.

This type of firm was long considered as a vehicle for portfolio capital flows. Yet insofar as management control was exercised from head offices at home, they are more appropriately regarded as a form of multinational. The reclassification of free-standing firms engaged in FDI prompted the large upward revision of the amount of FDI in the world

continues

> ## Box 2.3 Free-standing companies and the first global economy (*continued*)
>
> economy before 1914. In fact, there remain many uncertainties about the management structures of these firms. In some cases, most managerial decision-making was located in host economies. Some firms were engaged in a form of property development. Once the short-lived need for their specialized project management skills dried up, management control shifted to locals, and the investment ceased to be FDI.
>
> Nominally independent free-standing companies were often part of wider business networks. There were 'clusters' linking different firms around original promoters, financial intermediaries, solicitors, accountants, mining engineers, merchant banks, trading companies, and influential individuals. Common to all clusters was the provision of services. The small head offices of the free-standing companies typically outsourced many managerial functions. Insofar as firms formed parts of networks, the description 'free standing' might be misleading.
>
> (*Source*: Wilkins 1988a; Corley 1994; Sluyterman 1994; Casson 1994a; Hennart 1994a; Jones 1998a; Wilkins and Schroter 1998.)

2.2.2 The drivers of multinational growth

The growth of multinationals over the course of the nineteenth century was driven by a number of factors.

Firstly, the diffusion of modern economic growth created an accelerating search for raw materials and foodstuffs and for markets for manufactured products. The process which had begun with the Industrial Revolution in Britain intensified over time. The new capital-intensive industries such as chemicals, machinery, and packaged food products which grew towards the end of the nineteenth century were large consumers of raw materials. Chemicals and electricals production consumed large amounts of minerals such as copper, aluminum, and zinc. The automobile industry which appeared in the early twentieth century needed tin for solder and for the alloys used in bearings. In the late nineteenth century petroleum, initially used as kerosene for lighting and heating, began to be used as an alternative to coal to drive trains and steamships, while it was the only fuel that could be used in automobiles. While the United States had a rapidly increasing market and was rich in resources and land for growing food, European countries, including Britain, had to seek markets and resources across borders.

The policy environment was critical in the emergence of the modern multinationals also. While the absence of major international wars reduced the risks of cross-border business, the spread of international property law guaranteed property rights virtually worldwide. Seventeenth-century European governments had started the process of reducing the risks of trade by signing bilateral commercial treaties that protected alien property, but it was only in the nineteenth century that these treaty standards hardened into international law, the core principle of which was that the property of foreigners could not be taken without prompt, full compensation. Uncompensated seizure was considered robbery, and the use of unilateral force was considered a legal and legitimate response. The principles of this law were strongly supported by European governments, and enforced on much of the rest of the world by the British and, later, the United States. Western concepts of property rights were imposed through treaties, the securing of extraterritorial rights (especially at Far Eastern ports) and by the spread of colonial rule. Down to 1914, there were no large-scale **sequestrations** of foreign property (Lipson 1985).

As the nineteenth century progressed, liberal economic policies took hold in many countries as governments withdrew from economic activities. Government intervention was, by later standards, minimal. Most governments treated foreign-owned firms more or less like domestic firms. The growth of trade protectionism from mid-century represented a partial departure from liberalism. The McKinley Act of 1890 raised US tariffs to an average level on protected commodities of 50 percent. However, as governments sought to restrict foreign goods but not foreign companies—or people—this served to stimulate multinational manufacturing, as firms were able to respond to restrictions on their exports by opening factories in international markets instead.

Geographical distances were dramatically reduced by improvements in transport and communications. In 1800 land transport was based on dirt roads and water transportation. Both were slow and dependent on the weather. The international spread of railroads from the 1830s brought a new speed and reliability. The earliest railroads were built in Britain and the eastern United States in the 1830s, but their subsequent spread was rapid. During the first half of the century improvements in sailing-ship technology produced a sharp fall in ocean freight rates. From the mid-century the use of steamships also expanded. The opening of the Suez Canal in 1869 provided a shorter route between Europe and Asia. Sea journey times and costs continued to fall with the opening of the Panama Canal in 1915. By then, travel by ship across the Atlantic took only six days (Wilkins 2004). The result was a revolution in the speed and reliability that people and goods could be transported across distances, and a fall in the cost of such transportation.

There were major improvements in communications also. The telegraph was the most important nineteenth-century innovation. In 1852 London and Paris were joined by electric telegraph. The first successful trans-Atlantic cable connection was in 1866. In 1870 Bombay and London were linked by cable. The cable from Europe reached Australia in 1872. Information could now cross continents in minutes.

These transport and communication improvements opened new markets, and made the exploitation of natural resources in distant lands more feasible. Ores and metals could be shipped economically from Bolivia, central Africa, and Malaysia to the major markets in Europe and North America (Schmitz 1979). Before the nineteenth century the best chance of sustaining direct investments was if a government awarded a monopoly or special privileges. Improvements in transport and communications made it feasible, if still difficult, to manage cross-border operations.

Finally, the expansion of multinationals was facilitated by the appearance of new types of firms. In the eighteenth century most firms everywhere were small and family-owned. Owners were usually responsible for paying all of a firm's debts. There were high levels of volatility. The largest private enterprises of the eighteenth century were the European chartered trading companies. During the nineteenth century legal reforms permitted new forms of corporate governance. During the first half of the century many states in the United States permitted limited liability. Limited liability became fully available in Britain in 1861. Earlier forms of corporate governance, such as partnerships, persisted, but limited liability facilitated capital raising, and opened the way for the growth of larger firms.

The subsequent emergence of the modern industrial enterprise was also important (see Box 2.4). The modern industrial enterprise came to play a central role in creating the most technologically advanced fast-growing manufacturing industry of each generation. Large corporations already accounted for most US multinational investment before 1914. However, much multinational business did not take this form (see Chapter 7).

Box 2.4 The rise of managerial capitalism

Chandler (1962, 1977, 1990) has described the emergence of the modern industrial enterprise in the nineteenth century. At the beginning of the century, production and distribution of goods all over the world was carried on by small enterprises whose managers were also the owners. Business enterprises in the nineteenth century normally operated a single unit of production or of distribution. The flow of goods between these enterprises was coordinated by the 'invisible hand' of the market. From the middle of the nineteenth century there was the development of large corporations administered by a hierarchy of salaried professional managers. Ownership was separated from control.

Chandler identified changes in technology and in markets as two crucial variables in explaining the shift from these personally managed enterprises to the modern corporation. The coming of modern transportation and communication in the nineteenth century—especially railroads, telegraphs, steamships and cables—made possible **mass production** and mass marketing for the first time. The first corporations with managerial hierarchies appeared in the United States in the 1850s and 1860s to coordinate the movement of trains and the flow of goods on the new railroad networks and messages over the new telegraph system.

Transportation improvements coincided with the development of new technologies in certain industries which permitted much greater reduction in cost per unit of output as volume increased. The first industries to secure these economies of scale included oil refining, metallurgy and food processing, where continuous flow techniques were applied. Mass production in turn required assured mass markets, with the result that manufacturing enterprises in these industries typically built their own extensive marketing organizations. In those industries that integrated mass production and mass distribution, managerial hierarchies emerged to provide a 'visible hand' to coordinate the flows of goods within the enterprise.

The large managerial enterprise which emerged in the capital-intensive manufacturing industries of the late nineteenth and early twentieth century achieved economies of scale from their size and integration and **economies of scope** from diversifying into new products and, eventually, countries. The success of individual firms depended on their organizational capability, which in turn rested on their willingness to make three inter-related investments in production facilities, marketing, and in management. Firstmover firms had considerable advantages over subsequent challengers. In many cases their industry quickly became and remained oligopolistic.

Chandler regarded the United States as the seedbed of **managerial capitalism**. It was the United States that took the lead in the creation of large corporations. The United States had many more and many larger managerial hierarchies than those of other nations. In

Germany there was also a growth of large corporations in the capital-intensive industries, though family ownership and management was stronger. German firms also tended to collaborate in cartels. Chandler described this system as cooperative managerial capitalism. In Britain manufacturing firms remained smaller, and continued to be dominated by their founding families. Chandler argued that British **personal capitalism** caused a lag in that country's competitive abilities in the capital-intensive industries of chemicals, machinery and electric equipment. However, many historians dispute the view that family business was inherently less successful than managerial capitalism. Wardley (1991) also showed that large-scale companies did emerge in Britain particularly in the service sector.

2.3 Globalization challenged and reversed, 1914–50

The outbreak of World War I in 1914 began a process which saw the beginning of the end of the first global economy. There had already been signs of a backlash against globalization in the previous decades. The most visible sign was the shift towards trade protectionism. By 1914 Britain, the Netherlands, and Denmark were the only free-trading countries left. There was also the beginning of a backlash against immigration. The United States began to attempt to control Asian immigration from the 1880s. In 1901 Australia implemented its 'White Australia' policy which virtually blocked immigration from Asia or the Pacific Islands.

The world economy became progressively unstable. There was a severe recession soon after the end of World War I in 1918, although countries such as the United States, Australia, Canada, Brazil, and India saw a rapid growth in manufacturing as a result of import substitution. The onset of the Great Depression in 1929 resulted in a worldwide economic shock. US real GDP fell by almost a third between 1929 and 1933. While much of the industrialized world in the 1930s experienced high levels of unemployment, declining primary commodity prices caused sharp falls in real incomes for the producer countries in Latin America, Asia, Africa, and Australia.

The backlash against the global economy was evident in multiple areas. The nationality of firms was identified as an issue during World War I, as governments sequestrated affiliates of enemy-owned companies in their countries (see Chapter 10). The Russian Revolution in 1917 was followed by the sequestration of foreign property. Russia had been a leading host economy for multinationals before World War I. Perhaps two-thirds of French and Belgium foreign investment had been located in that country. Singer Sewing Machines had built one of the largest modern industrial enterprises in Russia. All was now lost. The Soviets acknowledged a legal obligation to compensate foreign property owners, but only if Western countries paid for the damage their armies had caused after they intervened in the civil war which followed the Communist Revolution. Throughout the 1920s, the League of Nations (the predecessor to the United Nations) held conferences designed to clarify the obligations of host states to foreign capital, but the European states were unable to secure their aims in the face of resistance from Latin American and other 'peripheral' countries (Lipson 1985).

Elsewhere, during the 1920s there was an increase in the growth of restrictions on foreign companies. By the following decade political nationalism was rampant. Xenophobic dictatorships ruled Germany, Italy, and Japan. Many governments of developing countries began to question foreign control over their natural resources. The Mexican **nationalization** of foreign oil companies in 1938 was a landmark event which asserted national sovereignty over natural resources.

During World War I the international monetary system was severely disrupted by inflation and the suspension of the Gold Standard. Though many countries returned to the Gold Standard in the mid-1920s, world finance and economic conditions had changed greatly. Countries both overvalued and undervalued their currencies in relation to gold, providing a further source of instability. Capital flows often assumed a speculative and short-term form. The war transformed Germany from a major creditor country to a debtor, whereas the United States emerged as the world's largest creditor. US foreign investment rose from $7 billion to $17 billion between 1919 and 1929, but—exceptionally for the United States—portfolio lending grew faster than FDI (Lewis 1938).

The Great Depression was followed by the collapse of the international financial system. The repatriation of the large amounts of American portfolio lending from Europe provoked a major financial crisis in central Europe and Germany in 1931. The Gold Standard was fatally undermined when Britain abandoned it in September of that year, followed by the United States two years later. Regional currency blocs developed, each supported by extensive exchange controls. A US Dollar area included Latin America; a Sterling bloc included most of the British Empire and some northern European countries; a German bloc extended over parts of central Europe; a Yen bloc included parts of Asia; and a residual 'gold bloc' included France and some other Western European countries. In this environment, cross-border capital flows fell sharply, and were largely confined within currency blocs (Kenwood and Lougheed 1992).

After World War I, trade protectionism spread. By the early 1920s, US tariffs had been raised to their highest-ever levels by the Fordney-McCumber tariff. Australia, India, and some Latin American countries were among those that used tariffs, import quotas and other trade barriers to help infant industries and foster their manufacturing sectors by import substitution. International trade recovered from the wartime nadir during the 1920s: by the end of that decade the ratio of world trade to world product had probably returned to its 1913 level (Kenwood and Lougheed 1992). But the Great Depression led to the collapse of the international trading system. The Smoot-Hawley Act of June 1930 substantially increased the US tariff level, and other countries followed in the classic 'beggar my neighbor' pattern. By the end of the 1930s almost half of the world's trade was restricted by tariffs.

It was physically easier for human beings to travel and communicate. Automobiles became an item of mass consumption, at least in the United States. Telephone systems spread. Air travel became faster, safer, and more regular. However, the backlash against the global economy was particularly strong in the area of migration. During World War I many countries, including the United States, made the use of passports for entering and leaving countries compulsory for the first time. Work restrictions dated from the same period. In 1917 the United States required foreign nationals to have visas issued by US census offices. In 1921 an Immigration Act reduced the annual number of immigrants from over one million to a maximum of 357 803. The maximum number of immigrants from any nationality was set at 3 percent of the foreign-born of that nationality residing in the United States in 1910. In 1924 a further act set a quota of 2 percent and took the base year back to 1890. This was before the large southern and eastern European immigration of the 1890s and 1900s. All Asians had been excluded in 1917 (James 2001).

During the interwar years the first global economy disintegrated. Between 1914 and 1950 the commodity price gaps between continents reverted to their 1870 levels. Capital markets reverted to market segmentation (Obstfeld and Taylor 2003; Lindert and Williamson 2003). Mass migration fell sharply. The annual migration rate to the United States fell from 11.6 immigrants per thousand population in the first decade of the twentieth century to 0.4 immigrants per thousand population in the 1940s (Chiswick and Hatton 2003).

2.3.1 Multinationals during the Great Depression and world wars

Multinationals continued to operate, and even to expand, as the first global economy disintegrated. However, there were some major shifts in response to the stocks of the era. The United States emerged from World War I as the most dynamic direct investor in the world economy, though its stock remained well below European levels. US FDI almost doubled in the 1920s. In contrast German FDI all but disappeared following its sequestration during and after World War I by the victorious Allies. The sequestration of foreign capital in Russia in 1917 not only eliminated a large share of total French and Belgian FDI, but dampened new multinational investment from those countries. In 1938 the estimated total world stock of FDI was around $26 350 million. The United States, Britain and the Netherlands together may have accounted for over three-quarters of the total amount (see Box 2.2).

The Great Depression and its aftermath finally halted the overall growth of world FDI. **Exchange controls** were a major disincentive to engage in new FDI, as dividends and profits could not be repatriated, though they could give rise to 'enforced investment' as funds that could not be repatriated were ploughed back into business. This helps to explain the almost 50 percent increase in the level of US FDI in Germany between 1929 and 1940 (Wilkins 1974a). A picture of stagnation emerges for the only economy for which FDI estimates exist, the United States. The stock of **outward** US FDI fell, though **inward** FDI into the US between 1935 and 1940 may have risen from $1.6 billion to $2.9 billion (Lipsey 1988). The ratio of FDI to total US output tumbled from 4.7 percent to 1.4 percent between 1914 and 1929, but may have climbed back to 3.2 percent by 1939 (Wilkins 2004).

Even during the 1930s there were exceptions to stagnation. There remained opportunities for multinational growth in markets protected by high tariff barriers. Falling world food and raw material prices caused cheaper imports and higher real incomes in some countries, at least for the proportion of the working population which remained in employment, and this created growing markets for new consumer products like vacuum cleaners and refrigerators, and processed food products. Although international trade slumped in the 1930s, some multinational trading companies found rich opportunities. Japan's large trading companies grew alongside Japanese exports, opening up new markets in Latin America, the Middle East and the **Soviet Union**, and creating 'global sales networks' (Kawabe 1987).

World War II and the immediate aftermath saw—not surprisingly—little new multinational investment. Both sides in the conflict sequestrated the assets of the other. The entire stock of German and Japanese FDI was lost. The spread of Communism to eastern Europe in the late 1940s, and to China in 1949, resulted in further falls in the stock of FDI as those countries progressively nationalized privately owned firms, foreign and domestic. The United States was the only country to significantly increase its actual FDI during the war, yet this was dwarfed by the dramatic growth of the domestic economy. The ratio of inward FDI to total US output was around 1.3 percent by 1945 (Wilkins 2004).

The numbers of multinationals which were large hierarchical corporations continued to grow in the interwar years. Their operations became more complex, involving more countries and more products. New US industries became involved in multinational expansion on a substantial scale for the first time, notably automobiles, food, and consumer chemicals (Wilkins 1974a). There were further developments in corporate organization. In the United States, a number of large corporations including Du Pont, General Motors (GM), and Standard Oil of New Jersey responded to the managerial problems caused by scale and diversification by moving from centralized or wholly decentralized organizations towards semi-autonomous product divisions. This **multi-divisional structure (M-form)**, which was spread rapidly through US industry, combined coordinated control, implemented through financial reporting and capital allocation, with sufficient decentralization to make further product and geographical growth possible. The M-form had the capacity to manage scale and complexity by separating strategy from operations (Chandler 1962). Both GM and Standard Oil of New Jersey were major US multinational investors in the interwar years.

There was no clear-cut correlation between the spread of the M-form and the further growth of multinationals. Most US corporations had still to adopt the M-form in the interwar years. Ford, which had extensive multinational operations, remained personally managed by its owner, Henry Ford. Some scholars have now questioned whether, even at GM, the M-form worked in practice as it was described in theory (Freeland 2001). Nor can it now be seen as a uniquely American phenomenon. It is evident that German companies, including the steel firm Thyssen, had developed a similar organizational form before World War I (Fear 2004).

The biodiversity seen in the organization of multinationals persisted. It does seem that the creation of new free-standing firms fell greatly. Many European free-standing firms active in the United States disappeared or passed into local ownership during and after World War I. In Latin America, a swathe of British free-standing firms were acquired by US companies. Yet in some sectors (such as banking and utilities) and some regions (such as Southeast Asia and Africa) the free-standing type structure survived. Some networks of loosely coordinated firms evolved tighter organizational structures over time (Greenhill 1995). Even a new generation of free-standing firms appeared on the New York stock market as US investors floated companies that owned sugar plantations and mines in Latin America (Wilkins 1993a; Hennart 1994b).

The macroeconomic conditions of the interwar years, and the heightened risks of investment, also encouraged entrepreneurs to pursue collaborative strategies as an alternative to FDI. Numerous international cartel agreements were formed in both manufacturing and natural resources, as firms sought to maintain prices in conditions of overcapacity. In many developed countries merger waves had led to the creation of larger firms. Collusive behavior on an international scale was made much easier by the existence of oligopolistic and cartelized domestic markets, as it was far easier to organize industries when there were only a handful of major corporations than in a situation of hundreds or thousands of competing firms.

After 1930, multinationals were less drivers of global integration, than part of the process of disintegration. International cartels restricted flows of international trade, although there is some evidence that they continued to provide a channel for flows of knowledge (see Chapter 4). Although extensive multinational operations remained in place, they functioned in more 'national' ways. Trade barriers and exchange controls led to the increased autonomy of national affiliates, which increasingly became responsible for most of the value-added chain of their products. Nationalism encouraged firms to strengthen their 'local' identities in their host economies. In Europe, US companies such as IBM, Ford, and GM responded to European competition by developing new products for major markets which were distinct from those produced for their domestic American market.

2.4 **Restoring a global economy, 1950–80**

The 1950s onwards saw the beginning of the reconstruction of a new global economy. Between 1950 and 1973 the annual real GDP growth of developed market economies averaged around 5 percent. This growth was smooth, with none of the major recessions seen in the interwar years. World War II left the United States in a uniquely powerful position. While Europe and Asia had experienced extensive destruction and loss of life, no battles had been fought on the soil of the United States. The US dollar became the world's major reserve currency. US corporations assumed leading positions in many industries. Europe and Japan had to spend the immediate postwar decade undergoing extensive reconstruction, heavily dependent on official aid from the United States, yet over time Europe and Japan closed the technological and productivity gap with the United States. The emergence of a US deficit on its balance of trade in the 1960s, and the devaluation of the US dollar, and the end of its convertibility into gold in 1971, provided symbolic signs of the ending of an era.

There remained many restrictions on the flow of capital, trade, and people across borders. Foreign companies were entirely excluded from the Communist world. In the twenty years after 1945 the European colonial empires were dismantled. In some cases, decolonization was followed by an aggressive reaction against the businesses of the former colonial power, and sometimes all foreign investment. The relatively small number of expropriations without compensation until the late 1960s—when a period of large-scale expropriation began—reflected the power and determination of the United States to protect foreign investments, but Western countries were unable to re-establish an international legal regime which guaranteed the property rights of international investors. Even in the developed countries, receptivity towards multinationals fell. In Europe and the United States, whole sectors were closed to foreign companies. The Japanese economy grew so fast that it had become the world's second largest capitalist economy by the 1970s, but its governments systematically discouraged wholly owned FDI, and restricted it to a low level (see Chapter 8).

During the 1940s and early 1950s only the US dollar was available as a major convertible currency. Elsewhere exchange controls regulated capital movements. They were often the instruments used by governments to screen or monitor FDI flows. The worldwide controls over capital movements were related to balance of payments concerns and the system of fixed exchange rates established at Bretton Woods. It was not until 1958 that most European countries adopted nonresident convertibility, which permitted foreigners to move funds for current account purposes freely from one country to another. This was the key development in the establishment of a liberal and open international economy. It had an immediate impact on FDI flows, with an increase of US FDI into Europe (Wilkins 1974a). However, most developing countries continued to exercise tight controls over capital movements. Even most developed countries retained some exchange controls.

It was only after the collapse of the Bretton Woods system of fixed exchange rates in the early 1970s that controls over capital movements began to be slowly dismantled. The advent of floating exchange rates permitted a huge explosion in international financial markets from the 1970s, but these capital flows were different than before 1914, for they largely occurred between rich countries. In 1900 Asia, Latin America, and Africa had accounted for 33 percent of global liabilities. In the 1990s, they accounted for 11 percent (Obstfeld and Taylor 2003).

World trade barriers were reduced under the auspices of the General Agreement on Tariffs and Trade (GATT) signed in 1947. This process peaked in the 1960s, when the Kennedy Administration in the United States made major efforts to secure radical reductions in tariff rates. During the middle of this decade there was a comprehensive reduction of barriers to trade in manufactured goods. By the end of the 1960s, however, the US-inspired drive for trade liberalization showed a loss of momentum, as US balance of payments deficits began to cause concern about the scale of foreign imports. Nontariff barriers spread in the following decade. Most developing countries in Latin America, Asia, and Africa became progressively closed to international trade from the 1950s to the 1980s. Even the richest and most developed countries maintained very high levels of protection for agricultural products, far higher than before 1913 (Findlay and O'Rourke 2003).

The formation of regional trading blocs was both a part of the process of reducing trade barriers and a limitation on it. The European Economic Community (later known as the EC, and, from 1993, the **European Union**) was formed in 1957, and initially consisted of six Western European countries. It developed common tariffs against external imports. An extreme case was the Common Agricultural Policy, adopted in 1966, which severely restricted US agricultural exports to Europe. However, within Europe, free trade was established between the member countries, even though nontariff barriers persisted. The creation of such a large 'Common Market' attracted many US companies to Western Europe.

Technology made it easier than ever before for companies to move people, knowledge, and goods around the world. There were new waves of innovations in transport and communications. In 1958 the first commercial jet made an Atlantic crossing. This was followed by a phenomenal increase in air traffic. The development of telex was a considerable advance over telephones in facilitating international communications and coordinating of multinational business. In 1965 the first satellite for commercial telecommunications was launched. During the 1970s the use of the facsimile machine took off. The movement of goods across the world was facilitated by the development of larger ocean-going ships or super-freighters, and the growth of containerization.

The flow of migrants across borders remained constrained by immigration policies. Although the number of migrants were considerable—there were 3.2 million immigrants to the United States in the 1960s—they were much smaller relative to the host population than in the early twentieth century. The proportion of foreign-born in the US population was less than 5 percent in 1970. There was also a major shift in the geographical source of emigrants. Europeans were much less important, although they moved within their home region. The proportion of Europeans and Canadian to total immigrants in the United States fell from 78 percent in the 1940s to 13 percent in the 1980s. Over the same decades the proportion of Latin Americans rose from 18 percent to 47 percent, and the proportion of Asians from 4 percent to 37 percent (Chiswick and Hatton 2003).

By 1980, the integration of worldwide capital, commodity and labor markets remained limited compared to the late nineteenth century.

2.4.1 The resumption of multinational growth

The expansion of the world economy prompted a recovery in the growth rate of world FDI. The system of international cartels was dismantled. By 1960 the world stock of FDI had reached $60 billion. By 1980 it was over $500 billion. These were the decades when the term 'multinational' was invented, and when economic theorists turned their attention to explaining their existence.

Between 1945 and the mid-1960s the United States may have accounted for 85 percent of all new FDI flows. By 1980 it held 40 percent of total stock. In the twenty years after the end of World War II both German and Japanese FDI remained low, but growth during the 1970s gave the two countries an overall share of world FDI of 8 percent and 7 percent respectively. The German share finally surpassed that of the Netherlands by that date. By 1980 almost two-thirds of world FDI was located in Western Europe and North America. Latin America and Asia had declined very sharply in their relative importance as host economies. By 1980 there was no multinational investment in China, and almost none in India. Even Japan in that year accounted for less than 1 percent of world inward FDI stock.

The relative shift of world FDI to Western Europe and North America reflected the many barriers to foreign multinationals elsewhere. In agriculture and mining, and later in petroleum, foreign firms lost the ownership of production facilities in many countries, even if they remained very powerful in the transportation, processing, and marketing of commodities. By 1980 manufacturing FDI was larger than the natural resource and service sectors combined. In services, while transport and utility investments were no longer important, from the 1960s multinational banks, trading companies, and international commodity dealers began rapid international expansion.

As suggested in Figure 2.1, there were two different trends evident in this era. On the one hand, much of the multinational investment dating from the first global economy in resources and utilities was swept away. The high levels of integration seen in many commodities was broken by nationalizations and other forms of government intervention. Formerly large host economies including Russia, China, and even India—which retained a quasi-capitalist economy—were isolated from the world economy. On the other hand, new types of firms expanded abroad. These included management consultants which transferred knowledge across borders, and fast food restaurants and hotels, which transferred lifestyles. They were particularly important in diffusing US management and marketing techniques to other economies, although they were typically adapted in their new hosts. In Europe, firms also began to respond to European integration by building European-wide organizations, and integrating previously autonomous national subsidiaries (see Chapters 4 and 5).

By 1979 the overall size of multinational investment was still smaller in relation to the world economy as a whole than in 1914. This reflected the barriers to foreign ownership erected in many countries, and in many sectors, such as utilities, and the disappearance of the hugely capital-intensive investments in mining and petroleum. During the first global economy, much of the growth had been driven by the exchange of manufactured goods made in the developed world for the resources found elsewhere. The emergent new global economy was driven by trade, investment, and knowledge flows between Europe, North America, and Japan.

2.5 The new global economy: borderless, regional, or semiglobal?

During the 1980s the pace of globalization intensified. By then the overwhelming influence of the United States on the world economy had given away to a situation whereby wealth was distributed more equally between the Triad of North America, Western Europe, and Japan, which accounted for around three-fourths of world manufacturing production. Paradoxically, the United States became the single 'superpower' following the end of the Cold War. Although the importance of the Triad in the global economy persisted or even grew after 1980, there were significant shifts. Japan's share of world manufacturing increased from 5 percent in the early 1960s to 20 percent thirty years later, but thereafter the Japanese economy stagnated for a decade in the wake of the collapse of its speculative 'bubble economy'. In contrast, during the 1990s the United States experienced a surge of growth, apparently driven by the productivity gains of a 'New Economy' associated with a boom in Internet and other high technology companies. This growth also ground to a halt at the end of the decade. The twenty-first century began with a major recession, scandals over auditing irregularities in large firms, major acts of international terrorism, and war.

National restrictions over cross-border capital flows were largely swept away as financial deregulation spread. The most striking changes were in emerging markets. Countries abandoned state planning and import substitution and sought export-led growth. Multinationals were increasingly seen as a means to develop new technologies, products and skills. China's adoption of market-oriented policies in 1979 is the appropriate chronological starting point for the new, or second global economy. The collapse of Communism in Russia and eastern Europe a decade later reopened further huge parts of the globe to foreign firms. Deregulation and privatization opened further opportunities, including in services such as air transport, tourism, and telecommunications which had long been closed to foreign companies. Multinationals now faced few risks of expropriation, but the international property rules of the nineteenth century were not restored. In China, eastern Europe, and elsewhere, multinationals faced enormous uncertainties regarding their legal rights and the enforcement of contracts.

However, governments did not withdraw from the market for capital flows in the way they had before 1914. Practically every government on the planet offered incentives for multinationals to invest. There also continued to be barriers to multinational investment in many resource and service industries (see Chapter 8). Although only some developing countries had exchange controls, world exchange markets continued to see continual and sometimes massive intervention in efforts to influence exchange rates.

A worldwide trend towards tariff reduction made possible further growth in trade, and deeper levels of economic integration. By the end of the century, tariffs on manufactured goods were lower than in 1913, although this was not true for a number of populous developing countries, including India and China. Nontariff barriers also fell from the late 1980s. However, there was no return to nineteenth-century free-trade. International trade in many commodities was distorted by tariffs and subsidies. Both the United States and the EU gave their farmers huge subsidies to grow cotton, oils, and many other commodities rather than import the much cheaper products of developing countries. The rich countries were also quite prepared to erect tariffs if domestic vested interests seemed threatened. The United States heavily protected its domestic textile industry, and in 2003 imposed 'emergency' tariffs to protect its steel industry.

In part, falling tariffs reflected the further growth of regional trading blocs. The EU was enlarged in 1973, 1981, 1986, 1995, and 2004. Barriers to the movement of goods and services within Europe declined sharply, and over time, barriers to the movement of capital and people were also removed. EU law took precedence over that of member states. In 2002, twelve members of the EU even abolished their national currencies and adopted the new Euro currency. The United States, Canada, and Mexico formed the North American Free Trade Agreement (NAFTA) in 1994, although this remained primarily a free trade area. In the following year the Mercosur customs union was launched by Brazil, Paraguay, Uruguay, and Argentina.

The real costs and risks of managing at a distance were sharply reduced by changes in communications and transport technologies. Developments in information technology revolutionized communications. The use of 'geo-stationary' satellites, which orbited the earth at heights of between 12 000 and 25 000 miles, permitted simultaneous cheap voice, data, and video links worldwide. Optical fiber cables provided an alternative means of transmitting very large volumes of information at very high speeds. The 1980s saw the appearance of the personal computer (PC).

The Internet began to be created after 1969 through the interlinking of computer networks in the United States, but it remained exotic for several decades. In 1990 the World Wide Web was born when a researcher at CERN, the high-energy physics laboratory in Geneva, Switzerland, developed hypertext markup language (HTML). Four years later the Internet was formally separated from the US government's auspices and became open to commercial activity. The number of Internet users in the United States increased from 6 million to 159 million between 1993 and 2002. There was a rapid worldwide diffusion. The number of Internet users in China increased from 2000 to 59 million over the same period, although in sub-Saharan Africa there were only 6.2 million by 2002 (http://devdata.worldbank.org).

Although information could cross borders almost instantaneously, people could not. There remained tight restrictions on migrant flows. The majority of immigrants to developed countries during the 1980s and 1990s were admitted through family reunification schemes or as refugees (Chiswick and Hatton 2003). Although both Europe and Japan had ageing populations combined with birth rates falling below replacement rates, there were few pressures on governments to relax controls, and xenophobic reactions to ethnic minorities became more rather than less frequent. However, diaspora formed a dynamic component of the global economy (see Box 2.5). There was also considerable illegal migration, especially from eastern Europe and Latin America. Emigrant remittances grew as important components of global capital flows. In 2003 estimated emigrant remittances to Latin America and the Caribbean reached $38 billion. This was more than the total of inward FDI and official aid (*Financial Times*, 26 March 2004).

Box 2.5 Diaspora and globalization

Originally the term diaspora referred specifically to the Jewish population exiled from Judea in 586 BC by the Babylonians, and in AD 235 by the Romans. The Jewish diaspora became one of the oldest, although following the Holocaust in Nazi Germany and the creation of the state of Israel in 1947, the Jewish population became more concentrated. In 2000 there were around 13 million Jews worldwide; 4.6 million lived in Israel, and 6 million in the United States. In recent decades diaspora has been used more widely to refer to any people or ethnic population which left their traditional and ethnic homelands and became dispersed throughout other parts of the world. The largest diaspora include Africans, Armenians, Chinese, Greeks, Lebanese, and Indians.

The networks established by diaspora communities have been important drivers of international business. During the late nineteenth century the Greek diaspora spread over the Mediterranean and Russia was active in wide-ranging international commercial and shipping business. About 600 000 Greeks lived in southern Russia in the first decade of the twentieth century. This community engaged in a wide range of commercial activities, creating a cosmopolitan business network based on kinship ties extending over central Europe and reaching even France and Britain.

Between the sixteenth and nineteenth centuries a Chinese diaspora developed through emigration to southeast Asia. Their ancestors form significant minority populations in the modern states of Malaysia, Indonesia, Thailand, and elsewhere, and a majority of the population of Singapore. More recently Chinese emigration has been directed primarily to the United States and Canada. There are currently an estimated 35 million ethnic Chinese living abroad.

The Chinese diaspora has never been homogeneous. It is divided into different language groups, such as Hokkien and Cantonese. In Southeast Asia (especially Thailand), ethnic Chinese adopted local names and speak the local language. Ethnic Chinese became prominent in commerce and finance, often dominating the business sectors of their host Southeast Asian countries. Family and dialect links enabled ethnic Chinese merchants to operate across borders throughout Asia. After 1980, ethnic Chinese firms based in Hong Kong and Taiwan, and later elsewhere, became the leading foreign investors as China liberalized its economy. They enjoyed connections (*guanxi*) in China, which reduced the transactions costs of investment by offering contacts with public authorities and inside information, and were welcomed by the Chinese government.

The modern Indian diaspora was a product of nineteenth-century British imperialism. Beginning in the 1840s, indentured laborers were transported from India to the British Caribbean, where they filled a gap left by the abolition of slavery. Subsequently they settled in South Africa, as workers in the sugar cane fields of Natal. Indian merchants became prominent in British colonies in Southeast Asia and East Africa. Sindhi, Gujarati and Punjabi merchants had extensive businesses throughout Southeast Asia in the interwar years. After Indian Independence in 1947, there was significant migration to Britain. Around one million ethnic Indians lived in Britain by the end of the century. During the 1990s there was an annual influx of 30 000–45 000 primarily professional Indian emigrants into the United States, which became prominent in the IT, professional, commercial, and academic sectors. Overall, there are currently an estimated 20 million ethnic Indians living outside India.

Overseas Indians were much less prominent as investors in India than their Chinese counterparts. They were less numerous, more of a professional group, and often lacked the family network connections and financial resources to invest in India. In 2003 the Indian government announced it would grant dual nationality to some overseas Indian residents abroad in order to encourage greater investment from this source.

(*Source*: Minoglou and Louri 1997; Brown 1994, 2000; Rauch 2001; McCabe, Harlaftis, and Minoglou, 2005.)

The pressure on rich countries to permit higher immigration was relaxed because technological change permitted companies to export jobs to locations with lower labor costs rather than import workers from such countries. From the 1990s there was a growth in offshoring, involving the relocation of labor-intensive service industry functions from rich countries to remote locations with skilled workforces but much lower wages. Among the functions to be offshored first were back-end processing, call centers, accounting, and software maintenance and development. The geographical flows of offshoring were heavily influenced by language. US businesses dominated the global share of offshoring, and British companies accounted for much of the remainder. It was located mainly in countries where English was the main business language, especially India, but also the Philippines and Israel.

The benefits of global capitalism were not spread evenly between nations and within nations. For many citizens in North America, Europe, and Japan, human indicators such as life expectancy continued to improve. Rapid income gains were also experienced by some East and Southeast Asian economies. The lead was taken by the 'four tigers'—Hong Kong, Singapore, South Korea, and Taiwan—which from the 1960s achieved high rates of economic growth and structural transformation. Between 1966 and 1990 Singapore grew by an average 8.5 percent per annum, or three times as fast as the United States. The 'four tigers' were followed by a second wave of Asian economies, including Malaysia and Thailand, although a major currency crisis in 1997, which began in Thailand, provided a major shock. Subsequent currency crises in Russia in 1998 and Argentina in 2001 demonstrated the vulnerability of the global system to such shocks.

The sustained growth of the Chinese economy marked the most important shift of economic power in the new global economy. China's real GDP between 1979 and 2003 grew at 9 percent per annum. China's re-entry into the global economy had profound implications for the rest of the world. By 2004 China's steel production was larger than the United States and Japan combined, and the country had become the world's second largest importer of oil after the United States. Foreign trade growth averaged almost 15 percent between 1979 and 2003. In 2001, by which time China's GDP was larger than that of Italy and approaching the size of France and Britain, the country joined the WTO. China was by then the largest manufacturer in the world of many products, including DVD players, cellular phones, desktop PCs, cameras, and refrigerators. However, China's GDP per head, at purchasing power parity, was only one-sixth that of the United States in 2004. After 1991, policy liberalization in India was also followed by a more gradual but significant improvement in that country's economic performance (Bhalla 2002).

There were also visible losers. While globalization was good for Asia, most of Africa experienced declining incomes. In the 1990s half of Africa's population lived in absolute poverty. While some Latin American countries including Chile appeared to benefit, others such as Argentina were rewarded for their participation in the global economy by economic crisis and the threat of social meltdown. At the end of the twentieth century most of the world's population beyond Western Europe and East Asia lived in countries where income levels were a lower percentage of the US level than in 1950 (Crafts and Venables 2003). Some scholars ascribed this situation to poorly functioning institutions which were hard to change because of embedded customs and traditions (North 1990). Others pointed to the downsides of globalization. Economic restructuring, liberalization and competition led to increased insecurity and impoverishment for some. Even in developed countries workers with few skills, and even skilled industrial and white-collar workers, faced uncertain futures (Streeten 2001).

Unlike the first global economy, a substantial part of the world was left out of the globalization process. Most economic activity was concentrated in North America, Europe, and East Asia. Rugman (2000) talked of 'regionalization' of production rather than globalization. Ruigrok and Tulder (1995) preferred the term 'Triadization'. Ghemawat (2003), stressing the incomplete nature of cross-border integration, opted for 'semiglobalization'.

2.5.1 Multinationals and the new global economy

Multinationals became the leading driver of the integration of the global economy. During the 1980s the average annual growth rate for FDI outflows reached 14 percent.

Between 1996 and 2000 it reached 40 percent per annum. This was far faster than both the annual growth of world exports (4.2 percent) and of world output (1.2 percent). The huge sums of multinational investment were the result of cross-border mergers and acquisitions which had become the principal vehicle for FDI. These were driven by the new opportunities for globalization, Internet-related technological change, and the very high levels of stock valuation seen in global equity markets. The total stock of world FDI reached $6.8 trillion by 2001, before stagnating over the following two years as world share prices fell.

In 2004 the United States remained, by a considerable margin, the largest home economy. Yet the once-dominant trio of the United States, Britain, and the Netherlands only accounted for two-fifths of world FDI stock. German, French, and other European firms also held large shares of FDI. The surge in Japanese FDI, which had begun in the 1970s, increased rapidly following a sharp appreciation of the yen in 1985. Japan held almost 13 percent of world FDI in the early 1990s, but a decade later this share had fallen to 5 percent. There was also a relatively small amount of FDI from emerging markets, including South Korea (see Chapter 9).

The stock of multinational investment remained largely located in North America and Western Europe, but there was a striking rise of flows into China. For much of the 1990s China was the second largest recipient of FDI worldwide after the United States. This sum did not include Hong Kong, which reverted from being a British colony to part of the People's Republic of China in 1997, albeit administratively distinct for fifty years. From 1979 until 2000 China absorbed, on a cumulative basis, over $346 billion of FDI (Huang 2003). Although inward FDI only represented around 5 percent of Chinese GDP during the second half of the 1990s, and amounted to less than one-seventh of total investment, foreign multinationals accounted for one half of gross exports. In India, the amount of FDI was so small even after 1991 that it had little impact on overall growth. However, Indian diaspora may have been significantly directing **outsourcing** opportunities to their country of origin. The fast development of the IT industry in Bangalore has been attributed to business linkages with Indians working in Silicon Valley (Carana Corporation 2004).

While services represented around a quarter of the total world stock at the beginning of the 1970s, they accounted for at least one half by 2000. Although there are a large and diverse group of service sector activities, 85 percent of service FDI was in trade-related activities and financial services. The same percentage of the stock was located in developed countries, where they took advantage of the growing demand for consumer services from rising real incomes, the growing technological, information and knowledge component of many activities, and the new opportunities offered by deregulation and liberalization.

By 2004 if the level of world FDI was related to the world output, the globalization of international business was approaching that obtained before World War I. Corporations had a much greater flexibility to locate different parts of their value-added activities in different parts of the world. Production of goods and services became internationalized at a deeper level than in the past. A striking manifestation of these trends was a rapid growth of **intrafirm trade** in manufacturing, especially in high technology industries such as automobiles and machinery which had experienced the greatest rationalization on a world scale. In 1970 intrafirm trade was estimated to account for around 20 percent of world trade. By 2000 the share was over 40 percent. Multinationals were the drivers of world trade growth.

As the integration of international production by multinationals proceeded, organizational forms evolved. Although in many industries giant corporations were created by mergers, boundaries of firms also became more porous, as they had been in the first global economy. During the 1970s and 1980s many large US and European-owned M-form corporations suffered from growing managerial diseconomies caused by size and diversification. Large corporations, although spending large sums on R & D, experienced growing problems achieving successful innovation (Christensen 1997). The result was a general trend towards divestment of 'non-core' businesses, outsourcing of many value-added activities once performed within corporate borders, and the formation of many alliances with other firms, which acted as suppliers and customers, or as partners in innovation. The new global economy was complex. Large corporations were powerhouses of innovation spending and market power. Yet the economy could also be seen as a 'worldwide web of interfirm connections' (Mathews 2002).

It remained less evident that the global economy had spawned a multitude of 'global firms'. Trade flows remained more regional than global. Only a handful of large multinationals really operated on a 'global scale'. In most instances, firms continued to generate a high proportion of their revenues from their home regions. A study of the 500 largest companies in the world in 2000 identified 380 for whom the geographical distribution of sales existed. Defining 'global' as a firm having 20 percent of its sales in each three parts of the Triad, but less than 50 percent in any one region, Rugman and D'Cruz (2000) could only find nine 'global firms'. These were mostly in the computer, telecom, and high-tech sectors, such as IBM, Sony, and Intel, but included Coca-Cola. In the new global economy, one study concluded, the multinational was a 'national corporation with international operations' (Hu 1992). As global competition intensified, geography and location remained central to corporate strategy.

■ SUMMARY

Globalization has a long history. However, the flows of people, trade, and capital across borders has not been a linear one, but one with major ebbs and flows. The process accelerated rapidly in the nineteenth century as technological change resulted in sharply falling transport and communication costs. The spread of modern economic growth following the Industrial Revolution created a worldwide search for markets and raw materials. Imperialism forcibly overcame resistance to the spread of global capitalism. By 1914 a remarkably integrated global economy was in place. Entrepreneurs and firms were the drivers of this integration. Chapters 3, 4, and 5 will examine in closer detail how their strategies were pursued in different sectors, Chapters 6 and 7 will show how they built organizations which could manage operations over distance.

Beginning with World War I, the first global economy was progressively destroyed by political and economic shocks. Much European FDI was eliminated through wartime sequestration and the Russian Revolution. Barriers to the mobility of people were erected which have never been removed. Barriers to investment and trade grew to dramatic heights. Multinationals proved flexible. Many existing organizations remained intact, although there was not a great deal of new investment during the 1930s and 1940s. Multinationals responded to the new environment by becoming more 'national' in their operations. They also entered numerous cartel agreements to control prices and restrict output.

Between the 1950s and 1970s there was a rebuilding of the global economy. Trade barriers and exchange controls, if not immigration controls, were removed between North America and Western Europe. However, China, Russia, and other Communist countries remained entirely divorced from global capitalism, and many developing countries erected barriers against it. The very large amounts of multinational investment in resources and related services in developing countries dwindled in importance through localization and nationalization. There were worldwide restrictions on multinational investments in many services. The Japanese 'economic miracle' of these years included the explicit exclusion of foreign firms. However, multinationals also resumed strategies of integrating economies by building regionally integrated businesses in Europe. Service providers diffused knowledge from the United States to the other capitalist economies.

From the 1980s the integration of global capital and commodity markets intensified. Multinational investment drove this process. Its importance to world output finally surpassed that reached in 1913. By the new century two-fifths of world trade alone was intrafirm. Multinationals were the primary drivers of the integration of China into the world economy. However, the influence of location and geography seemed as strong as ever. As Chapters 9 and 10 will explore, multinational investment remained extremely unevenly spread around the world.

There were always winners and losers as global capitalism spread. In the eighteenth century a booming Atlantic economy created lucrative opportunities for merchants, some of whom grew rich transporting African slaves across continents. In the late twentieth century China boomed, but incomes in Africa fell. Later chapters will explore how far the strategies of multinationals explain the pattern of winners and losers from globalization.

PART II Exploiting Opportunities

3 Natural resources

3.1 Multinationals and resources

Multinational investment in natural resources exploitation began early and grew rapidly during the nineteenth century. This was the first sector where entrepreneurs discerned and exploited opportunities to create value by operating across borders. These strategies were among the principal drivers of integration during the first global economy. They created some of the world's largest multinationals whose leadership of their respective industries was to persist until the present day.

The forms taken by multinationals reflect the highly heterogeneous nature of natural resources. The two main subsections of renewable resources (agriculture and forestry) and nonrenewable (mining and petroleum) have different characteristics. The distribution of hard minerals and petroleum around the world is fortuitous and asymmetric with respect to final markets. There are significant scale economies in the exploitation of minerals. Minerals can also only be used once in their original form. This makes questions of ownership and optimal exploitation of the resource of great strategic importance. These characteristics tend to create a different industry structure than in renewable resource industries, where there are often multiple sources for many agricultural commodities, and where products can often be developed by small investors with relative ease (McKern 1993).

There are industry-specific variations even within the wider renewable/nonrenewable categories. Mining industries generally share a number of common features: these include the importance of geology, the capital-intensity and high-risk nature of their business, and that most metals are homogeneous products sold in world markets. But there are also important differences between minerals. Minerals differ widely in their availability. Bauxite, the raw material from which aluminum is normally derived, is not widely distributed, at least in terms of sufficient richness for commercial use. In contrast, tin and zinc are far more widely found round the world.

3.2 Origins

3.2.1 Mining

There has been cross-border trade in precious metals and other commodities since the ancient world, but this had only exceptionally involved the ownership of mines in distant lands. This changed in the nineteenth century. Mining was one of the first activities to attract free-standing firms. Not surprisingly in view of the problems of distance and the risks involved in mining, as well as the still poor conditions of transport and communications, these firms were usually small and transient. There were exceptions, however, which were to prove remarkably long-lasting (Box 3.1). From the middle of the nineteenth century there was growing intra-European mining FDI which took the form both of **horizontal integration**, as mining firms engaged in FDI in foreign countries, and backwards vertical integration, as metallurgical companies sought mineral deposits.

A massive growth in world FDI in mining from the 1870s was spearheaded from Britain, which became the center of the international mining industry. Hundreds of free-standing firms were organized to exploit opportunities in nonferrous metals, especially copper, mostly in Spain and the United States. The Rio Tinto Company, founded in 1873 to buy mines from the Spanish government for the then large sum of $18 million, constructed a mining and metallurgical complex in southern Spain within a decade. It secured for a time a leading position in the world markets for sulfur and copper. Subsequently the emergence of new producing regions, especially in the United States, eclipsed Rio Tinto's Spanish production, but it dominated the world pyrites industry before 1914 (Harvey 1981). Region after region was incorporated into the world mining industry. In the late nineteenth century South Africa, with its rich deposits of gold and diamonds, had become a magnet for foreign entrepreneurs. By 1914 two-fifths of British capital invested in mining was in the South African gold industry (Harvey and Press 1990).

A trio of German metal trading companies became large-scale corporate players in world metals as Europe became increasingly dependent on foreign ores and metals. These were Aron Hirsch and Sohn; Beer, Sondheimer & Co.; and Metallgesellschaft, the

---

Box 3.1 The St. John d'el Rey Mining Company: a nineteenth-century free-standing mining company in Brazil

This company was formed in 1830 by a small number of investors to lease and operate mines in southern Minas Gerais in Brazil. The company operated without limited liability until the British law was changed in 1856. It paid its first dividend to stockholders in 1842. The London board of directors met bimonthly to discuss company business, and there was a small clerical staff in the head office. The chief operating officer in Brazil was known as the Superintendent who headed the mining operations. In Brazil, supervisory positions were held by British nationals, while lower level labor was undertaken by slaves (until 1882) and free Brazilians. By 1913 the company operated the deepest mine in the world employing over 2,500 workers, including 150 European expatriates, and was the producer of the vast majority of Brazil's gold, acquired large real estate holdings around the gold mine, built hydroelectric plants, and owned and operated a private electric railway. During the 1950s inflation and a weak international gold market resulted in deteriorating financial performance. In 1960 the company was taken over by a group of New York financial investors.

(*Source*: Eakin 1989.)

largest of the three. Metallgesellschaft, founded in 1881, moved from trading in metals into the mining, processing, and distribution of copper, lead, and zinc. It invested in the United States and Mexico as well as Europe. Its US subsidiary, the American Metal Company, formed in 1887, invested in coal mining, but its main focus was smelting and refining. In 1912 Metallgesellschaft built the largest refinery in Europe in Belgium to process ore from the Belgian Congo. The German metal traders succeeded separately and jointly in vertically integrating on an international scale the mining, smelting, refining, sale, and manufacturing of all the most important nonferrous metals. In certain metals, such as lead, zinc, copper, and nickel, their control was such as to amount to a preponderant influence upon international prices (Becker 1998).

During the late nineteenth century US-based companies also crossed borders to invest in mining and smelting in Canada, Mexico, and Central America. After World War I, they ventured greater distances, investing widely in Latin America. The largest US FDI in Latin America was in nitrates and copper in Chile; copper, lead, and zinc in Peru; tin in Bolivia. However, US firms were active in almost the full range of minerals including asbestos, chrome, coal, diamonds, gold, nickel, platinum, silver tungsten, and vanadium. The major US enterprises involved included American Smelting and Refining (ASARCO), Kennecott, American Metal (whose ownership passed from German to US hands as a result of World War I), Anaconda, and Alcoa, which grew as a giant aluminum company (Wilkins 1970, 1974a; Navin 1978).

3.2.2 Petroleum

It was in petroleum that some of the world's largest multinationals were to develop. The first oil well in the world was drilled in Pennsylvania in 1859. At this time the primary use of petroleum was as kerosene used in heating and lighting, although by the turn of the century it was also being used as fuel oil as a substitute for coal and as gasoline, the fuel for the newly invented internal combustion engine. The United States remained the world's oil producing country through to 1914. The dominant business enterprise was the Standard Oil Company, which became the largest corporation in the United States, and in the world. Standard Oil's power rested on control over much of the pipelines and refinery capacity in the United States. It also became a major oil exporter. From the 1880s refineries were built abroad to refine imported American oil. By 1907 Standard Oil controlled fifty-five foreign companies capitalized at around $37 million, although it only made modest investments in oil production outside the United States.

Standard Oil's spectacular growth was halted by US **antitrust** legislation. In 1911 the United States Supreme Court decided that Standard Oil was a monopoly which infringed that country's unique (at that time) antitrust laws. It was dissolved into 34 separate companies, nine of which had foreign facilities. Standard Oil of New Jersey (later known variously as Jersey Standard, Esso, and Exxon) obtained the largest foreign assets, including oilfields and refineries in Rumania and Canada; refineries in Germany and Cuba; and marketing operations in Canada, most of Latin America, and Western Europe. Among the other firms formed out of the dissolution were Standard Oil of New York (Socony, and after a merger with the Vacuum lubricants company, Mobil), which took over Standard's Far Eastern distribution companies, and Standard Oil of California (Socal and, later, Chevron). There were also new American entrants into multinational oil, especially the Texas Company (later Texaco) which began to establish overseas sales offices from 1905. By 1913 it was selling oil through its own outlets in Europe, Latin America, Asia, and elsewhere (Wilkins 1970).

The growth pattern of the European-owned oil industry was different. Until the discovery of North Sea oil in the 1970s, Western Europe possessed no indigenous oilfields. As a result, Europe's oil companies emerged from trading and distribution, or else from free-standing companies established to search for oil in foreign countries. In the absence of antitrust legislation, European oil companies demonstrated early an inclination towards market-sharing agreements.

The oilfields of eastern Europe, and especially Russia, played an important part in the growth of European oil companies. The primitive Russian oil industry was transformed by the introduction of modern technology by members of the Swedish Nobel family, who had settled in Russia in the 1870s. They began a process which made Russia the world's largest oil producer by the turn of the century. Their company—which produced around one-tenth of total Russian oil in the late nineteenth century—was not a 'Swedish multi-national', for although members of the Swedish family managed it, they did so from headquarters in Russia with no control from a Swedish parent company. Its equity was held in various Western European countries, as well as in Russia, with German banks as the single most important institutional shareholders (Fursenko 1991).

European banks became powerful drivers of cross-border investments in petroleum. In 1886 the Paris branch of the Rothschild banking family, which had already built a business importing and refining American oil in France, purchased a Russian oil producer which was built into being the largest exporter of Russian kerosene. The Rothschilds also created distribution companies in Western Europe. In 1903 Deutsche Bank, one of German's largest banks, acquired control of a leading Rumanian oil producer, and built a vertically integrated oil business which included distribution companies in a number of European countries (Pohl 1989). In 1906 the Deutsche Bank, Nobels, and Rothschilds established the jointly owned Europäische Petroleum Union (EPU), which owned its own distribution companies and oil tankers throughout Europe. However, the investments were to prove transient. In 1912 the Rothschilds sold their Russian oil interests to the fast-growing Shell Group. The sequestration of German foreign assets during World War I, and the Soviet nationalization of Russian oil in 1917, eliminated both the Deutsche Bank and the Nobels from the industry.

The origins of the two largest European-owned oil companies were also found before 1914. In 1907 a merger of Dutch and British oil companies created the Shell Group (Box 3.2). There was also a cluster of British entrepreneurial ventures. During the 1900s Balfour Williamson, a diversified merchant house with interests along the West Coast of the Americas, developed the largest oil company in California. The engineering contractor Weetman Pearson discovered oil in Mexico in 1908. Both businesses were later acquired by Shell, in 1913 and 1919 respectively. A third company remained independent, and ultimately became British Petroleum (BP). This originated in a syndicate formed to exploit an oil concession granted by the Iranian government in 1901. In 1908, after a long search during which the venture was often on the verge of financial collapse, oil was discovered. The Anglo-Persian Oil Company was formed as a free-standing company with

Box 3.2 The origins of the Shell Group

The Shell Group originated in separate British and Dutch oil companies. The 'Shell' Transport and Trading Company's origins lay in the activities of a London merchant who began his career in the 1830s selling boxes made from shells brought from the East. The business expanded the number of commodities sold, and the Samuel family established a large shipping and trading business in the Far East. During the 1880s the firm began selling the Russian oil of the Rothschilds to the Far East, breaking the monopoly previously held by Standard Oil. Fears that Russian supplies might be reduced led to a search for oilfields nearer Asian markets. In 1898 a major oilfield was discovered in the Dutch colony of Borneo. The 'Shell' Transport and Trading Company was founded in 1899.

The Royal Dutch Petroleum Company was established in the Netherlands in 1890 on the basis of a concession to drill for oil in the Dutch East Indies. Henri Deterding, who became chief executive in 1901, was an ambitious entrepreneur who sought to build an oil company to rival Standard Oil. In 1907 he obliged Shell, weakened by managerial failures and unsuccessful business strategies, to enter a merger agreement. This created the world's first binational corporation. The decision was taken to retain separate Dutch and British holding companies, with separate shareholders. This option was probably chosen to allow the new group access to British diplomatic and political protection, and to retain its position as a supplier to the British navy and army. The British executives of Shell Transport were retained for similar reasons. The Dutch held 60 percent and the British 40 percent of the combined shareholding. Deterding dominated decision-making before his retirement in the 1930s.

After 1907 the Shell Group built integrated distribution businesses in many markets. It acquired major production interests in Russia (1912), California (1913) and Mexico (1919). Its share of world oil production reached 9 percent in 1914, which was four times larger than Standard Oil of New Jersey. By the end of the 1920s Shell was selling gasoline throughout the United States through its 65 percent owned affiliate, Shell Union. During this period Shell also developed major production assets in Venezuela, which had become the world's second largest oil-producing country by 1928.

(*Source*: Gerretson 1958; Beaton 1957; Jones 1981.)

a head office in London in the following year. In 1914 the British government—anxious to secure reliable supplies of cheap fuel oil for the Royal Navy and concerned about British dependence on oil from foreign countries supplied by foreign firms—took a majority shareholding in the company (Jones 1981; Ferrier 1982).

World War I demonstrated both the strategic and commercial importance of oil, and raised fears about the exhaustion of existing oil supplies. The result was a worldwide search for oil in the face of a perceived oil shortage. US, British, and Anglo-Dutch companies dominated this global search. There was intense competition by companies, supported by their respective governments, for concessions in the Middle East, where extensive oil reserves were widely suspected beyond Iran. However, it was not until 1927 that oil was discovered in Iraq. By then fears of oil shortages were being replaced by overcapacity, a problem worsened with the outbreak of the Great Depression. It was 1934 before a pipeline was completed which enabled the export of Iraqi oil. The first major discoveries in Saudi Arabia and Kuwait came only in 1938.

3.2.3 Renewable resources

As the nineteenth century proceeded, entrepreneurs searched with growing urgency for new supplies of food and commodities. The urban populations of Western Europe and the United States consumed growing amounts of foodstuffs. Manufacturing industries needed inputs. Powerful global markets, usually physically located in London, developed for commodities such as wheat, which was typically grown by independent farmers and then traded. In other foodstuffs, multinational strategies were used to develop and exploit supplies. Many British free-standing companies invested in cattle ranges in the United States, acquiring major properties in Texas, Wyoming, Colorado, and New Mexico, though by 1914 most of these ranches were back in American hands (Wilkins 1989). British entrepreneurs also established large land companies in Latin America, especially in Argentina from the 1880s, intended to raise livestock. Large US meat packing companies, such as Armour and Swift, established packing plants in this region also. They came to dominate their beef exports, but did not integrate into ranching (Wilkins 1970).

In some commodities foreign-owned plantations became very important. The demand for rubber had been initially met by wild or natural rubber collected by labor-intensive methods in Brazil. Following the transfer of rubber seeds from Brazil to Singapore, individual British planters began to establish plantations in the British colonies in Malaya. From the mid-1890s the worldwide surge in demand for rubber led British trading companies active in Malaya to diversify into plantation rubber, acquiring estates, and establishing free-standing companies. By 1914, by which time Southeast Asia accounted for two-thirds of world rubber output, companies such as Guthries and Harrisons & Crosfield controlled large acreages of rubber plantations in the region (Jones 2000).

Manufacturing companies also integrated backwards into rubber plantations. Before 1914 Dunlop, the British tire and rubber manufacturer, acquired rubber estates in Malaya, while US Rubber invested in Sumatra, in the Dutch East Indies. During the interwar years other manufacturers followed this route. Among other US rubber manufacturers, Firestone leased a small Liberian plantation in 1925, while Goodyear acquired plantations in Sumatra and the Philippines. In 1927 Ford also began to establish plantations in Brazil. Despite losses caused by pests and other difficulties, Ford's plantations continued until 1945 (Wilkins 1974a; French 1991).

Tropical fruits and tea were among the other commodities which witnessed a massive growth in importance of foreign-owned plantations. During the late nineteenth century bananas became, and remained, the most important traded fruit in the world, and the most important fruit in the diet of most western countries. A handful of vertically integrated multinationals came to acquire a predominant influence on the world banana trade. The largest of these was the US-owned United Fruit (renamed Chiquita in 1990) (see Box 3.3). By the interwar years United Fruit exercised a duopolistic control over the world banana export trade along with another US company, Standard Fruit (Box 3.3).

Box 3.3 The world banana industry and the origins of Chiquita

The United Fruit Company's origins went back to the Boston Fruit Company, which had begun by purchasing bananas in Jamaica for shipment and sale in Boston. In the late 1880s this company purchased Jamaican banana plantations. By the time the United Fruit Company was formed in 1899 the business owned or leased over 320 000 acres of land in the Caribbean, including Jamaica, Cuba, Costa Rica, Columbia, and Nicaragua. This land was primarily used for growing bananas, although there was also orange groves, coconut trees, rubber trees, sugar production, cacao, and cattle land. By 1914, United Fruit accounted for over two-thirds of all bananas consumed in North America.

Initially, United Fruit purchased the bulk of its fruit from independent farmers, but in 1911 it was decided to make large land acquisitions to build plantations. By 1913 the company owned or leased over 850 000 acres. United Fruit made contracts with the host governments in the region. In an agreement with Costa Rica in 1900, United Fruit agreed to increase banana consumption, and in return received government land and a 10-year exemption from export taxes. United Fruit invested in all stages of the operation, and became the first vertically integrated fruit company. Bananas and other fruit were transported from the plantations to the ports in company-owned railroads. By 1914 United Fruit controlled over 800 miles of railroads in Central America. Fruit was shipped in company-owned vessels.

The size of United Fruit dwarfed that of its host economies in Central America. The company was widely known as 'El Pulpo', the Octopus that strangled all it touched.

(*Source*: May and Plaza 1958; Bucheli 2005; Davies 1990; Wilkins 1970.)

The role of foreign companies was almost as great in tea. China was traditionally the largest world producer and exporter of tea. Foreigners were not permitted to own land in the country. As a result, merchants from the tea-drinking countries, especially Russia and Britain, bought tea from local producers, and concentrated on the export, transport, and marketing of Chinese tea to foreign markets. In contrast, plantations became the main form of tea production in South Asia. Following the discovery of tea plants in Assam, the East India Company started experimental tea gardens in 1835. Expatriate British planters developed a plantation industry. Over time plantations were acquired by the expatriate British 'managing houses'. British trading companies such as James Finlay and Harrisons & Crosfield also integrated backwards from tea trading into tea plantations. By the end of the century India had replaced China as the world's largest producer. There was no equivalent of United Fruit in tea production, but the companies engaged in it were large. By the 1940s James Finlay owned 90 000 acres of tea plantations in India and employed 130 000 plantation workers. These firms also invested in marketing channels, developing distribution facilities in Britain, the United States and elsewhere (Jones 2000).

In other commodities, including cotton, tobacco, and coffee, production remained in the hands of local commercial or peasant farming. In such commodities, foreign companies became prominent at the marketing and processing stage. In vegetable oils there was a mixture of investment in production and in intermediary trading. Before World War I the British soap manufacturer Lever Brothers—a predecessor of Unilever—made substantial investments to secure supplies of the vegetable oils needed in soap manufacturing. A large concession was secured in the Belgian Congo to develop palm oil culture, initially using natural palms rather than plantations. In British West Africa, the colonial authorities prohibited the leasing or purchase of land. Lever's response was to buy the expatriate merchants which specialized in purchasing palm fruit and kernel from African producers. This became the basis for the largest European-owned trading company in Africa, the United Africa Company, created in 1929 (Fieldhouse 1978, 1994).

3.3 Determinants

3.3.1 Entrepreneurship, technology, and risk

The fundamental reasons behind the rapid growth of international business in natural resources lay in the industrialization in Europe and the United States which provided a large market growth for minerals and foodstuffs, and so prompted a global search for sources of supply. Until the early nineteenth century the world's demand for nonferrous metals, for example, had been met by long-established mining regions in Europe—Cornwall, Spain, Sweden, and Saxony—as well as Latin America. But as demand soared, and newer metals such as aluminum and nickel were required, these traditional sources of supply were inadequate. New discoveries were made in remoter parts of the globe, and their exploitation was often undertaken using direct investment strategies of one kind or another. The exploitation of natural resources in distant regions was facilitated by improved communications and falling transport costs.

FDI in natural resources arose from entrepreneurial perceptions of these profitable opportunities. The initial exploitation of overseas natural resources in the nineteenth century was typically in the hands of large numbers of small firms or individual prospectors. Mining was—and remains—a high-risk industry not only because of the exploration process, but also due to uncertainties regarding cost and completion time if a mine is constructed, and the subsequent performance of a mine or oilfield. Price fluctuations provided a further dimension of risk. Entrepreneurs seeking to exploit resources on the world's frontiers encountered a formidable combination of logistical problems arising from inadequate or nonexistent infrastructure and, often, political instability or the lack of a modern legal structure.

There was a high level of firm creation and destruction. Fraud and financial malpractice were common. In nineteenth-century mining and petroleum, the borders between speculative, fraudulent, and entrepreneurial activities were thin. In Britain 8,400 companies are known to have been formed between 1880 and 1913 for mining and mine exploration abroad, the great majority of which generated little or no serious activity (Harvey and Press 1990). The individuals behind these companies can be conceived as Kirzner-style entrepreneurs taking advantage of the opportunities of the period, but by transferring technologies and organizational methods across the world they were also Schumpeterian innovators, as much destabilizers of the environment as taking advantage of it. The risks of such investments, and the high rewards if successful, were exemplified by the development of the Mexican oil industry by Weetman Pearson (see Box 3.4).

Box 3.4 Weetman Pearson and the Mexican oil industry

Weetman Pearson began working for his family firm of S. Pearson & Co. based in Yorkshire, England in the 1870s. It became one of the world's largest engineering contractors. Pearson built the Hudson River Tunnel connecting New York with Jersey City, and in 1896 completed a huge scheme to drain Mexico City. Subsequent projects in Mexico included the construction of a modern harbor at Vera Cruz and a 200-mile railroad across the Tehuantepec Isthmus. These successful infrastructure projects resulted in a close relationship with the dictatorial regime of Porfirio Diaz.

Pearson's staff discovered petroleum deposits when they were looking for rock for the Vera Cruz harbor construction. A missed train connection, which left Pearson spending a night at the Texan town of Laredo on the Mexican border, which was in the grip of an oil boom, led him to perceive the possibilities that could arise from discovering oil in Mexico. From 1902 Pearson was able to use his contacts with the Mexican government to secure large oil concessions. Pearson received a 50-year exemption from all taxes. Ahead of finding oil, he invested in downstream facilities by building a refinery and buying oil tankers to transport oil, and signed contracts to supply oil products to distributors in Europe. No oil was found. By 1908 Pearson had pledged his entire personal fortune in the Mexican oil venture, which had been obliged to buy Texan oil on the open market for refining and re-export to Europe. Finally in 1910, after Pearson had hired a new team of American geologists and drilling had moved to a new region, a hugely prolific oilfield was discovered. By 1914 Mexico had become the third largest oil-producing country in the world—Pearson owned 60 percent of total production.

The prior investment in downstream capacity enabled Pearson to build a large integrated oil business which was incorporated as Mexican Eagle in 1910. However, the political risks grew following the overthrow of Diaz in 1911. There was a civil war between 1914 and 1917. The Mexican constitution in that year stated that the state owned the subsoil rights. In 1919 Pearson sold his Mexican oil interests to Shell for £7.7 million. Mexican oil output fell from 25 percent of world output in 1920 to 3 percent in 1930. In 1938 the industry was nationalized. Shell received compensation in 1945.

(*Source*: Spender 1930; Jones 1981.)

Foreign entrepreneurs held several advantages over nationals in developing countries in the exploitation of their resources. The markets for minerals and commodities were overwhelmingly in the developed economies. European and US firms had much better knowledge of conditions in the final market, and greater ease of establishing and maintaining relations with customers in the consumer countries. Their reputations served as guarantees of quality to consumers.

The existence of natural resources in their home economies provided foreign companies with access to skills and technologies which could be exploited abroad. This was obvious in the case of the United States, which in 1900 was the world's largest producer of copper, lead, and petroleum, and second largest in bauxite, gold, and zinc. The importance of French companies such as Pechiney in aluminum reflected France's position as the world's leading producer of bauxite until the 1940s. Britain was the world's largest producer of tin, copper, and lead before the 1850s. The use of skilled miners and technology from the old mining region of Cornwall became a prominent feature of British mining ventures. The importance of countries as major consumers of particular commodities yielded advantages to their firms. The extensive British ownership of tea plantations reflected that country's very high level of tea consumption. By the interwar years the British drank over half of the world's tea output.

Multinational firms had better access to advanced technology, and were better able to recruit professionals trained in Europe or the United States. Advances in mining and other technologies enabled Western firms to discover and exploit new sources of minerals, sometimes replacing indigenous producers in the process. The importance of technological advantages can be seen in the case of Malayan tin. Local Chinese entrepreneurs developed the Malayan tin industry during the nineteenth century. The large surface deposits of alluvial tin were easily mined using labor-intensive working methods, and Western mining companies had no advantage. The situation changed as the more easily accessible and rich ore deposits were exhausted. During the 1900s British companies introduced a new technology—bucket-dredging—which had been first developed in New Zealand in the 1880s. Dredges could operate in swampy areas where drainage was impossible and work low-grade deposits profitably through economies of scale. Few Chinese miners adopted dredging, which was more capital-intensive than previous methods. FDI in Malayan tin surged, and by the end of the 1920s, tin production by Western-owned firms in Malaya exceeded that of Chinese enterprises (van Helten and Jones 1989).

Access to finance also provided advantages for multinationals. The London Stock Exchange was not only the world's leading source of mining finance, but also offered a vibrant entrepreneurial environment. The importance of London as an international financial and trade center enabled it to function as the center of a 'global information network'. British merchants, shippers and other businesses throughout the world sent back to London details of investment opportunities, offers of mining concessions, and information about local contracts (Harvey and Press 1990a).

The capital-intensive nature of mining operations helps to explain the involvement of banks and investment houses in the mining groups which emerged in the late nineteenth century. From the late 1880s the London and Paris branches of the Rothschilds held a large interest, amounting to around one-third of the ordinary capital in 1905, in the Rio Tinto Company. For a time in the late 1890s the Rothschilds also controlled the Anaconda Copper Company in the United States, the then largest copper-producing company in the world (Wilkins 1989). The Mellon banking family loaned the aluminum company Alcoa much of its start-up capital, and controlled a substantial minority stake in the firm for many years. The links between the Rothschilds and Rio Tinto, and the Guggenheims and Kennecott and ASARCO, lasted through much of the twentieth century (Bosson and Varon 1977).

Typically ownership advantages in management were evident. In petroleum and aluminum, US companies grew as large enterprises at home before venturing abroad. These firms exploited abroad organizational capabilities developed at home. The clusters of plantation companies in the business groups around British trading companies had competences based on network forms of organization and socialization methods of control (see Chapter 6).

3.3.2 **Internalization factors**

The large numbers of European free-standing firms active in resources reflected the existence of high transactions costs in capital transfers in the nineteenth century because of the risks that debtors might not repay their obligations. Information asymmetries and opportunistic behavior made the effective monitoring and screening of borrowers costly. A strategy of taking collateral as security for a loan was possible, but not effective for investments in mining and agriculture in which capital sunk into unsuccessful projects could not yield saleable assets.

The free-standing firms in resources can be regarded as providing an institutional alternative to capital markets with high transactions costs. They were created in capital-rich countries to bring additional funds to firms located in capital-poor countries which could not obtain local financing. Rubber plantation companies—and their tin equivalents—in early twentieth century Malaya, owned either by European expatriates or local Chinese, were unable to find sufficient local sources of capital and needed the resources of London capital market. However, their reputations and the nature of their collateral were insufficient to attract London investors. The solution was to reorganize the ventures as free-standing firms, through which British lenders could monitor the use of their funds and exercise some managerial control over the venture (Hennart 1991a).

Transactions costs theory explains patterns of vertical integration in minerals and agricultural products. The presence of physical asset specificity often led to vertical integration rather than the use of markets. This can be seen in the differing patterns of growth of the Bolivian and Southeast Asian tin industries. The former was characterized by greater vertical integration than the latter. The different types of tin found in the two regions help to explain these differences. The tin found in Southeast Asia, including Malaya, was alluvial. It was low grade but easy to mine as it was found close to the surface. The ores could be easily concentrated, and the concentrates were homogeneous and contained few impurities, and were easy to smelt. Mining firms and smelters felt no pressure to integrate but used the market to exchange products. Bolivia's lode deposits, on the other hand, were found underground. The ores were more complex and contained impurities. Smelting lode concentrates was difficult, and had to be tailored to the particular characteristics of an ore. The smelters in this sector were characterized by physical asset specificity. The costs of switching partners were high, while there could be fears that the more flexible party would opportunistically renegotiate the terms of trade. The result was an incentive for vertical integration between mining and smelting in the lode sector of the tin industry (Hennart 1986, 1987).

Problems of quality control arising from situations of information asymmetry encouraged vertical integration in tropical fruit products such as bananas. Export bananas are a highly perishable crop that must be harvested at least once every 7–10 days throughout the year. Moreover, as a tropical fruit, feasible production locations are at a distance from the major consumer markets. The bananas must arrive green at the final destination for subsequent ripening. This involves major investments in specialized refrigeration and ventilated ships, and ripening, storage and transportation facilities in the importing countries (Roche 1998). The growth of large vertically integrated firms was a response to the need to ensure adequate supplies. Consistent quality was better assured by vertical integration because it reduced the incentive to cheat at each stage. Improvements in quality control enabled the multinationals to introduce consumer brands, whose bananas sold at a premium price compared to the unbranded bananas which could be supplied on an irregular basis through an arm's length export trade (Hennart 1987, 1991a).

It was the coordination of production and marketing where the economies of integration and internalization were found in the banana trade. Production itself offered few economies of integration. Consequently United Fruit both owned plantations and contracted with local producers, largely peasants. In Colombia local planters accounted for around 80 percent of United Fruit's exports by 1930. Under the terms of their contracts with the company, the local planters were obliged to sell all their fruit to United Fruit, but United Fruit was not obliged to buy any. The fruit belonged to the company as soon as it was cut from the tree. However, ownership reverted to the planter if the fruit was subsequently rejected on quality control grounds, or if the ship carrying them sank, or if it was damaged in unloading on the docks, or if it was rejected by US health authorities when it was imported into the United States. Local planters also had to agree not to sell any of their fruit to any other company, including the fruit United Fruit had rejected. In return, United Fruit gave loans to the local producers. In the absence of local credit initiations, it became the main banker in the Magdalena region where banana production was located (Bucheli 2005).

3.3.3 Concessions and politics

Relations with governments played a key role in the growth of multinationals in resources. Mining, petroleum, and plantation investments in developing countries often operated on the basis of concessions from host governments, which were often colonial administrations. The lack of bargaining skills and technical know-how on the government side, and the control over technology, capital, and markets on the company side, made most of these concessions appear in retrospect remarkably favorable to the foreign companies. Before 1914 most agreements awarded the concessionaire virtually unrestricted rights in exploiting one or more natural resources. The concessionaire was typically granted extensive rights over a key large land area, often for fifty or more years. The financial obligations imposed on investors were rather limited, and often royalty payments were based on volume of output, rather than on value. It was not until the 1950s that the concept of taxation of concession income began to gain wide acceptance (Smith and Wells 1975).

The concession system effectively placed much of the world's best plantation land and mineral resources in the hands of the first mover companies which had secured them before 1914. Subsequently, it was difficult for new entrants to make great progress, especially because of the economic conditions and falling price of commodities in the interwar years. Greater opportunities emerged in the 1950s, when host governments began to negotiate and/or cancel concessions, but by this time the **first movers** were frequently large vertically integrated corporations possessing further large barriers to entry.

Governments provided competitive advantages for their firms in certain products believed to have a strategic value. The growth of European-owned petroleum companies was encouraged by European governments. The most important example was the British government's investment in the Anglo-Persian Oil Company in 1914. Subsequently the British government provided the funds necessary for Anglo-Persian's growth, a market for its products, and assistance in growing as an integrated oil company by selling it the sequestrated British Petroleum Company, the Deutsche Bank-controlled petroleum marketing and distribution company in Britain (Jones 1981; Ferrier 1982). Although Anglo-Persian retained quasi-management independence from the government, its support at a critical time provides the main explanation of how a wholly British-owned company became one of the world's seven oil majors. During the 1920s several other European governments also created their own companies, notably France's Compagnie Française des Pétroles (CFP) in 1924 (Melby 1981).

During the interwar years the granting of oil concessions became a major part of contention in international diplomacy. In the Middle East, most of whose states were under British or French 'protection' after the war, there were prolonged diplomatic rivalries as the US State Department supported the efforts of US oil companies to gain access. As fears of shortage turned into a problem of surplus oil by the end of the 1920s, the Middle East was divided into monopoly concessions operated by international consortia. Under the terms of the Red Line Agreement of 1928, control of the Iraqi oilfields was in the hands of the Iraq Petroleum Company, jointly owned by Shell, Anglo-Persian, CFP and a consortium of five US companies, including Jersey Standard. These seven oil majors came to be called the 'seven sisters'. The concession for Saudi Arabian oil was held by Aramco, owned jointly by Jersey Standard, Socal, Socony, and Texaco (Wilkins 1974a; Venn 1986).

3.4 International collusion

During the interwar years, and especially the 1930s, extensive international cartel agreements were formed in many natural resources. These agreements were driven by the sharp falls in commodity prices. However, there were considerable differences in their effectiveness and longevity. While in some commodities collusive arrangements proved difficult to sustain even over the short term, at the other extreme a small number of commodities remained controlled by international cartels for decades. The major determinants of successful cartelization included the number of producers, the barriers to entry and the support of governments. Also important in facilitating cartels was nonsubstitutability with other products and nondifferentiation, which meant that producers could not engage in non-price competition while still maintaining high prices.

In the petroleum industry, the pressures towards cartelization that had been present since the late nineteenth century became much stronger in the interwar years, and US companies became involved. As in many other commodities, expanding production in the early 1920s resulted in a growing problem of oversupply within a few years. The result was worldwide marketing agreements symbolized by the Achnacarry Agreement in 1928 (see Box 3.5).

Box 3.5 The Achnacarry Oil Agreement, 1928

In 1928 the chief executives of the world's three largest oil companies—Jersey Standard, Shell and Anglo-Persian—met at Achnaccary castle in Scotland, ostensibly for hunting, but in practice to plan a worldwide oil cartel.

The Achnacarry or 'As Is' agreement was designed to bring surplus productive capacity into balance with demand by controlling competition. Each company was to accept its existing market share and not seek to increase it. They were to make their existing distribution facilities available to other producers at below the cost that a producer would incur by creating new facilities. New facilities were only to be built to meet increases in consumption. Each market was to be supplied from the nearest producing area with the object of securing the maximum economies in transportation and preventing different production areas competing for the same business. Each member of the cartel was allocated a quota for each product in each market, and would direct oil shipments on the geographically most favorable basis. Prices were to be based on those at the US Gulf of Mexico.

It was intended that this agreement should apply to all countries, except the domestic market of the United States, where they faced objection under the antitrust laws. However, arrangements were also made to control US exports through the formation of associations consisting of US oil companies accounting for around almost one half of US oil exports.

In practice, it proved difficult to achieve the desired stabilization of prices in the world oil industry. Attempts to control US production—whose overcapacity was made worse by the discovery of the huge East Texas field in 1930—failed, partly because of US antitrust laws. The failure to cartelize the US domestic market left the oil majors trying to organize cooperation in individual markets. Even this proved difficult. The inability to control US oil exports, as well as those from Soviet Russia and Rumania, undermined the 'As Is' agreements, which had to be renegotiated.

(*Source*: Bamberg 1994.)

Cartels could not survive unless new entrants could be controlled. The failure to control this problem weakened the oil cartels of the 1930s. The attempts to cartelize the world copper industry were unsuccessful also, largely because of the rapid growth of production from the Copper Belt in Africa and Canada (Navin 1978). The cartelization of the tin industry, which took place in response to a dramatic price fall at the end of the 1920s, was more successful. A Tin Producers Association was formed in 1929 which established voluntary output controls. A year later the governments of British Malaya, the Dutch East Indies, Nigeria, and Bolivia signed a Tin Agreement, which established compulsory production quotas. This cartel was successful in sustaining prices and became the basis of one of the world's longest running commodity agreement, which endured until 1985. A major reason for the success of international collusion in tin, as opposed to copper, lay in the willingness of the governments of the major tin-producing countries to support it using their statutory powers (Hennart 1986). It was a similar story in tea. The International Tea Agreement in 1933 was successful in stabilizing prices. This was enforced by government legislation, which was facilitated by the fact that the market was dominated by only three countries—India, Ceylon, and the Dutch East Indies—and by large tea firms (Gupta 1997).

In the world aluminum industry, cartels were successful because of the concentration of ownership. Alcoa, the dominant US producer, stayed out of formal membership of the international cartels for antitrust reasons. Instead it engaged in implicit collusion with the cartels, supported by equity investments in various European producers, as well as in bauxite and waterpower properties in Europe. In 1931 the 'Aluminum Alliance' was formed, designed to stabilize markets in the wake of the Great Depression. Alcoa participated in this Alliance through its nominally independent Canadian subsidiary—Alcan—to which it had transferred virtually all its foreign properties three years previously (Stocking and Watkins 1946).

The long-running international cartels in gold and diamonds show the significance of dominant firms in sustaining collusive agreements. Anglo-American Corporation, which was South Africa's largest gold mining company by the 1950s, was a major influence in both cartels. Anglo-American was controlled from its inception in 1917 by the South African-based Oppenheimer family, which exercised control through a complex web of cross-shareholdings in partially owned companies. The Oppenheimer companies were highly centralized; effectively immune from takeover; and virtually free from government interference.

Anglo-American was able, through its leading position in the South African gold industry and that industry's importance in world gold production outside the Soviet Union, to exert a considerable influence over gold prices. This control was facilitated by long-term collusion with the Soviet gold industry, which like Anglo-American had an authoritarian and secretive structure able to sustain collaborative agreements over the long term. Although no formal cartel agreement was made, for decades after World War II the Soviets and South Africans met to regulate the supply of gold so as to keep prices high and curb speculation (Spar 1994).

In diamonds, more formal collusion became a feature of the industry. This collusion was driven by the nature of the industry. While mining diamonds was highly capital- and labor-intensive, there was no guarantee that the stones they retrieved would be valuable. Indeed, much of the value rested in the image that diamonds were rare. By the 1890s a cartel of diamond merchants in South Africa, then the only source of diamonds, had already been formed. In 1929 Anglo-American acquired one-third of De Beers, the dominant producer in that country. An international diamond cartel was organized by De Beers' London-based Central Selling Organisation (CSO), established in 1934, which controlled at least 80 percent of world trade in rough (uncut) diamonds. De Beers sought to purchase a large percentage of world output. The rough stones were then sold through the CSO to an elite group of the world's diamond merchants, who were obliged to purchase the rough diamonds in a quantity and at a price set by De Beers.

De Beers' influence was initially based on South Africa's unique role as a diamond producer, but by the end of the century South Africa only accounted for 11 percent of total world gemstone production. De Beers responded by developing collaborative links and long-term contracts with the new diamond producers. After the discovery of a large supply of diamonds in Siberia in the 1950s, the Soviets entered the diamond cartel.

De Beers purchased most of the Soviet production of gems, and then marketed the stones through the CSO. The diamond cartel became an almost uniquely successful commodity cartel which kept the supply of diamonds limited and their price high for decades (Spar 1994).

During the 1990s there were serious challenges to this cartel. The collapse of the Soviet Union resulted in the growing threat of unofficial Russian sales reaching the market. In the United States, the Department of Justice blocked the company from selling diamonds directly into the country on antitrust grounds, while in 1994 it was indicted in an Ohio court on a charge of fixing industrial diamond prices. It was only in 2003, following the adoption of a new marketing strategy involving a joint venture with the luxury goods group Moët Hennessy Louis Vuitton (LVMH) aimed at promoting De Beers' brand name in the US diamond jewellery market, that De Beers could establish a direct presence in the United States. In 2004 De Beers paid a $10 million fine to settle the price-fixing case (*Financial Times*, 12 July 2004).

3.5 The growth of large integrated firms

3.5.1 Mining

By the middle decades of the twentieth century ownership and control of the world mining industry was highly concentrated. Horizontal integration had occurred as firms sought to utilize their skills and expertise developed in one country to others, and to diversify sources of supply. This was the traditional strategy for the growth of mining firms. Vertical integration also occurred as firms sought to control all or some of the stages of production from mining or drilling, through processing and refining, to distribution and manufacture of final products. Driving this concentration process was the growing capital-intensive nature of mining, and the longer gestation periods following an initial investment before a product could be produced and sold. There were, however, marked differences in industry structure between minerals (Box 3.6).

The world aluminum industry was controlled by a small number of large vertically integrated multinationals. During the interwar years they collaborated closely in extensive international cartel agreements, but these arrangements were subsequently disrupted by regulatory intervention. In 1945 Alcoa was the subject of a historic US antitrust decision when it was ruled that although Alcoa had not intended to create a monopoly, the fact remained that it had a monopoly on the American domestic market which was in violation of antitrust law, and it would be in the nation's best interest to break it up. In the wake of this decision, US government-financed wartime aluminum plants which had been run by Alcoa were sold off to two new rivals: Reynolds Metals and Kaiser Aluminum and Chemical. In 1950 the US courts also obliged the separation of Alcoa and Alcan, its Canadian affiliate, on the grounds that the same nine shareholders controlled almost 45 percent of Alcan's stock and over 46 percent of Alcoa's stock (Smith 1988). During the 1950s and 1960s these four North American firms coexisted with France's Pechiney and Alusuisse of Switzerland to form a 'big six' in the world aluminum industry.

Box 3.6 Market shares of large multinationals in selected minerals in the 1950s

Commodity	Combined share of world production (%)
Aluminum	
Alcoa, Reynold Metals, Kaiser	90
Aluminum, Alcan, Pechiney,	
Alusuisse	
Copper	
Kennecott, Anaconda, Phelps Dodge,	65
Roan-AMC, Anglo-American, Union	
Minière, International Nickel	
Tin	
London Tin Corporation, Patiño,	45[1]
Billiton	
Iron Ore	
Bethlehem Steel, Republic Steel, United States	10
Steel	

[1]Before 1952.

(*Source*: Vernon 1983 for aluminum; United Nations 1980 for copper; Hennart 1986 for tin; author's estimates for iron ore.)

These six multinationals were internationally vertically integrated across all three stages in the production of aluminum. They controlled almost all the world's bauxite reserves, which were largely concentrated in a number of developing countries, especially in the Caribbean and later in Africa. Once mined, the bauxite was transferred internally between the affiliates of the six multinationals for refining into alumina. Little refining was undertaken in the bauxite-producing countries, although Alcan, whose longer shipping routes made cutting transport costs important, built alumina plants in Jamaica and Guyana during the 1950s. A number of other alumina refineries were built in the Caribbean region during the following decade, as host governments pressured companies for local processing. At the next stage a smelting process converted alumina into aluminum. This electrical process was highly energy-intensive, so smelting facilities were located near low-cost sources of energy. Until 1970 the only aluminum smelter built in the Caribbean was a small one in Surinam owned by Alcoa (Rodrik 1982).

In 1956 the six major multinationals produced most of the world's alumina and accounted for 85 percent of the smelting capacity of the world outside the Communist countries. The strength of these companies was mainly derived from control of this processing stage. More than three-fourths of world trade in bauxite and alumina occurred internally between the affiliates of multinationals, and no open competitive markets for these materials developed (Cobbe 1979; Vernon 1983).

The rationale for such extensive vertical integration in aluminum lay in its extremely capital-intensive nature and the existence of high economies of scale associated with the refining process. There were substantial advantages to operating smelters at as near full capacity as possible, which necessitated a continuous supply of raw material. The need for security of supply of bauxite also explained why each company used bauxite from a number of sources. A particular feature of the industry was the high asset-specificity in bauxite refining, arising from the cost savings that could be obtained when refineries were built to process a single type of bauxite. As bauxites are heterogeneous, each refinery needed to obtain its bauxite from a limited number of mines, and switching costs were high. There was an obvious incentive for vertical integration by refiners to avoid opportunistic behavior by suppliers of ores (Cobbe 1979; Hennart 1987).

Large vertically integrated multinationals were also for a time a prominent feature of the world copper industry. Based in the world's leading producer and consumer of copper, large US companies secured world leadership in the industry. In copper, unlike aluminum, control of rich ore deposits was a decisive competitive advantage. In 1911 the three largest US copper groups controlled between them 48 percent of world copper refining output (Schmitz 1986). The largest US copper companies all became involved to some degree in FDI—even though the North American copper market can be regarded as segmented off from the rest of the world—but the degree of internationalization and integration differed considerably. Kennecott originated as a copper mining company. It integrated into semi-fabrication in 1929, but until 1958 the company's ores were smelted and refined by ASARCO, an outcome of the Guggenheim participation in both companies. ASARCO originated as a lead smelter, and became involved in smelting of copper in 1899. It entered the copper mining business in 1922 with an investment in Peru, and subsequently it purchased mining interests in Canada, Mexico, and Australia, but it did not mine copper in the United States until 1954. ASARCO diversified abroad much more than either Kennecott or Phelps Dodge, but was less integrated into fabrication. Phelps Dodge started as a copper trader and began copper mining in the 1880s. Unlike Kennecott, it integrated into fabricated copper at a relatively early stage, and by the early 1930s was refining most of its smelter output. Phelps Dodge became the first fully integrated US copper company (Navin 1978; Read 1986).

Barriers to entry to the copper industry were lower than in aluminum. Copper smelters and refiners were less capital-intensive. The ongoing discovery of large sources of copper not only undermined the interwar cartels, but provided the basis for challengers to the American leadership. A vast mineral zone was discovered in the Belgian Congo before 1914. By 1929 the Union Minière du Haut Katanga, which exploited these deposits, emerged as one of the world's leading suppliers of copper. The development of the Zambian copper deposits in the interwar years provided further opportunities for new entrants. Nevertheless in the 1950s the seven largest copper mining companies accounted for around two-thirds of total copper output of the market economies.

The importance of large integrated multinationals in the world tin industry peaked in the interwar years. In Malaya, which dominated world production, many of the British free-standing companies active in tin production came under the control of the London

Tin Corporation (LTC), which was formed in 1925. By 1937 the LTC controlled, through its subsidiary Anglo-Oriental, about one-third of Malaya's tin output. This company also controlled tin companies in Thailand, Burma, and Nigeria. Although the alluvial nature of Southeast Asian tin provided no strong incentive for integration forwards into smelting, LTC became part owner of one of the two large smelters which smelted the whole of Malaya's output of tin concentrates.

In contrast, a vertically integrated multinational developed from the Bolivian tin industry. The Bolivian entrepreneur Patiño displaced the foreign companies which had initially developed the Bolivian industry and by 1910 had become the largest Bolivian producer of tin concentrates. This output was at first sold to smelters in Britain and Germany. In 1916 Patiño secured control of the British smelter, in partnership with the US-owned National Lead Company, a major consumer of tin. This was a rare case of a tin user acquiring interests in mining or smelting. The high physical asset-specificity of the smelters required to deal with Bolivia's lode ores provided an incentive for this strategy. In 1929 Patiño also obtained control of one of the two Malaya smelters (Thoburn 1981; Hennart 1986). During the 1920s the main corporate vehicle for this Bolivian company, the Patiño Mines and Enterprises Consolidated, was registered in the United States, apparently to assist the raising of capital (Klein 1965; Wilkins 1993b).

By the 1930s three groups—LTC, Patiño and the Dutch government and private company (Billiton) interests which controlled the Dutch East Indies tin industry—accounted for almost half of the world's mining and tin smelting outside the Soviet Union (Hennart 1986). This concentration facilitated the cartelization of the industry, and Patiño and LTC were behind the first producers cartel. But during the early 1950s—much earlier than in most other minerals—host governments began to take control of the production of tin. In 1952 Bolivia became the first country to take over its tin industry. The Patiño group remained important in the marketing and smelting of tin, but lost its ownership of mines. From 1953 the Indonesian government began excluding Dutch companies from mining, a process which was completed by the end of the decade.

The role of multinationals in iron ore remained less than in bauxite, copper or even tin. Large US and European steel corporations established in the nineteenth century grew up close to their own domestic sources of iron ore and coking coal. They integrated backwards within their own economies and became integrated from mining through fabrication, but plentiful domestic supplies and high transport costs did not provide incentives to invest abroad. The iron and steel industry became characterized by powerful domestic firms which were vertically integrated within their own borders, which were protected by high tariffs and—in the interwar years—extensive international cartels. Both international trade and investment in iron ore were low. In 1950, measuring by the iron content of ore, less than 20 percent of the world output of iron ore was exported, and over half of those exports were in intra-European trade (Cobbe 1979).

From 1950 the leading US steel companies began to invest on a substantial scale in mining ore internationally. The principal reasons for the change of strategy included a feared exhaustion of domestic iron ore supplies; improvements in bulk shipping capacity which reduced the cost of long ocean hauls; and the discovery of new iron ore locations. By 1964 US-controlled companies controlled three-fourths of Canada's iron ore producing capacity. Bethlehem Steel developed mines in Chile, Venezuela, and Liberia;

Republic Steel mined ore in Liberia and US Steel invested in Venezuela (Wilkins 1974a; McKern 1976).

Barriers for entry into production of iron ore were relatively low. The growth of the Japanese steel industry in particular provided vast opportunities for new independent producers. The iron ore industry developed as one where international vertical integration from iron ore to steel remained low, but where two-fifths of trade took place under long-term arm's-length contracts between major producers and consumers (principally Brazil and West Germany, Australia and Japan), while another two-fifths was sold on more short-term contracts (Brown and McKern 1987).

3.5.2 Petroleum

In 1950 the seven major oil companies or 'seven sisters'—five American (Jersey Standard, Gulf Oil, Texaco, Standard Oil of California, and Mobil) together with BP and Shell—accounted for 85 percent of gross crude oil production and 72 percent of refinery throughput in the world excluding North America and the Communist countries (Penrose 1968). In a ranking of the world's largest industrial firms by revenues in 1956, all of the 'seven sisters' were among the world's top twenty-five enterprises. Jersey Standard and the Shell Group were in second and third place respectively. In comparison, Anaconda, at that time the world's largest mining company, was ranked the world's 55th largest industrial firm by this measure (Schmitz 1995).

The large petroleum majors were vertically integrated internationally, operating at all stages of the industry, beginning with the exploration and production of crude oil and ending with the distribution of the finished product to the final consumer. In the 1950s they controlled 90 percent of the oil moving in international trade. They were also extensively diversified into petrochemicals, fertilizers, and other industries which used petroleum derivatives as raw materials. Vertical integration in the industry arose—or was said to arise—from the benefits to companies from assured outlets for crude; the more efficient operation of refineries as a result of assured and managed flows of crude oil; and the greater ability to adjust to short-run changes in the demand for different products in different areas (Penrose 1968).

The economics of the industry encouraged such concentration. The investments required to develop an oil field or build a refinery were extremely large. Once these sums had been committed, operation of the facility entailed high fixed costs. As a result, small variations in price or in output had a relatively powerful effect on profits. Short-term elasticities of both supply and demand have been low, which meant that they were both very slow to respond to price changes. Both the interwar cartels and the extensive vertical integration can be seen as responses to these conditions.

During the postwar years oil majors were behind the rapid expansion of the Middle East oil industry. Between 1948 and 1972 Middle Eastern crude oil production grew from 1.1 million barrels to 18.2 million barrels. Almost all of this low cost production was controlled by the 'seven sisters', plus France's CFP. Huge finds were also made in Nigeria, and smaller ones in Canada. By the 1960s there was excess capacity and falling real prices in the industry. This cheap energy helped drive the fast economic growth seen in these years.

Despite the growth of Middle Eastern oil, the United States remained both a large producer as well as the world's largest market for petroleum. This attracted new multinational investment. In 1958 BP, the only one of the seven majors to lack any presence in that country, entered a joint venture with the US's seventh largest oil company, Sinclair Oil, designed to supply BP's cheap Middle Eastern oil to Sinclair for refining and marketing in the United States. The US adoption of mandatory oil import quotas in 1959 blocked the initial strategy, but the two companies did undertake exploratory work in Alaska. Ultimately BP went ahead with exploration alone, securing large acreage at Prudhoe Bay, where the largest oil field ever found in the United States was discovered in 1968/69. In 1970 BP acquired a shareholding in Sohio, a large regional refiner and marketer which lacked crude, and in a complex arrangement transferred its Alaskan oil interests into it on the understanding that it would receive majority ownership when production reached a certain level, which it did in 1978. Full ownership was taken of the company in 1986 (Bamberg 2000, 2001).

3.5.3 **Renewable resources**

In plantation agriculture, large vertically and horizontally integrated multinationals continued to exercise a major influence on trade and production in commodities between the 1950s and 1970s. In addition to being one of the world's largest consumer goods manufacturers, Unilever became one of the world's largest agribusinesses. Its huge affiliate in the Belgian Congo was converted over time to intensive plantation production, not only of palm products but also of other tropical products. By 1959 this affiliate had a planted area of 140 000 acres producing 54 000 tons of palm oil, as well as smaller quantities of cocoa, coffee and tea, and was probably the world's largest single plantation enterprise. Unilever also had smaller plantation investments in seven other countries. Unilever was the world's largest single producer of palm oil; it was responsible for around 12 percent of total world exports of palm oil in 1960 (Fieldhouse 1978).

In the world tea industry, the influence of free-standing firms and trading companies was superseded over time by larger corporations, both local and foreign. In India, most of the expatriate managing agencies which had held a large share of Indian tea production were acquired by local entrepreneurs between the 1950s and 1970s. James Finlay's large India tea plantations were sold to the powerful Tata business group during the 1970s. Subsequently Tata Tea established marketing operations in the United States, acquired the large British tea marketing company Tetley in 2000, and developed an integrated multinational tea company with a significant presence in over thirty-five countries by the new century. However, it was Unilever which became the world's largest tea company through a series of acquisitions. Unilever became the inheritor of the legacy of the nineteenth-century British entrepreneur Sir Thomas Lipton. It acquired T.J. Lipton, the largest tea company in the United States, during World War II, and the wholly separate Lipton International, an international tea marketing company, in 1971. In 1984 Unilever made a further acquisition of British-owned Brooke Bond, which had large plantations interests which amounted to 3 percent of Indian national production of tea, 15 percent of Kenya's, nearly 40 percent of Tanzania's, and about 2 percent of total world tea production. This acquisition raised Unilever's share of world tea consumption and trading to well over 20 percent.

Meanwhile, the banana industry continued to be dominated by a few large integrated firms, which had advantage of access to the best plantation sites, often held by concessions, and which had control of refrigerated transport and contacts with retailers. There were modifications to the corporate structure of the banana industry over time. Following antitrust proceedings, United Fruit was enjoined not to acquire further banana companies, and in 1967 it had to spin off part of its business to form a new company. It was acquired by another company and renamed United Brands in 1970, and Chiquita in 1990. The company experienced a series of mishaps during the 1970s, including a hurricane which destroyed 70 percent of its Honduran plantations, and a Federal court conviction for bribery of a Honduran government minister. Subsequently the company complained that it was disadvantaged by the EU banana regime which favored imports from former colonial territories. In 2000 it still accounted for 25 percent of the world banana market, but its struggle to change EU quota policy—in which it enlisted the support of the US government—proved costly. In 2001 Chiquita had to file for Chapter 11 debt restructuring (Bucheli 2005).

The second member of the banana duopoly, Standard Fruit, was acquired in 1968 by Dole (then known as Castle & Cooke), a Hawaiian shipping and food processing company. Subsequently Dole preferred to adapt to EU regulations rather than fight them, investing in African production and diversifying its operations. A third major competitor emerged in the industry, when the Del Monte Corporation, a large US multinational fruit and vegetable processor, diversified into bananas after an unsuccessful takeover bid by United Fruit in 1967. Del Monte acquired the West Indies Fruit Co, a banana company based in Tampa Florida, set up its own plantations in Costa Rica, and acquired the United Fruit business in Guatemala. The company was owned by the US conglomerate RJR Nabisco between 1979 and 1989, when the canned fruit and fresh produce businesses were sold separately. In 1996 the Abu-Ghazaleh family acquired the latter, and took it public (Roche 1998). In 2000 Dole and Del Monte accounted for 25 percent and 19 percent respectively of the world banana market.

In sugar cane large integrated multinationals continued to expand during the middle decades of the last century. The sugar industry consisted of two complementary agricultural crops: cane from tropical areas and beet from temperate ones. The beet sugar industry and refineries were in the hands of strong national oligopolies usually supported by protectionist policies. Historically these firms undertook little FDI. Sugar cane was produced by estates which sold their raw sugar on the world sugar commodity markets in New York, London, and Paris. There had been substantial FDI in sugar plantations since the late nineteenth century. US sugar refiners, for example, owned nearly 40 percent of Cuban output in 1958 (Wilkins 1974a). Booker McConnell, initially a British trading company, accounted for 70 percent of the sugar output of Guyana in central America in the 1950s, which was shipped to Britain in company-owned vessels (Chalmin 1990). Tate and Lyle, Britain's leading sugar refiner, began buying sugar estates in the West Indies in 1937, and over the following three decades acquired large estates and factories in Jamaica, Trinidad—where it accounted for 80 percent of the local production—Guyana, Zambia, and Zimbabwe.

3.6 New entrants and the decline of integration

3.6.1 The ownership of resources

From the 1950s the development of multinationals in natural resources represented a considerable contrast with manufacturing. As a relative proportion of world FDI, the significance of the natural resource sector progressively declined. While manufacturing multinationals began to integrate their production internationally, in most resources there was a strong trend towards the fragmentation of vertical integration, and the decline of intrafirm trade flows.

A major reason for the decline of vertical integration was the policies of host governments to increase national ownership and control over natural resources. This trend led to expropriation of foreign assets, especially from the late 1960s. The extension of national control over resources was often accompanied by the formation of 'producer associations'—or cartels of national producers—designed to enhance the bargaining power of host countries against the vertically integrated companies. The classic example was the Organization of Petroleum Exporting Countries (OPEC) founded in 1960 by Iran, Iraq, Kuwait, Saudi Arabia, and Venezuela. In 1973/74 OPEC emerged as the role model for producer cartels following unilateral huge rises in the price of oil from $3 a barrel to $11.75. It became apparent over time that this cartel was no more successful than the 'seven sisters' in regulating prices over the long-term, yet OPEC—which in 2003 had eleven member countries and was headquartered in Vienna, Austria—retained a powerful influence over worldwide production levels.

The ownership of world minerals and petroleum was transformed. In tin, the Bolivian and Indonesian nationalizations of the 1950s were followed by the extension of state ownership, or at least state participation, in production in many other countries. A landmark event was the takeover in 1976 of the London Tin Corporation—the largest tin mining MNE—by the Malaysian government to form the Malaysia Mining Corporation (MMC). In copper, there was widespread nationalization during the 1960s and 1970s by the established producing countries of Chile, Peru, Zambia, and Zaire (Shafer 1983). By the early 1980s about one half of the mineral production capacity located in developing countries was state-owned (Radetzki 1989). Between 1971—when Algeria and Libya nationalized their oil industries—and 1976 virtually every major oil-producing developing country nationalized their oil industry.

Multinationals became increasingly dependent on arm's-length transactions for their raw material needs. While in 1960 the leading seven copper corporations still controlled between 60 percent and 70 percent of copper production, two decades later the seven largest private companies controlled less than 23 percent of copper production. The copper industry was integrated, but mainly within national boundaries, where state-owned enterprises accounted for over 40 percent of copper mining capacity and substantial percentages of smelting and refining capacity (UN 1980). In 1970 the seven major oil companies owned 69 percent of world crude production. By 1979 their share had fallen to 24 percent. The system of integrated supply was replaced by government-to-government deals.

Foreign ownership of plantations was greatly reduced also. In some cases this was through outright nationalization, the fate of Booker McConnell's sugar plantations in Guyana in 1976. In other cases governments pursued localization strategies. In Malaysia almost the entire foreign-owned plantation sector was 'localized' during the 1970s and 1980s. State-owned companies were used as vehicles to buy the equity, and then 'localize', many of the large British-owned plantation groups, such as Sime Darby (Jones 2000). Nevertheless, the foreign ownership of plantations did not disappear even at the height of the fashion towards 'localization'. The large tropical fruit multinationals retained control of large plantations; they still accounted for around 60 percent of banana production in Latin America at the end of the 1990s (Roche 1998). Foreign companies continued to own and control tea and other plantations in East Africa, whose governments looked upon them as valuable sources of employment.

Nor did the loss of ownership over the production of many commodities automatically imply a decline in the control which multinationals exercised over them. While the ownership of plantations declined, multinationals continued to exert considerable influence over developing country agriculture through various forms of contract. In the banana industry, the multinationals developed the 'Associate Producers' system under which they sold or leased some of their plantations to local independent producers. The Associate Producers remained dependent on the companies through the latter's control over production inputs and technical assistance, and through the long-term contracts in which the multinationals set the purchase price of a given grade of banana. They also retained control over transport and distribution in the main markets—so that third party companies could not purchase the surplus fruit and the local producers could not dispose of unsold supplies. This kind of contract farming enabled multinationals to avoid conflicts over land ownership and labor issues, and lessened the risk of expropriation because fewer assets were located within the host country (United Nations 1987; Glover 1986).

3.6.2 New entrants

The emergence of new competitors to incumbent multinationals changed the corporate structure of world resource industries as much as host government policies. In the oil industry, the postwar years saw the rise of competitors to the 'seven sisters'. These included US European state-owned oil companies such as France's CFP—which was virtually the eighth member of the seven sisters—and Azienda Generale Italiana Petroli (AGIP) of Italy, which was part of Italy's state energy-holding corporation, Ente Nazionale Idrocarburi (ENI). During the 1950s AGIP developed an innovative strategy for negotiating oil concessions with producer states which offered them a 'partnership' in the exploitation of their natural resources. The same strategy was applied when the Italian company sought concessions to build refineries and distribute its refined products in developing countries. AGIP also formed distribution companies in many European countries and Africa. Using imported Soviet oil, AGIP offered the lowest gasoline prices in Europe. Among other independents which competed for concessions and markets were US companies such as Getty Oil, Occidental, Amerada, and Continental. The independents weakened the influence of the oil majors on world prices, and increased the bargaining power of the producer governments.

The competitive structure of the industry became more complex as both the large mining and petroleum incumbents diversified into other industries. Mining companies evolved as holders of broad portfolios of investments in a range of minerals, although investments beyond mining were rarely sustained. The oil majors, which were cash rich as a result of the high oil prices after 1973, and feared being excluded by direct contact between oil producing and consuming nations, also diversified. In 1970 Shell acquired Billiton, a long-established Dutch company which had diversified from tin mining in the Dutch East Indies into bauxite, and subsequently into other minerals. The Atlantic Richfield Company—the pioneer oil explorer in Alaska—acquired Anaconda in 1977. In 1980 BP acquired a large British mining group, Selection Trust, while its Sohio affiliate acquired Kennecott in the following year. There were also large investments in coal, nuclear power, and chemicals.

These diversifications by the oil majors were rarely successful, and sometimes financially disastrous, fully demonstrating the capabilities of firms to destroy as well as create value by expanding across borders. In most cases, firms lost interest as the profitability of petroleum was restored after the traumatic years of the 1970s and early 1980s. In 1989 BP sold most of its mining and minerals business to Rio Tinto Zinc (RTZ), the British mining company. Five years later Shell sold its Billiton metals and mining assets to Gencor, a South African mining group. By the end of the century the oil majors had divested most activities outside the petroleum industry except in oil-related chemicals and alternative energy sources.

Among new entrants were locally owned companies which had acquired the production assets of the multinationals. By the early 1980s state-owned entities controlled about one half of the mineral production capacity in developing countries (Radetski 1989). In most cases state mineral enterprises did not undertake FDI nor attempt to integrate forwards, but there were exceptions, especially in copper. Both Codelco of Chile and ZCCM of Zambia made investments in European downstream processing of copper. Codelco became the world's largest copper producer on the basis of copper mines formerly owned by the US multinationals in Chile. ZCCM, in contrast, became a byword for the management problems and resulting inefficiency of state-owned firms (Radetski 1989).

In aluminum, state-owned companies in Venezuela and the Arabian Gulf built large smelters, while Japanese companies invested in smelting capacity in foreign countries or supplied technology to foreign smelters in return for long-term contracts to supply the Japanese market. However, despite such new entrants and nationalizations in the major bauxite exporting countries of Guyana and Jamaica, in 1982 six major multinationals still controlled 46 percent of world bauxite production, and 50 percent and 45 percent respectively of the refining and smelting of alumina and aluminum (Brown and McKern 1987). During the 1990s about two-thirds of world alumina was still traded among affiliates.

Multinationals often developed contractual and equity relationships with state-owned mining enterprises. While the state companies could sell products such as copper for which there existed a competitive world market, in the case of products like bauxite in which no open market existed, they often needed to form joint ventures with foreign companies. Joint ventures became increasingly common in aluminum, and often worked to the advantage of the multinationals, which were able to negotiate favorable supply and management arrangements (Rodrik 1982).

In the petroleum industry, a few state-owned companies became vertically integrated multinationals. The Kuwait Petroleum Company (KPC) pursued one of the most ambitious strategies. During the 1960s the Kuwait government obliged the company which controlled its oil production—a joint venture between BP and Gulf Oil—to relinquish part of its concession to a state company, which also established a refinery in Kuwait. During the early 1970s foreign ownership of Kuwait's oilfields was completely eliminated, and in 1980 the KPC was established to manage the various government oil activities. During the 1980s KPC expanded into exploitation and distribution abroad, buying Gulf Oil's refining and marketing networks in various European countries. KPC survived the temporary Iraqi occupation of its home country in 1991, and continued to expand over the following decade.

State-owned entities were far from the only new entrants. In the banana industry, the Ecuadorian firm Noboa was able to challenge the tropical fruit multinationals. In Ecuador, restrictions on land ownership by foreign firms meant that the banana industry was developed by local firms. Noboa began business in 1952 selling to Standard Fruit, and soon afterwards began exporting using its own banana ships. Noboa rapidly increased Ecuadorean production from the 1980s. By end of the century Noboa held around 11 percent of the world banana market (Roche 1998).

3.7 Consolidation and privatization since the 1990s

From the 1990s there was considerable consolidation and restructuring in the resource industries. In the petroleum industry, a period of low oil prices—below $10 a barrel—towards the end of the decade stimulated mergers and acquisitions which created a small group of 'super majors'. Exxon Mobil was created by merger in 1999. A year earlier BP acquired the US-owned Amoco, the sixth largest publicly traded oil and gas company in the world, in the largest cross-border transaction in business history until that point. In 2000 BP acquired another US oil company, Arco, and the smaller British-owned Burmah Castrol. The French-based Total Fina Elf was created through the mergers of France's Total and Elf Aquitaine and Belgium's PetroFina in 1999 and 2000. ChevronTexaco was created by the merger of two major US companies in 2001. Only the Shell Group, the fifth 'super major', did not follow this trend. It successfully cut costs by internal restructuring, but during 2004 the company became embroiled in a corporate governance scandal having admitted to the overvaluation of its reserves by 20 percent.

The super majors were enormous in scale and scope (Box 3.7). In 2002 Exxon Mobil operated in 200 countries. BP marketed its products in over 100 countries and had production in twenty-three countries; 44 percent of its sales were in the United States, 41 percent in Europe, and the remainder in the rest of the world. These giants coexisted with smaller companies. US-based integrated oil and gas companies, such as Amerada Hess and ConocoPhillips, explored for oil and natural gas worldwide, but their refining and marketing operations were generally limited to the United States. European companies included Italy's Eni, which was a fully integrated oil and natural gas company, whose production locations included West Africa, the Arabian Gulf, Brazil, and the

Box 3.7 The world's largest international petroleum and mining companies, 2003

Company	Home economy	Revenues ($ billion)
Oil super majors		
Exxon	US	246.5
BP	UK	232.5
ChevronTexaco	US	121.7
Shell	Netherlands/UK	121.2
Total Fina Elf	France	104.6
Large mining companies		
Alcoa	US	21.5
Anglo-American	UK	18.6
BHP Billiton	UK/Australia	15.6
Alcan[1]	Canada	13.6
Rio Tinto	UK/Australia	9.2

[1] In 2003 Alcan acquired Pechiney, which had revenues of $14.4 million in that year.

(*Source*: Company Annual Reports.)

Caspian Sea. State-owned international integrated oil companies included Saudi Aramco, Petroleos de Venezuela (PDVSA), the National Iranian Oil Company (NIOC), Petroleos Mexicanos (PEMEX), and the KPC.

A similar process of consolidation evident in mining saw the emergence of a small number of diversified large and multinational companies. These included the long-established Rio Tinto. This British company finally sold its original Spanish mines in 1954 after many difficulties with that country's Fascist dictatorship. By then it had already invested in the Zambian Copper Belt in the interwar years. In 1962 Rio Tinto partly merged with the Consolidated Zinc Corporation, an Australian mining company, to form the Australian-based CRA, and began to diversify further into copper, uranium and tin, and more widely into cement, chemicals, and oil and gas. After 1988 the nonmining businesses were sold, but the mining business grew further through the acquisition of BP's international mining interests in 1989, and of the Nerco and Cordero coal mining businesses in the US in 1993. In 1995 Rio Tinto and CRA were unified through a dual listed company structure, Rio Tinto plc in Britain and Rio Tinto Ltd in Australia, which operated as a single business entity with the same board of directors. The corporation was one of the world's leading producers of iron ore, bauxite, copper, diamonds, coal, and uranium.

Cross-border mergers of companies based in Canada, Australia, and South Africa created giant mining groups. In 1993 South African-based Anglo-American Corporation placed its non-African operations in a separate, Luxembourg-registered company known as Minorco, and in 1998 merged with that entity to form a new British-registered company, Anglo-American plc. This involved buying out of minorities and unravelling of cross-holdings, including that with De Beers. Anglo-American took a 45 percent share in De Beers, which remained controlled by the Oppenheimer family. In 2001 Gencor, another leading South African mining company which had previously bought Billiton from Shell, shifted domicile to Britain, and was then acquired by Australia's BHP. The new enterprise, which was among the world's top producers of iron ore and coal, was a dual-listed Anglo-Australian company run as a single entity with the same board of directors and management. In 2000 a three-way merger between Alcan, the Canadian aluminum producer, and the Swiss and French companies Alusuisse and Pechiney was blocked by European competition authorities, but the merger of the first two companies went ahead, and three years later Alcan succeeded in acquiring Pechiney.

There were new opportunities for multinational companies as former Communist countries opened their borders to them, and as former state-owned assets such as Zambia's ZCCM were **privatized**. The Caspian Sea was opened up to exploration by foreign oil companies following the breakup of the Soviet Union in 1991. Three years later the Azerbaijan government signed a thirty-year agreement with a consortium known as Azerbaijan International Operating Company (AIOC), consisting of the state oil company, BP, Amoco, Russia, and Turkey's national oil companies, and several other foreign companies. There were also some large foreign investments in Russia, despite political risk and corporate governance scandals. In 1997 BP paid $570 million for 10 percent of the Russian oil company Sidanko, only to see many of the firm's assets taken by Tyumen Oil Company (TNK), a Russian competitor as a result of bankruptcy litigation in the country's opaque courts. During 2003 BP invested a further $6.15 billion in a joint venture with its former adversary TNK. In the same year Shell invested around $10 billion in a company formed with the Japanese trading companies Mitsui and Mitsubishi to develop oil and gas on the island of Sakhalin.

Box 3.8 Coffee and globalization

The globalization of coffee consumption and production took place over centuries. The coffee tree probably originated in the Ethiopian province of Kaffa. The outer cherry flesh of coffee berries was eaten by slaves taken from present-day Sudan into Yemen and Arabia, through the great port of its day, Mocha. Coffee was cultivated in Yemen by the fifteenth century. During the seventeenth century Dutch and Italian merchants took the product to Europe, and it also reached North America. In 1616 Dutch merchants also took trees back to Holland where it was grown in greenhouses. At the end of the seventeenth century the Dutch planted coffee in Java, Indonesia. The Dutch planted coffee in their South American colony of Surinam in 1718, to be followed by plantations in French Guyana and the first of many in Brazil at Para. In 1730 the British introduced coffee to Jamaica.

Brazil became established as the world's major coffee-growing region, accounting for three-fourths of world production in 1900. Brazilian planters used African slaves before the Emancipation in 1888, and thereafter southern European immigrants. Coffee production was also encouraged in some European colonies in Africa and Asia. Unlike sugar or rubber, foreign planters or companies made few investments in coffee estates. Coffee did not, unlike tea, require immediate processing after harvesting, so was there no incentive for plantations with their own processing establishments. Foreign firms, especially German, Dutch, and British merchants, became important in the processing and exporting stage. In Brazil ten export houses sent out two-thirds to 90 percent of the crops until the 1920s, and continued to control over half after that. There was a similar concentration in the roasters of coffee beans in the consumer countries. During the nineteenth century the United States became the largest market for coffee. By the 1950s, the five largest roasters in the United States, including General Foods which controlled the Maxwell House and other leading brands, roasted over one-third of all the coffee.

In 1938 Nestlé invented powdered instant coffee after eight years' research, following a request from the Brazilian government to develop coffee cubes as a way of using up a large coffee surplus. It was launched in the United States in 1939. In the 1990s Nestlé accounted for over one half of the world instant coffee market, and General Foods for one-third. Instant coffee provided one-third of all coffee drunk in the United States in the peak year of 1978. After World War II the mechanization of coffee processing eliminated the human factor in coffee roasting, and a new emphasis on convenience rather than quality, facilitated the growing influence in the industry of a few large multinationals which offered lower quality, ground-roasted, canned or instant coffee. They collaborated with the wide-spread government-supported collusion in the industry. Between 1962 and 1989 the International Coffee Agreement awarded annual quotas to countries.

The complex world coffee supply chain spanned producers, local traders, exporters, roasters, and retailers, but most of the value was captured by the large multinational roasters which benefited from economies of scale and **brand** recognition. In 2000 around 80 percent of coffee was sold as roast and grounded. Philip Morris was dominant in this market in the United States, while in Europe Philip Morris, Sara Lee/Douwe Egberts and Nestlé were the market leaders. In instant coffee, Nestlé held over one half of the world market, and Philip Morris over a fifth. The multinationals provided price leadership in the coffee market. Between 1975 and 1993 the international price of coffee fell by 18 percent on world markets, but the prices paid by US consumers rose 240 percent. During the late twentieth century international chains of coffee bars, such as Starbucks, partially re-energized the demand for coffee in developed markets, but their impact on coffee markets remained small.

(*Source*: Clarence-Smith and Topik 2003; Koehn 2001).

Nevertheless, mining and petroleum companies continued to face many governmental restrictions. Mineral and petroleum wealth remained highly politically sensitive. The Middle East was still closed to foreign firms and 'global forces' because of upstream nationalizations, various embargoes and sanctions, and OPEC output restraint. As a result, international companies focused on the development of high cost petroleum deposits elsewhere, even though Middle Eastern oil was much cheaper to develop.

In foods and beverages, large multinationals exercised a pervasive influence on many commodities, including coffee (see Box 3.8).

Multinationals exercised a strong and growing influence on global patterns of foods production. In Latin America and other emerging markets, there was a rapid growth of nontraditional agricultural exports such as off-season fruits and vegetables and speciality horticultural crops. This growth was in response to demand in rich countries caused by consumer demand for more healthy products, as well as improved refrigerated shipping infrastructure which made it easier to transport fresh commodities. The large tropical fruit multinationals were well-placed to distribute these products to international supermarket chains (Raynolds 1994). However, large retailers, in their quest for cost reduction, also built long-term direct supply relationships with locally owned producers and exporters. This was in part due to increasing concentration of retailing in developed countries and the growth of international sourcing of fruits and vegetables.

Fish farming also developed rapidly. Although the most dynamic initial growth of the industry was not due to multinationals—the highly successful Norwegian industry was developed by local fishing interests—multinationals were also active in its first stages. In 1968 Unilever started to invest in the breeding of salmon when it developed its own fish farm in a remote Scottish loch on the basis of knowledge acquired from Norway. During the 1980s its Marine Harvest subsidiary expanded to Chile, before being sold in the following decade, becoming part of Nutreco, based in the Netherlands. During the 1990s multinationals drove the fast growth of fresh fish exports. Nutreco became the largest producer of farmed salmon in the world, accounting for 16 percent of total production in 2004. It owned farms in Norway, Scotland, Ireland, Canada, Australia, and Chile. In Chile, the role of multinationals grew rapidly through the acquisition of local companies which held concessions for salmon. By 2000 about 40 percent of Chilean production was foreign-controlled (United Nations 2002).

■ SUMMARY

During the nineteenth century multinational investment played a key role in the global search for raw materials and foodstuffs for the markets of the industrialized world. Numerous entrepreneurial firms were formed to engage in this search. Western-owned firms brought a large proportion of the world's resources under their ownership. These firms employed a variety of strategies including vertical integration, networks, and long-term contracting to secure and retain control of resources in the face of unpredictable changes in markets, technologies, and political conditions. First mover advantages were reinforced by monopoly concessions which typically included highly favorable fiscal provisions.

In many commodities there were strong internalization arguments for integration and, together with the capital-intensive nature of mining, this led to the emergence of large corporations. By 1914, a high proportion of the world trade in commodities such as petroleum, aluminum, and bananas was intrafirm. During the interwar years—and sometimes later—these firms also cooperated in extensive international cartels designed to stabilize markets, though this aim was rarely achieved over the long-term.

From the 1950s the position of incumbent multinationals was partially eroded by host government intervention, the increased bargaining strength of hosts, and the diffusion of technology and management skills. Vertical integration down to the production level was weakened or eliminated in most commodities. However, large multinationals often retained powerful positions in world commodities through their control of transportation, processing, and marketing, and by horizontal diversification. These firms were often able to control quality and quantity of production by the use of contracts.

During recent decades privatizations and the opening of once-closed markets again created multiple opportunities for multinationals in the resource sector. Multinationals again invested in minerals and petroleum in the former Soviet Union as well as many emerging markets. Cross-border mergers and acquisitions produced a new generation of global giants. Yet there was no return to the pre-1914 world. Multinationals often acted in joint ventures or used contracts rather than wholly owned natural resources. And resource investments were no longer the driving force of globalization.

4 Manufacturing

4.1 Multinationals and manufacturing

Multinational strategies have figured prominently in nearly all of the world's most dynamic manufacturing industries since the late nineteenth century. The firms that pioneered the capital-intensive technologies of the Second Industrial Revolution of the late nineteenth century—chemicals, electricals, and machinery—rapidly expanded into international markets. The automobile producers followed in their path, as did their post-World War II successors in computers, pharmaceuticals, and telecoms.

The scale and significance of multinational manufacturing raises key issues in international business. Why did entrepreneurs choose to build factories in foreign countries rather than export their products or license their technologies? How and why did multinational investment become so important in the world's leading industries? How were complex technologies and brands transferred between countries by firms?

4.2 Origins and growth

4.2.1 Overview

There appears to have been no case of multinational manufacturing before the nineteenth century. The first instances appeared during the 1830s. Among the pioneers were Swiss cotton firms, which built plants in neighboring southern Germany (Schröter 1993b). These investments, like many of the earliest attempts, were short-lived, but mid-century saw direct investments in manufacturing which were more durable. During the 1850s Siemens and Halske, the German firm which pioneered the development of telegraph and cable equipment, established workshops in St. Petersburg, Russia and London, England to install and maintain products manufactured in Berlin. In 1863 the company went further, and built its own cable factory near London, designed to ensure independence from the prices and quality of existing suppliers (Feldenkirchen 2000). Singer, the sewing machine company, has often been regarded as the first successful US multinational manufacturer. By 1914 it had built an extensive international business (see Box 4.1).

There were many examples of multinational manufacturing before 1914. In Europe, a 'foreign' investment could be very geographically proximate. Swiss investments in foreign countries were sometimes within walking distance from the Swiss border.

Box 4.1 The multinational expansion of Singer Sewing Machines 1867–1914

Singer's growth was based on the invention at the beginning of the 1850s of the world's first commercially successful sewing machine. By 1867 Singer had become the largest manufacturer of sewing machines in the world, and it opened its first foreign factory in Glasgow, Scotland. It began by assembling parts imported from the United States. Over time it manufactured the heavy stands of the machines, and assembled them with imported machine heads. Finally, it began to manufacture entire machines and supply them worldwide. In 1885, Singer opened a new factory near Glasgow. This was the largest sewing machine factory in the world. There were other factories in Canada, Austria, and Germany, and in 1901 a Russian factory was opened outside Moscow.

Building on its practice in the United States, Singer used its own sales offices to market sewing machines, selling its products through hire purchase. Following innovations in the British market, Singer pursued a marketing strategy of intensive marketing through individual canvassers. By 1890 Singer's sewing machines were sold virtually worldwide and almost entirely by its own employees. As its markets in North American and Western Europe became saturated, Singer employed its sales strategies to great effect in new markets, especially Russia. Singer's sales in Russia rose from 70 000 machines in 1895 to almost 700 000 machines in 1914. Singer's Russian company had an elaborate network of offices and around 4,000 depots, stores and shops, and employed over 27 000 people. Thousands of Singer agents—who received a weekly salary plus commission—were responsible for selling machines, collecting installment payments, and even doing minor service on machines.

Singer's sewing machines became one of the world's first global products. They provided a means to fulfill a universal need—to wear clothes—in a novel way, by putting in people's homes a machine formerly only in factories. The machine did not break down, was mobile, and could be used by women. By 1914 Singer accounted for a staggering 90 percent of all the sewing machines sold in the world.

(*Source*: Davies 1976; Carstensen 1984.)

Basel-based chemical and pharmaceutical companies Geigy and Hoffman-la-Roche built factories in Grenzach, which was effectively a suburb of the Swiss city, but located just over the German border (Schröter 1993c). US FDI in Canada was also sometimes just over the border. Ford's first Canadian factory was across the Detroit River from its US operations (Wilkins 1970).

There was an extraordinary diversity of firms engaged in multinational manufacturing. There were large and small firms, managerial and family firms, free-standing companies and more 'conventional' multinationals. While many US firms manufactured internationally by 1914, in sheer numbers Western European companies were pre-eminent. Even manufacturers from Japan—then a very poor economy compared to Europe and the United States—made small investments in textile spinning and weaving in China in the 1900s, and Kikkoman opened a soy sauce factory in Denver, Colorado in the 1890s (Wilkins 1986b, 1989).

Multinationals were active primarily in the products which developed during the Second Industrial Revolution rather than the First. By the end of the nineteenth century textiles still accounted for around two-fifths of total British exports, with iron and steel and machinery accounting for a further one-fourth. These were the products in which the United Kingdom held a comparative advantage in the world economy. Yet the British firms in these industries undertook almost no FDI, in contrast to their counterparts in branded consumer products, cotton thread, tyres, and artificial silk. Multinational manufacturing developed in industries in which technology, brands, and product differentiation were key features.

4.2.2 Chemicals and machinery

Multinational strategies were prominent in the high technology industries of this era—chemicals and machinery. The late nineteenth century saw remarkable developments in the chemical industry, associated with the application of scientific research to industrial processes. Thousands of new products were invented. The German chemical companies grew as large managerial enterprises which made long-term investment in research and production. In some sectors the German superiority was crushing. In artificial dyestuffs the total value of the production of the eight German firms (including their foreign subsidiaries) amounted to three-fourths of total world production in the 1900s. German firms were vigorous exporters of their new products, but they also invested abroad on a substantial scale (Schröter 1990).

The leading German dyestuffs firms, BASF, Bayer, and Hoechst, established their first foreign subsidiaries in Russia and France in the 1870s and 1880s, followed later by the United States and Britain. Bayer, the largest firm, had taken a minority interest in a US manufacturing company in 1871, and although this particular investment was later disposed of, Bayer became a substantial manufacturer in the United States. In 1914 Bayer owned three of the seven dyestuff plants in the United States, and it also manufactured there the new pharmaceutical products which it had developed, notably aspirin. The German companies supported their manufacturing operations in the United States with extensive nationwide sales organizations (Wilkins 1989). In Russia, five German manufacturers established six dyestuffs factories which accounted for around 80 percent of the German dyes sold on the Russian market in 1913 (Plumpe 1990).

Bayer and Hoechst had large pharmaceutical operations, but there were also specialized German pharmaceutical firms which went abroad before 1914. E. Merck began manufacturing pharmaceuticals (including morphine, codeine, and cocaine) in the United States in 1899, and started production in France in 1912 (Hertner 1986). Further, FDI was undertaken by the leading German electrochemical firms, such as Degussa, the largest German producer of cyanides by the electrolytic process. By 1914 this firm's US subsidiary had four manufacturing plants in operation producing a variety of cyanides, bleaching agents, sodium, and chloroform (Wilkins 1989; Chandler 1990).

Among non-German firms, the first Swiss chemical FDI occurred in 1882 when a dyestuffs firm built a small factory near Lyon, France to supply the textiles industry. Ten years later this factory was sold to another Swiss firm, Geigy, which had already begun manufacturing in Russia in 1888. By 1914 Geigy, Ciba, and Sandoz had small-scale manufacturing in the United States, Britain, France, and Germany, while the Swiss pharmaceuticals manufacturer Hoffmann La Roche had opened a factory in Britain in 1909 (Schröter 1993c). The Belgian chemical firm Solvay & Cie also developed a large multinational business to exploit its invention of a continuous process to make caustic soda, which was used in the manufacture of glass, textiles and other chemicals (Bolle 1968). In contrast, the US manufacturers of industrial chemicals and pharmaceuticals rarely ventured beyond their home market before World War II. Meanwhile, British chemical firms lagged in technology, and had no basis on which to expand abroad (Chandler 1990).

The machinery industries of the late nineteenth century resembled chemicals in the proliferation of new products. Unlike chemicals, it was an industry in which US-based companies became prominent international investors. They pioneered the mass production of machinery by fabricating and assembling interchangeable parts, and as a result US firms became world leaders in many products. A considerable proportion of US manufacturing FDI in Europe originated from this sector. Otis Elevator became the first worldwide producer of lifts, with factories in Britain, Germany, France, and Canada by 1914. National Cash Register became the world's first-mover in cash registers, and had factories in Germany and Canada by 1914.

In electrical engineering two German firms (Siemens and Allgemeine Elektricitäts-Gesellschaft (AEG)) and two US firms (General Electric (GE) and Westinghouse) formed a global **oligopoly** which dominated the world electrical industry. In 1913 German firms accounted for more than a third of the world's production of electrical goods, and almost a half of world electrical exports (Feldenkirchen 2000). By 1914 Siemens had ten foreign factories spread over five countries. AEG, founded in 1883, acquired factories in Russia and Austria-Hungary, and established joint venture production subsidiaries with GE in Italy and Siemens in Russia. From the formation of GE in 1892, the US firm expanded abroad, building a network of overseas subsidiaries in which it had equity stakes, though not always controlling ones, mostly operated by its Thomson-Houston subsidiary. A contrasting strategy was that of Westinghouse, who constructed a number of large overseas factories, beginning with a giant plant in Manchester, England in 1899. By 1914 other large factories were owned in Germany, France, Russia, and Canada. Size was no guarantor of profitability, and during World War I the firm divested from European manufacturing (Wilkins 1970).

Swedish electrical engineering companies also became internationally important in a number of specialist products. ASEA, which pioneered methods of electrical transmission in the 1890s, acquired a British manufacturing company in 1898. L. M. Ericsson developed a large overseas business—exporting 95 percent of its production at the turn of the century—and then built factories in the United States, Russia, Britain, and elsewhere in Europe, manufacturing telephone exchanges and sets for local markets (Olsson 1993).

4.2.2 Branded consumer goods

Multinational manufacturing was found in many branded consumer goods by 1914. British companies manufactured dog food and toffee in the United States, and marmalade in Germany. A German firm manufactured malt coffee—a cheap coffee-substitute made from barley—in Austria, Sweden, Russia, and Spain. US, British, and German multinationals made gramophone machines and records all over Europe, as well as in India, Brazil, and Argentina (Wilkins 1989; Hertner 1986; Jones 1985).

The predecessors of two of Europe's largest consumer goods firms—Nestlé and Unilever—already had substantial multinational investment by 1914. Nestlé originated as one of a cluster of Swiss firms producing condensed milk, baby food, and chocolates. The Anglo-Swiss Condensed Milk Company, which despite its name was a purely Swiss company, established a British factory to produce condensed milk in 1872, and an American plant ten years later. This enterprise also expanded elsewhere, although in 1902 divested from the United States by selling its business to the US company Borden. Three years later Anglo-Swiss merged with another Swiss firm Nestlé, which had itself established foreign condensed milk factories by the turn of the century. By 1914 the combined business manufactured condensed milk and baby food products in Britain, the United States, Australia, Norway, Germany, and Spain. Nestlé also had a large shareholding in a Swiss chocolate company which manufactured chocolate in the United States and elsewhere (Wilkins 1989).

The predecessors of Unilever were large-scale multinational investors also. Van den Bergh and Jurgens, the leading Dutch margarine companies, established factories in Germany and Belgium; by 1914 each Dutch firm had seven margarine factories in Germany. In Britain, the Dutch companies invested in distribution, forming relationships with retailing groups which led, by 1914, to the acquisition of full control over several chains of retail shops. Lever Brothers, the British predecessor to Unilever, erected or purchased soap factories in numerous countries between 1890 and 1914, in several of which it controlled multiplant operations (Wilson 1954).

4.2.3 Significance by 1914

There was extensive multinational manufacturing by 1914, especially in chemicals, machinery, and branded consumer products. Amidst the galaxy of small or failed investments, some manufacturing companies had established extensive multicountry and multiplant manufacturing (see Box 4.2).

These companies were usually first movers in their industries. They often established market positions which proved hard to challenge unless the companies fell victim to complacency. The foreign affiliates of these companies sometimes became large business enterprises, employing a thousand or more workers, and even larger numbers when the firms also undertook FDI in marketing and distribution. Saint-Gobain's German factories accounted for almost two-fifths of the French firm's total glass production in 1913 (Daviet 1989). By the same date Singer's sales in Russia alone accounted for over 30 percent of its total worldwide sales (Carstensen 1984). In 1914 almost one-fifth of Siemens's total workforce of 80 000 were employed outside Germany (Weiher and Goetzeler 1977).

In terms of market share, foreign-owned manufacturing affiliates sometimes secured prominent positions in their host economies. In the United States, the production of a number of products was either wholly dominated by, or substantially in the hands of, foreign multinationals, including cotton thread, rayon, magnetos, and dyestuffs (Wilkins 1989). In Germany, foreign-owned companies were pre-eminent in products as

Box 4.2 Some large multinational manufacturing enterprises, c. 1914

Company	Nationality	Product	No. of foreign factories in 1914	Location of foreign factories
Singer	US	Sewing machines	5	UK, Canada, Germany, Russia, Austria-Hungary
J & P Coats	UK	Cotton thread	20	US, Canada, Russia, Austria-Hungary, Spain, Belgium, Italy, Switzerland, Portugal, Brazil, Japan
Nestlé	Swiss	Condensed milk/ baby food	14	US, UK, Germany, Netherlands, Norway, Spain, Australia
Lever Brothers	UK	Soap	33	US, Canada, Germany, Switzerland, Belgium, France, Japan, Australia, South Africa
Saint-Gobain	France	Glass	8	Germany, Belgium, Netherlands, Italy, Spain, Austria-Hungary
Bayer	Germany	Chemicals	7	US, UK, France, Russia, Belgium
American Radiator	US	Radiators	6	Canada, UK, France, Germany, Italy, Austria-Hungary
Siemens	Germany	Electricals	10	UK, France, Spain, Austria Hungary, Russia
L. M. Ericsson	Sweden	Telephone equipment	8	US, UK, France, Austria-Hungary, Russia

(*Source*: author's estimates)

diverse as elevators and margarine. In Britain, they were the major forces in dyestuffs and electrical engineering.

4.2.4 The interwar followers

During the interwar years manufacturing firms went to more foreign countries, and built more plants, and made more products in individual foreign countries. Yet multinational strategies became more complex. Managers had to negotiate their way through a web of exchange controls and tariffs. They often found themselves negotiating with governments. There was a growing rate of failures, and of divestments.

World War I produced winners and losers among the established manufacturing multinationals. The winners included the firms owned by the European countries which had managed to stay neutral, notably Sweden, Switzerland, and the Netherlands. The growth of the Swedish company SKF to become the world's largest ball-bearing manufacturer was greatly facilitated by being able to undertake production on both sides during the war. War time profits enabled the Swedish company to buy up the entire German ball-bearing industry in the 1920s (Lundström 1992).

Sweden was also home to Swedish Match. During the 1920s this firm expanded rapidly from its Swedish base, led by its charismatic chief executive Ivar Kreuger. By 1930 companies owned at least 50 percent by Swedish Match accounted for more than 40 percent of total world match production and manufactured in over thirty countries.

Swedish Match's growth was based in part in its willingness to make sovereign loans in return for being given match monopolies. In Germany and much of eastern Europe, Swedish Match operated state match monopolies. Loans were financed from borrowing from the United States. Kreuger had a close relationship with various leading American financiers, who regarded the seemingly respectable match company as a safe intermediary to lend funds to Europe. It later emerged that the whole business rested on fraudulent balance sheets. The Great Depression exposed the weakness of the corporate edifice. Kreuger committed suicide in 1932. However, Swedish Match survived. It had seventy manufacturing companies in thirty-one countries in the mid-1930s (Hildebrand 1985).

The multinational growth of German companies was radically affected by the expropriation of most of their assets by the victorious Allies. Former dynamic international strategies became more risk-averse, as well as resource-constrained. In chemicals and pharmaceuticals, the loss of intangible assets such as brand names and patents was perhaps even worse than that of physical assets. Bayer only recovered the right to use its own brand name in the North American market in 1994. E. Merck & Co. also had its US pharmaceuticals business expropriated. Although family members bought it back from the US government in 1919, the US-based Merck & Co. became fully American with no links to its former German parent. In electrical engineering, Siemens not only lost its foreign factories and patents, but had to compete in international markets with its former British affiliate which had become an independent company.

During the interwar years German manufacturing companies often preferred to participate in international cartels and other arrangements which did not involve the investment of large sums of capital abroad rather than risk multinational investment. Yet large German enterprises often rebuilt extensive international distribution networks. By 1936, Siemens & Halske had sixteen plants in Europe, as well as factories in Japan and Argentina. However, World War II again led to the loss of all its foreign assets—alongside those of all other German companies—and even the loss of the right to use its name in more than forty countries (Feldenkirchen 2000).

The growth of large multinationals was facilitated by the merger waves of these years. In chemicals, there was a large-scale consolidation of the industry. In Britain, four separate companies merged to form ICI, which provided the basis for the renewal and growth of the British industry. IG Farben was formed in the mid-1920s by the merger of eight German firms including Bayer, BASF and Hoechst. By the end of the 1930s this company had 726 subsidiaries or partly-owned affiliates in foreign countries. Two-thirds of these were sales agencies, and most of the remainder were engaged in the finishing and packaging of pharmaceuticals and dyes (Schröter 1984). The formation of Unilever in 1930 saw the creation of a second Anglo-Dutch giant alongside Shell (see Box 4.3).

Most multinational manufacturing was located in other developed economies. Over 80 percent of total US FDI in manufacturing in 1929 was located in Canada or Western

---

Box 4.3 The foundation and early growth of Unilever

Unilever was formed in 1930 through a merger of Lever Brothers and the Margarine Unie, itself a recent merger of Dutch firms including Van den Berghs and Jurgens, as well as Schicht, one of the leading oil and fats businesses in central Europe. The business was controlled by two holding companies—Unilever Limited registered in London and Unilever NV registered in the Netherlands—with identical boards of directors. An arrangement known as the Equalisation Agreement stipulated that British and Dutch shareholders would receive dividends of equal value. Unilever had two chairmen and two head offices, in London and Rotterdam. The basic structure remained in place in 2004.

Unilever's businesses included not only soap and margarine factories, but also African trading companies, plantations, ships, retail shops and much more. On its creation Unilever already possessed extensive multinational manufacturing on four continents, although Britain, the Netherlands and Germany provided the largest share of corporate profits. During the interwar years new factories were opened in, among other countries, India, Thailand, Indonesia, China, Argentina and Brazil.

Unilever also built a large business in the United States. Lever Brothers began manufacturing soap in the United States in the late nineteenth century. During the interwar years it mounted a successful challenge to Procter & Gamble, the largest incumbent firm. By 1940 Lever's share of the US laundry soap market reached 30 per cent, compared to Procter's 34 per cent. Unilever acquired full control of the leading US tea company T. J. Lipton in 1943, and acquired the toothpaste company Pepsodent in 1944. The basis of Unilever's post-war frozen products business was also laid with the purchase from General Foods of the rights to manufacture and sell quick-frozen foods under the Birds Eye name.

(*Source*: Wilson 1954; Jones 2002.)

Europe. European firms invested primarily either in other European countries or in the United States, although British companies such as Dunlop, the tire manufacturer, and Cadbury and Rowntree, the chocolate manufacturers, also increasingly turned to Australia, New Zealand, Canada, and South Africa, which were small, but developed and risk-free, markets within the British Commonwealth (Jones 1986a).

Manufacturing investments in developing countries were not unknown, especially in larger markets with tariff barriers. In interwar India, British companies built factories in soap, tyres, chemicals, and tin containers, among other products (Tomlinson 1989). In China, British trading companies including Jardine Matheson and Swires invested in cotton textiles and sugar refining before World War I. During the interwar years a new generation of multinational manufacturers entered that country. Lever Brothers began manufacturing soap in Shanghai in 1923, and Chinese soap sales constituted around 2 percent of Unilever's worldwide total within one decade. Swedish Match had a large manufacturing business in Shanghai (Osterhammel 1989; Cochran 2000). The British American Tobacco Company had a vast cigarette manufacturing operation (see Box 4.4). In Latin America, Brazil was a popular location. Unilever began manufacturing toilet soap in 1929, followed six years later by toothpaste. During the 1930s, Goodyear and Firestone built tire plants, and Du Pont began making chemicals.

> ## Box 4.4 British American Tobacco and China before 1949
>
> The origins of BAT lay with the American Tobacco Company, which had exploited the commercial possibilities of the invention of continuous-process cigarette machinery to become the biggest cigarette enterprise in the United States by the turn of the century. The acquisition of a leading British producer in 1901 led to a violent reaction from British competitors organized into the Imperial Tobacco Company. In 1902 a compromise was reached. The US market was reserved for the American Tobacco and the United Kingdom for Imperial Tobacco, while they created a new company, BAT, to control tobacco production and marketing in the rest of the world. Although British-based, BAT was initially US-controlled and managed, but this US influence was diluted after American Tobacco was ordered to be dissolved under US antitrust law in 1911. By the early 1920s BAT had become British-controlled.
>
> BAT built an extensive multinational manufacturing business. China was its largest single market for the first 25 years after BAT was founded. American Tobacco began exporting to China in the 1890s. James B. Duke, that company's founder, had a strong conviction about the huge potential market opportunities of that country. An initial factory in Shanghai was followed by others after 1905. By 1914 BAT was manufacturing in China between one half and two-thirds of the 12 billion cigarettes it sold in that market. The firm was fully integrated from control over the growing of tobacco through all stages of production and forward to distribution and marketing in China. A key factor in the firm's success was its distribution. BAT developed accounting and control systems that both monitored its cigarettes and minimized the risk of bad debts. It fostered competition within its own sales teams by creating parallel distribution mechanisms, in particular through the creation of a joint venture with a Chinese firm, Wing Tai Vo Corporation, which accounted for one-third of all BAT sales during the interwar years. BAT was able to market its goods and generate sales even in the remotest parts of the country.
>
> By 1937 BAT's annual sales had reached 55 billion cigarettes throughout China. It had factories in several locations. However, the Japanese invasion of China in 1937 eroded the firm's sales. In 1941 all BAT's assets were expropriated by the Japanese. BAT returned to China after 1945, but the Communist Revolution in 1949 sealed its fate. In 1952 BAT divested from China. BAT began exporting cigarettes to China again only at the end of the 1970s. It opened a factory in 2003.
>
> (*Source*: Cochran 1980; Cox 2000.)

4.2.5 Automobiles and food in the interwar years

The interwar years saw divergences in the international business strategies pursued in different manufacturing industries. In industries characterized by high levels of oligopoly, such as chemicals and electricals, international collusion became extensive (see Section 4.4). In other industries, including automobiles and branded and packaged foods, multinational strategies were preferred.

The automobile industry originated in France in the late 1890s, and automobile manufacture soon spread in Europe. European companies concentrated on making small numbers of expensive cars for the wealthy, but became quite active in cross-border investments. France's Renault established distribution operations in the United States and elsewhere, and built small assembly plants in Italy, Spain, Britain, and the United States. Germany's Daimler began manufacturing in Austria in 1902, while Italy's Fiat built factories in Austria, the United States, and Russia before 1914 (Fridenson 1986; Laux 1992).

During the 1900s the automobile industry was revolutionized by Henry Ford in the United States with the development of a standardized product—the Model T—manufactured on a moving assembly line. Ford was able to achieve large economies of scale from production in large volume, interchangeable parts and flow production. As a result, costs were dramatically less than for cars produced—as in Europe—in small batches by skilled craftsmen. This laid the basis for the American domination of the industry for the next half century. The world had about 20 million motor vehicles during the 1920s, and Americans owned about 17 million of them. In 1950 the United States still possessed 60 percent of the world's 80 million motor vehicles (Rubenstein 2001).

High distribution costs encouraged manufacturers to locate final assembly operations in the country where the vehicles were sold. Before 1914 Ford built assembly plants in Canada and Britain, as well as a small unit in France. During the 1920s the American industry (or parts of it) underwent further transformation, as Alfred P. Sloan undertook large-scale organizational innovation at GM, which led to the development of the multi-divisional organizational structure (see Chapter 7). GM had replaced Ford—burdened by the eccentric policies of Henry Ford, who had taken his company private in 1920—as the US market leader by 1930 (McCraw 1995).

Ford and GM became the only two manufacturers which sold large numbers of vehicles in more than one country. During the 1920s, GM made a series of international acquisitions, including Opel, one of the ten largest industrial companies in Germany and the manufacturer of Germany's best-selling car, and the smaller Vauxhall in Britain. Both companies assembled cars beyond Europe, in Argentina, Australia, Brazil, and Mexico. European companies also assembled internationally. France's Citroën—for a time Europe's largest automobile firm—opened factories in Germany, Britain, Belgium, and Italy during the 1920s, though many were sold following its financial collapse and takeover by Michelin in 1935.

First-mover advantages could be overturned by inadequate strategies, suboptimal organization, or exogenous circumstances. In interwar Europe, Ford was afflicted by the same organizational failings as its US parent. Its once dominant market share in Britain was disseminated by British-owned competitors. In 1928 Ford built a new British factory at Dagenham, near London, which became the largest car factory in the world outside the United States, but it was poorly located, and too large for the market at that time (Church 1994).

The automobile industry carried in its wake component and supplier firms. Automobiles provided a huge demand for rubber tyres. A number of large firms developed in the industry, which soon expanded across borders. France's Michelin and Britain's Dunlop both manufactured in several foreign countries before 1914, and the number of their foreign plants expanded greatly in the interwar years (Jones 1984). During the interwar years the leading US tire manufacturers followed the US car makers abroad, building plants behind tariff barriers. Between 1927 and 1938 Goodyear opened factories in Australia, Britain, Argentina, the Dutch East Indies, Brazil, and Sweden. US Rubber, Firestone, and Goodrich had similar strategies (French 1987; 1991). US manufacturers of wheels, batteries, roller bearings, spark plugs, window glass, and other components also invested abroad (Wilkins and Hill 1964).

Branded food products received considerable multinational investment as companies established factories to serve national markets. Corn Products Refining Company (later CPC and subsequently Bestfoods), a leading US corn refiner, built extensive European and Latin American corn refining businesses, and acquired a share in the German-owned Knorr soup and bouillon company in 1926. From the 1920s Kraft, manufacturer of dairy products and processed foods, built extensive international operations in Europe, especially in Germany and Britain. On a smaller scale, firms such as Quaker Oats, Kellogg's, Heinz, Carnation, Pet Milk, and Wrigley set up foreign production facilities, often initially in other English-speaking countries with similar market conditions.

The international operations of Coca-Cola, which had originated in Atlanta, Georgia in 1886, expanded rapidly after 1930 when the Coca-Cola Export Corporation was established to sell and promote its soft drink in all countries except the United States, Canada, and Cuba. By 1940 Coke could be purchased in seventy countries. Coca-Cola employed the same franchise system that it used domestically. The firm established its own syrup factories abroad which supplied local independent bottlers which were given exclusive licenses for their territories. World War II generated a major growth momentum. Following Pearl Harbor, the company pledged to make Coca-Cola available at five cents a drink to every American in the armed forces. By 1946 there were 155 Coca-Cola bottling plants around the world, over one-third of them shipped from the United States at government expense (Giebelhaus 1994).

European food manufacturers continued to invest across borders in the United States and elsewhere. During the 1920s Nestlé began manufacturing chocolate, and in 1938 it launched Nescafé, the soluble powder that was to revolutionize coffee-drinking habits worldwide. By that year Nestlé operated 105 plants outside Switzerland (Heer 1966). Among smaller food specialty manufacturers, the British-owned Reckitt & Colman manufactured mustard and condiments in New York. Foreign-owned makers of alcoholic beverages, including a substantial number of British brewers, lost their business following the introduction of Prohibition in the United States in 1920. However, after the repeal of Prohibition in 1933, Canadian companies, including Seagram and Hiram Walker, established substantial alcoholic beverage businesses in the United States, as did the Cuban-based Bacardi (Wilkins 2004).

4.3 Determinants

4.3.1 Ownership factors

The manufacturing companies which undertook multinational investment from the nineteenth century possessed (in greatly varying degrees) the range of ownership advantages identified in theory. As in natural resources, entrepreneurial ability was often a decisive advantage. It was rarely the inventors of new products who built the successful enterprises of the late nineteenth century: rather it was the entrepreneurs who matched inventions with investment (Chandler 1990). The entrepreneurs who built large corporations, such as James B. Duke or Henry Ford, had global ambitions, and their personal influence on the international strategies pursued by their firms is evident. Swedish Match's Ivar Kreuger also demonstrated that global ambitions were sometimes pursued by unscrupulous means.

The creation of large corporations with managerial hierarchies provided new types of ownership advantages for firms in the new capital-intensive, technically advanced and fast-growing industries of the late nineteenth century (see Chapter 2). These firms developed the capacity to create knowledge, and they invested in the organization required to exploit this knowledge commercially. German firms became leaders in the commercialization of scientific research, as chemical and pharmaceutical firms such as Bayer built corporate research laboratories which developed a stream of new products. In the United States, GE's research laboratory was created in 1901, and undertook pioneering research in lighting, vacuum tubes, X-rays, and other products. The laboratories of GE were responsible for a remarkable number of innovations in electricals, communications, and even chemicals during the interwar years (Chandler 1990).

In branded and packaged consumer products ownership advantages were often derived from skills in marketing, especially branding, advertising and product differentiation. The use of brand names proliferated from the late nineteenth century, and the development of multinational manufacturing was closely related to this phenomenon. Homogeneous products such as soap were turned into intangible assets by brand names. The names of manufacturers such as Kellogg or Heinz became brands in themselves (Wilkins 1994b). These brands lay at the heart of the competitive advantages of firms. Yet during the first global economy there were few 'global' brands. Most multinationals owned numerous local or regional brands in different markets.

Firm size itself was of less importance as an ownership advantage. Many European firms at early stages of their corporate careers made both distribution and manufacturing investments overseas. Swedish, Swiss, and other European companies faced such small home markets that they went abroad almost immediately after they were founded (Olsson 1993; Lundström 1986a). Even in the US case, 'small' firms made direct investments. US FDI in the German machinery sector before 1914 included several investments from small companies. The investing US firms were sometimes smaller than their German competitors (Blaich 1984).

Access to capital was important. British free-standing companies benefited from the relative cheapness of capital and the ease of raising funds on the well-developed London capital market (Wilkins 1988b). Firms could secure access to capital by other means than through capital markets. In Continental European countries where the ties between banks and industry were close, banks facilitated multinational manufacturing. In Sweden, Germany, and Switzerland the role of banks in financing the international expansion of companies was an important, if passive, factor (Jones and Schröter 1993a). In Sweden—which like the United States was a net capital importer before 1914—banks served as both advisers and financiers to Swedish companies going abroad (Lundström 1986b).

In the 1920s the small size of the German capital market and high interest rates may have constrained German firms to raise capital to undertake FDI, but larger enterprises were able to raise considerable sums by issuing long-term debentures on foreign capital markets. Foreign subsidiaries were used to finance foreign investments, especially after the introduction of German exchange controls. In the second half of the 1920s IG Farben set up foreign holding companies to finance its foreign activities. In 1928 it established IG Chemie in Switzerland. IG Farben transferred its foreign investments to this Swiss company, including its important US interests which were placed under the control of the American IG Chemical Corporation (AIG). IG Chemie and AIG were used to raise considerable sums from foreign capital markets (Schröter 1984).

While it is plausible to maintain that manufacturing multinationals before World War II possessed some ownership advantage that they exploited in foreign markets, the significance of these advantages needs to be put in perspective. The concept works best when applied to major corporate innovators such as GE. But the scale of the ownership advantage possessed by most manufacturing multinationals was not of such magnitude. The existence of numerous failed and unsuccessful multinational investments indicates that often companies misjudged their competitive strengths and organizational abilities, or else dissipated any initial advantages.

4.3.2 **Locational factors**

Before World War II the most important locational factor which encouraged manufacturing firms to exploit their ownership advantages abroad through FDI rather than exporting was tariffs. While manufacturers of cheap and undifferentiated products could shift their exports to developing countries and colonial markets if protectionism damaged markets in the United States or Europe, the makers of high-technology products and branded consumer goods needed markets with high per capita incomes and industrial sectors. If their exports were rendered uncompetitive, the choice was to jump tariff barriers and engage in local manufacture, or else lose the market. The level of tariff protection often explains not only when and where firms undertook foreign manufacture, but also what stages of production were involved.

Yet, tariffs were not a universal determinant. Free-standing enterprises did not have a domestic business engaged in exporting prior to foreign production, so there was no question of jumping tariff barriers. Britain, which was largely free trade before the 1920s, was the most popular destination for US manufacturing FDI after Canada, attracting a disproportionate share of the American investment in Europe (Jones 1988).

A number of nontariff barriers to trade stimulated manufacturing FDI. While outright government restrictions on foreign multinationals were few before the 1920s, national feelings sometimes led governments to favor local producers, or else led foreign companies to undertake local manufacture in order to appear as national enterprises. Nationalistic pressures intensified in the interwar years. GE took shares in local electrical companies in recognition of the growth of national feelings and hostility to foreign products. Some governments put foreign companies under direct pressure to manufacture locally (Wilkins 1970, 1974; Jones 1986a).

Patent legislation also influenced the choice between exporting and FDI. US electrical FDI in Canada was stimulated by patent legislation which stipulated that patents were null and void if not worked within two years of issuance, while imports also nullified patents. After British patent law was modified in 1907 to prescribe that a foreign patent, after its transfer to Britain, had to be exploited there or else be revoked, German dyestuffs firms established plants in that country (Hagen 1997a, 1997b).

As manufacturing FDI seldom occurred in very labor-intensive industries, labor costs were rarely an influence except in the limited number of instances when Western firms established production facilities in developing countries. The overall size and per capita income of markets was a far more important locational factor. While protectionism stimulated FDI in the United States, companies were drawn to the most fast-growing and largest market in the world (Wilkins 1989). Producing in a market gave firms greater sensitivity to local tastes, and a better ability to respond quickly to market needs. Local production also offered one of the most effective responses to competitors based in major markets. If a US company attacked a European market, a European competitor might retaliate in the United States. In the interwar years the increasing domination of certain industries by large companies gave a strong element of oligopolistic rivalry to corporate strategies. While in some industries the oligopolists cooperated in cartels, in others they competed by erecting factories in different host economies.

4.3.3 Internalization and knowledge transfer

During the nineteenth century manufacturers experimented with different means to exploit their knowledge across borders. After the invention of the sewing machine in the 1850s, Singer first attempted to exploit the invention outside the United States by licensing. A licensing agreement was made with a French company in 1855 under which Singer sold its French patent to an independent French merchant in return for cash and the payment of a royalty. The French firm declined to pay Singer all its fees, handled competitive sewing machines and declined to disclose information on sales. Singer never again sold a patent to an independent business. When the French firms' patent from Singer expired in the 1870s, Singer went into direct competition with it using its own marketing company (Wilkins 1970).

The Singer example provides clear support for a transaction cost explanation for the growth of multinational manufacturing. Licensing agreements may increase the transactions costs with the misuse or dissipation of property rights whenever they cannot be fully protected through a contract or where the litigation procedure is costly or ineffective. The reason why multinational investment was especially prominent in the industries of the Second Industrial Revolution rather than the First was the complexity of writing contracts for complex technologies and for brand names.

However, it is not necessary to assume market failure through opportunism to understand why firms in the nineteenth century sought to transfer knowledge by extending their boundaries rather than using markets. Second Industrial Revolution industries involved new technologies and processes. In most cases there were no firms in foreign countries to license these technologies to. The prevailing condition of transport and communications also made it difficult or impossible to disaggregate different parts of the value chain. Multinational investment presented a superior organizational means to transfer knowledge internationally.

Transactions costs can often explain the changing modes used by multinationals to operate in foreign markets. A study of a sample of 119 British manufacturing firms which made a direct investment between 1870 and 1939 showed that 94 percent of firms for whom information was available exported their product before undertaking FDI. Virtually every company had agency agreements with foreign companies before investing abroad. These agency agreements often involved high transaction costs in terms of enforcement by the principals, as many agents sought large discounts or were inefficient in various ways. Such problems led firms to replace agents with selling companies (Nicholas 1982; 1983).

4.4 The interwar cartels

By the 1930s a considerable proportion of world manufacturing was controlled by international cartels. A number of characteristics of the period encouraged this trend, including depressed market conditions, growing political risk, and exchange controls. Interwar European governments often supported the spread of cartel agreements. The German government had a long tradition of supporting cartels. German criticism of cartels grew during the Great Depression, but the Nazi government after 1933 was an enthusiastic supporter of such arrangements. During the 1930s British governments positively encouraged the participation of British companies in cartels in some, if not all, industries (Wurm 1993). The formal participation of US companies in international cartels was made difficult by US antitrust laws, but firms such as GE often became important participants in them nonetheless (see Box 4.5).

International cartels proliferated in industries where there were a relatively small number of producers, especially those manufacturing semi-finished products and capital goods, including engineering, iron and steel, and chemicals. The larger the number of firms in an industry, and the greater the variety of products, the greater were the problems faced by organizers of cross-border collusive agreements. They were rare in most finished consumer goods, where there was a considerable variety of products, and in industries like textiles with large numbers of producers, and in fast-growing industries such as automobiles.

The 'classic' interwar cartel was concerned with price and output, but an enormous variety of individual arrangements existed. A common type of price agreement permitted each national group of producers to decide the price to be charged in their home market, prices which were followed by exporters to that market. The international cartels in matches and electric lamps were of this type. A second type of cartel—common in steel products—involved the fixing of export prices for a market or several markets. Cartels designed to restrict the quantity or value of sales were frequent. These often featured sales or export quotas, expressed as a percentage of total sales or exports. It was common for home markets to be reserved entirely, or in part, to the nationals of that market. In some cases foreign firms were allowed to supply particular markets to the extent of a certain

Box 4.5 GE and world electric lamp cartel

The Convention for the Development and Progress of the International Incandescent Electric Lamp Industry was signed in 1924. A Swiss corporation—Phoebus S.A.—was established to administer production quotas, prices, exchange of technical information, and sharing of patent rights. Within Phoebus, the General Assembly of members set policy; an Administrative Board issued rules to implement that policy; and a Board of Arbitration adjudicated disputes. There was also a testing laboratory to assure consistent quality among members' products. A marketing division promoted the use of electric lighting, especially the lamps of cartel members. Companies' production was held to the share of the lamp market that they held in 1922/23. The overall aim of the cartel was to assure each company as much of its home market as it wished plus a fixed share in other, common, markets.

GE took the initiative to establish the cartel, and was a decisive influence on its policies, but was never one of the member companies, which came to include the major European lamp manufacturers and, later, Tokyo Electric of Japan. GE wished to avoid any US antitrust scrutiny, and preferred to match the cartel's policies informally. The American firm was able to effectively enforce its wishes, in part because of its enormous importance in the world industry, arising from its strong patent position, and the fact that its home market accounted for almost half of total world sales in the 1930s. GE also held equity in the major corporate members. In 1929 its holdings included 29 percent in Osram of Germany, 17 percent in Philips of the Netherlands, 25 percent in AEG of Britain, 44 percent in Compagnie des Lampes of France, and 40 percent of Tokyo Electric of Japan. GE also joined in joint ventures with cartel members. It manufactured lamps in China with Osram and Philips, and in Mexico with Osram.

The world electric lamp cartel controlled about three-fourths of world output of electric lamps between the mid-1920s and World War II, although the success in keeping prices arbitrarily high meant that some new entrants were attracted into the industry.

(*Source*: Reich 1992.)

proportion of home consumption—and these supplies could either come from imports from the parent or from its own production subsidiaries in that market. However, some cartels, for example, in wire products, specifically prohibited FDI in specified markets.

Many international cartels divided up sales territories. A classic formulation would be for the British participant to be allotted the British Empire market, and the American firm the North American market, leaving the German participant with Continental Europe. The wide-ranging agreements in the interwar chemical industry between ICI, Du Pont and IG Farben took this form. In some industries patent agreements were an important feature of the international cartel system. This was the basis of the relationship between Du Pont and ICI which provided for the sharing of know-how and R & D results.

International cartels differed extensively in their durability. Terms of agreement varied from three to five years, but were also found for one year only. Many broke down during the term of the agreement, and renewals often involved changes in the original terms.

Given that a central preoccupation of cartels was to prevent cheating and opportunistic behavior by members, it was not surprising that the majority of cartel agreements provided for sanctions. Fines were imposed for companies exceeding quotas, and compensation was paid for underselling or underproduction. Sometimes compensation payments were available to manufacturers which refrained from extending capacity.

The interwar international cartels developed complex organizational forms. The administration of cartels was sometimes handled by representatives from the member corporations, who implemented the decisions made at regular meetings of members' representatives. This system was more effective for straightforward matters such as setting minimum price levels, than for when more complex arrangements were being administered. In such cases, separate companies were sometimes formed, independent from the member companies, to provide the administration. There were also cases when joint sales organizations were established, which collated orders and distributed them among member corporations (Hara and Kudo 1992). The more highly organized cartels placed their headquarters in small European states such as Switzerland, Belgium, Luxembourg or Liechtenstein, both to avoid scrutiny from governments and to take advantage of more liberal company laws.

Although much of the literature on collaborative agreements highlights their unstable nature, some interwar cartels were both durable and effective in achieving their specific goals. The international dyestuffs cartel accounted for around 70 percent of world sales in 1938, and was successful in maintaining prices. It has even been suggested that the use of a large part of the earnings of the dyestuffs cartel to finance R & D implied that the effects of cartels on welfare may not have been as negative as might be anticipated (Schröter 1990).

World War II massively disrupted the international cartels. It severed the long-standing relationships which had existed between German firms and their US and British counterparts. The importance of German firms in the cartel system linked it in the public mind to the Nazi war machine. This was one factor behind a resurgence of aggressive US antitrust policies against cartels after the war had ended. There were a series of major antitrust actions in the United States against US companies active in international cartels. Even non-US companies faced the risk of being taken before US courts if they had any agreement with a US corporation, even if it did not affect the United States itself. However, in practice, international cartel agreements in industries such as chemicals were weakening even without this regulatory onslaught, as the new economic conditions of the postwar world made a resumption of direct investment strategies more attractive.

4.5 Renewal and growth

4.5.1 Overview

From the 1950s the growth of manufacturing FDI resumed. International cartels were dismantled in most industries. US-owned firms became pre-eminent in multinational manufacturing. They invested abroad in a range of products, though machinery, chemicals, transportation equipment, food products, and primary and fabricated metals were especially important. US companies were the world's technological innovators in many industries. They were the leaders in capital- and technology-intensive production methods. The United States became the world center of innovation—in 1967 the United States accounted for almost 70 percent of the R & D undertaken in the OECD—and US industrial productivity was the highest in the world. As late as the 1970s the United States was also the home of more than half the companies worldwide with 20 000 employees or more (Chandler 1994).

US multinationals built most of their factories in Canada and Western Europe during the immediate postwar decades. The economic recovery of Western Europe, its growing attractiveness as a market, and the emergence of a regional market with the formation of the European Economic Community (subsequently the European Union) in 1957 made Western Europe an attractive location for US manufacturers. During this decade a world-wide 'shortage' of US dollars—which had become the world's major reserve currency—encouraged US corporations to establish factories in Europe to supply customers in countries that lacked dollars to buy American products (Wilkins 1974a).

European manufacturing FDI was initially more muted. British and Dutch firms were the most active in manufacturing abroad. British companies were especially strong in food, drink, and tobacco. Since the interwar years they had a strong bias towards investing in the developed **Commonwealth** markets of Canada, Australia, New Zealand, and South Africa. In the case of the Netherlands, a small group of large firms (the first two of them Anglo-Dutch)—Shell, Unilever, Akzo, and Philips—accounted for most of the large amount of FDI in chemicals, petroleum, electrical engineering and food products (Gales and Sluyterman 1993; Hoesel and Narula 1999; Sluyterman 2003). In contrast, the manufacturing firms of many other European countries, including France and Germany, undertook comparatively little multinational investment until the 1970s, preferring to use export strategies to take advantage of the fast world trade growth and the opportunities offered by European economic integration (Neebe 1991). It was only during the 1970s that French and German manufacturers began to engage in FDI on a substantial scale.

The focus of much of the multinational investment which took place in the three decades after World War II concerned US firms investing in Europe. In soap and detergents, from the 1950s Procter & Gamble (P&G) invested in France, Belgium, the Netherlands, Germany, and elsewhere in Europe. P&G had only invested in Canada and Britain before 1945. This was a highly concentrated industry: Unilever, P&G, Colgate, and Henkel accounted for 60 percent of world sales of soap and detergents during the 1960s. The position of these firms derived from the barriers to entry arising from economies of scale in production, research and marketing in the detergents industry. P&G was able to build large market positions in Europe, and substantially erode the market position of the largest European incumbent, Unilever, in part because of a technological lead in synthetic detergents (Dyer, Dalzell, and Olegario 2004).

Japanese manufacturers also rebuilt their businesses after the destruction of World War II, primarily using export strategies. After Japan re-entered the world economy in 1949, there was a rapid growth of exports—four-fifths of which were manufactured goods by the mid-1950s. In 1950, half of Japanese exports were textile products, but by 1975 this had fallen to 5 percent, as machinery and transport equipment became the leading exports. The fixing of the exchange rate at Yen 360/US $1 between 1949 and 1972 helped to create this growing export competitiveness.

The success of Japanese exports provoked a wave of 'new protectionism' from the 1970s. As the US trade deficit mounted, US administrations became involved in growing trade disputes with Japan. The United States pursued 'orderly marketing agreements' in sectors such as textiles, automobiles, and electronics. As in the past, trade restrictions encouraged multinational investment. There was an immediate upsurge of Japanese FDI in the electronics and automobiles industries (Encarnation 1992). Subsequently the growth of European import restraints—and Japanese concerns about being excluded from integrated European market being created by the Single European Market project after 1985—also stimulated Japanese FDI into European manufacturing (Strange 1993). Meanwhile, the success of the postwar Japanese economy in rising real incomes also raised labor costs. Combined with the revaluation of the Japanese Yen after 1972, Japanese manufacturers began to shift assembly and lower-value added processes to offshore plants in the developing world, especially in Southeast Asia.

Multinational investment in manufacturing in developing markets was not substantial after World War II, but there were a few examples. In West Africa, there were multinational investments in textiles, brewing, and other industries, but by the 1960s investors were already being deterred by political and economic instability. During that decade Brazil, which was almost certainly the largest developing host country, attracted considerable investment as a result of its import substitution policies. These years also saw the beginning of outsourcing to cheaper locations in Southeast Asia. However, many countries remained closed or unwelcoming to foreign firms. China no longer permitted FDI, while India's preference for local equity participation, exchange controls and trade protection, and high rates of taxation curbed the interest of foreign firms in the country.

4.5.2 Chemicals and automobiles

The postwar decades saw a sharp expansion of world markets for chemical products: the growth of demand for chemical products has consistently exceeded overall rates of growth in the developed world. The interwar preference for cartels was abandoned in favor of large-scale multinational investment. By 1970 FDI by US chemical companies (excluding the large investments made by oil companies in petrochemicals) reached $13 billion, or one-third of their domestic plant investment. No other US industry approached either the total sum or the ratio (Chapman 1991).

The new strategy of US chemical companies was evident in the case of Du Pont, whose FDI—and even exports—had been marginal to its overall business before the mid-1950s. The catalyst was the ending of collaborative links with British-owned ICI in 1952—which had to be finally severed because of antitrust rulings—followed a few years later by ICI's decision to acquire a dye plant in the United States. Du Pont retaliated and in 1958 opened a new factory in Britain, designed to supply the European market. Between 1959 and 1972 Du Pont's total FDI increased from $300 million to more than $1.6 billion, by which date its foreign sales reached one-fifth of the firm's total sales volume (Taylor and

Sudnik 1984). Du Pont's foreign expansion was part of a wider trend by US chemical companies to invest abroad. While Du Pont and Monsanto concentrated on plastics and synthetic fibers—or downstream operations—Union Carbide and Dow were particularly prominent in petrochemicals.

International competition to US firms revived faster in chemicals than in almost any other capital-intensive industry. British and Dutch companies such as ICI, Shell, and Akzo were initially prominent, but they were not alone. The German chemical industry, which was radically changed after the end of World War II by the breakup of IG Farben and the re-emergence of BASF, Bayer, and Hoechst as independent companies, returned to foreign production. The German firms initially reinvested in Latin America, often repurchasing plant they had lost in the war, and then invested elsewhere in Western Europe and North America. The leading three Swiss chemical companies—Ciba, Geigy, and Sandoz—abandoned their cartel in 1950, partly because of US antitrust pressure on their American subsidiaries, and reverted to extensive FDI. The merger in 1970 of Ciba and Geigy created a $1.4 billion company with widespread manufacturing operations in Europe, North America, and Brazil (Taylor and Sudnik 1984).

The fastest growing part of the chemicals industry was petrochemicals, an industry which developed in the interwar years out of the technological convergence of the oil and chemical industries. Initially it was an almost exclusively US industry: in 1950, 98 percent of world production of ethylene, a key petrochemical product, was located in the United States. Subsequently, the petrochemicals industry grew exponentially with surging demand from the automobile, textile and construction industries, the growing use of synthetic materials, and falling costs of petroleum raw materials. World ethylene capacity grew twenty-six-fold between 1950 and 1970. While in 1950, 98 percent of this capacity was in the United States, by 1970 the share of the United States was 48 percent, Europe 33 percent and Japan 14 percent. More than one-third of world ethylene capacity outside the United States and Japan was foreign-owned in 1970.

The oil companies, with their long experience of multinational operations, were initially the most active direct investors. Exxon and Shell—whose US subsidiary has undertaken pioneering research in the industry—made large-scale FDI in European petrochemical manufacture in the 1950s. They were subsequently joined by the US chemical companies, and later the major European chemical companies, which began to switch from coal to petroleum as the basic raw material for organic chemical manufacture (Chapman 1991).

In the automobile industry, the scale of FDI reached unprecedented levels as rising world incomes created an ever-expanding market for automobiles, while the proliferation of import barriers and local content requirements discouraged importing. Competitive struggles between the major US firms in the American domestic market were reproduced abroad. Chrysler, the third biggest US producer after Ford and GM, had almost no FDI before 1945, but thereafter perceived the need to match its two US competitors in the world market if it was to sustain its position in its domestic market. Given its late entry into multinational manufacturing, Chrysler's strategy was one of acquisition of foreign firms. By 1973 it had purchased full control over French, Spanish, and British manufacturing companies and secured control of around 7.5 percent of total Western European vehicle production.

The focus of non-US automobile manufacturers was initially on exports rather than direct investment. In Western Europe, there was a process of consolidation of fragmented low-volume manufacturers. German firms consolidated into Volkswagen (VW), Daimler-Benz, and BMW. The former, which focused on producing a single small car known as the Beetle, grew rapidly to become Germany's largest producer but it, like all other European producers including Renault, Peugeot, and Fiat, largely relied on exports before the 1970s.

The most dramatic change in the post-war automobile industry was the rapid growth of Japanese-based manufacturers. Toyota and Nissan, Japan's two largest producers, had been founded in the interwar years, but the industry had to be rebuilt after the destruction experienced during World War II. The subsequent growth of the Japanese firms as successful challengers to the corporate giants Ford and GM provided a compelling example of how incumbents can be overturned if new entrants can generate sufficient organizational and technological competences.

Over several decades Toyota developed a new production system which came to be known as 'post-Fordist', or **'lean production'**, and included the use of 'just-in-time' (JIT) systems and quality control. Instead of integrating all parts of automobile manufacture within the corporation, Toyota purchased many components from tiers of suppliers with whom close relationships were maintained. Over time, around 70 percent of the entire value of a finished car was contracted out to suppliers, a much higher figure than in the mass production system. This Toyota production system, which was eventually adopted by manufacturers worldwide, was able to deliver some of the advantages of both large size—economies of scale and scope—and those of small firms, including flexibility and entrepreneurship (Womack, Jones, and Roos 1990; Gerlach 1992; Fruin 1992).

Japan's share of world automobile output rose from 1 percent to 25 percent between 1960 and 1990, while the share of the United States fell from 50 percent to less than 20 percent. During the 1970s the Japanese automobile companies penetrated the US and European markets, benefiting from an increased demand for small cars which US manufacturers were too slow to meet. Before 1982 there was not a single Japanese automobile production plant outside Japan, but this changed after the US government imposed a Voluntary Export Restraint (VER) whereby the Japanese government 'voluntarily' agreed to prevent Japanese car makers from increasing exports to the United States. Honda, which had a relatively small domestic market share in Japan compared to Nissan and Toyota, and insufficient quota allocation under the VER, responded by building a motorcycle plant at Marysville, Ohio. An automobile plant was established adjacent to this, which produced its first car in 1982.

The following decade saw a rapid growth of Japanese investment in the US, and later, European. A Nissan plant opened at Smyrna, Tennessee in 1983. Toyota entered the United States more cautiously by establishing a 50/50 joint venture with GM to produce cars at an old GM assembly plant at Fremont, California. This New United Motor Manufacturing, Inc. (NUMMI) plant, designed to test the feasibility of transferring the Toyota system to the United States, began production in 1984, and within a few years it took only half of the previous workforce to assemble the same number of cars. By 1990 there were nine Japanese-owned assembly plants in the United States, employing 30 000 workers and with an annual production of 1.5 million cars. Together with imports,

Japanese companies controlled around one-third of the US car market. The 'big three' US producers were turned into a 'big five', comprising GM, Ford, Chrysler, Honda, and Toyota. By 1990 more than 300 Japanese or joint venture automotive parts suppliers had also been established to supply parts to transplant auto assemblers in the United States (Kenney and Florida 1993; Womack, Jones, and Roos 1990).

Automobile production spread beyond North America, Europe, and Japan. During the 1950s Brazil and Mexico obliged foreign companies to manufacture rather than merely assemble automobiles using strict domestic content rules. Led by VW, the result was a rapid expansion of motor vehicle production in Brazil, which reached over 1 million vehicles by 1980. In South Korea, the government selected large domestic conglomerates known as the **chaebol** to develop an automobile industry (see Chapter 9).

4.5.3 Electronics

US companies were pre-eminent in the new and fast-growing electronics industries. The first companies to appreciate the opportunities for the commercial applications of computers were business machinery firms, including IBM, National Cash Register (NCR), and Remington Rand, whose origins dated back to the nineteenth century. These companies benefited from the huge wartime demand for typewriters, adding and calculating machines and punched card tabulators, which were the contemporary tools of data management and processing. The US government became the largest customer in the world for such equipment, and its funding and encouragement of specific types of research—held to be essential for national security—led directly to the development of electronic digital computers, and miniaturized electronics. Later the sheer size of US industry—as well as its readiness to accept the new technology—created a formidable non-military domestic market. (Cortada 1993; Chandler 2001).

The US business machine companies took advantage of their unique nation-specific ownership advantage in the form of their domestic market. Remington Rand developed the first computer designed for business use, the Univac. IBM's subsequent recognition of the importance of electronics for the data processing industry resulted in the firm undertaking massive investment in research and production. By 1958 IBM had secured a predominant position in the US market, accounting for over 80 percent of the nearly 6,000 computers installed in that year. In the face of a proliferating number of incompatible computers, IBM's strategy focused on the creation of a single family of compatible computers which would enable it to reach as wide a commercial market as possible by utilizing the cost advantages of the economies of scale. The result was the extraordinarily risky decision to launch System 360 in 1964, a broad line of compatible mainframe computers with peripherals for a wide range of uses. This proved an immense marketing success, and became the benchmark against which all other machines were measured. By the time IBM introduced its 370 range in 1970, it was the world's largest computer and electronic computer manufacturer, and one of the largest manufacturing enterprises in the world. By 1970 IBM had operations in nearly 100 countries, and its non-US businesses represented 50 percent of corporate profits (Dassbach 1989).

During the 1980s, the electronics industry was further transformed by the development of the personal computer (PC), which had first appeared in a primitive form in the previous decade. In 1981 IBM launched its own PC, and took the decision to outsource both its disk operating system and its microprocessor to two new firms, Microsoft (founded in 1975) and Intel (founded in 1968). IBM rapidly became the industry leader in PCs and established the Microsoft/Intel combination as the industry standard, but because IBM did not have exclusive rights to their components, Microsoft and Intel were able to sell their proprietary technologies to manufacturers of IBM 'clones' such as Compaq and Dell. Over the following decade IBM found its competitive position in the PC market undermined by these new companies which exploited new distribution channels such as mass retailers. In contrast, Intel and Microsoft's capabilities were protected by copyright and other measures. The Microsoft/Intel combination became the entrenched industry standard.

Intel became the world's largest producer of microprocessors, while Microsoft acquired a near monopoly in personal computer operating systems after launching Windows 3.0 in 1990 and Windows 95 in 1995. Bundled into the latter was the Microsoft Explorer 2.0 browser for the emergent Internet, which had shortly before become available for commercial use. Microsoft and Intel, and their products, had a profound impact on world business, but the former in particular was far removed from an old-style manufacturing multinational. It contracted out almost all of its manufacturing business worldwide, and was primarily a service company. In 2004 around one half of its employees (27 000 out of a total workforce of 55 000) worked outside the United States. It had offices in sixty countries, and operations and logistics centers in Ireland and Singapore.

The semiconductor industry was a critical component of the electronics industry. The critical innovation was the fabrication of the first successful transition at Bell Laboratories—owned by American Telephone and Telegraph (AT&T)—in 1948. These first transistors used germanium as their base material, but in 1954 Texas Instruments (TI) introduced the silicon transistor which had superior characteristics, and within a decade production of silicon transistors had overtaken that of germanium ones. At the end of the 1950s researchers at TI and Fairchild Semiconductors independently discovered the means of combining transistor and other discrete electrical components into a single, or integrated circuit (IC). This opened up the modern era of integrated circuits. A third US company, Motorola, which originated as a manufacturer of car radios in the 1920s, was less of an innovator, but moved successfully into semiconductor manufacture from the late 1950s. As in computers, US semiconductor firms derived strong competitive advantages from their home market. In 1960 the United States accounted for over three-fourths of world consumption of semiconductors, a reflection of the importance of military and aerospace demand in the initial growth of the industry (Langlois 1988).

US firms moved quickly to exploit their technological innovations abroad. In Europe they jumped tariff barriers and built fabrication facilities. TI was responsible for the first FDI by a US semiconductor firm when it established a manufacturing plant in Britain in 1957. The company hoped to qualify as a local producer by this strategy, and thus receive production contracts from the British government, Europe's largest defence spender. By 1974 US semiconductor producers had established dozens of subsidiaries in Europe engaged in assembly, and sometimes manufacturing (Langlois 1988). In Asia, US firms took advantage of low labor costs to locate assembly operations.

The semiconductor industry came to consist of two separate categories: memory chips and microprocessors. The latter developed during the 1970s, and involved the incorporation of sophisticated solid-state circuits onto a single chip. In the United States, TI and Motorola were joined by Intel, and two start-ups from Silicon Valley, Advanced Micro Devices and National Semiconductors. Beyond the United States, established electronics firms moved into semiconductor manufacture, especially Japanese computer makers such as Fujitsu, NEC, Toshiba, Hitachi, and Mitsubishi, and European electronics firms including Philips and Siemens.

Between 1985 and 2000 semiconductors became the most dynamic products in world trade, as annual exports grew from $26 billion to $235 billion. By 2000 they represented 5 percent of world trade. Production came to be organized globally. Assembly stages were often placed in emerging markets, while the higher value added activities were located in developed countries. In 2001 Intel's sales of $23 billion made it the world's largest manufacturer of semiconductors: they were three times its nearest competitors, Toshiba, NEC, and TI. Intel's growth in semiconductors contrasted with Motorola, which in 2003 separately listed its semiconducter division after years of declining market share.

Intel kept its high-value elements of semiconductor production predominately in the United States—two-thirds of Intel's manufacturing workforce was in the United States in 2001—while conducting the more labor-intensive assembly and testing activities in lower cost sites. It built wafer fabrication plants in Israel (first opened 1985) and Ireland (first opened 1993), as well as opening assembly and testing plants in Barbados (1977, later closed), Philippines (1979), Malaysia (1988), and Costa Rica and China (1997). US export restrictions prevented Intel from establishing advanced facilities overseas to produce the silicon wafers from which individual chips were carved.

In consumer electronics, multinational strategies played a central role. In the immediate postwar decades radio and television sets were the major products. In the United States, Radio Corporation of America (RCA) was the leading firm. It played a central role in the commercial role of color televisions in the 1950s. RCA licensed key color television technologies to foreign companies, including Philips—the largest European firm in the sector—and the Japanese firms Matsushita and Sony. Sony had been organized in 1946 to manufacture audio magnetic tape recorders, taking its current name in 1957.

The initial leaders in the industry experienced different fates. During the second half of the 1960s RCA diversified into computers and beyond electronics altogether. This strategy triggered a process of decline. In 1986 the residual consumer electronics was acquired by GE and sold to France's Thomson SA two years later. The experience of the Japanese companies stood in complete contrast. Matsushita, drawing in part on the technological competences of Philips with whom it collaborated in a 65/35 percent joint venture between 1952 and 1992, began selling its radios and televisions outside Japan under the Panasonic brand as early as 1959. During the 1960s it began selling color televisions in the United States: by 1975 it held 8 percent of the national market. Matsushita also opened plants in Southeast Asia and other developing countries. During the 1970s it responded to protectionism by establishing assembly operations in major markets. In 1974 Mitsushita acquired Motorola's television business and began manufacturing in the United States, and in 1976 built a plant in Britain to supply the European Union. Sony also established its sales subsidiaries in the United States, followed by Europe, during the

1960s. In 1972 it built a television production plant in California, and by 1975 had captured nearly 6 percent of the US television set market. Within a few years only one US-owned television manufacturer remained in business.

During the 1970s Japanese companies commercialized a stream of new consumer electronics products. Matsushita set the world standard for videocassette recorders with its VHS format. Sony, which had pioneered miniaturization technology, launched its Walkman in 1979, and between 1979 and 1982 collaborated with Philips to develop the CD player. This again set the world standard for CDs, and was rapidly exploited by Sony with new production plants in the United States and Europe. In 1986 Sony and Philips introduced the CD-ROM, and in the early 1990s Sony launched the DVD.

The growth of the consumer electronics industry was characterized by complex international business strategies involving both close collaboration—as seen in the close relationship between Philips with both Sony and Matsushita—and fierce competition involving the establishment of worldwide production facilities. The new transistor and printed circuit-based technologies required large production runs. The Japanese firms moved much of the production of electronics to low wage countries from the 1970s. There were numerous acquisitions of smaller electronics manufacturers. Sony and Matsushita also acquired the Hollywood film studios Columbia Pictures and MCA in 1989 and 1991 respectively. Despite the subsequent losses caused by these purchases, Sony and Matsushita—as well as a cluster of other Japanese companies including Sanyo and Sharp—came to dominate the world electronics industry.

In contrast, Philips was burdened by a large number—around 200 in 1980—of expensive European production sites. It had over 500 plants worldwide, far more than its US and Japanese competitors, who built fewer plants with more capacity. During the mid-1980s it made heavy losses due to a failed innovation, and was then weakened by loss of market share in Europe to the Japanese companies. In 1992 Philips sold its share in the joint venture with Matsushita to the Japanese company, along with most of its US business. Divestment from consumer electronics followed in a few years (Chandler 2001).

4.5.3 Integrating markets

During the post-war decade a number of new US entrants to the European market, including Du Pont, Monsanto and Dow in chemicals, were among the first companies to treat Europe as a region, rather than a collection of fragmented national markets. In contrast, US companies which had pre-existing operations inherited—like their European-based counterparts—a legacy of separate national markets combined with tariff and quota constrained European trade. The European business of Ford was extremely fragmented after World War II (see Chapter 7). The Treaty of Rome in 1957 gave Ford an opportunity to restructure its European operations. The company perceived that European integration could produce a large market similar to that of the United States. Ford faced a particular problem that its German business was marginalized within the German market. Ford initially planned to import or assemble cars from its much stronger British affiliate, on the assumption that Britain would soon join the Common Market. When the French vetoed British membership in 1963, Ford was obliged to pursue alternative strategies (Tolliday 1999).

In 1967 Ford of Europe was formed, as a wholly owned subsidiary of the US parent, and it began a process of integrating previously autonomous national affiliates. In time, the new organization become the locus of strategic decision-making and financial planning. Product development was integrated through design and development of the first Europe-wide model—the Capri—in 1969. Falling trade barriers permitted growing cross-border movements in components and final products. Ford of Europe developed as a regionally integrated manufacturing operation with growing levels of intrafirm trade. By the mid-1970s Ford had secured a considerable productivity advantage over GM in Europe, which was much slower to integrate its European affiliates (McKinlay and Starkey 1994).

Subsequently Ford, and to a lesser extent GM, pursued integration strategies. Ford attempted to produce a world car—the Escort—in 1981, but the plan failed because it did not establish a single organizational structure for product development and design. From the mid-1980s Ford developed a new 'world car' designed to be sold around the world, which was launched in Europe as the Mondeo in 1993. This time Ford closely integrated the design and production worldwide. In 1995 Ford merged its North American and European units into a single operating unit designed to achieve common governance of product, manufacturing, supplier, and sales activities along global product lines. However, even in automobiles, Ford's structure remained exceptional.

Many other large companies took longer to integrate their European operations. Pre-existing national businesses found it especially hard to move in this direction compared to newcomers. National differences in tastes, as well as legislation, varied considerably between industries. While markets and competitors in computers became rapidly international, European markets for many consumer products remained more local for much longer.

4.5.3 Outsourcing and free trade zones

From the 1960s there was a shift of some manufacturing to cheaper wage economies, some of which established free trade zones. Taiwan and South Korea were earlier pioneers of such zones. They offered tax holidays and other incentives for foreign firms to locate factories in them, which appeared as an attractive strategy to develop export industries without some of the political and other costs that a general liberalization of trade policy would entail.

US semiconductor firms were among the first to relocate some operations. Fairchild Semiconductor—a pioneering firm which subsequently lost momentum and was acquired by a French company in 1979—led the way with a plant in Hong Kong in 1963, followed by one in Singapore. By 1974, twenty-six US semiconductor firms had established fifty-six offshore assembly facilities, especially in Mexico, Singapore, and Malaysia. In that year almost four-fifths of American production was assembled abroad (Langlois 1988; Yoffie 1993). The nature of the semiconductor industry made it ideal for such outsourcing. Transport costs to foreign markets were low because of the high value per weight of semiconductors, while workers in Asia and Latin America could be trained quickly to undertake the tedious assembly work required.

> **Box 4.6 The impact of the *maquiladores* on Mexican employment**
>
> The origins of Mexico's *maquiladores*—foreign-owned factories that assemble imported components for export—date back to 1965, when the United States and Mexico started a Border Industrialization Program, designed to reduce regional unemployment in the northern territories of Mexico. Initially they were restricted to regions near the border with the United States, but from the mid-1970s these restrictions were relaxed. US-owned firms including GE, RCA, IBM, Coca-Cola and Ford were the first to locate their production in Mexico. There was a rapid growth of production following the 1982 Mexican debt crisis, when wage rates fell sharply. During the early 1980s Japanese firms, and within a few years Korean firms also became major investors. Employment in the *maquiladores* rose from 100 000 in 1982 to 500 000 in 1992. The implementation of NAFTA in 1994 resulted a further boost. By 2000 employment had reached 1.3 million, and the sector accounted for over 40 percent of total Mexican exports. Exports to the US increased from $42 billion in 1993 to $166 billion in 2000. Ford's Mexican plant was the third largest foreign-owned manufacturing operation in Latin America. Nearly one-fifth of those exports came from Ford, GM, Daimler Chrysler, VW, and Nissan.
>
> The Mexican case also illustrated the increasing mobility of assets in the twenty-first century. Assembly operations could be shifted between locations. China overtook Mexico as the largest exporter to the United States after Japan during 2000. Mexican factories faced especially strong competition in clothing and textile, leather and shoes, and electronics. Between 2001 and 2003 employment in the Mexican *maquiladores* fell by 200 000.
>
> (*Source*: United Nations 2002.)

Initially US firms established wholly owned affiliates and most corporate functions remained with the parent. Wafers manufactured in the United States were air-freighted to Asia, assembled into circuits, and then air-freighted back to the parent firm for testing and distribution. Over time local firms developed manufacturing skills and acted as subcontractors, and—especially when Japanese semiconductor multinationals expanded into Asia from the 1970s—more sophisticated parts of the production process—such as R & D and wafer fabrication—began to take place in Asia.

Even before the formation of NAFTA in 1994, many (and later others) firms also began to locate assembly operations in *maquiladores* in Mexico (see Box 4.6).

4.6 Global networks

During the last decades of the twentieth century, manufacturing FDI grew at a fast pace. There were major changes to industrial structures. In some industries there was further consolidation, though in others there was a diffusion of market power. The dominant mode of FDI became mergers and acquisitions. During the second half of the 1990s there were huge cross-border mergers, especially in automobiles, pharmaceuticals, food, beverages and tobacco.

Personal care was one industry which moved from fragmentation to concentration. During the 1950s personal care was highly fragmented, reflecting strong national differences in concepts of beauty and personal happiness. Income differences also caused wide divergences in the consumption of 'luxury' products such as shampoos, skin care creams and lipstick. The United States accounted for around one half of the world markets. US manufacturers of mass market products such as Avon and Revlon had established some international operations, but there were few international products or brands. Until the 1970s, L'Oréal the leading French cosmetics manufacturer had 90 percent of its sales in France.

From the 1980s there was rapid international consolidation in this industry. The largest consumer goods manufacturers, P&G and Unilever, were already among the world's largest manufacturers of toothpaste and shampoos (Miskell 2004). During this decade they purchased US cosmetics companies, including Richardson Vicks and Cheseborough Ponds, owners of mass brands such as *Oil of Olay* and *Pond's Cream* (Dyer, Dalzell, and Olegario 2004). A number of specialist cosmetics firms also expanded across borders. These included US-based Estée Lauder, which had opened its first foreign branch in London in the late 1950s. By the 1990s it was selling brands such as *Clinique* and *Estée Lauder* in 100 countries, and international revenues represented 40 percent of total sales. L'Oréal, which was majority owned by the founding family and (after 1974) by Nestlé, also rapidly expanded internationally with a portfolio of skincare brands ranging from *Lancôme* in the prestige sector of the market to *Pléntitude* which was sold in mass channels.

By the new century, the global market for cosmetics and toiletries was over $170 billion. The industry expanded rapidly as disposable incomes rose. By 2004, China, where cosmetics sales had been almost nonexistent under the Communist government until the early 1980s, had become the world's third largest market after the United States and Japan. Overall, L'Oréal held the largest share, around 9 percent, of the world market. P&G, Unilever, Shiseido and Estée Lauder also accounted for substantial market shares. A culturally-specific industry had become partially 'globalized'.

During the 1990s there were extraordinary changes also in the global automobile industry. In 1998 Germany's Daimler acquired Chrysler, the third largest US manufacturer. In the following year Renault paid $5.4 billion for a controlling 37 percent share of Nissan, which had come close to bankruptcy after years of mismanagement and substandard strategies. In 2000 DaimlerChrysler, which had earlier come close to investing in Nissan, acquired one-third of another poorly performing Japanese manufacturer, Mitsubishi Motors, for $2.1 billion. Both firms also invested in Korea's large domestic automobile industry, which had also been in difficult circumstances since the Asian financial crisis in 1997. Renault acquired 70 percent of Samsung Motors, and Daimler-Chrysler took 10 percent in Hyundai Motors. In 2004 the world's largest automobile manufacturers, in order of sales, were GM, Ford, Toyota, VW and DaimlerChrysler, although Toyota's market capitalization (nearly $120 billion in May of that year) was more than GM, Ford, and DaimlerChrysler combined.

As always, differences in firm capabilities led to quite different outcomes from apparently similar strategies. Within five years Nissan's competitiveness had been fully restored after a 'turnaround' led by a Brazilian-born Renault executive. The sales of the two companies together made the alliance the fifth largest global automobile manufacturer by volume. In contrast, DaimlerChrysler was unable to exercise control over Mitsubishi Motors whose performance continued to deteriorate. In 2004 the German company decided not to provide further funds for the loss-making Japanese company, and sold its stake in Hyundai.

4.6.1 International production systems

From the 1980s international production systems developed, within which multinationals located different parts of their value chain across the globe, serving as powerful agents of international integration. Many companies integrated their production systems on a regional basis. Firms sought to base activities in locations where innovation levels and entrepreneurship were clustered (Porter 2000). Functions such as finance and R & D were also dispersed from head offices in some cases (see Chapter 7).

There were many changes to both the governance and the value chain of international production as the boundaries of firms became less sharp. However, there were also considerable firm and industry-specific variants. While some firms opted for largely equity control, in others more externalized forms of control were used. However many manufacturers sought to outsource some activities as they focused on 'core competences'. Leading manufacturers in a range of industries began to exit from manufacturing altogether. Contract manufacturers emerged to specialize exclusively in providing turn-key manufacturing services. However, even when international production systems became highly externalized, multinationals typically continued to control key functions, such as brand management and product definition, and setting quality standards.

In some cases, the entire product range was outsourced. Cisco Systems, which had been founded in 1984 and became the worldwide leader in networking for the Internet, opened offices worldwide to sell its equipment, but manufactured almost nothing. During the 1990s Cisco retained its knowledge base in the fast changing technology by buying start-ups financed by venture capitalists in California. In this respect, even Cisco's innovation was 'outsourced'.

In many industries multinationals focused on the more knowledge-intensive functions, especially R & D and brand management. Industries such as garments, footwear, toys, and housewares saw the growth of 'buyer driven commodity chains' in which large retailers, brand-name merchandisers and trading companies drove the establishment of decentralized production networks mainly in emerging markets. By the new century most manufacturers of standardized garments had shifted their production to off-shore low cost sites. In 2003 Levi Strauss, the world's largest branded clothing maker, closed its remaining four North American manufacturing and finishing plants, shifting all production to Latin America and Asia. Fashion-oriented retailers, selling exclusive designer products, tended to source from premium quality producers in countries such as France and Italy (Gereffi 1994).

General retailers, such as Wal-Mart, and garment specialty retailers, such as The Gap, designed and marketed clothing but did not manufacture themselves. It some cases they used contract manufacturers. In others, use was made of 'full package providers' who were independent intermediaries who supplied products according to the buyer's design.

One example was the Hong Kong-based Li & Fung which from the 1980s began to take control of complete garments programs for a season for particular buyers. Manufacturing was contracted out to locations that are the most cost-efficient, and the company came to preside over a large network of contract suppliers in China, elsewhere in Asia and in various African countries.

4.6.2 **Pharmaceuticals and telecoms**

Pharmaceuticals underwent substantial restructuring from the 1990s. The industry had started to grow quickly after World War II. Each decade saw new generations of drugs, including antibiotics, contraceptives, and numerous drugs to fight cancer, ulcers, cholesterol, high blood pressure, impotence, and much more. During the 1950s US pharmaceutical companies began establishing research and development facilities in Europe. The research activities of US-owned affiliates was one factor which stimulated British companies to emulate their strategies. From the 1960s the British industry, which had lagged behind its US and German competitors in research and innovation, was transformed. A cluster of successful British-owned pharmaceutical companies, including Beecham, Welcome, and Glaxo developed over the following decades.

Pharmaceuticals remained a fragmented industry longer than other high technology industries. In the mid-1990s, no company held a 5 percent share of the world market. However, as the costs of the industry accelerated with growing complexity in drug development and approval cycles, there was a growth in strategic alliances—which increased from 121 to over 400 between 1986 and 1993—followed by a wave of domestic and cross-border mergers and acquisitions.

The industry was reshaped by the creation of US and European giants. In 1994 Bayer acquired the North American self-medication business of Sterling Winthrop. Two years later the Swiss firms Ciba-Geigy and Sandoz merged to form Novartis. During 1999 British-owned Zeneca acquired the Swedish Astra to form Astra Zeneca; Hoechst and Rhône-Poulenc merged to form the Franco-German-owned Aventis; and a domestic merger in France of pharmaceutical subsidiaries of L'Oréal and the oil company Total created Sanofi-Synthélabo. A series of mergers between British and US firms culminated in the creation of GSK in 2000 (Box 4.7). In 2004 Sanofi-Synthélabo acquired Aventis to form the world's third largest pharmaceutical company. Among the purely US-owned companies, Pfizer acquired Warner-Lambert in 2000, but Merck—the US's and the world's largest pharmaceutical company—grew organically rather than by merger.

Multinational strategies had always featured in the telecom industry. Ericsson, based in the small Swedish market, established manufacturing operations in Russia and sales subsidiaries in China and Mexico as early as the 1890s. By the time of World War I this firm also had factories in Britain, France, Austria-Hungary, and the United States. Around one-third of Ericsson's total production was manufactured in eleven factories outside Sweden in the 1930s. After World War II new factories were built in Brazil, Mexico, Australia, and elsewhere. Ericsson also entered the telephone operating business in a range of countries in the interwar years, but subsequently it was divested as it did not wish to compete with its customers. By 1990 it only operated telephones in Argentina. By that year Ericsson was the fourth largest telecom manufacturer, holding around

> ### Box 4.7 Making a pharmaceutical giant: GlaxoSmithKline (GSK)
>
> Glaxo began as a merchant business in New Zealand in the 1870s. The company later migrated to Britain, and became that country's leading manufacturer of powdered infant milk. During the interwar years Glaxo diversified into vitamins, and launched its first pharmaceutical product in 1924. Until the 1960s the pharmaceutical business rested on licensing products and processes from Glaxo's much larger US competitors. A change of strategy led to a growth of spending on research. In 1981 Glaxo launched Zantac, a treatment for ulcers, which skilful marketing made into the world's best selling drug. This enabled Glaxo to plough profits into research, and to expand a small US affiliate which had been acquired in 1977. In 1994 Zantac generated over 40 percent of Glaxo's sales. By then Glaxo was the world's second largest pharmaceutical company after Merck. As Glaxo grew in technological competences, its international strategy changed. During the postwar decades Glaxo established mainly sales and marketing organizations abroad, primarily in the British Commonwealth. In 1962 Glaxo's Indian business was its largest foreign affiliate. Thereafter the firm began to expand in Europe, the United States, and Japan.
>
> During the 1990s Glaxo was a major participant in the restructuring of the world industry. In 1995 it acquired the smaller British company Wellcome, which specialized in antiviral medicines. In 2000 Glaxo Wellcome merged with SmithKline Beecham, a firm created by a merger between US and British companies in 1989. The new GSK had sales of nearly $32 billion in 2002, and held 7 percent of the world prescription drug market. It had 99 manufacturing sites in 39 countries, and R & D facilities in seven countries. GSK was headquartered in Britain with its operations based in the United States.
>
> (*Source*: Jones 2001.)

7 percent of the world market, and having 70 000 employees, most of them outside Sweden (Olsson 1993).

During the 1980s the industry underwent a major change with the development of cellular or mobile telephony. The mobile phone industry had two components: mobile communication infrastructure and mobile handsets (or cellular phones in the United States). The early mobile networks were for the most part incompatible between countries. In the United States, several competing systems and standards evolved in different parts of the nation. Subsequently second generation systems, which used digital rather than analog technology, were introduced. A pan-European system known as global system for mobile (GSM) communication was launched in 1990, and accounted for seven-tenths of the world's subscribers by the new century. The remainder used two competing US standards or the Japanese standard.

The market for telecom equipment came to be dominated by a small number of large multinationals. In 2000 Ericsson's sales of over $30 billion included nearly one-third of the world mobile infrastructure equipment market and 10 percent of the world cellular phone market. However competitive pressures led it to divest rather than further expand international manufacturing. During the 1990s it reduced the number of its production plants from seventy to less than ten worldwide. The residual plants either focused on the development and design of new products, or on standardized products. The latter were concentrated in a few low-cost sites, including China, Poland, and Estonia. A decision to concentrate on mobile telecom infrastructure led to the sale of many of its plants at the turn of the century and the outsourcing of its non-core manufacturing to contract electronic manufacturers such as Flextronics and Solectron. In 2000 Ericsson and Sony established a London-based joint venture, Sony Ericsson, to exploit the opportunities of third generation mobile systems, whose implementation had begun in Japan.

Ericsson's strategies were broadly emulated by its major competitors in the world telecom industry, including Nokia (see Box 4.8), the Canadian firm Nortel, the US firms Lucent, Cisco Systems, and Motorola, and Germany's Siemens, all of whom had telecom equipment sales in excess of $22 billion in 2000. These firms all moved, although at varying rates, to outsource production to contract manufacturers. They also progressively outsourced innovation to cheaper locations, including Russia and India. Wipro, an Indian firm based in Bangalore, developed a substantial business doing research for most of the large telecom manufacturers.

Box 4.8 The multinational growth of Nokia

The Nokia wood-pulp mill was founded in southern Finland in 1865. A new town grew up around the mill and took its name. Nokia developed as a forestry and power generating company. In 1898 the Finnish Rubber Works opened in the town, and used the Nokia brand for its rubber products. In 1912 the Finnish Cable Works was established, the first Finnish company to manufacture electrical wires and cables. In 1966 Nokia, the Finnish Rubber Works, and the Finnish Cable Works merged, though they had been acting as a loose group since 1922. Subsequently Nokia expanded internationally with large acquisitions, especially in electronics during the 1980s. It acquired the largest Scandinavia television manufacturer, a Swedish electronics and computer firm, and German and French consumer electronics firms, becoming Europe's largest manufacturer of television sets. This expansion, heavy losses on mobile phones, and an extremely severe recession in its home market, produced a major financial crisis in the early 1990s. In 1992 a new strategy was adopted to focus entirely on telecom equipment, then one-third of total sales. Within a few years power, tires, cables and television had been sold.

The development of Nokia's mobile phone business began in the 1960s with the manufacture of radio telephones. Nokia was an early entrant into digitalization. In 1969 it was the first company to introduce digital transmission equipment that conformed to international standards, and it made Europe's first digital telephone switch in 1982. The Scandinavian countries were the first to develop a common wireless network. The Nordic Mobile Telephone (NMT) system, opened in 1981, was the world's first multinational cellular network. Nokia made one of the first phones on the network. Over the following decade this standard was adopted by many other countries, and Scandinavia became the largest user of mobile phones. From the beginning, Nokia was one of the main developers of GSM technology. In 1981 it developed the first operational network to the (DSM) standard. Nokia became one of the leading suppliers. As privatization and deregulation changed European telecommunications markets, Nokia targeted new service operators, and also sold networks to emerging markets such as China and India. By the mid-1990s

continues

> **Box 4.8 The multinational growth of Nokia (*continued*)**
>
> Nokia was the largest mobile phone manufacturer in the world. By the end of that decade it accounted for one-fourth of total Finnish exports and around one-third of Finnish research and development spending.
>
> Nokia built a highly international business. By 2004 it manufactured in ten countries outside Finland. Telecom infrastructure was made in China, Malaysia, and Britain. Mobile phones were made in Brazil, China, Germany, Hungary, Mexico, Korea, and the United States. Nokia's share in world mobile phone manufacture reached 35 percent, although it faced intense competition from major competitors led by Motorola, Siemens, Sony Ericsson, and Samsung.
>
> (*Source: www.nokia.com*; Häikiö 2002)

■ SUMMARY

From the nineteenth century, multinationals occupied an important place in the international diffusion of manufacturing knowledge, processes, and products. Multinational manufacturing grew rapidly between the 1880s and 1930, despite the disruption caused by World War I, but the Great Depression partially halted this growth by creating conditions that favored the alternative of international collusion. The firms which engaged in multinational manufacture often possessed ownership advantages in technology, organization and other factors, while high transactions costs encouraged them to exploit through direct investment rather than market-based arrangements. Tariffs, patent legislation, market size, and competitive behavior were important locational determinants.

After World War II the growth of multinationals resumed. Multinational strategies were prominent in electronics, computers, chemicals and other fast-growing industries. During the 1960s European and Japanese companies, which had been initially preoccupied with the reconstruction of their domestic economies, and then took advantage of falling trade barriers by exporting, resumed multinational manufacturing strategies. These years saw the origins of integrated production systems, and from the 1980s this strategy was intensified. Mergers and acquisitions greatly increased concentration ratios in industries such as pharmaceuticals and telecoms.

Multinational manufacturing presented complex management challenges. There were many failures and poor-performing investments in each generation. Organizational solutions varied over time and between nationalities. By the middle of the twentieth century multinational manufacturing had become dominated by large corporations. Subsequently a process of geographical and functional integration led to the growth of global manufacturing. Yet the boundaries of the multinationals undertaking this integration became more flexible. Outsourcing and alliances fragmented international value chains. In some high technology industries, even innovation was outsourced to start-ups and new ventures.

5 | Services

5.1 Multinationals and services

The transportation, information, energy and financial infrastructure of the first global economy were put in place by business enterprises. They financed, insured and transported world trade in manufactures and resources. In subsequent generations, service enterprises renewed their role as the enablers of global capitalism. They sometimes performed central roles as coordinators of cross-border investments in manufacturing and resources.

The service sector is highly diffuse, and includes trade, finance, personal and business services, construction, transportation, communication, and public utilities. Not only do these different services have different characteristics, but in many cases they consist of subsectors which also differ considerably from each other. A further complexity arises from the distinction between FDI in services and FDI by service sector companies. Since the nineteenth century both manufacturing and petroleum companies have diversified into distribution and transportation, while service multinationals have diversified far beyond services.

5.2 Origins and growth

5.2.1 Trade and shipping

The range of international business in services in the nineteenth century was striking, but the large investments in trade and distribution were especially important. Manufacturing firms made numerous investments in sales and distribution companies in foreign markets to assist their exports. These investments often proved a first stage of multinational involvement, and were followed in time by assembly or production facilities.

The nineteenth century saw the growth of multinational trading companies which offered an alternative organizational form to the vertical integration of manufacturers and petroleum companies. The chartered trading companies of earlier centuries seldom outlived the withdrawal of their monopoly privileges. By 1914 the only survivor was the Hudson's Bay Company, which had evolved into a successful retailing business, although it only stopped trading in fur in 1991. However, there was a rapid spread of private merchants at the world's entrepots and ports. They were often part of wider family or ethnic networks, and over time some merchant houses evolved into large multinational trading companies (Jones 1998b, 2000).

During the late nineteenth century trading companies handled the flow of manufactured goods from the developed world to the developing regions and the reverse flow of commodities. European companies were especially prominent, reflecting the fact that over 60 percent of world trade was European in 1913, consisting of both intra-European trade and European trade with the rest of the world. These trading companies also created trade flows by investing in plantations, mining, and other activities. These investments were placed in independent companies which often drew heavily on local sources of funds—sometimes the profits of past commercial activities by European expatriates, and in other cases indigenous capital—for finance.

The scale of a few businesses reached considerable proportions. In Latin America British merchant houses such as Balfour Williamson and Anthony Gibbs were active in mining, petroleum, flour milling, banking, and many other activities. Both companies invested in the United States. Balfour Williamson was a leading pioneer of the Californian oil industry during the 1900s. Gibbs became a large-scale wool shipper and rancher in Australia. In Asia, there was considerable investment by European trading companies in plantation crops including tea and rubber. Jardine Matheson, John Swire and other merchant houses made diversified investments in the British colony of Hong Kong and the coastal regions of China (see Box 5.1).

The ownership of trading companies was not limited to countries with colonial empires. Denmark was the home to a cluster of trading companies engaged in trade with Russia, such as the Siberian Company, and to the East Asiatic Company, founded in 1897 to trade with Asia, especially Thailand, where it invested in teak production. Swiss-based trading firms included Volkart, a major exporter of cotton and coffee from India (Guex 1998). Greek merchant houses built extensive businesses stretching from Russia through the Mediterranean to Western Europe (Minoglou and Louri 1997).

There were few US-based multinational traders. The international trade of the United States was far less than Europe, while US companies often vertically integrated rather than using trade intermediaries. In Japan, in contrast, trading companies assumed an unusually important role. After the Meiji Restoration in 1868 several dozen companies were founded. The first one was Maruzen, established in 1869, which specialized in the import of books and fancy goods from Europe and the United States. Mitsui Bussan, the first Japanese general trading company or **sogo shosha**, was founded in 1876. This differed from 'speciality' trading companies because it came to trade in many products in many regions. It opened its first overseas branch—in Shanghai—in 1877, for the purpose of selling Japanese coal in China. By the eve of World War I, Mitsui Bussan had more than thirty foreign branches and offices in Asia, Europe and the United States, and it traded more than 120 different kinds of goods. It handled around 20 percent of Japan's total exports and imports. In the 1900s the firm also invested in Chinese cotton textiles production, and opened a flour mill in Shanghai (Yonekawa 1990).

The importance of trading companies in Japan rested on that country's peculiar historical circumstances. The country had been a closed economy for over two centuries before 1853. The result was a severe lack of information about foreign markets and a severe shortage of people with requisite language and trading skills to undertake foreign

Box 5.1 Jardine Matheson and China

Jardine Matheson's origins went back to a series of partnerships founded from the 1780s by British merchants resident in Canton. In the 1820s two Scottish merchants involved in the trade between Calcutta and Canton, William Jardine and James Matheson, joined these partnerships, and in 1832 they founded Jardine Matheson, registered in Hong Kong. By the end of the decade it accounted for around half the foreign trade of China. Its largest business was selling Indian opium to China. This business remained important until the 1870s, when it was undermined by new competitors selling Indian opium and the availability of cheaper Chinese-produced opium.

From the 1860s Jardine Matheson evolved as a diversified conglomerate. Branches were established all over China, and in Japan and New York. In 1865 Jardine formed a company to build a 12-mile railroad in Shanghai (China's first). In 1870 a silk factory was established in Shanghai, followed by a sugar refinery and ice factory in Hong Kong. Large investments were made in wharves and warehouses in Shanghai and Hong Kong, and in 1881 the Indo-China Steam Navigation Company, an ocean shipping venture, was founded. In 1895 a cotton mill (again China's first) was built in Shanghai, and in 1897 a textile spinning and weaving factory opened in Hong Kong. The latter also diversified into shipping and sugar refining, but also established silk, cotton, ice and other factories in China and Hong Kong. In 1898 the British and China Corporation was founded jointly with the Hongkong Bank to build railroads in China.

In London Jardine Matheson was represented by Matheson and Co—they had identical shareholders after 1906. This acted as a merchant bank, and also functioned as an international venture capitalist. During the late nineteenth century Matheson was involved in copper mining in Spain and California, banking in Iran, gold mining in South Africa, and oil in Peru. It also acted as agent for Jardine Skinner, a British merchant house in Calcutta, which had close trading but not equity links with Jardine Matheson. The shareholding structure of Jardine Matheson was complex, but control rested with the Jardine and Keswick families.

(*Source*: Jones 2000).

business. Sogo shosha used such scarce human resources most effectively by employing them in diverse goods, areas and functions. A shortage of knowledge about foreign countries also explains why most Japanese manufacturers did not integrate vertically by establishing their own distribution facilities abroad (Yoshihara 1987). Their use was also appropriate to the industrial structure of Japan, which—with the significant exception of textiles—consisted of industries where economies of scope were more achievable than economies of scale (Fruin 1992).

The growth of the first sogo shosha, Mitsui Bussan, was facilitated by the Japanese government, anxious to reduce Japan's dependence on foreign merchants (Yamazaki 1987). Mitsui Bussan was also part of the Mitsui **zaibatsu**, one of the diversified family-controlled holding companies which were important features of the Japanese business system before World War II. Much of Mitsui Bussan's business involved dealing in commodities such as raw silk, raw cotton, cotton yarn, coal, machinery and sugar, which were produced by enterprises which also belonged to the Mitsui zaibatsu, or else were financially supported by Mitsui Bank (Yamazaki 1987). Mitsubishi—which founded its own sogo shosha in 1918—was another of Japan's big zaibatsu.

Trading companies survived the multiple shocks of the interwar years, though not without casualties. In Japan, the trading companies were adversely affected by the post-war recession, the disruption caused by the devastating Tokyo Earthquake of 1923, and the stagnation of Japanese foreign trade during the 1920s. In 1927 Suzuki Shoten, a large sogo shosha, went bankrupt. The survivors adopted new management methods and strategies. Mitsui Bussan developed new risk management strategies, which included financial control systems which enabled the calculation of income and expenditure for every commodity, and it also avoided the speculative activities which were common among trading companies. The firm began to recruit graduates from the elite Tokyo University after 1905. As manufacturers started to undertake their own distribution, Mitsui Bussan responded by investing in Japanese manufacturing companies and putting directors on their boards (Sakamoto 1990). By the 1930s the sogo shosha could benefit from the rapid growth of Japan's exports. They expanded the range of commodities in which they traded, and opened up new markets in Latin America, the Middle East and the Soviet Union. These 'global sales networks' enabled them to develop third country trade (Kawabe 1990).

While the interwar years also saw some bankruptcies among European trading companies, many also proved resilient. There was diversification into the distribution of new products, including automobiles, and sometimes into local manufacturing. In China, Jardine Matheson invested in engineering, cotton manufacturing, the export of dried eggs, and brewing. During these years Swiss-owned André grew as a major international grain trader, opening branches in Argentina and the United States. The ability of trading companies to 'reinvent' their businesses was one of their most noteworthy characteristics (Jones 1998, 2000).

There were often close ties between trading and shipping companies. The former would act as agents for the latter, while some shipping companies also functioned as trading companies. Shipping was divided into two sectors: liner ships, which carried passengers and general cargoes, such as finished manufactured goods, on a fixed schedule, and tramp ships, which carried bulk cargoes, including coal, ore, and grain. During the nineteenth century the division was not rigid, and British companies, who collectively owned over 40 percent of world tonnage, operated in both sectors. British shipping companies carried a high proportion of the world's trade, including perhaps as much as a half of the foreign trade of the United States.

The Scottish-based Mackinnon 'Group'—a collection of interlinked partnerships—constructed a diversified intercontinental enterprise in liner shipping and related business between the 1840s and the 1890s. Its extensive steamship operations, which included important shipping companies such as British India Steam Navigation Co., extended over four continents. This venture also owned trading firms in the Arabian Gulf and East Africa, and invested in the production of commodities to be carried on its steamers, including tea estates, coal mines, and jute and cotton mills in India, and a meat-freezing factory in Queensland, Australia. The merger of the British India Steam

Navigation Co. and the P & O Steam Navigation Co. shortly before World War I created the largest shipping enterprise in the world (Munro 2003).

The international shipping activities of other countries grew in relative importance from the late nineteenth century. By 1914 German and US companies owned 11 percent of world tonnage each, and Norwegian, French, and Japanese a further 4 percent each. From the 1880s Japanese shipping companies developed international shipping routes, first in Asia and later to the United States. Osaka Shosen Kaisha (OSK) was organized in 1884, and Nippon Yusen Kaisha (NYK) in the following year. NYK inaugurated shipping lines between Japan and the United States and Europe. To facilitate this business, the firm set up offices in major US and European ports (Wray 1984; Wilkins 1989).

Firms from other sectors also invested in shipping. In the oil industry, the earliest tankers were commissioned in the 1870s by the Nobels, the Swedish oil producers in Russia. Subsequently oil companies came to own and operate large tanker fleets. The United Fruit Company established a fleet for the bulk transport of tropical agricultural products. Both oil and agribusiness had characteristics which favored integration into shipping. The rate of production was difficult to vary in the short run and beyond a certain point, the marginal cost of storing products was high. Consequently the coordination of shipping and transportation in these industries relied heavily on forward planning. Long-term chartering of fleets was a theoretical alternative to ownership in such circumstances, but the transport of both oil and agricultural products required special technologies which were embodied in the design of ships. For various reasons, established shipowners were reluctant to invest in such dedicated ships (Casson, Barry, and Horner 1986).

5.2.2 **Financial services**

Bankers had engaged in the finance of cross-border trade and international lending for centuries, and the history of international banking can be legitimately traced back to the Italian bankers of the Middle Ages, through the bankers of south Germany in the sixteenth century, and the Dutch bankers of the eighteenth century (Cameron and Bovykin 1991). These bankers generally operated internationally through partnerships and family connections rather than direct investments.

Business institutions which were much closer to modern-style multinational banks appeared in Europe in the 1830s, when the first British 'overseas banks' were established. These free-standing banks were promoted and owned largely in the United Kingdom, where they had (usually) their corporate headquarters, but did not conduct domestic banking activities in Britain. Nor did they have equity links with domestic British banks until after 1914. The first banks established branches in the British colonies in Australia, the West Indies, and Canada. By mid-century they were operating in Latin America and South Africa, as well as in the ports of Asia. Their names, such as the Standard Bank of South Africa and the Imperial Bank of Persia, reflected their specialization on particular regions or countries (Jones 1986b). By 1913 just over thirty British overseas banks operated almost 1,400 branches outside the United Kingdom, spread throughout Australasia, Asia, Africa, and Latin America.

The British overseas banks rarely entered a completely 'virgin' territory, but they often introduced a degree of stability and financial sophistication which had not previously existed. They provided trade finance and related foreign exchange, and financed a considerable share of the international trade of the southern hemisphere countries and Asia. Over time they progressed from multinational service banking—servicing the requirements of corporate clients and expatriates from the home economy—to multinational retail banking—or serving local customers through the same deposit and loan facilities as domestic banks. Although equity capital was used to initially finance a new branch, once a business was established, local lending was financed by local deposits and—where permitted—the issue of bank notes. There was, as a result, only a limited amount of FDI involved in their operations (Jones 1993).

Specialist overseas banks were also created in France, Germany, and other European countries to operate in colonial territories and in Latin America. European banks also established branches in other European cities, especially London, the major international financial center before 1914. In most cases, the overseas banks owned in continental Europe had much closer links with pre-existing domestic banks than in the British case (Meuleau 1990; Hertner 1990).

Both Japanese and United States banks had limited international business before 1914. Japan's first multinational bank was founded by the government in 1880. This was the Yokohama Specie Bank, the predecessor to the Bank of Tokyo, which by 1914 had around twenty foreign branches, spreading from China to Europe and the United States (Tamaki 1990). There was only a handful US bank branches abroad before 1914. Subsequently, the number of foreign branches of US banks reached over 180 in 1920, before falling back to 107 by 1925. Citibank, which opened its first foreign branch in Buenos Aires, Argentina in 1914, became the pre-eminent bank. By 1930 it had almost one hundred foreign branches, two-thirds of them in Latin America (Wilkins 1993a; Huertas 1990).

Multinational banks sometimes diversified outside their core business. The 'mixed' banking system prevalent in Continental Europe resulted in closer links between banks and industry than in the United States or Britain, and this was reflected in their foreign as well as domestic activities. The Deutsche Bank was involved in railway construction in the Middle East, controlled a Rumanian oil company, and—together with other German banks—became extensively involved in public utility investments before 1914.

Insurance attracted early multinational investment. From the late eighteenth century the British-owned Phoenix Assurance Company began opening agencies in other European countries, and later elsewhere. It opened a New York fire and marine agency in 1804. After the end of the US Civil War a substantial number of British companies entered the US market, as well as a number of Canadian and German firms in the 1870s. By 1913 there were almost ninety foreign companies active in fire and marine insurance in the United States, including firms from Britain, Germany, Russia, France, Switzerland, Japan, and even Bulgaria. In 1910 foreign companies accounted for over 50 percent of the US marine and inland insurance, and 24 percent of US fire and marine insurance (Wilkins 1989; Pearson and Lonnborg 2003). In life insurance, US companies—notably New York Life, which began selling insurance in Canada in 1858—joined British, Dutch, German, and other European firms in expanding across borders (Wilkins 1970; Gales and Sluyterman 1993; Schröter 1993a).

Insurance companies used several modes to access foreign markets. Some firms underwrote international insurance without any foreign presence; others used independent agents; in other cases wholly owned agencies or joint ventures were formed. From the 1880s the largest British firms began to establish subsidiary companies in the United States, usually registered as American companies in New York.

There was a wide range of regulatory regimes in insurance markets, but even tight controls did not necessarily prevent foreign companies from securing business. Although Russia restricted direct underwriting by foreign companies in 1847, for example, this encouraged the use of reinsurance, sometimes sold by specialist multinational reinsurance broking firms (Pearson and Lonnborg 2003). However the widespread concern to restrict the provision of life insurance to national companies reduced multinational investment in that sector. In addition, high European inflation during World War I caused major losses to the US life insurance companies, because many of their policies were in gold, while depreciated currencies made the cost of paying them exorbitant. After the war the US companies withdrew from foreign markets other than Canada (Wilkins 1974a).

In fire, accident, and other types of insurance, there remained international opportunities, and there were also opportunities in motor insurance, which attracted new entrants into multinational motor insurance in the interwar years (Westall 1992). The origins of America International Group (AIG), which was to become the world's largest insurer, was with an American entrepreneur, C. V. Starr, who established an insurance agency in Shanghai in 1919. Initially acting as an agent for US fire and marine insurance companies, Starr formed a life insurance company which within a decade had offices opened not only in China, but elsewhere in Asia. In 1926 an office was also opened in New York under the name AIU, and subsequently a large Latin American business began to be developed.

5.2.3 Energy and communications

There was widespread multinational investment in energy, transport and communications in the first global economy. The building and operation of utilities in the nineteenth century was undertaken not only by specialist enterprises, but also by firms engaged in other types of business. Mining, petroleum, and agribusiness companies frequently invested in utilities to provide the infrastructure to support their businesses. Trading companies became involved in establishing and managing utilities, sometimes for extended periods, in Latin America and Asia.

The gas industry provided early instances of multinational investment. The Imperial Continental Gas Association was formed in Britain in 1825. It acquired an existing gas works in Ghent, in the Netherlands. Britain was the world pioneer of gas lighting, and this and similar companies drew on this expertise. Like other free-standing companies, it did not manufacture gas in the United Kingdom. Subsequently this venture expanded by securing municipal contracts to supply gas lighting to other European cities. At the turn of the century it operated gas utilities in ten major European towns outside the United Kingdom—of which Berlin was the largest operation—and twenty-nine smaller towns, and had a total workforce of almost 8,000 (Hill 1950).

By the middle of the nineteenth century a worldwide boom was underway in building railroads. Foreign capital financed much of the construction of the world's railroads, though it was largely portfolio in nature. The government controlled the large railroad systems built in both Russia and British India, which were financed in part by bonds issued abroad. In the United States, the railroad system was a private sector one, owned and managed almost entirely by American companies, though American railroad securities were widely held abroad. Railroads were by far the largest single sector to attract foreign investment in the United States between 1875 and 1914, when the total foreign investment in American railroads was over $4 billion. But the only clearly identifiable FDI in this huge sum was that of Canadian railroad companies, principally the Canadian Pacific and the Canadian Grand Trunk, which crossed the United States border to complete their own systems, though sometimes other foreign portfolio holdings were so large that some managerial control could be exercised (Wilkins 1989).

In contrast, foreign investment in Latin American railroads often took the form of FDI. Beginning with the Panama Railroad Company, a New York chartered venture which built a railroad across the Panama Isthmus in 1851, there was US FDI in the railroad systems of Mexico and Central America, as well as Canada (Wilkins 1970). By the end of the century the largest amount of US FDI in Mexico was in railroads, though subsequently the government bought out much of the American investment, and control of the system passed into Mexican hands. Elsewhere in Latin America, foreign ownership of railroads became considerable in the late nineteenth century, and then tended to decline, though the foreign role was persistent in Cuba and Argentina. In the latter country, British-owned and managed railroad companies became dominant in the wake of the Baring Crisis, a disastrous financial crisis in 1890, when the state-owned railroads were privatized. Between 1900 and 1914 total route mileage doubled, almost entirely in British-owned railroads, although three French-owned railroad companies were also active (Lewis 1983a; Regalsky 1989).

Foreign companies played a central role in the spread of electrification. Between the late nineteenth century and 1914 residents of most of the world's cities were provided with access to electricity, in the homes or at work, or else in the form of street lighting or on tramways. The main forces behind this process were German electrical engineering firms. In Europe and Latin America, these firms obtained concessions to build electrical installations or plants. Subsequently they created companies to which such concessions were transferred. These companies then ordered equipment from their German parents. The German electrical producers also purchased existing horse tramway companies, and electrified them, again using their own products. These firms were controlled by vast holding companies (see Chapter 6). The outcome of this strategy—which contemporary German observers called *Unternehmergeschäft*—was to create a large market for electrical products by promoting the electrification of a whole region. Swiss, Belgian, and French electrical companies followed similar strategies ((Jacob-Wendler 1982; Schröter 1993a; Hertner 1984, 1987b; Lanthier 1989). In Latin America, Canadian companies also became important agents of electrification (see Box 5.2).

Among the many other utility investments before 1914, Belgian companies were prominent in building and operating tramway systems. By the eve of World War I there

Box 5.2 Canadian business and the electrification of Brazil and Mexico

Canadian firms undertook major investments in the provision of electricity and tramways in southeast Brazil. The Sao Paulo Tramway, Light and Power Company was formed in 1898, followed by the Rio de Janeiro Tramway, Light and Power Co. Ltd. six years later. These linked enterprises were large electricity generators, and created integrated, electrified tramway systems in their cities. Waterpower, gas, and telephone enterprises were also operated. In 1912 a Toronto-based holding company, the Brazilian Traction, Light and Power Co. Ltd. was formed which owned the shares of both companies). Another Canadian company, the Mexican Light and Power Company, which was founded in 1902, operated a large-scale hydroelectric system and an urban tramway system in Mexico City.

Both the economic and social impact of the Canadian utilities was considerable. Access to the safe urban transportation provided in Brazil by tramway utilities such as Canada's Brazilian Traction helped to advance the emancipation of Brazilian women—or at least those of the middle and upper-class—who had endured a cloistered existence in the nineteenth century.

The 'nationality' of these Canadian utilities was ambiguous. An American engineer was the most influential individual behind the Brazilian and Mexican ventures, providing both entrepreneurship and technical expertise. The tiny Toronto and Montreal headquarters of the companies consisted of a handful of financiers. The key purchasing functions—the acquisition of the capital goods required to build the hydroelectric and tramway systems—was located in New York. Most capital was raised beyond the limited Canadian capital market. Funds were raised on a large scale in London, using some of the most prestigious British financial houses, and later on other European capital markets also.

In later decades political pressures mounted against the Canadian firms. The Canadian-owned utilities in Mexico were taken over by the government in the late 1940s. Brazilian Traction's position was stronger. In 1946 it produced 60 percent of Brazil's total power, supplied 75 percent of the nation's telephones, and was the largest private sector employer, with 50 000 Brazilian workers. During the 1950s Brazilian Traction shifted the domicile of its subsidiaries to Brazil, and adopted other Brazilianization measures. After 1964—when the government purchased American & Foreign Power's Brazilian business—it was the sole foreign utility in the country. Finally in 1979 the Canadian utility sold its Brazilian assets to the national power company, in an amicable agreement.

(*Source*: McDowall 1988; Armstrong and Nelles 1988.)

were twenty-three Belgian tramway companies active in Russia (McKay 1970). By 1914 British-owned and managed gas, electricity, tramway, bus, and dockyard companies were found all over Latin America, and especially Argentina, Brazil, Chile, and Uruguay. They were often dominant influences on their local economies (Rippy 1959; Finch 1985).

The creation of a global communications network began with the laying of submarine telegraph cables during the 1850s. British companies, notably the Eastern Telegraph Company, were pre-eminent in the industry. They controlled key patents, were supplied with plentiful funds from the British capital markets, and were heavily subsidized to build cable lines linking the various components of the British Empire. The transiting of transatlantic cables through Britain enabled the British government to intercept and censor messages from the United States, a practice that continued until the 1960s. In South America and Asia, the British exploited cable lending concessions to prevent US companies from establishing cable routes to the regions (Hills 2002).

British and German wireless companies were first movers in transoceanic radio communication. The leading enterprise was again a British firm, Marconi. The firm specialized in ship-to-shore and ship-to-ship transmissions, but shortly before the war it also began commercial transoceanic transmissions. Marconi's US affiliate, established in 1899, became the leading firm in radio communications in that country, with no locally-owned competitors (Wilkins 1989).

From the late nineteenth century the global spread of telephones, an American invention, was undertaken by multinational investment. The initial strategies of American Bell and Edison to introduce telephones in Europe and elsewhere often involved taking minority interests in companies operating franchises for particular cities (Wilkins 1970). Subsequently there were direct investments in telephone utilities in Latin America and other developing regions. In the 1900s Swedish-owned Stockholms Allmäna Telefon (SAT) secured concessions to operate the telephone systems of Moscow, Warsaw in Poland, and in Mexico (Lundström 1986a).

World War I focused new attention on the importance of both telephones and electrification, and afterwards US companies assumed a newly critical role in their spread. During the 1920s utilities received more US FDI than any other sector (Wilkins 1974a). The American & Foreign Power Company was formed in 1923 out of a GE subsidiary, although equity links (but not cross-directorships) were subsequently severed. It undertook substantial FDI, especially in Latin America, but also in China, where a major acquisition in 1929 in Shanghai gave it the largest power station in that country. The firm manufactured and sold electricity and gas, ran tramways, and even supplied telephone services (Wilkins 1974a).

This period also saw the fast international growth of the International Telephone and Telegraph Corporation (ITT). This was a 'free-standing' firm in the sense that it did not operate a business inside the United States, although it was headquartered and managed there. It was founded in 1920 by the merger of two small telephone companies in Puerto Rico and Cuba, the former acquired as a result of a bad debt. Under the leadership of Sosthenese Behn, ITT borrowed extensively on the US capital markets to finance the purchase of foreign telephone companies and the foundation of new ones. In 1925 ITT acquired the international division of Western Electric, the largest US producer of electric products, and with it a network of subsidiaries manufacturing electrical products and telephone apparatus, in Europe, Argentina, Australia, Japan, and China (Wilkins 1974a). By the end of the decade the firm operated telephone and telegraph in several Latin American countries, and had extensive cable and radio investments. Its total worldwide employment, almost entirely outside the United States, approached 100 000 (Abo 1982).

European-owned utilities were more subdued in international markets. The once-extensive Belgian FDI in Russian utilities was eliminated by the Communist Revolution.

In postwar Latin America, many British-owned utilities sold out to American interests (Finch 1985; Miller 1993). The system of financial holding companies for electrical utilities was changed rather than entirely destroyed by World War I. By the early 1920s the holdings of the German electrical companies Siemens and AEG had passed under the control of Swiss banks. Under new ownership, the *Unternehmergeschäft* strategy was continued, with the ownership links in the holding companies being used to generate orders for the Swiss electrical companies (Segreto 1987, 1992, 1994).

5.2.4 **Construction**

The provision of cross-border construction and engineering services across borders was an important element in the building of the first global economy during the nineteenth century. Among the pioneers were British railroad contractors Brassey and Peto & Betts. They grew rapidly during Britain's huge railroad building boom of the 1840s—probably accounting for as much as a third of British railroad construction—and thereafter undertook massive construction projects first in Continental Europe, and then in India, Canada, Latin America, and elsewhere. However this first wave of investments came to an end with the bankruptcy of Peto & Betts in the international financial crisis in 1866, and the death of Brassey four years later (Linder 1994).

French civil engineering firms became involved in major infrastructure projects, especially for harbour facilities and tunnel construction, in a growing number of countries from the middle of the nineteenth century. After initially undertaking projects in neighbouring Belgium and Switzerland, they invested more widely in the Mediterranean region and Eastern Europe. From the 1900s French firms secured large orders from the construction of railways, urban sanitation systems, and harbor facilities in Latin America (Barjot 1986).

The scale of international contracting reached formidable proportions in the decades before World War I. A new wave of British contractors appeared, including S. Pearson and Son (see Chapter 3). Pearson's tunneling in New York City provided a rare instance of a European firm undertaking significant construction work in the United States. Another British contractor, Lucas & Aird, built water and gas works in Europe, India, Argentina, Brazil, and other countries, as well as the giant Aswan Dam in Egypt. German-owned Holzman built railroads in Iraq and German East Africa, as well as harbors in Morocco and Russia. The Danish firm of Christiani & Nielsen, founded in 1904, expanded elsewhere in Scandinavia, Russia, Germany, and Britain building bridges and reinforced concrete structures. After World War I its international expansion intensified, and included the establishment of affiliates in Latin America (Linder 1994; Boje 2000).

During the 1920s cross-border activities in construction again grew rapidly. Holzman had established an affiliate in Argentina in 1913 which by 1930 had become the largest construction firm in Latin America employing 5,000 persons. During the 1920s the German firms founded further companies in Chile, Peru, and Brazil. US construction firms including Ulen and J. G. White were active especially in Latin America. Warren Brothers, the largest highway construction firm in the United States, performed road and paving building throughout Latin America, and had foreign subsidiaries in Europe and Australia (Linder 1994).

5.2.5 **Significance**

Service multinationals were extremely important in the making of the first global economy. They were transferors of organizational and technological systems, alongside consumption patterns and culture, across borders. They facilitated the incorporation of peripheral regions into the world economy. Yet the provision of many services was not a capital-intensive process, and frequently involved only small amounts of FDI. Trading companies and banks were as much coordinators and mobilizers of local resources as foreign investors.

5.3 **Determinants**

There were multiple determinants of the growth of multinational investment in services. A distinction can be made between trade-supporting, location-bound services, and foreign-tradeable services, though the same firm could be involved in the provision of different types of service.

5.3.1 **Trade-supporting services**

A great deal of multinational service investment involved the servicing of international trade. Many of the activities of trading and shipping companies, banks and insurance companies, and utility and contracting firms, were related to the facilitating of trade flows in one way or another. The unprecedented growth of world trade in the nineteenth century, and the integration of new countries and regions into the world trading system, provided many opportunities for such trade-supporting investments.

Intermediaries such as trading companies were used to facilitate trade flows because they reduced search, negotiation, transaction, and information costs. European manufacturers in the nineteenth century did not use trading companies when buying and selling elsewhere in Europe or North America, but trading companies were active in Asia, Latin America, and Africa where the business cultures, institutions and languages were very different from Europe (Yoshihara 1987). This resulted in significant obstacles to trade arising from lack of trust and lack of information. The risks of dealing in these areas were particularly high because much of the trade involved primary commodities, which were subject to price fluctuations and to interruptions in supply because of climatic or other natural factors. Without trading companies, the high costs of acquiring knowledge about foreign markets would have been indivisible, and would have fallen totally on individual exporters. Trading companies reduced risks by gathering information, and by forming relationships with other enterprises. Japan's trading companies were joined in numerous transactions with other Japanese service sector ventures in banking, shipping and insurance (Wilkins 1986).

These concepts also explain why trading companies often diversified into non-trading activities. Knowledge and know-how about markets could be employed to pursue other profit-making opportunities by exploiting economies of scope. Transactions costs arising from opportunism and information asymmetry provided incentives for trading firms to integrate backwards or forwards. Given that the business of trade intermediaries was to put buyers and sellers into contact, there was always a risk that their clients would deal directly with one another. In order to survive, therefore, trading companies had incentives to pre-empt being excluded from transactions by taking equity stakes in suppliers and customers, or investing in entirely new activities (Jones 2000).

Much of the FDI in utilities was also trade-supporting category. The utility investments undertaken by German electrical manufacturers were a means of creating overseas markets for their goods. Although British FDI in utilities never originated from British manufacturers, British merchants and land companies were prominent. In Latin America —and elsewhere—railroad ventures and other utilities were promoted by British merchants and landowners already active in the region. They sought expanding market opportunities for their crops and animals, and often invested in several companies. There were many links at director level between British companies in Latin America active in railroads, other utilities, banks and shipping. There was sometimes quasi-integration to provide services from the agricultural estate to the port of export (Lewis 1983a).

The main locational determinant of this kind of investment in utilities was the absence of adequate infrastructure to support accelerating trade flows. It flourished where trading opportunities existed, and where either governments or local entrepreneurs did not invest in infrastructure. In some contexts, mining or tropical fruit MNEs had little alternative but to make utility investments in order to engage in the successful export of their commodities. The foreign-owned utility companies derived ownership advantages from access to capital and technology, and from links with other foreign enterprises in the host economies.

5.3.2 Location-bound services

Multinational investment in location-bound services can be partially explained in terms of entrepreneurial perceptions of profitable opportunities in supplying services where consumption could not be separated from production. The investments were undertaken for offensive, profit-seeking motives. British gas companies in Europe were not a 'trade-supporting' investment: they sought profitable opportunities in the provision of gas lighting in European cities. This service had of necessity to involve production near the point of consumption because, unlike the natural gas era after 1945, 'town gas' was manufactured from coal, and was not transportable over long distances.

Foreign enterprises engaged in location-bound services held similar ownership advantages to firms undertaking market-oriented manufacturing FDI. They usually possessed organizational skills, including access to new technologies, which could be exploited in foreign markets, as well as access to capital. However, in much of the developing world in the nineteenth century, these enterprises were first-movers with no indigenous competitors. There was, as a result, no need for an 'ownership advantage' over local rivals. A lack of local competitors also made diversification strategies attractive. Firms which possessed knowledge about a particular host economy would be alert to further profitable opportunities, and to ways to exploiting them. These enterprises needed compensating advantages only when, over time, local rivals developed.

5.3.3 Foreign-tradeable services

For services for which a choice of exporting or direct investment existed, the problem is to explain why one mode of servicing a foreign market was chosen rather than another. The finance of international trade is an example. British trade with the United States and Continental Europe was financed using 'correspondent' relationships between independent banks. On the British side, much of this business was undertaken by the 'merchant banks' such as the Rothschilds and Barings. They acted as the London bankers for foreign banks in return for equivalent services in their countries. In contrast, much of Britain's foreign trade with developing regions was financed by the overseas banks with branches in those countries.

Internalization theory helps to explain why different modes were chosen for different geographical regions. International trade finance required detailed creditor information and debt collection facilities. The established and reliable domestic banking systems in existence in the United States and Europe meant that these functions could be undertaken using independent banks in other countries as correspondents. However, in most of the countries in which British overseas banks invested from the 1830s, it was hard to find local banks which could be trusted to act as correspondents, given that the banking systems were nonexistent or in their infancy. The transactions costs involved in the use of the market were likely to be high, and it was rational to internalize trade finance by establishing a multinational branch network.

Differential regulation was an important influence on the choice of modality in international banking. Before 1914 the development of US multinational banking to provide international trade finance and other services for US business was constrained by Federal and state regulatory restrictions on branch banking in general, combined with the specific prohibition on the opening of foreign branches by national banks, which included the largest American banks. There were even regulatory restrictions on the participation of American banks in international trade finance (Carosso and Sylla 1991). Canadian banks were sometimes able to take advantage of this situation by servicing US corporations in the West Indies and elsewhere (Quigley 1989). Foreign multinational banking within the United States was also made very difficult by US regulations. By the beginning of the twentieth century foreign banks were prohibited from opening branches in most US states, or else—as in New York—limited to opening 'agencies' which could not take deposits (Wilkins 1989).

5.4 Equity and non-equity strategies in a regulated environment

5.4.1 The changing structure of multinational services

In contrast to manufacturing and resources, there was not a spread of international cartels as a result of the Great Depression. There were few significant international cartels in services apart from in shipping, where from the 1870s shipping companies had begun to set uniform rates on shipping lines in 'conferences'. During the 1930s such conferences spread to cover each major shipping route, although tramp shipping remained totally uncartelized. Shipping conferences were exempted from US antitrust law, except that conferences serving US foreign trade had to have free entry for new members, while elsewhere would-be new members had to fight for membership. Paradoxically, while antitrust pressures after World War II helped to eliminate most international cartels in manufacturing, governments encouraged their growth and facilitated their survival in strategic international services such as air travel and tele-communications.

There was a significant shift in the nature of services provided by MNEs. Beginning in the 1930s, there was a sharp fall in investments in utilities while, especially after 1950, there were new waves of activity in business, trade, hotel, and restaurant services, and a renewed importance for trade and finance-related activities. There was also a marked shift in the location of service sector FDI from developing to developed economies. By the 1970s almost three-fourths of the total stock of service investment was located in the developed economies. In developed economies, financial, business, and professional services were particularly important, while in developing economies trade, tourism and basic financial services accounted for a higher proportion of FDI.

5.4.2 The impact of government intervention: utilities, airlines, and insurance

The growth of government intervention in, and regulation of, many services had the effect of closing certain sectors altogether to MNEs, while in others the nature of multi-national investment was strictly regulated.

From the 1930s foreign-owned utilities faced mounting political difficulties, especially in Latin America, whose effects were exacerbated by the general economic conditions of the period. Currency depreciations had a particularly adverse effect on utilities whose rate structures were controlled by host governments. The mushroom growth of ITT and the American & Foreign Power Company—both heavily exposed to Latin America—was halted and both enterprises had a struggle to survive. ITT was particularly badly affected by the Spanish Civil War (1936–39), as around a quarter of its total income had come from Spain (Abo 1982).

After World War II political pressures against foreign utilities intensified. The American & Foreign Power Company had its large operations in China and Cuba expropriated in 1949 and 1960 respectively, and was obliged to relinquish control over its Indian proper-ties following Indian independence. Throughout Latin America, electric power was a political issue which led to the foreign utilities either facing nationalization or extensive controls over their rates and profit remittances. The US utilities responded by diversifi-cation beyond utilities, to such an extent that they could no longer be regarded as international utilities. ITT diversified into car rentals (with the purchase of Avis in 1965) and hotels (with the purchase of Sheraton in 1968). By 1970 public utilities comprised a mere 4 percent of the total book value of US FDI (Wilkins 1974a). However Canadian-owned Brazilian Traction was able to retain its Brazilian businesses until 1979 (see Box 5.2).

The 1930s were dismal for the European railroad companies in Argentina. The onset of the Depression and the contraction of Argentinean foreign trade caused a sharp decline in their freight traffic, but the government prohibited them from dismissing workers or cutting their remuneration. Currency depreciation and the introduction of exchange controls from 1931 interrupted the repatriation of profits. In addition, the government launched an extensive road-building program, which facilitated competition from motor transport. The profitability of the foreign companies was virtually destroyed and they were unable to pay dividends to their shareholders through the 1930s (Heras 1987). Over the next three years after Juan Perón became president in 1946 the government purchased the British and the French-owned railroads in Argentina (Wright 1974). The remaining British railroad companies in Brazil were sold shortly afterwards (Abreu 1990).

Telecommunications became an industry in which MNEs could play little role in most of the world. Telecommunications monopolies in many countries—usually state-owned—blocked the entry of foreign operators. These monopolies cooperated in cartel agreements, which set the prices of international telephone calls. As the television industry spread in the 1950s and 1960s, almost every country in the world blocked foreign ownership of broadcasting media. There were also numerous restrictions on the country of origin of programs, often prompted by a desire to protect national cultures.

Air transportation also became rife with government restrictions against foreign companies. Multinational strategies were seen in the first stage of the commercial industry's development in the interwar years. The US pioneer was Pan American Airways, which began a service between Florida and Cuba in 1927, and over the following decade expanded its route network over Latin America, and subsequently began trans-Atlantic and trans-Pacific services. Pan American purchased Mexican and Colombian airlines as part of its expansion strategy (Wilkins 1974a). The airlines of European colonial powers, such as KLM of the Netherlands and Imperial Airways of Britain, developed long-haul operations to colonial territories. The Singapore-to-Australia service was operated by a joint venture between Imperial Airways and the Australian airline Qantas. The joint venture was registered in Australia and managed by Qantas, but Imperial Airways held 51 percent of the equity and its operations were coordinated with the Imperial Airways' London to Singapore services (Dierikx 1991).

The potential for substantial FDI in airlines was greatly constrained by governments. From the beginning civilian aviation was regarded as a matter of national prestige, as well as strategic concern. Airlines were used as instruments of national diplomacy. Pan American was given a range of government subsidies to encourage its spread in Latin America (Wilkins 1974a). European airlines were often government-owned and always in receipt of large subsidies (Dierikx 1991). After World War II the airline industry became highly cartelized with rigid government controls on entry, capacity, and tariffs. Flights between countries were a matter of intergovernmental negotiation. Traffic rights were negotiated on a bilateral basis, and as a rule only one 'national flag' operator was recognized per route. Foreign ownership of airlines was almost never permitted. As a result, from the 1950s international airlines expanded dramatically, but their direct investments were limited to offices and inventories abroad which did not involve large sums of money (Wilkins 1974a). Insurance companies faced growing regulatory barriers also. Foreign insurance companies were nationalized in many developing countries after World War II.

A growing insistence by governments that insurance companies should maintain reserves in each of the countries which they operated undermined the competitive advantages of large international insurance companies vis-à-vis smaller rivals (Michie 1992). There remained more multinational investment in non-life insurance than in the heavily regulated life insurance sector. The most internationalized sector was reinsurance, in which companies based in Germany, Switzerland, and the United Kingdom were prominent. Reinsurance was less heavily regulated than other types of insurance, and benefited from restrictions on other segments, because as more insurance was preserved for local companies, they found it necessary to take out reinsurance in order to cover themselves against catastrophes (Goodman 1993).

Yet it remained possible to build large multinational insurance businesses. Although the US international insurance business developed by C. V. Starr lost all its Chinese operations in 1950, the company expanded rapidly internationally elsewhere. By the end of the 1950s it was represented in seventy-five countries worldwide. In 1967 a new corporate structure was formed with the foundation of The American International Group, which consolidated the group's domestic and international affiliates.

5.4.3 Equity and non-equity modes

In many other services multinational strategies before the 1980s were less hampered by regulation. Table 5.1 identifies the typical mode employed to operate in foreign countries.

The use of FDI strategies by advertising agencies rested on considerable internalization advantages. The companies had a strong brand name and image, and there was a high cost of quality control if alternative strategies were employed. Locational factors, such as the need for on-the-spot contact with clients and adaptation to local tastes, made the export of the service difficult.

Given the origins of most modern advertising and marketing methods in the United States, it was US firms that were the most prominent multinational investors. They opened offices in Europe before World War I. During the interwar years they expanded further as agencies such as J. Walter Thompson, Lord & Thomas, and Paul E. Derrick opened foreign offices to service the accounts of their large domestic advertisers who had become MNEs. During the 1920s J. Walter Thompson had an agreement with GM that it would open an office in every country where the car firm had an assembly operation or distributor, and this drove its expansion in Europe and elsewhere. Once established in a country, however, the US advertising agencies developed local client bases (West 1987).

Table 5.1 International business in services: organizational modes

Service	Typical mode
Advertising/Consulting	FDI
Accounting	Partnerships
Construction management	Transitory FDI, but permanent offices
Hotels	Franchising/management contracts

After World War II US agencies exploited their innovations in advertising and market research in many countries. By the 1970s they were operating worldwide, which they often entered by servicing their US-based clients (Terpstra and Yu 1988). US multinationals often preferred to appoint one agency to deal with their entire international business. European-owned agencies were disadvantaged in this respect as their multinationals often preferred to treat each country in which they had a subsidiary separately, and appointed local agencies (West 1988). It was not until the 1980s that British and Japanese advertising agencies began to challenge the US pre-eminence in the industry.

Management consultants also expanded abroad using FDI. The profession of management consultancy emerged towards the end of the nineteenth century from fields such as engineering and accounting. The development of the concept of 'scientific management' by the US engineer Frederick W. Taylor at the start of the twentieth century led to the first organized growth of the field. During the interwar years the US-based consultancy established by the naturalized Frenchman Charles Bedaux opened several European offices, although its growth faltered during the 1930s, partly because of the emergence of locally owned firms. After World War II, local service providers continued to provide most consultancy services in Europe (Kipping 1997).

The focus of Bedaux, as well as other consultancies of that era, was efficiency. During the 1930s a new kind of consultancy firm began to appear in the United States which dealt with wider organizational and strategic issues. These companies included Arthur D. Little, Booz Allen & Hamilton, A. T. Kearney and McKinsey. From the late 1950s, these firms opened offices in Europe, offering local companies access to US managerial expertise. McKinsey opened its first foreign office in 1959 (see Box 5.3). The Boston Consulting Group, established in 1963, rapidly expanded abroad. By 1970 it had already opened in Britain, France, Germany, and Japan. Bain and Company, founded in 1973, opened an office in London five years later. Over the next two decades it opened offices throughout Europe and Asia.

In other professional business services, cross-border activities were more typically conducted by informal networks of independent firms. This organizational form became pre-eminent in accounting, engineering, architecture and surveying services, and legal services. These services not only required local specialized knowledge, but products required specific customization. A high degree of knowledge of local laws, standards and procedures was also required. International networks of independent national firms provided the advantage of a presence in all major markets without incurring the costs of coordination through ownership ties. These firms often used a common name, enabling local firms to gain in reputation. Various techniques were available to monitor behavior so as to prevent damage to the reputation of the firm: these included maintaining minimum standards of professional work and periodical quality reviews throughout the organization (Aharoni 1993).

The growth of international accounting partnerships provides an important example of this strategy. Before World War II a number of US and UK accountancy firms had operated under the same names in both countries, and these arrangements were formalized after the War. In 1945 Price, Waterhouse established a separate international firm on a worldwide basis through the integration of its existing national practices. A series of other mergers at international level followed. In 1952 the British-owned Deloitte merged with a

---

Box 5.3 Multinational strategies in management consulting: McKinsey & Company, Inc.

McKinsey was founded in the United States in 1926 to provide accounting and financial services. In 1933 Martin Bower, a Harvard-trained lawyer, joined the firm, and in 1937 his New York office became the basis for a new partnership. The firm's philosophy was to provide advice to the top management of firms. Bower emphasized that management consultants needed the same level of professionalism as lawyers, and this was achieved by constant formal and informal training within the firm.

From the early 1950s McKinsey recruited consultants from leading US business schools, especially the Harvard Business School. New associates were given the opportunity for promotion to principal and then to partner, for which they had to be elected by unanimous vote of the partnership. In 1954 a formal policy of 'up or out' for associates was adopted. McKinsey undertook a major consultancy project for the Shell group in 1958, and in the following year opened an office in London. By 1971 the firm had 17 offices on four continents. McKinsey consulted for US companies, but also sought to develop a local client base by establishing close relationships with local elites. It played a prominent role in the adoption of the M-form by many European companies during that period. The 'up or out' policy helped the firm extend its networks in international markets, as many former consultants went on to senior positions in industry.

By the 1990s McKinsey operated in over thirty countries. The firm supported new offices even when they were not profitable, and maintained only one profit and loss account for the whole firm. In Europe there were initially few business schools—McKinsey played an active role in the foundation of INSEAD in 1959—and in Germany and elsewhere high quality staff had to be recruited using the norms of the local labor market. A constant concern was to preserve the firm's culture and identity as the company expanded internationally. To maintain a culture of 'one firm', McKinsey exchanged professionals between offices and had interoffice personnel evaluations. New offices were opened by McKinsey partners rather than through acquisition.

(*Source*: Kipping 1999.)

US firm, which eight years later merged with another firm created by a British, US, and Canadian merger, to create Deloitte & Touche. In 1989 the addition of a Japanese partner produced Deloitte Touche Tohmatsu. In 1957 another Anglo-US-Canadian merger created Coopers & Lybrand, which eventually merged to create Pricewaterhouse Coopers.

The merger of accounting firms at international level enabled them to enter previously unserved national markets. The leading firms entered national markets through mergers with established national practices, and over time comprehensive international networks were built up. If no suitable practice existed for a merger, new firms were sometimes established, while in other cases national firms were recruited as representatives or correspondents rather than being integrated into the international firm. Although these international firms were partnerships, in most cases the partners from the US arm of the practice were particularly prominent (Daniels, Thrift, and Leyshon 1989).

The major exception to the partnership strategy in international accounting was that employed by Arthur Andersen, a US-based firm. Before 1945 this firm did not open any overseas offices in its own name, but entered into agreements with foreign firms that would represent it in particular countries. From the 1950s Arthur Andersen severed all its existing agreements with national practices, and began to open offices in foreign countries in its own name. However during 2002 Andersen disintegrated as a result of its role in the Enron corporate scandal, with many of its national units merging with the other large firms.

A few large firms accounted for a considerable share of all international construction management after 1945. US companies, including Bechtel, undertook the largest share of international construction contracts. They held considerable advantages in terms of specialist expertise, skilled personnel and reputation, and benefited in many developing countries from US government links on defence and political matters. Beginning in the United States as a railroad construction business in 1898, Bechtel's first international project was in 1940 when it was involved in a joint venture to construct a pipeline system in Venezuela. By 1979 the firm had offices in twenty countries, and one-fifth of its 35 000 permanent, nonmanual workers were based outside the United States (Stephenson 1984: Linder 1994).

Construction companies employed multiple modes of market servicing, depending on the type of project. Licensing was used for process plant projects whose proprietary technologies existed, and was generally employed in developed market economies. Management contracts and turnkey arrangements were used by firms engaged in industrial plant and heavy civil work, especially in developing economies lacking suitably qualified management. Turnkey projects involved contracts for the construction of operating facilities which were transferred to the owner, for a fee, when the facilities were ready to commence operations. Turnkey contracts in remote areas of developing economies sometimes involved building entire infrastructures—reminiscent of the early, pioneering days of international business. Larger companies such as Bechtel maintained permanent offices in some countries. Joint ventures with local firms were sometimes used to win contracts from host governments, and to reduce the risk of nationalization (Enderwick 1989).

In hotels, restaurants, fast food and car rental businesses, franchising and management contracts were the predominant modes used in multinational business. The hotel industry was primarily national before World War II, although Swiss-owned companies made direct investments in foreign hotels even before World War I (Wavre 1988). Subsequently, international business in hotels expanded alongside the improvements in transport and the growth of international tourism. A number of major US hotel groups—Holiday Inn, Inter-Continental, Hilton and Sheraton—emerged, alongside a smaller number of French and UK hotel firms, such as Club Méditerranée and Trust House Forte. The importance of these three home economies reflected the fact that their domestic industries were characterized by chains of hotels, which gave them experience in multiplant operations.

The use of management contracts and franchising arrangements enabled hotel companies to exploit a number of ownership advantages in foreign countries—which included their brand name which guaranteed a quality of service as well as access to international reservation systems—without the need for equity investments. The performance requirements of the international hotel group could be satisfactorily codified in a management contract or franchising agreement. Moreover, although most customers for hotels outside North America were foreigners, local knowledge of such things as decor, ancillary services and local inputs often made a substantial local managerial presence desirable (Dunning 1988a).

5.4.4 Multinational trading companies

Multinational trading companies survived the era of extensive government regulation and grew to a new importance. A surprising number of European trading companies formed in the nineteenth century outlived the end of colonialism. They continued to benefit from incumbency advantages, and their knowledge of local markets, and their longstanding relationships with business and political networks. In Asia, the British trading companies based in Hong Kong—the 'hongs'—were badly disrupted by the Pacific War and the 1949 Communist Revolution in China, after which they lost all their considerable assets in that country. Yet they survived, expanded into new regions of Asia and elsewhere, and became active participants in Hong Kong's rapid economic growth from the late 1950s. Both Swires and Jardine Matheson remained controlled by their founding British families, but this did nothing to prevent entrepreneurial diversification. During the late 1940s Swires established Cathay Pacific, which became one of Asia's most successful airlines. Swires has continued to manage, and partly own, Cathay Pacific until the present day (Jones 2000).

The major problem for European trading companies was their location in emerging economies. While Hong Kong offered a politically secure as well as low tax environment, most companies had their main businesses in other parts of Asia, in Latin America or Africa where governments were often hostile to foreign firms, or pursued import substitution strategies which made international trading business difficult. Between the 1950s and the 1970s the extensive British merchant houses in South Asia passed under Indian ownership, usually as a result of families selling their holdings to local entrepreneurs. In Malaysia, the government used state-owned companies to buy the shares of the British agency houses which owned large rubber and palm oil estates. A number of the former British companies, including Sime Darby and Guthries, became Malaysian-owned multinationals. Both British and Dutch companies, such as Hagemeyer, attempted to build new businesses in politically safer developed countries (Jones 2000).

New types of multinational trading companies emerged. Previously a number of European commodity traders such as Louis Dreyfus et Cie were active in the international grain trade, but postwar changes in the nature of commodity markets led to a rapid expansion of this business. The most important changes were the intervention of the state, especially in the creation of monopoly marketing boards and the nationalization of mines and plantations in many developing countries, and the emergence of genuine world markets, as indicated by the prodigious growth of the leading world commodity exchanges, such as the Chicago Board of Trade, the New York Sugar and Coffee Exchanges, and the London Metal Exchange.

During the 1950s US-based commodity firms entered the world markets. Cargill, one of the leading US grain traders, established an international company initially based in

Canada, which in 1956 was shifted to Switzerland. This company—Tradax—became the basis for the group's international expansion and developed as one of the largest grain companies in the world. Subsequently Cargill diversified into the production, processing and marketing of an extremely diversified range of food products, as well as coal mining and steel production, on almost a worldwide basis (Broehl 1992, 1998). By the early twenty-first century Cargill, which remained a private company owned by the Cargill and MacMillan families, had revenues of $60 billion—placing it among the twenty largest companies in the United States—and employed over 100 000 people in sixty countries. It controlled 25 percent of total US grain exports and over 20 percent of the US meat market, was the largest exporter from Argentina, and the biggest poultry processor in Thailand (*Financial Times*, 25 February 2004).

The core business of these traders was the purchase of commodities in one country and their sale in another, but this process involved many risks because of fluctuations in prices, exchange rates, freight rates and so on. The companies sought to control these risks by owning their own shipping fleets, some of which became substantial for a time during the 1960s and 1970s, although this strategy was reversed subsequently. They also developed specialist skills in financial management, to such an extent that there was a convergence between some commodity traders and financial institutions in the 1980s (Chalmin 1987). Most of the commodity companies were privately-owned.

The commodity traders dominated world trade in many commodities. For many years the world grain market was substantially in the hands of six large enterprises: Cargill and Continental from the United States, Louis Dreyfus (France), Bunge and Born (Argentina), André (Switzerland) and Tuppfer (Germany). In the 1970s these six firms accounted for 96 percent of US wheat exports, 80 percent of Argentinian wheat exports, and 90 percent of European wheat exports (Chalmin 1985). Changes in the structure of commodity markets and the high-risk nature of commodity dealing provided opportunities for new entrants to grow rapidly. The Swiss-based Marc Rich & Co (renamed Glencore International in 1994), was only founded in 1974, but twenty years later it was one of the world's biggest traders in oil, aluminum and alumina, as well as a diversified range of minerals and agricultural commodities. The high risks of trading also produced casualties. André went bankrupt in 2000.

In Japan, the dissolution of the zaibatsu after the war was accompanied by the break up of the sogo shosha. Mitsui Bussan was broken into 233 companies, and Mitsubishi Shoji into 139 companies. Subsequently most of these companies came back together. They were joined as sogo shosha by a number of other firms, which had formerly been speciality textile, steel, and machinery trading companies. A total of ten (nine after a merger in 1977) sogo shosha accounted for over 80 percent of Japan's total imports and exports during the 1960s, and although this percentage fell over time, even in 1990 they handled more than half of Japan's imports.

The re-emergence of the sogo shosha took place in the context of the postwar Japanese system of horizontal enterprise groups which replaced the dissolved zaibatsu. These groups, known as **kigyo shudan,** emerged from former zaibatsu, or from new groups of firms around Japan's banks. The kigyo shudan comprised of considerable numbers of firms engaged in a wide range of industries. They were joined by webs of cross-shareholding, and cross-directorships. Each kigyo shudan had a 'main' bank and a sogo shosha.

The primary function of the sogo shosha in the postwar decades remained trade intermediation. They traded in almost everything, handling between 25 000 and 40 000 different products, although the companies differed quite considerably in their product profiles. They earned the bulk of their profits from the movement of bulk commodities, assisting their clients on a commission basis in finding buyers or sellers. Japan's rapid industrialization from the 1950s made the country a leading importer of many primary commodities, providing the sogo shosha with enormous business opportunities in the area of procuring raw industrial materials and energy resources from overseas. They were also major participants in Japan's export growth. They performed the export function for many small manufacturers who were too small to engage in the export business themselves, and to whom they also provided credit.

The prominence of the sogo shosha in Japan's international trade rested on their continued ability to handle transactions of certain products at a low cost. The main product characteristics in which they held such advantages were standardized products, products handled in large lots or repetitively, products which were handled several times through the production cycle, and products where the achievement of economies of scale in trading were conditional on access to world markets (Roehl 1983). A considerable proportion of trade transactions were with other members of their kigyo shudan. The sogo shosha developed advanced information-gathering capabilities. They sought to acquire and process worldwide economic, and other information, which was provided free to clients. As computers and faxes became available, these information activities grew in scale, and in their significance as a source of competitive advantage for the sogo shosha.

The sogo shosha became Japan's leading multinationals, not only in international trading, but also in manufacturing, resource extraction and other non-trading ventures. They lost all their overseas assets after World War II, and it was not until 1949 that they were allowed their own overseas offices. Thereafter the trading companies rapidly reestablished their international networks of offices. During the late 1950s the sogo shosha began to form joint ventures or affiliate firms abroad, in part as a defensive reaction to the FDI undertaken by Japanese manufacturers. When Japanese cotton textile companies invested in Brazil and other Latin American countries in the 1950s, the sogo shosha lost their export markets. Threatened by this loss, the sogo shosha began to participate in overseas investments with the intention of protecting their foreign business. They developed an innovative system of organization involving the setting up of separate joint ventures with selected partners (Yasumuro 1984).

The number of sogo shosha joint ventures grew rapidly during the 1960s. Joint ventures in developed countries were often wholly owned by two Japanese partners, typically a sogo shosha and an industrial enterprise. These were usually concerned with marketing and servicing, and were usually designed to promote the export of manufactured goods from Japan. The most frequently used structure in developing countries were joint ventures with three partners, such as a sogo shosha, a Japanese industrial enterprise (or occasionally another sogo shosha), and a local firm. These were often involved in manufacturing and raw materials. The scale of involvement in manufacturing and natural resources was much higher than before World War II. Sogo shosha also became active in large-scale construction projects.

The sogo shosha coexisted with other Japanese enterprises engaged in international trade. There were large numbers of smaller, and more specialized, trading companies which dealt with narrower product ranges or geographical areas. Of greater significance were the in-house trading companies established by the Japanese consumer electronics and automobile manufacturers, which established their own sales organizations in the 1960s. Sogo shosha had fewer advantages in trading in goods characterized by high technology, aftercare services and by brands, and the manufacturers of these products did not require their assistance to sell or invest abroad. The result of the expansion of the sales and service networks of Japanese manufacturing companies in the developed market economies was a fall in the share of the sogo shosha in Japan's foreign trade, but they developed as new opportunities presented themselves in third-country trade, counter-trade and from the 1980s, in the emerging Chinese market. The sogo shosha also restructured themselves towards information and financial businesses.

The Japanese trading companies were enormous businesses. The revenues of C. Itoh and Mitsui & Co, the largest sogo shoshas in the late 1980s, were over $100 billion, or similar to the size of the GDP of Argentina. C. Itoh traded over $20 billion of agricultural products annually, which was equal to all the sugar, coffee, beef, rice, and wheat exported by all developing countries at that time (Morisset 1997).

During the 1970s the example of the sogo shosha encouraged emulation. Beginning in 1975, the Korean government began to designate the title of general trading companies as a strategy to increase the competitiveness of Korean exports. The designated companies—of which the Samsung Trading Company was the first in 1975—received subsidies, and were in turn set export targets. The Korean general trading companies accounted for 50 percent of total Korean exports by the mid-1980s, although they did not emulate the extensive diversification of the sogo shosha. There were less extensive attempts to copy the Japanese model in Thailand, Taiwan, and even the United States (Cho 1984). Sears, one of the largest US retailers, established Sears World Trade in 1982 which was explicitly patterned on the sogo shosha. However it was closed down four years later after making heavy losses.

5.5 Services and the second global economy

The growth of multinational services was rapid from the 1980s. In many sectors there was a strong trend towards consolidation. Government-imposed restrictions on involvement in services by foreign companies was swept away in developed economies and, at a slower pace, in emerging ones also.

Technological change was important too. As services became more tradeable, especially with the development of the internet, it might have been predicted that FDI would slow, as it ceased to be the only means of reaching customers in international markets. Yet the internet also facilitated the splitting of the production process of services, and enabled the location of some of it abroad. As a result, a number of countries developed as centers for international service functions. Among emerging markets, India grew as a location for software development and other international service functions. Software firms were clustered in a single location, Bangalore. During the 1990s Ireland grew rapidly as a location for IT-based services such as telecom, computer and other business services (United Nations 2002).

Deregulation and privatization reopened sectors for multinational investment. Foreign insurer's share of the Latin American market rose rapidly during the 1990s, reaching over 70 percent of life insurance premiums in Chile and Argentina by 2000 (Pearson and Lonnborg 2003). In 1992 AIG received the first foreign insurance license granted in forty years in China. In 1996 it moved back to the Shanghai office building where the company had originated in 1919, although it proved hard to expand share in a market dominated by huge state-owned companies.

Mergers and acquisitions led to the growth of a number of very large firms global insurance firms. At the beginning of the new century, AIG was the world's largest insurance company. In 2003 it had 80 000 employees and 350 000 affiliated agents in 130 countries. AIG's market capitalization of over $180 billion made it one of the largest corporations in the world by that measure, and somewhat bigger than Intel, Cisco Systems, or BP. ING (Netherlands), Axa (France) and Assicurazioni Generali SpA (Italy) were the world's next largest insurers.

Telecommunications and public utilities re-emerged as a sector in which multinational investment was possible. The privatization of telecommunications and utility monopolies in developing countries was accompanied by the liberalization of FDI rules. The former socialist eastern European countries and many emerging countries looked to foreign companies to modernize outdated facilities. Technological change and the growing strategic importance of telecommunications undermined government monopolies, and made governments more receptive to using foreign companies to access the latest technologies. At the same time former state-owned utilities, including Deutsche Telecom and Spain's Telefónica, put pressure on them to internationalize.

There was accelerating growth of FDI in telecommunications in both developed and emerging markets. Telefónica made large acquisitions in Latin America after 1995, becoming one of the world's largest telecom firms. Deutsche Telecom, created out of the German Post Office in 1990, was active in sixty countries in 1990 in a range of telecom products, including mobile phones (known as cell phones in the United States). The largest mobile telephone company was British-based Vodafone, created by a demerger from a wireless technology engineering company called Racal in 1991. Vodafone purchased AirTouch in the United States in 1999 and Mannesman in Germany in 2000. The latter acquisition's value of $200 billion was the equivalent of 6 percent of the combined GDP of Britain and Germany in that year. Vodafone had over 220 million customers worldwide by the new century, and the United Nations ranked it as the world's largest multinational in 2003. A decade earlier this position had been occupied by Shell (United Nations 1994, 2000, 2003).

There was also substantial multinational investment in water utilities in the 1990s, although this was a politically sensitive industry which posed acute management problems. French-owned companies were prominent and were able to draw on a long tradition of domestic experience. The provision of water in France was provided by private companies under contract to local governments from the middle of the nineteenth century. During the 1990s the leading French water companies made large international investments, both in response to the deregulation of water provision in many countries, and to perceived investment opportunities elsewhere. Vivendi transformed itself into a media company, acquiring the Universal entertainment business of Canada's Seagram. Suez acquired water companies in the United States, Britain and elsewhere, and invested in financial services.

The global expansion of the French water companies resulted in heavy indebtedness, and was followed by large-scale restructuring and divestment. In the case of Vivendi, a new company Veolia was formed in 2002 to own the water business. Both companies experienced serious management problems with US acquisitions. In 1999 Vivendi had acquired US Filters in the largest-ever French acquisition in the US, but Veolia had to sell it four years later with a loss of $4 billion. Suez was also obliged to sell its US-based water treatment company only a few years after its acquisition. However Suez and Veolia remained the world's two largest private water companies with 125 million and 110 million customers respectively in 2004. They were followed by Saur, a component of the French-owned construction group Bouygues, and RWE Thames Water, owned by RWE, the fifth largest German industrial company, whose ownership of American Water Works made it the largest private water supplier in the United States.

A feature of the deregulation policies of these decades was the growth of energy trading. This was the core business of Enron, a Texas-based company created in 1985 from the merger of two natural gas pipeline operators. Enron grew rapidly in the United States, and expanded internationally. In 1989 it began constructing a gas-fueled power plant in Britain, whose energy markets had been deregulated, and subsequently it entered energy trading in that country. In 1992 Enron acquired control of an Argentinean pipeline operator that supplied two-thirds of that country's gas demand, and further major investments were made in Latin America, especially in Argentina and Brazil. In 1991 Enron began the construction of a large power plant south of Bombay in India, but this became progressively enmeshed in political conflict. Shortly before its collapse in 2001 after accounting irregularities revealed a major corporate scandal, Enron was the US's seventh largest firm, with $40 billion in revenues. The firm marketed and traded natural gas, electric power, and other energy commodities throughout the Americas, Europe, India, and Australia. Within two years, little remained of this global giant.

In some services government regulation remained prominent. The world air industry continued to be regulated by complex national agreements on landing slots, such as the so-called Bermuda agreements that governed service between the United States and Britain. Most countries protected their airlines from foreign takeovers. The United States continued to restrict foreign airlines to owning no more than 25 percent of the share of the equity of a domestic airline despite the bankruptcy or near-bankruptcy of its major legacy carriers. In Europe, non-EU airlines were not allowed to own more than a 49 percent stake of a EU-owned airline. The need to protect landing slots meant that even when acquisitions were made complex holdings company arrangements were necessary. Air France's acquisition of the Dutch airline KLM to form Europe's largest airline in 2004 had to be structured to leave the Dutch company nominally independent in order to preserve its landing slots in foreign airports.

In order to get round national laws and regulatory problems, international airlines were obliged to enter alliances rather than make acquisitions (see Chapter 6). When airlines did make acquisitions, results were often problematic. In the early 1990s the Spanish state-owned airline Iberia acquired control of airlines in Argentina, Chile, and Venezuela, but the results were catastrophic for both the acquired airlines and for Iberia, which within a few years had to be rescued from bankruptcy by the Spanish government (Toral 2001). In 2000 Singapore Airlines purchased a 49 percent stake in Virgin Atlantic, but soon afterwards, the September 11 terrorist attack caused a dramatic fall in trans-Atlantic air travel, and synergies between the two airlines were slow to materialize.

Most governments also retained restrictions on foreign ownership of media companies. However this did not prevent the growth of multinational media companies. News Corporation expanded from its Australian base to buy newspaper and satellite television interests in Britain, and later the United States (Fleming, Merrett, and Ville 2004). The company developed satellite broadcasting networks in India and China, and in the United States owned Fox Entertainment, a national television network, the publisher HarperCollins, and a controlling stake in DirectTV, the largest satellite pay TV-operator. In 2004 News Corporation moved its primary listing to New York, reflecting the fact that more than three-quarters of the group's revenues were generated in the United States.

The Walt Disney Company, which originated as a film production company in 1929, also developed a global media business, typically using joint venture partnerships and licensing agreements. The company, which had opened its first Disneyland theme park in California in 1955 followed by Florida in 1971, opened the highly successful Tokyo Disneyland in 1983, which was owned and operated by a local company, Oriental Land, which paid royalties to Disney. In 1992 Disney opened another theme park near Paris, France, in which it retained part of the equity. Disney's other operations included cable channels such as The Disney Channel and ESPN—which were transmitted in a variety of local languages—stores, and multiple other media businesses.

5.6 Multinational banking

The structure of multinational banking as it had developed in the nineteenth century remained in place until the 1960s. The European overseas banks survived the Great Depression and World War II. British overseas banks—in some of which Britain's domestic banks had acquired shareholdings after World War I—owned several thousand branches in Australia, New Zealand, and South Africa, and parts of the developing world, where they provided a mixture of retail and trade finance services. Multinational business was almost non-existent in developed economies. US banks divested from many of their foreign branches in the 1930s. In the late 1950s only 7 US banks had any overseas branches, while foreign banks had virtually no business in the United States.

From the interwar years, and especially after World War II, banking became a highly regulated industry. Product innovation, even by locally owned banks, was difficult. Central banks assumed many of the tasks once undertaken by private banks. Exchange controls and restrictions on currency convertibility provided few opportunities for international banking. From the 1940s there was a spread of restrictions against foreign banks.

The prohibition of branch expansion by foreign banks became particularly common. In a number of developing countries foreign banks were nationalized, while in others they were subject to crippling discrimination. In the United States, foreign banks were virtually excluded by regulations. In Europe, they were either completely excluded or extremely constrained, while foreign acquisitions of domestic banks was almost impossible.

During the 1960s multinational banking underwent a transformation. The key development was the emergence—or re-emergence—of an integrated international money and capital market. The development of the **Eurodollar** market owed its birth in the late 1950s to restrictions on interest paid on deposits (Regulation Q) within the United States. The unwillingness of eastern European governments to hold their dollars in the United States, and British government restrictions on Sterling lending by its banks, helped to create the conditions where a market for dollars outside the United States—or 'Eurodollars'—emerged in London. The market grew in London, partly because of the large financial infrastructure associated with its traditional role as an international financial center, but especially because of the lightness of regulatory controls. There were no liquidity ratios, and there was freedom of entry and exit in London's Euromarkets. This made London an attractive location compared to the other more tightly regulated European financial centers such as Paris and Frankfurt, as well as Tokyo, which remained heavily regulated until the 1980s. London's ability to attract transactions in non-Sterling currencies enabled it to become the world's largest international financial center, even though Britain no longer had its nineteenth century role as a net overseas lender, and even though the British currency was only a minor international medium of exchange.

The Eurodollar market was able to capture a rising share of financial intermediation from sheltered and conservative domestic banking markets. It was regulated neither by the host country nor according to the currencies being transacted. In large transactions for corporations and governments—or wholesale banking—multinational banks could offer higher deposits and charge lower loan rates on business transacted in London. The emergence of Eurobonds in 1963 resulted in a similarly unregulated capital market. International banking had been closely tied to international trade flows and related exchange operations. Over time, the Eurocurrency, Eurobond and foreign exchange markets became largely uncoupled from international trade. Multinational banks became the dominant players in these new financial markets, while lending to corporations and governments was undertaken on a dramatically enhanced scale.

The Euromarkets were physically located in a number of financial centers, which combined the right mixture of regulatory and fiscal conditions, together with political stability. The 'hierarchy' of such financial centers had London as its apex, followed by New York and later Tokyo, extended down to major regional centers such as Singapore and Hong Kong in Asia, and at its base had 'offshore' centers such as the Cayman Islands and Panama, through which transactions were passed mainly for fiscal reasons. Light and flexible regulation was the key factor in the development of French financial centers. Once a center was developed, further growth occurred through economies of agglomeration (Reed 1981; Jones 1992).

A distinguishing characteristic of the global markets was their continued growth even after the original causes of their emergence were removed. During the early 1970s the

United States abolished Regulation Q and controls against capital outflows, but the oil price rises of the period provided a further stimulus to the system. There was a massive inflow of funds into the Eurodollar market from the oil-producing countries, while many non-oil-producing countries borrowed from the market to finance their deficit balance of payments. The world debt crisis, which began in 1982 when Mexico announced its inability to service its large debt, revealed the poor quality of much of this international bank lending.

From the 1960s there was a rapid growth of multinational banking, led by US banks. By 1975, 126 US banks had over 700 foreign branches. US banks led the growth of the Euromarkets through rapid product innovation, developing new lending instruments such as floating rate loans and syndicated credits. While in 1960 international operations were of marginal concern to US banks, by the mid-1980s the total assets of their international branches amounted to 20 percent of the total assets of all US banks. The primary activity of these branches was Euromarket operations. The determinants of much of this multinational banking lay in the advantages of direct representation is a virtually unregulated 'supranational' financial market. In these markets, multinational banks competed with other giant banks in a large, wholesale banking market (Gray and Gray 1981).

This type of multinational banking—which was entirely a post-1960 phenomenon—coincided with more traditional forms of multinational service and retail banking which was broadly similar in nature (if not scale) to that undertaken in the nineteenth century. The multinational bank branches located in financial centers operated in both the supranational financial markets and their national financial markets. There was a particular link with servicing the requirements of their parents' clients. During the 1960s US bank branches in London serviced the British subsidiaries of US nonbank corporations, although over time US banks also lent to local corporate clients (Kelly 1977).

Multinational retail banking also continued to be undertaken. During the 1960s Citibank began to diversify from servicing large corporations in foreign markets to retail banking. It opened branches to attract household deposits, undertook consumer lending, and acquired a number of foreign consumer finance companies (Cleveland and Huertas 1985). Foreign banks exploited ownership advantages in management, product differentiation and technology in retail markets, though these rarely compensated for the disadvantages of foreign banks at the local level. A number of the descendants of the European overseas banks also continued to undertake multinational retail banking as well as trade finance, especially in Asia and Africa, where they benefited from powerful incumbency positions. The most noteworthy survivor of this genre was HSBC, the successor to the Hongkong Bank (see Box 5.4).

The growth of multinational banking was facilitated by the progressive deregulation of financial services which took place in developed economies from the 1970s. This deregulation, which partly reflected the impact of the Euromarkets in undermining national regulatory controls, facilitated the entry of foreign banks into previously closed markets. In the 1960s foreign banks held an insignificant share of the American market. By 1992 non-US banks accounted for 45 percent of the commercial and industrial loan market. Foreign acquisitions of banks became feasible, though hostile takeovers were rarely permitted by regulators. Regulatory barriers between different financial services—such as commercial investment banking, and banking, and insurance—were also progressively

---

Box 5.4 HSBC: making a global bank

The Hongkong and Shanghai Banking Corporation was established by British and other international merchants in the British colony of Hong Kong in 1865. It was registered in Hong Kong. The bank (like many other British overseas banks) issued its own bank notes, and these were (and remain in 2004) legal tender in Hong Kong. Before 1914 branches were established in many of China's ports, Japan, and in neighboring countries, as well as in London, San Francisco and Lyon, France. The bank grew by financing trade and related exchange business, and also issued Chinese and Japanese government loans in London.

The Hongkong Bank remained overwhelmingly focused on East Asia until the 1950s. Although all its branches in China were lost in 1949, its business in Hong Kong grew rapidly. The British colony had low taxes and a booming export economy. The Hongkong Bank acquired equity stakes in Hong Kong-based shipping interests, and in Cathay Pacific, the colony's carrier. In 1959 and 1960 the Hongkong Bank acquired two smaller British overseas banks: the Mercantile Bank of India, which had branches in South and Southeast Asia, and the British Bank of the Middle East, which had a substantial business in the Middle East, especially in the oil-rich Gulf states.

The Hongkong Bank remained heavily dependent on Hong Kong in particular, and the Far East more generally. However in 1980 it acquired 51 percent of Marine Midland Bank of New York State, and this became wholly-owned in 1987. In 1992 Midland Bank, a large British domestic bank, was acquired. In 1993 HSBC, the parent holding company, shifted domicile to Britain. Over the remainder of the decade HSBC expanded in both developed and emerging markets. In 1999 HSBC was established as a uniform international brand name across the world. The bank expanded in South America, taking over Banco Bamerindus in 1997 and in the same year acquired full control of Banco Roberts in Argentina. In 2002 GF Bital, Mexico's fourth largest financial services group with 1400 branches, was acquired. HSBC also made two large acquisitions in the United States, Republic New York Corporation in 1999 and Household International in 2002.

By 2004 HSBC Group was the third largest commercial bank in the world by assets, and the fourth largest by market capitalization. It had 170 000 employees in 7,000 offices in over 80 countries.

(*Source*: King 1991; HSBC Annual Reports.)

---

dismantled. In 1999 the Glass-Steagal legislation of 1933 which had separated banking, securities, and insurance activities in the United States was overturned.

During the 1970s Japanese banks expanded internationally at an exponential rate. The liberalization of Japanese regulatory constraints enabled its banks to make their first substantial foreign investments. The leading commercial banks and securities houses established offices in the major European financial centers, as well as the United States (Mason 1992). The Japanese share of international bank assets rose from 23 percent to 35 percent between 1984 and 1990. The phenomenal growth of Japanese bank assets which drove their international expansion reflected the inflationary surge of land and stock prices in Japan between 1985 and 1990. The subsequent collapse of this 'bubble economy', combined with new international rules on capital adequacy, resulted in a sharp retrenchment of Japanese financial activities abroad.

By the new century banking remained less 'global' than many other industries. Cross-border mergers and acquisitions were rare. Many countries, and almost all developing ones, had some restrictions on foreign-owned banks, although there was a remarkable growth of foreign banks in certain Latin American countries. These included Mexico, where the banking system almost collapsed following a devaluation of the peso in 1994. Ten years later 90 percent of Mexican banking assets were foreign-owned. A small number of banks, led by Citibank and HSBC, had retail operations in many countries, but they held significant shares of retail markets in only a small number of them. Even within the European Union cross-border retail banking was not extensive. The 'liability of foreignness' exercised a strong influence in the industry (Miller and Parkhe 2002). A study of the cash management services provided to foreign affiliates of large multinationals showed that they preferred to use host country banks for cash management services because of their greater familiarity with the local market, culture, language and regulatory conditions (Berger et al. 2003).

There were rapid shifts in competitive advantage during late twentieth century. In 1994 the world's ten largest banks by total assets consisted of eight Japanese banks, followed by a French and a Chinese bank. Citibank, the largest US bank, was ranked twenty-sixth in the world. By 2003 Mizuho Financial Company, created by a merger of three Japanese banks in 2000, was the world's largest bank by assets, but Citigroup was the second largest, and by far the largest in terms of market capitalization. UBS (Switzerland), Deutsche Bank (Germany), HSBC (UK) and BNP Paribus were also in the top ten. The growth of such global giants was driven by domestic mergers and acquisitions, which had a particular impact on consolidating the once fragmented US market. The largest US mergers included Citicorp and Travellers Corporation (1998) and Bank of America and FleetBoston (2003). In terms of ownership of international bank assets, in 2002 German banks held the largest share (19 percent), followed by the United States (11 percent), Switzerland (11 percent), Japan (10 percent), and Britain (9 percent).

5.7 Multinational retailing

Multinational retailing has a long, but erratic history. From the 1850s there were cases of firms establishing single-unit luxury goods boutiques in London, Paris, and New York. In London, the jewellers Tiffany and Cartier opened small shops. In menswear and womenswear, the Swiss-owned Etam and the Dutch-owned C & A opened businesses elsewhere in Europe in the interwar years (Godley 2003). Singer and Kodak were among manufacturers which also established retail businesses.

The US-owned F.W. Woolworth built an extensive multinational retailing operation on the basis of the 'five-and-dime' variety store concept on which it was founded. Woolworth opened its first British store in 1909. By the 1960s it had 1,068 branches, and was Britain's largest retailer, employing 60 000 people (Godley 2003). After World War II, other US mass merchandisers invested internationally. In 1942 Sears, Roebuck, the largest

> **Box 5.5 Seven Eleven Japan**
>
> The US-owned Southland Corporation developed the 7-Eleven convenience store from the late 1940s. It franchised its stores, and largely expanded abroad using franchising also. In 1973 it licensed Seven Eleven to Japan, wholly owned by the large Japanese retailer Ito Yokado.
>
> Seven Eleven Japan took over the convenience store concept, but adapted it for the Japanese market. In the United States, Southland built stores and then franchised them. Its stores were located in suburbs and sold a range of useful products at slightly higher prices. Its major product innovation was the frozen carbonated drink *Slurpee*, invented in 1935. In Japan, Seven Eleven took advantage of restrictive legislation which sought to protect mom and pop stores by limiting the growth of large stores. It franchised to existing stores, which limited political opposition, while enabling the company not to invest in real estate. Its stores were located in urban areas, and featured a sophisticated use of information technology, which permitted them to identify the exact requirements of consumers at each store. Seven Eleven Japan became the largest food retailer in Japan.
>
> In 1991 Ito Yokado and Seven Eleven Japan paid $430 million to acquire 70 percent of Southland Corporation. They had already acquired Southland's stores in Hawaii in 1989. By then the US company was close to bankruptcy. The convenience food sector in the United States had become much more competitive. It had not made investments in information technology, but instead diversified beyond retailing into oil refining and auto parts. The company had become heavily indebted after thwarting a takeover bid in 1987.
>
> (*Source*: McCraw 1995.)

US retailer, opened a small store in Cuba. Subsequently it opened stores in Canada, Latin America, and Europe (mainly Spain) (Hollander 1970; Truitt 1984). Rising incomes, increased urbanization and growing consumer spending encouraged US firms to open stores in Europe. Safeway Stores, which had Canadian shops from the 1920s, began opening shops in the 1960s in Britain, Germany, and Australia (Wilkins 1970).

Although cross-border retailing grew in the postwar period, most firms remained oriented towards their domestic markets (Hollander 1970). In a number of cases licensing strategies were employed (see Box 5.5).

This reflected the perceived risks of international markets. There were frequent failures as multinational retailers underestimated the problems caused by consumer resistance to change, the competitive response of local retailers, and operating difficulties in foreign environments. Woolworth, for example, suffered from the trend towards more specialized retailing from the 1960s. For a time its international stores subsidized the ailing US operation, but in the 1980s it had to sell its British general merchandise stores. During the same decade Sears Roebuck divested from Spain and Latin America, and Singer sold its worldwide chain of sewing machine shops.

There were sometimes hostile reactions to multinational retailers when they were seen as threats to local mom and pop stores. During the 1990s Tesco, which became the largest British food retailer, expanded in eastern Europe, Poland, and Hungary, and in Asia, including South Korea and Thailand. Tesco's strategy seemed successful—by 2004 the firm had approaching one half of its store space overseas—yet it was not immune from such difficulties. In 2001 there were violent attacks against Tesco's Lotus stores in Thailand, which it had entered in a joint venture with the local conglomerate CP Group, but taken control after the Asian financial crisis in 1997.

In every generation there were new generations of multinational retailers which sought to translate their success in their home markets into international markets. This often proved unusually difficult. The British food and clothing retailer Marks & Spencer, which held for many years a quasi-cult status in its domestic market, made a series of misjudgements in foreign markets. In the United States it bought Brooks Brothers, an upmarket clothing retailer, and another chain in 1988. Stores were established in France and elsewhere in Europe. However all these ventures were subsequently divested.

In other instances, periods of sustained growth and success were followed by unexpected difficulties. This was the fate of the Dutch retailer Royal Ahold. In the Netherlands it owned Albert Heijn, the leading retail food chain in the Netherlands. From the 1970s Ahold also invested abroad, usually in joint ventures or by acquisitions. The first acquisition in the United States was in 1977, and it made its largest acquisition—of the Massachusetts-based Stop and Shop—in 1996. It grew to employ over 100 000 people and was the second largest food retailer in the United States. By 2002 Ahold owned 6,500 stores in thirteen European countries, and 600 stores in ten Latin American countries, as well as a chain of TOPS supermarkets in Thailand, Malaysia and Indonesia. However the discovery of overstated earnings in its US affiliates in 2002 brought the company to the brink of ruin, and prompted major divesting.

French companies pioneered the hypermarket, a combination of a supermarket and low-priced discount store. Carrefour began business in 1960, and three years later opened its first hypermarket outside Paris. A feature of the company was a high degree of decentralization which gave store managers responsibility for store profits and formulating forecasts. Carrefour invested abroad at an early stage, and was the first foreign retailer to enter some markets. In 1969 Carrefour opened a hypermarket in Belgium, and from the mid-1970s expanded into Latin America. In twenty-five years Carrefour had over 220 stores in Brazil and 150 in Argentina. In contrast to Royal Ahold, Carrefour preferred to open new stores which it wholly owned. By 2003 Carrefour owned around 9,600 stores in thirty countries, but it remained capable of misjudging markets. In South Korea and Japan (where it opened in 1996 and 2000 respectively), consumers expected upscale foreign brands rather than discounted local products, and Carrefour made heavy losses before shifting strategies.

In the United States, discount stores began to be established during the 1950s as low-cost competitors to department stores. The most successful was Wal-Mart, founded in 1969, which initially grew in small towns in the rural southern states of the country. By 1985 it owned over 850 discount stores in the United States, and it was the largest company in the world by sales by 2000. However the firm was quite late to expand abroad, perhaps because of a perception that its traditional advantages in the United States—including highly efficient distribution and low advertising—were not easily transferable to many foreign locations.

In 1991 Wal-Mart began its first international venture when it formed a joint venture with Cifra, Mexico's largest retailer, in which it later acquired a majority control, becoming the dominant retailer in Mexico with over 550 stores by 2002. Elsewhere Wal-Mart's performance was mixed. In Germany, it acquired two retail chains in 1998, but experienced major profitability problems over the following years. It was more successful in Britain, where it acquired the local retailer ASDA, becoming the largest superstore owner. In Asia there were mixed outcomes. A joint venture agreement with Thailand's CP group to operate in China in 1994 was dissolved within eighteen months. An attempt to sell its products through a local supermarket in Japan failed. It re-entered Japan in 2002 in a partnership with Seiju, the fifth largest Japanese supermarket. The most serious problems were in Indonesia, where operations closed in 1997 amidst legal suits with a joint venture partner. Overall Walmart had 1,170 stores in nine countries by 2001 (Bell, Lal, and Salmon 2004).

A new generation of multinational niche retailers emerged. IKEA, the Swedish pioneer of flat-pack furniture, expanded rapidly in Europe from the middle of the 1970s, and opened its first store in the United States in 1985. The US specialty retailer Toys "R" US began international expansion after 1984, and within a decade owned over 200 stores in fifteen countries outside the United States. The Gap, founded in San Francisco to sell denim jeans at affordable prices in 1969, opened its first international store in London in 1987. Its international stores grew from 46 to 382 over the course of the 1990s.

5.7.1 Fast food

The fast food industry, whose multinational growth dated from the 1960s, typically employed franchising and management contracts. Although the concept of 'fast food' is strongly identified with the United States, one of the first movers in international business was British-owned J. Lyons. This firm acquired the international franchise of the Wimpy Bar, an American hamburger operation, and while the US venture remained modest, the British firm exploited the Wimpy concept on a large scale, first in Britain and then, by the 1960s, elsewhere in Europe, in Australia, South Africa, Thailand, Congo, and Hong Kong. Lyons, itself a licensee, in turn licensed its foreign operations (Hollander 1970).

However, it was US-owned firms which subsequently came to dominate the industry. A prominent example was McDonald's (see Box 5.6). It formed a cluster of multinational fast food chains including Kentucky Fried Chicken (KFC) and Burger King, the latter being owned for a number of years by the British alcoholic beverages group Diageo.

The growth of fast food retailing was surprising given the culture-specific nature of food tastes. There was a delicate balance to be drawn between local adaptation and standardization. McDonald's and other US firms marketed, in part, a brand image of an American lifestyle, which too much adaptation to local conditions could dilute. However some adaptation to local tastes and preferences was usual. Fast food retailers could even stumble in culturally similar markets. In 1992 the Hong Kong-owned fast food chain Café de Coral invested in mainland China, but its prices were too high for most consumers. It returned to China only in 2003, by which time KFC and McDonald's had 900 and 560 outlets respectively.

Box 5.6 McDonald's and the growth of multinational fast food

McDonald's was named after two brothers who opened a drive-in store in California in 1937 selling hotdogs and milkshakes. After World War II they shifted to a self-service format which sold hamburgers, drinks and French fries prepared in advance. In 1954 the McDonald's brothers gave Ray Kroc, a milkshake-making machine salesman, exclusive rights to franchise the McDonald's system across the United States. Kroc strengthened the franchise system with strict operating standards, and opened the first 'real' McDonald's in 1955 in a suburb of Chicago in 1955. McDonald's became the largest fast food restaurant in the United States. It held over one-third of the US market in the 1990s.

McDonald's opened its first foreign restaurant in Canada, in 1967, and from 1970 began opening in Europe and elsewhere. It entered most foreign countries through forming 50/50 joint ventures with local partners who ran the foreign operations. The first European stores, in Germany and the Netherlands, changed food menus and store designs to meet the perceived needs of local customers, but customers preferred the unadapted American experience. Thereafter national companies employed the McDonald's operating system and marketed the standard fast food menu, although there were limited local adaptations, such as McLaks, a grilled salmon sandwich sold in Norway.

The company's marketing strategy was tailored to different national situations. In some countries the joint venture company owned and operated the restaurants, while in others they licensed to local franchisees, as in the United States. The Japanese joint venture, started in 1971 and controlled by the local partners, was a particular success, and became that country's largest restaurant chain.

During the 1990s McDonald's increased its international expansion in response to perceived market saturation in the United States. The first restaurant in Russia opened in Moscow in 1990, only blocks from Lenin's tomb. In the same year McDonald's opened its first restaurant in China. By 2003 it had 550 restaurants in 70 Chinese cities owned by two joint ventures in China; it was not until that year that the first unit franchise was given. McDonald's opened in India in 1996, again using master franchises. As most Indians did not eat beef or pork, McDonald's could not sell its flagship product, the *Big Mac*, but marketed mutton and chicken patties, known as *Maharaja Mac* and *Chicken Maharaja Mac*.

By 2004 McDonald's had over 30 000 outlets (13 000 in the United States) in 120 countries—the few exceptions included North Korea, Vietnam, and Iran. Its restaurants employed 250 000 people outside the United States, and international business accounted for almost one-half of McDonald's revenues. During 2003 the first quarterly loss since going public in 1965 raised concerns about its future growth, perhaps as consumers switched to more nutritious meals. McDonald's responded by diversification into the faster-growing fast casual market (such as the Prêt a Manger sandwich chain in Britain). In France, McDonald's put salads and fresh fruit on its menu, and served *Evian* mineral water.

(*Source*: Love 1988.)

■ **SUMMARY**

Multinational service companies flourished in the first global economy. Trading and shipping companies, banks and utilities facilitated the expansion of world trade, constructed the infrastructure of a global economy, and spread technologies. Trading companies developed a long-term role as coordinators of economic activities in the resource and manufacturing sectors. Much of this multinational investment was related to servicing trade between the developing and industrialized countries.

As the twentieth century progressed, and especially from 1930, governments blocked multinational investment in many services and constrained its growth in others. Foreign-owned utilities, banks, insurance companies, and airlines were highly restricted. Yet there remained new opportunities, especially in developed economies, in professional business services and the provision of consumer services including fast food restaurants and hotels. Moreover, the changing nature of trade flows and increased government intervention did not make trading intermediaries redundant. After World War II, the sogo shosha and the commodity trading companies grew rapidly, and increased their significance in the world economy. Multinational banking underwent an unprecedented growth from the 1960s, but its significance was wider still. A great deal of the growth of multinational banking was related to escaping from regulatory controls. The deregulation of financial services which followed helped undermine government intervention elsewhere. The global money and capital markets, often operating in a wholly unregulated environment, became of central importance in the new global economies.

The spread of deregulation and liberalization provided the conditions for a rapid relative rise in the importance of services in international business. By the new century at least one half of total world FDI was located in services. Companies such as Citibank, AIG and Wal-Mart were among the largest in the world. Yet globalization was patchy. The international airline industry remained heavily regulated by governments which blocked most cross-border mergers. There were numerous restrictions on foreign firms in other services, especially but not only in developing countries. In multinational banking and retailing, among many services, the 'liability of foreignness' remained very evident.

PART III | Building Organizations

6 Crossing borders

6.1 Expanding abroad

Chapters 6 and 7 examine how firms have built the organizations that enabled them to exploit opportunities both at home and abroad, and in different industries. This chapter examines the strategies that firms have used to exploit and enhance their competitive advantages by crossing borders. It begins with corporate strategies for entering and exiting countries. It then turns to collaborative strategies with other firms. Finally, the chapter considers the role of subsidiaries in the evolution of multinationals.

6.2 Entering and exiting markets

6.2.1 The evolution of multinationals

Firms have employed a range of modes to enter foreign markets. The 'classic' organizational form was a wholly owned affiliate, but this has always coexisted with a range of equity and nonequity modes including joint ventures, cartels, licensing, franchising and long-term contracts. Firm-, industry-, location-, and time-specific factors influenced which mode was employed at any one time.

Multinationals follow an incremental process as they enter and evolve in a foreign market (Johanson and Vahlne 1990). Manufacturing companies often progressed from exporting, to selling through agents, to the establishment of a distribution company, to local production. A company makes an initial commitment of resources to a foreign market, and through this investment gains local market knowledge. Gradually, and through several cycles of investment, the multinational develops local capabilities and market knowledge. This evolutionary pattern might also be understood using transactions costs theory. While low volume transactions can be mediated through markets, recurrent transactions encourage the use of intermediate modes such as licensing and agents. As the use of agents and licensing involves the risk of opportunistic behavior, there are incentives to shift to hierarchical modes (Nicholas 1983, 1986).

This pattern was followed by nineteenth-century pioneers of multinational manufacturing such as Singer and Lever Brothers, and has been repeated ever since. However, there was nothing inevitable about the process. Firms have passed through stages at different speeds, many have not completed the cycle, or else have divested. Historically, many forms of multinationals have not passed through this process at all. The free-standing companies which were so prevalent in the first global economy did not follow an evolutionary path from exporting, to agents, to direct investment. Nor did firms investing in resources or many services. As acquisitions became the primary mode of multinational entry over the course of the twentieth century, some firms entered a foreign country with a huge pre-existing organization.

The move from one mode to another was often triggered by exogenous events, including the imposition of tariffs, or shifts in the competitive structure of an industry. The changing strategies of IG Farben, the German chemicals company formed by merger in 1925, in interwar Japan illustrate the impact of exogenous factors on choice of mode. Initially this firm exported its chemical products to that market. It invested in distribution in order to facilitate this strategy, but declined to license its technology to Japanese firms for fear of losing control over it. Tariffs rendered this export strategy difficult from the early 1930s, as did the growth of a local chemical industry. Government restrictions made it impossible for IG Farben to manufacture in Japan, so it shifted to offering licenses to Japanese firms. The German firm felt able to shift its strategy in part because its position had been secured by its central role in worldwide chemical cartels. It was therefore in a position of strength to negotiate price and market agreements with Japanese companies (Kudo 1994).

The internal dynamics of decision-making within firms was a major determinant of entry modes in foreign markets. Each firm had its own unique combination of resources, including entrepreneurial ability. Although systematic patterns can be observed, diversity has been the norm rather than the exception.

6.2.2 Greenfield versus acquisition

The establishment of a wholly owned subsidiary in a foreign country is done either by creating a new firm through a greenfield investment or by acquiring another firm. A number of theories have sought to explain the choice that firms have made between these two modes. It has been suggested that firms initially going abroad prefer to enter foreign markets by acquisition in order to reduce uncertainty, while large and established multinationals might be more willing to undertake greenfield investment. Late entrants into oligopolistic markets might prefer acquisitions in order to speed up their response to the entry of leaders in foreign markets, higher acquisition rates might occur in faster-growing markets because they provide a quicker means of entering such markets, although acquisition has also been suggested as a suitable method of entry when a target market is static or declining, as additional production capacity is not required, while greenfield strategies may be more attractive when a market is growing (Dubin 1976; Knickerbocker 1973).

Greenfield investment was the predominant mode of entry into foreign markets in the nineteenth century. Many of the manufacturers which crossed borders, typically possessed new technologies which limited the opportunities to acquire appropriate companies in foreign markets. In the new and emergent industries of the first global economy, there were far fewer potential acquisitions. The mining, banking or trading companies which sought opportunities in developing countries had no local firms to buy. Nevertheless, a market for corporate control had developed in advanced economies by the second half of the nineteenth century. Mergers and acquisitions became drivers in the domestic growth of firms in the United States. One estimate is that the ratio of mergers and acquisitions to the US GDP had reached 10 percent at the beginning of the twentieth century (United Nations 2000).

Although most acquisitions in the United States at this time were domestic, foreign firms often entered that country through acquisitions, which were sometimes substantial. In 1889 a British group acquired control of the largest flour producer in the country to form Pillsbury-Washburn Flour Mills, which became the largest milling enterprise in the world. However, within a decade management control was again in American hands. European consumer goods companies also entered the United States through acquisition. Lever Brothers acquired soap companies in Boston and Philadelphia in the late 1890s. In 1917 Nestlé began manufacturing in the United States after acquiring two companies which owned twenty-seven factories between them. In some instances foreign firms entered the United States by acquiring other foreign-owned firms. Shell became a major Californian oil producer by buying the affiliate of British-owned trading company Balfour Williamson in 1913 (Wilkins 1989, 2004). US corporations also made use of acquisition strategies to expand abroad. The American Tobacco Company frequently purchased majority interests in foreign manufacturers (Wilkins 1970).

During the 1920s the number of cross-border acquisitions grew. Swedish Match acquired firms in much of the world, even in Japan where the market for corporate control was limited (Lindgren 1979). General Motors, unlike Ford, entered foreign markets including Canada, Britain and Germany through the acquisition of local firms. In 1928, Chrysler, another US automobile company, inherited a multinational business through the acquisition of another US firm, Dodge, which manufactured trucks and automobiles in Canada and Britain. As US corporations grew in size, they often made their first foreign investments through acquisitions. American Home Products, a giant drugs company formed in 1926, immediately acquired a series of British manufacturing companies. P & G began its expansion beyond North America by acquiring a British soap manufacturer in 1930 (Wilkins 1974a).

A number of aggregate studies have confirmed the widespread use of acquisition strategies quite early in the history of multinationals. Figure 6.1 examines the mode of entry of 634 new manufacturing subsidiaries established by US firms in Britain between 1908 and 1962.

This data confirms both the substantial number of acquisitions, and reveals that the ratio of greenfield to acquisition fluctuated over time. The ratio was higher in the 1920s, and between 1950 and 1962, than in the 1930s. This might be explained as oligopolistic bunching, as both the 1920s and 1950s witnessed a surge of new US entrants. During the 1930s British real incomes also grew, so the increased use of greenfield investments might have been related to a growing market. However, the strongest correlation with shifts in entry mode was with the domestic market for corporate control. During the 1920s, and

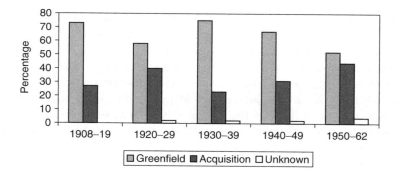

Fig. 6.1 Mode of entry used by US manufacturing companies to enter Britain, 1908–62.
Source: Jones and Bostock (1996).

again during the 1950s and 1960s, there were large-scale merger waves in Britain (Jones and Bostock 1996).

The use of acquisition strategies accelerated after World War II. US manufacturing firms made increased use of acquisitions worldwide (Vaupel and Curhan 1969, 1974; Curhan, Davidson, and Suri 1977). They became a means of consolidating highly fragmented industries such as ice cream. From the late 1950s, Unilever, which had only previously sold ice cream in Germany and Britain, built an international ice cream business by acquiring small, and often family-owned businesses throughout Europe, as well as in the United States, Australia and elsewhere. By the 1980s, Unilever held 30 percent of the European ice cream market (Reinders 1999).

Acquisitions were much less frequent in developing countries. Buying companies often involved complicated and time-consuming negotiations with family owners as well as much political sensitivity. Yet, they were not entirely absent. In Brazil, where Unilever had a small soap and detergents manufacturing operation since the interwar years, the Anglo-Dutch company acquired its main competitor Companhia Gessy Industrial, which was about twice Unilever's existing size in that country, in 1960. The new Gessy Lever, created by merging the two companies, became the dominant manufacturer of soap and detergents.

The use of acquisition strategies was facilitated from the mid-1950s as the phenomenon of the 'hostile' takeover bid made against the wishes of incumbent directors became established in the British and US business systems (Roberts 1992). However, hostile acquisitions remained rare in Continental Europe and Japan. Most large European companies only began making hostile acquisitions in the 1980s or even later. Vodaphone's acquisition of Mannesmann in 2000 was the first large-scale hostile acquisition of a German company by a foreign firm.

Despite the large Japanese greenfield investments in automobiles and electronics during the 1980s, acquisition was the predominant means of entering the US market. Businesses were often built up through successive acquisitions over time. During the late 1960s, BP discovered oil in Alaska through its own exploration. It acquired a shareholding in Standard Oil of Ohio in 1970, and transferred its Alaskan assets to it on the understanding that its initial 25 percent of equity would rise to 54 percent as crude production increased. In 1987, BP acquired full ownership. In 1998, BP acquired the US oil company Amoco, the sixth largest publicly traded oil and gas company in the world, in the largest cross-border transaction in business history until that point. Two years later BP acquired another US oil company, Atlantic Richmond. During four decades, BP grew as one of the largest oil companies in the United States as a result of both greenfield investment in oil exploration and acquisitions.

Many European companies grew in the United States in a similar fashion. Nestlé's businesses expanded in size and scope through a series of acquisitions of US firms: Libby, the fruit juices company in 1971; Stouffer's frozen foods in 1973; Carnation in 1985; and the pet foods company Ralston Purina in 2002. Unilever's renewal of its US business from the late 1970s was the result of both the exertion of tighter management control and the acquisition of firms in industries in which it had limited prior presence. In 1978, Unilever made the largest acquisition to date by a foreign company when it acquired National Starch, a specialty chemicals company. The acquisition of Cheseborough Ponds in 1986 provided Unilever with a large personal care business, both in the United States and internationally. The following years saw acquisitions of other personal care companies, including Elizabeth Arden (1989), Calvin Klein (1989), and Helene Curtis (1996), and ice cream companies, including Breyers (1991), and Ben and Jerry's (2000). In 2000, Unilever paid $24 billion for the US foods company Bestfoods (Jones and Gálvez-Muñoz 2001; Jones 2005).

By the 1990s, cross-border mergers and acquisitions had become the main driving force of world FDI (see Box 6.1). However, there were considerable variations in the use of this strategy. This reflected continuing differences between countries in the ability of foreign firms to make acquisitions (Healy and Palepu 1993). There was also some evidence concerning the impact of culture on corporate strategies. A study of foreign entries into the US market during the 1980s suggested that cultural distance from the United States deterred greenfield entry, as did a cultural aversion to uncertainty (Kogut and Singh 1988).

Although acquisitions provided an important means to enter or expand in foreign markets, their role was much wider. They were increasingly used to access assets in foreign locations which could enhance the ownership advantages of the multinational as a whole. These assets were often innovation capabilities. In consumer products, companies also sought desirable brands. The acquisition of local brands which could be globalized became a driving force behind mergers and acquisitions in the alcoholic beverages industry (Lopes 2002). In the personal care industry, foreign firms acquired US brands from the 1980s that were then exploited worldwide. L'Oréal, the French-owned cosmetics company, became a master of this strategy. In 1996, L'Oréal acquired Maybelline, the owner of a large but downmarket cosmetics business primarily in the United States. The brand was revitalized, and then transferred to international markets. In 1998 and 2000 L'Oréal acquired the Afro-American cosmetics companies Soft Sheen and Carson, whose brands were subsequently transferred to African markets. Through this process, classic 'American' brands became components of the brand portfolios of global firms, often owned outside the United States.

Acquisitions involve risks which derive both from the process itself—sellers of a firm typically have better information than buyers—and from the post-acquisition problems of managing pre-existing firms. Only around one half of all corporate acquisitions were

Box 6.1 The growth of cross-border mergers and acquisitions since the 1980s

The value of cross-border mergers and acquisitions rose from $115 billion to $1,144 billion between 1988 and 2000. They accounted for between 25 and 30 percent of total mergers and acquisitions worldwide. There were two periods of extensive merger activity: 1987–1990, and 1996–2000. These involved thousands of firms, but a small number of mega-deals accounted for much of the total value. In 1988, twenty-two acquisitions worth over $1 billion represented 43 percent of the total value of all cross-border mergers and acquisitions. In 1999, 109 such mergers represented almost 70 per cent of the total value. The three largest acquisitions in that year involved European acquisitions of US firms. Vodafone acquired AirTouch Communications for $60.3 billion; BP acquired Amoco for $48.2 billion and Daimler-Benz acquired Chrysler for $40.5 billion. Cross-border mergers and acquisitions subsequently declined sharply in response to poor economic conditions and declining stock prices. In 2002, the value of cross-border mergers and acquisitions was $370 billion.

Cross-border mergers and acquisitions by value were heavily concentrated in Europe and the United States, although there was a spectacular, if temporary, fall in acquisitions in the latter during the early 2000s (see Box Fig. 6.1). The level of acquisition activity in developing and transition markets was less affected by market instability. There were substantial numbers of acquisitions in central and eastern Europe, many of them privatization-related, although their total value was not great.

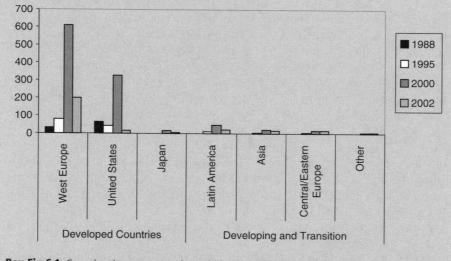

Box Fig 6.1 Cross-border mergers and acquisitions by sales 1988–2002 ($ billion). (*Source*: United Nations 2000, 2003; Evenett 2004.)

deemed to be 'successful'. Value added often went mainly to the shareholders of acquired firms. Acquisitions were often conducted by managers seeking to maximize their own utilities rather than shareholder value. One study estimated that around one-third of all acquisitions made by US firms in the 1960s and early 1970s were later sold because of poor performance (Ravenscraft and Sherer 1987).

Cross-border acquisitions faced additional risks because of differences in cultures, legal environments and accounting standards. In aggregate, foreign acquirers often paid too much for acquisitions in the United States or acquired US firms with below average profitability (Seth, Song, and Pettit 2000, 2002; Laster and McCauley 1994). It was also common for foreign firms to experience post-acquisition management problems in the United States, including difficulties retaining senior management. The high level of job mobility in the United States made this a problem for all acquisitions, but foreign acquirers were particularly affected (Krug and Nigh 1998). Senior US executives were often not comfortable with foreign firms, perhaps because their own career prospects were limited, or because of cross-cultural tensions.

For whatever reason, the history of failed acquisitions of US firms was long and substantial. During the 1970s and 1980s the leading British domestic banks made spectacularly unsuccessful acquisitions in the United States, culminating in divestments. The Midland Bank, the world's largest financial institution before World War I, was effectively destroyed by its acquisition of a Californian bank in 1980, and was eventually acquired by HSBC. Most of the other large British acquisitions of US banks were subsequently sold (Jones 1993). The list of other foreign firms which made unsuccessful acquisitions in the United States over the last three decades extends from French automobile manufacturer Renault to Matsushita's acquisitions in Hollywood (Jones and Gálvez-Muñoz 2001). Foreign firms tended to enter late in US merger waves, and to buy at the top of markets. A leading example at the end of the US stock market boom of the late 1990s was Deutsche Telecom's acquisition of the mobile phone operator VoiceStream Wireless for $34.6 billion. This left the German firm with a huge burden of debt, a falling share price as US investors sold stock, and acute management problems in turning around the business, which was rebranded as T-Mobile in 2002.

Cross-border acquisitions pose acute organizational issues. The process involves the integration of firms with wholly different corporate cultures and routines than the acquirer, and these characteristics are rooted in different national management systems. Frequently the managers of the acquired and acquiring firm speak a different language. Further complexities arise because if an acquired foreign firm is totally absorbed into the systems and structures of the parent, it will probably lose the distinctive attributes that made it desirable, such as local knowledge and contacts. If it is not integrated at all, transfers of knowledge and corporation-wide efficiency will suffer.

During the last decades of the twentieth century, post-acquisition management inside many large multinationals moved from being an *ad hoc* process to being almost routinized. Unilever, which acquired 540 companies between 1965 and 1990, developed systematic procedures to absorb acquired firms which were known inside the firm as 'Unileverization'. This involved the introduction of corporate accounting systems, and changes to salaries and pensions to conform to corporate practice. Unilever also strove to retain good managers, including former family owners, at least for a time. The pace of 'Unileverization' speeded up overtime. During the 1970s it could take up to a decade. However, within two years of Unilever's acquisition of the US personal care company

Cheseborough Ponds in 1986, only 6,000 of the original 23 000 staff remained. Sales of unwanted assets reduced the acquisition cost from $3.1 billion to $2 billion (Jones 2005).

6.2.3 Divestments

There has been nothing inevitable about the growth of multinationals. Size has never been a guarantor of longevity. Singer, which built a pioneering multinational business before 1914, did not exist at the end of the century. ITT, which had built a spectacular international utility business in the interwar years. subsequently became a large-scale multinational manufacturer, and in the 1960s claimed to employ more people abroad than any other US company (Wilkins 1974a). But its subsequent evolution first into a diversified conglomerate, then into a hospitality and gaming business whose assets included the Sheraton hotel chain, finally culminated in its acquisition by a smaller real estate investment trust in 1998. During the space of the single decade of the 1990s Enron grew, flourished, and collapsed as a major multinational. The handful of large multinationals who remained industry leaders over the last century were powerful, but exceptional, corporations.

Nor was there anything inevitable about the success of affiliates. Wars, nationalizations and financial crises caused many casualties, but the great majority of failures were the result of normal market processes. Multinational activity has always been a continuous process of entries, exits, expansion, and decline. During the nineteenth century, this cycle was followed by thousands of European free-standing companies. During the 1930s many US corporations divested their European businesses in response to financial difficulties in their domestic business or in response to growing political risk. The historical experience of US manufacturing investments in Britain illustrates this turnover of firms. Both in 1908–19 and 1950–62 the proportion of exits to entries was 11 percent. In the 1920s it fell to 6 percent, but during the 1930s and 1940s it was almost 30 percent. Of the 121 new US entrants in the 1920s, 14 percent did not survive for two decades. The proportion rose to 20 percent of the 112 new entrants of the 1930s (Jones and Bostock 1996).

Many of multinational investments have been short-lived and transient. One study during the late 1960s suggested that divestments were 16 percent of newly founded US subsidiaries (Caves 1996). A higher proportion of acquired subsidiaries subsequently exited than those established through greenfield investment. The substantial number of exits provides strong evidence concerning the 'liability of foreignness'. When newly entering a foreign market, foreign firms have to collect information on local conditions that come to a large extent free to local firms. This may result in overpaying for acquisitions, or mismanaging them. Foreign firms sometimes face hostility and discrimination from governments and consumers.

There are two major qualifications to the 'liability of foreignness' argument. Firstly, it applies best to the initial entry stage of firms into a foreign market. The liability can be expected to narrow over time as firms embed themselves into their host economies. In the nineteenth century, foreign firms often used intermediaries, such as *compradores* in Chinese-speaking communities, to maintain contacts with the indigenous business and political system. 'Local' managers continue to perform such a function in contemporary multinationals. The successors to the British overseas banks formed to operate in Australia in the 1830s, retained London head offices until the 1970s—when ANZ finally moved domicile to Australia—but the business was run for generations by Australian managers and staff (Merrett 1985). In the twentieth century, the affiliates of large multinationals such as Ford or Shell were so long-established in many economies that their 'liability' compared to local firms was unlikely to be substantial.

Secondly, there was no automatic link between divestment and management difficulties. A number of aggregate studies of multinational divestments during the 1980s and 1990s showed that while most were poorly performing, a significant number were profitable. The financial strategies of parents and changes in strategy were also important considerations in exit decisions. The fact that a significant proportion of exits take the form of sell-offs rather than liquidations lends credence to the view that divestment is caused by factors other than managerial failure or underperformance (Hennart, Roehl, and Zeng 2002). A study of the fates of 405 Japanese-owned plants that were operating in the United States in 1980 showed that only 209 were still in existence in 1998. However, many of the sales were by Japanese trading companies to their domestic joint venture partners. The trading companies often entered such arrangements to safeguard or open new trade channels, and exit was as likely to mean that this goal was achieved as indicating failure (Hennart, Roehl, and Zeng 2001; Hennart and Kryda 1998).

The argument is supported by case study evidence on individual companies. In 1978 Unilever's acquisition of National Starch in the United States enabled the Anglo-Dutch company to build a profitable worldwide specialty chemicals business, largely managed by the competent American management it had acquired. By the 1990s Unilever was ranked among the world's fifty largest specialty chemical companies. The subsequent sale of National Starch to the British chemicals company ICI for over $8 billion in 1997 was made not because it was unsuccessful, but because it looked out of place with the desired position of Unilever as a fast moving consumer goods company, while the company did not wish to make the large amounts of investment needed to remain competitive in a high technology business (Jones and Gálvez-Muñoz 2001).

In the current state of research, it is not possible to establish whether divestments have become more or less common over time. There were considerable numbers of 'failures' as firms began expanding across borders in the first global economy (Godley 1999). The 1930s were another period of difficulty. During the postwar decades it is not unlikely that divestments were lower. Large multinationals might have held substantial advantages over local firms, especially in capital-intensive industries, but they may also have been tolerant of poor financial performance. As global competition intensified towards the end of the century, many restrictions on firms' strategies were removed by deregulation, and all corporations came under pressures from stockholders for improved financial performance, so it is not unlikely that divestments became more common.

6.3 Alliances and constellations

Historically, firms often crossed borders in alliance with other firms. They formed joint ventures, participated in cartels, licensed technologies to other firms, and engaged in long-term contracting. These modes were used as both substitutes for, and complements to, multinational strategies. They were often similar to the 'alliance constellations' identified in management literature (Gomes-Casseres 2003).

The boundaries of firms were porous during the first global economy. Numerous forms of interfirm collaboration took place. In France, Belgium, and other European countries with 'mixed' banking systems, banks and manufacturing companies typically cooperated together in consortia or alliances in Russia and elsewhere (Crisp 1976; Bussière 1983). Partnerships with local companies were common in industries which involved contracts with public authorities or else when there was reason to believe that a local identity would yield competitive advantage. They were often used by armaments companies before World War I (Davenport-Hines 1986; Beaud 1986).

There were strong national patterns in the propensity to collaborate. In the United States, antitrust legislation constrained the freedom of firms to collaborate. Elsewhere there was almost no similar restrictions until after World War II. In the Japanese case, the leading banks and shipping, insurance and trading companies frequently collaborated when they established foreign operations before 1914 (Wilkins 1986). European companies also regarded collaboration as a legitimate, and often a preferred mode, of operating abroad. The German and Swiss leaders of the European chemicals industry before 1914 were joined in multiple cooperative arrangements. The German dyestuffs firms were divided into two *Interessengemeinschaften*—BASF, Bayer and Agfa formed one, and Hoechst, Casella and Kalle the other—and their FDI often took the form of joint ventures between allied firms (Hertner 1986).

There were many types of interfirm network at this time. A striking example was the collaboration between Swire's (the Far Eastern trading company), Alfred Holt (a leading ocean shipping company), and Scott's (a Scottish shipbuilding company). The three British families entered a web of interconnected business activities during the 1850s and 1860s. Scott's built ships for the Holts, and took shares in their shipping company, while Swire's became agents for the shipping company. During the 1870s a member of the Scott family became a partner of Swire's, and invested in the regional shipping company which they established. There were two noteworthy features of this alliance. Firstly, the relationship developed in dynamic ways with frequent interactions strengthening the level of trust between the different parties. There were extensive information flows within the network, they assisted each other, identified new opportunities, and in effect learned collaboratively. Secondly, this network persisted over generations. Scott's built its last ship for Swire's in 1969 and for Holts in 1980. Shareholding relationships continued into the 1970s, when Scott's was nationalized alongside the entire shipbuilding industry (Boyce 2001; Jones 2000).

While the above case demonstrated the use of collaborative agreements for learning, risk-sharing was frequently an important motive behind alliances. During the interwar years, financial pressures and risk sharing was particularly prominent in joint ventures and collaboration, including cartel agreements. Joint ventures were employed in a number of industries where there was a high degree of political risk and capital demands also grew. During the 1930s, joint ventures were widely used in production, refining and marketing operations in the Middle East and elsewhere, sometimes because of political futures. The formation of the Kuwait Oil Company in 1934, jointly owned by Gulf Oil and Anglo-Persian, reflected the concerns of the British authorities that controlled Kuwait to prevent a wholly-owned US company from controlling the oil fields. In other cases risk-sharing drove collaboration, as when Standard Oil of California and Texaco formed a joint venture in 1936 to search for oil in Saudi Arabia (Wilkins 1974a).

Capital shortage often led firms into collaborative arrangements. The predecessors of IG Farben had lost their investments and their trademarks in the United States as a result of World War I. Following its formation in 1925, the German firm sought to re-establish its position without too much capital expenditure using technological advantage as a bargaining tool. IG Farben acquired equity stakes in US chemical and pharmaceutical companies, but only took full ownership in a limited number of cases. This strategy enabled the German company to reacquire a strong market position without extensive capital investment (V. Schröter 1986).

Licensing was used by firms to access foreign markets without a large managerial or financial commitment. During the interwar years the small Dutch family firm of Océ van der Grinten, which developed an innovative process for manufacturing copying paper, expanded abroad by making licensing agreements with firms throughout Europe, the United States, Latin America and Japan. Many of these licensees were also small family firms. This strategy provided both income and an export market for the specialty chemicals used to make the bulk copying paper. Managers from the Dutch company made regular visits to their licensees, and were able also to accumulate knowledge about foreign markets. This strategy continued in place until the 1960s, when Océ, which had grown in size and become a public company, began establishing its own factories (Sluyterman 1992). The longevity of Océ's licensing strategy was striking, but not a unique case (see Box 6.2).

Although the three decades after the end of World War II are regarded as the high point of the influence of large and integrated corporations, collaborative arrangements continued to be important. They remained a distinctive feature of the international petroleum industry until the 1970s. In manufacturing, joint ventures were used to access new markets or technologies, though with strong industry variations. Typically, large firms which possessed important intangible assets in product and/or possessed technologies were reluctant to risk the loss of such assets to their partners (Stopford and Wells 1972). Many studies suggested that firms possessing strong R & D capabilities preferred to establish wholly owned subsidiaries abroad (Gomes-Casseres 1989; Kogut and Chang 1991). There was some evidence also that multinationals used joint ventures to overcome marketing barriers in foreign markets arising from access to distribution channels or lack of brand recognition (Chen and Hennart 2002).

Joint ventures were widely used by Japanese companies to access foreign markets. These were sometimes with related members in a business group—joint ventures between trading and manufacturing companies were very frequent—and often with local firms as well (Hennart 1991b). US multinationals had a lower propensity to engage in joint ventures than those of other nationalities, but smaller firms in particular made use of them to access foreign markets (see Box 6.3 for the case of Xerox).

> ## Box 6.2 Licensing and strategic alliances in the international music industry before the 1950s
>
> During the first half of the twentieth century, leading US and British firms in the music recording industry collaborated in a web of licensing and equity relationships. The industry originated in the late 1870s following Thomas Edison's discovery that recorded sound could be reproduced. Subsequently, hand-driven machines known as gramophones were developed to play the music recorded on disks. In 1896 Eldridge Johnson, a New Jersey engineer, developed a motor for this machine, and later developed an improved recording process. In 1901 Johnson formed the Victor Talking Machine Company. Two years previously the newly formed Gramophone Company in Britain purchased the rights to Johnson's processes for Europe and the British Empire also featured extensively in the international music industry.
>
> In 1901 a formal agreement between Victor and the Gramophone Company defined the marketing, financial and research relationship between the firms. The two firms shared a common trademark and research laboratory and had an understanding not to compete with one another in the world's markets. The British company was allocated all markets in Europe, the British Empire, and Japan, and the American company everywhere else. An exchange agreement gave them access to each other's recording catalogues. The agreement provided the basis for the Gramophone Company to establish factories elsewhere in Europe and in India by 1914.
>
> The relationship between the firms persisted despite changes in ownership and equity. In 1920 Victor acquired majority control in the Gramophone Company. In 1929 Victor itself was acquired by RCA, then a distribution company collectively owned by leading US electrical machinery firms. Meanwhile, a merger between the Gramophone Company and another British music company to form Electrical and Musical Industries (EMI) in 1931 led to a reversion to British ownership. During the 1930s EMI moved away from its past dependence on US technology and launched successful research programs in stereo recording. However, even in the early 1950s over half of EMI's records sales were from RCA recordings. The agreement between RCA and EMI ended in 1953.
>
> (*Source*: Jones 1985.)

Collaborative arrangements were often employed when there were radical shifts in industry dynamics. They featured extensively in the early stages of the development of the Eurocurrency and Eurobond markets in London (see Chapter 5). Banks of several nationalities formed jointly owned 'consortium banks' which allowed them to explore the opportunities of the new markets while defraying some of the risks. They were particularly attractive to European banks which lacked international experience and were seeking ways to respond to the large US money center banks. The consortium banks became large institutions responsible for major product innovations. Orion Bank, initially formed by Chase Manhattan and the Royal Bank of Canada in 1970, briefly became one of the world's top international investment banks during the second half of the 1970s. It pioneered the swaps market by launching the first currency swapped

Box 6.3 Xerox's use of joint ventures to access international markets

In 1956 the Haloid Co (which became the Xerox Corporation in 1960) formed a joint venture with Britain's Rank Organisation. The (then) small US corporation needed a partner to penetrate foreign markets with its new photocopiers. The British company, an entertainment and leisure group, wanted to diversify out of the declining cinema industry in Britain. Rank Xerox, a 51/49 percent joint venture between the Americans and the British, proved a highly effective vehicle to penetrate many eastern hemisphere markets for office copiers. In 1962, Xerox also formed a 50/50 joint venture with Fuji Photo Film—Fuji Xerox—that was used to penetrate Asian markets.

In 1969, Xerox secured voting control over Rank Xerox, and thereafter was in effective management control over the British affiliate, but it was only in 1995 that Xerox raised its share of the equity in Rank Xerox from 51 percent to 71 percent. In 1997 Xerox acquired full ownership of its European business.

Fuji Xerox evolved as a dynamic and innovative manufacturing company in its own right. By the 1980s the joint venture was considerably more successful than its American parent which failed to respond effectively to the rise of new competitors such as Canon, Ricoh, IBM and Kodak. As a result, there were considerable tensions arising both from the geographical restrictions where Fuji Xerox could market its products, and from duplication in product development. In 2001 Xerox sold half of its equity holding in Fuji Xerox to Fuji Photo Film for $1.3 billion. Xerox retained 25 percent ownership interest, and product and technology agreements between Xerox and Fuji Xerox continued.

(*Source*: Fuji Xerox 1994; Annual Reports.)

Eurobond issue in 1979. However, over the following decade, in the wake of the world debt crisis which left many of them with large bad debts, all the consortium banks were closed down or absorbed into one of their parents (Roberts 2001).

Joint ventures were frequently used in developing countries in the postcolonial era. This was partly driven by firms seeking market knowledge in unfamiliar environments. This motive led the British-based brewer Guinness into a joint venture with Unilever's trading company, the United Africa Company (UAC) in West Africa. The traditional Irish beer had been introduced to the region by slave traders in the eighteenth century. Nigeria became Guinness's largest international market after World War II. The beverage was marketed as a cure for various diseases, as well as a means to increase male sexual potency. In order to expand sales further, the company sought local production. In 1961 Guinness formed a joint venture with UAC to brew the stout in Nigeria, which became its first overseas brewing business. The initial shareholding was Guinness 57 percent and UAC 33 percent, and a Nigerian local government the remainder. The joint venture was highly profitable, even after price controls began to be imposed during the 1970s. Guinness entered other West African joint ventures with UAC, as did the Dutch brewer Heineken.

This collaboration, like many others, encountered the problem that the longer-term benefits were not evenly distributed among the partners. When UAC attempted to persuade its partners to go into ventures with them in other geographical regions, they showed little interest, while over time the brewers accumulated knowledge of West African markets. During the 1990s Unilever divested entirely from the brewing joint ventures, but the brewers retained highly profitable affiliates in West Africa. In the 2000s the Nigerian market was dominated by Guinness Nigeria, which was majority owned by Diageo (the successor to Guinness) and Nigerian Breweries, majority owned by Heineken. Nigeria remained the third largest market for Guinness after Ireland and Britain (Fieldhouse 1994).

Public policy encouraged the use of joint ventures in developing countries. There was often pressure on foreign firms to take local partners. During the 1970s, India, Iran, Brazil, and Mexico were particularly insistent on local equity participation. There was a strong trend even for US firms to enter minority-owned joint ventures in developing countries. Smaller latecomer US firms were especially willing to accept such deals in order to access markets (Franko 1989; Gomes-Casseres 1990). Public policy also provided a major reason for the use of the joint ventures or minority-owned affiliates by foreign firms in Japan. The 'cultural distance' between Western countries and Japan provided a further stimulus (Mason 1992).

From the 1980s there was a new wave of corporate collaboration as numerous international strategic alliances were formed. These alliances took numerous forms, including international joint ventures, but nonequity arrangements were common. The agreements were initially heavily concentrated in a number of technology-intensive industries—computers, motor vehicles, electricals, telecommunications, biotechnology, chemicals, aerospace—characterized by high entry costs, globalization, scale economies, rapidly changing technologies and substantial operating risks. Strategic alliances enabled companies to share the risks of new research and to get faster access to changing technologies, as well as opening up the projects of technological cross-fertilization. Technological convergence also favored the creation of networks of joint ventures based on complementary technologies (Inkpen 2001). The relaxation of US antitrust enforcement from the early 1980s facilitated this renewal of business collaboration.

A classic example of the use of international joint ventures for corporate learning was illustrated in the formation of NUMMI, the GM and Toyota joint venture formed to manufacture automobiles in Fremont, California, in 1984 (see Chapter 4). Toyota sought to establish a manufacturing beachhead in the United States. GM was concerned to learn the Toyota production system. The longevity of this joint venture was striking. Twenty years later Toyota had their own wholly-owned plants elsewhere in the United States, while GM had vastly improved its production methods. The two firms were fierce competitors in the global automobile industry. Yet NUMMI continued to function as California's only car assembly plant, manufacturing Toyota's *Corollas* and GM's *Pontiac Vibes* on the same assembly line.

In some industries, the formation of alliances represented striking changes in corporate strategies. The changing environment was symbolized by IBM, which like other high technology companies had been traditionally highly reluctant to collaborate with other firms. It now entered alliances with numerous partners around the world, pooling technology and customer bases. In the international food industry, where the protection of brands among other factors had traditionally encouraged firms to prefer wholly owned subsidiaries, strategic alliances proliferated between the largest multinationals. Nestlé entered alliances with General Mills and Coca-Cola, and Unilever with PepsiCo.

There was a striking growth of international alliances in some service industries. In the airline industry, government restrictions severely restricted international acquisitions (see Chapter 5). Instead, there was a growth of international agreements that shared codes, marketing, maintenance, and terminals. In 1989, one of the first such agreements between Delta, Singapore Airlines, and Swissair was cemented by small exchanges of equity. In 1992 there followed a similar agreement between KLM and Northwest Airlines of the United States. The industry became characterized by global alliances led by the world's largest airlines. Star included United Airlines and Lufthansa, Oneworld included British Airways and American Airlines, and SkyTeam included Delta and Air France. There were frequent shifts in such alliances, however, and their scope was limited. Joint aircraft purchasing by alliance partners has never materialized.

International joint ventures and strategic alliances had high dissolution rates. A variety of studies suggested that anywhere between one-third and two-thirds broke up (Franko 1979; Kogut 1989; Child and Faulkner 1998). NUMMI was an exception rather than the rule. There were a variety of explanations for this instability. They might be regarded as inherently unstable. The partner firms remained competitors, and effectively were a form of cooperation within a competitive context (Kogut 1989). Insofar as the motive for alliances was learning, there was in-built possibility that partners would engage in learning races with one another, or behave opportunistically (Khanna, Gulati, and Nohria 1998). In the mid-1980s, at the height of American alarm about Japanese competitiveness, it became a refrain that joint ventures led to a one-way transfer of knowledge from the American to the Japanese partners (Reich and Mankin 1986).

The management of international joint ventures and alliances was difficult. There were often tensions when the original conditions changed, which they always did. Misunderstandings were magnified by cross-national or cross-cultural differences in the organization of firms and the behavior of managers. It was often hard to sustain the trust required to keep the collaboration functional. Hofstede's cross-cultural model suggested that some cultures were more 'compatible' than others in terms of uncertainty avoidance, masculinity, power difference, individualism, and long-term orientation (see Chapter 1). It was possible that joint ventures between firms from culturally compatible home countries might be more durable than those from widely differing cultures. Hofstede explained the long-running Anglo-Dutch collaboration seen in Shell and Unilever in such terms. In his schema, the cultural values of Britain and the Netherlands were quite similar, except that the British were more 'masculine' and the Dutch more 'feminine'. In gender terms, Shell and Unilever represented a form of marriage between different but compatible partners (Hofstede 1980).

The impact of culture on international collaboration has proved difficult to demonstrate empirically. The apparent cultural similarities between Britain and the Netherlands were no guarantee of successful business collaboration. In Unilever, relationships between the two nationalities were distant and sometimes tense, at least before the 1970s (Jones 2002). In 2004 the British chairman of Shell resigned after what was interpreted by some as a 'coup' by Dutch directors concerned about his leadership ability (*Financial Times,* 6/7 March 2004). The acquisition of the Dutch airline KLM by Air France in the same year had been preceded by long, but unsuccessful, negotiations with British Airways.

In general, it has proved hard to isolate the impact of culture from the many other factors affecting joint venture longevity. In order to reduce the number of variables, one study compared the longevity of two types of joint venture formed to operate in a single host economy, the United States, after 1980: the first, owned by different Japanese firms, and the second, by American and Japanese firms. This research suggested that the longevity of Japanese–American joint ventures was lower than wholly Japanese joint ventures. While this lent support to the culturist hypothesis, it was left unclear if the conclusions were generalizable to other host economies, let alone chronological periods. The impact of other factors, especially corporate culture, was left unexplored (Hennart, Roehl, and Zeng 2002).

Given the many motives in entering international strategic alliances, it was not evident that the termination of an alliance meant that it was 'unsuccessful'. It was often simply that both sides had achieved their goals, or else that circumstances had changed. In other cases there were excessive costs related to the problems of managing across the boundaries of firms, and to tensions between the advantages of gaining access to another firm's capabilities, and the risks of potential loss of control. The historical evidence, fragmentary as it was, suggested that alliances and joint ventures could be effective in transferring knowledge across borders. It remains unclear if they were more or less effective than transfers inside hierarchical firms.

6.4 Subsidiaries and hybrids

In most studies of multinationals the primary unit of analysis has been the parent company. The function of subsidiaries was typically seen as exploiting the ownership-specific advantages of their parents. Firms became multinationals by changing the location of some of their activities, often retaining key functions at home. Yet this greatly undervalues the importance of subsidiaries as firms, and their significance within multinationals. Foreign-owned companies often grew as large businesses in their own right. Over time they assumed many higher order activities, including technology and human resources. They formed important components of many national business systems. US-owned firms accounted for 30 percent of the total assets in Canadian manufacturing industry, and 42 percent by 1977 (Taylor and Baskerville 1994). Table 6.1 shows the importance of foreign firms in Australia's largest 100 nonfinancial companies at various benchmark dates.

Multinational subsidiaries, like locally-owned firms, evolve over time. Sales affiliates developed production. Production plants spawned research capabilities. An initial entry into a country with a small greenfield investment or a modest acquisition would grow incrementally, either through the plough-back of profits or further acquisitions. A study of US manufacturing investments in Britain between 1907 and 1962 showed how, typically, US companies began manufacturing in Britain with a single plant. Over time further plants would be built or acquired. There was an evolution from single product to

Table 6.1 Foreign ownership of Australia's largest
nonfinancial companies 1910–97

Date	Number	% Total assets
1910	31	49
1930	20	25
1964	36	41
1997	30	22

Source: Fleming, Merrett, and Ville (2004).

multiproduct businesses. Many firms grew their businesses by making further acquisitions. Yet there was no single growth model. Some firms grew in a linear fashion; others stagnated, contracted, or disappeared (Jones and Bostock 1996; Bostock and Jones 1994).

The evolution of multinational subsidiaries was driven by a combination of 'push' factors from head offices and 'pull' factors from the affiliates themselves (Birkinshaw and Hood 1998). Their roles could change radically over time. After Standard Oil acquired Canada's dominant oil company, Imperial Oil, in 1898, it was virtually dismantled as a firm. Its refineries were largely closed down, and its marketing and distribution was managed from New York City. However, the dissolution of Standard Oil in 1911 and the entry of Shell into the Canadian market caused Imperial's role to be re-evaluated. Standard Oil of New Jersey, the successor company, sent its most able executive to run the Canadian company, and control of sales and distribution shifted to Toronto. It was decided to use Imperial Oil as a vehicle for international expansions which was secure from US antitrust officials, and a subsidiary was established to develop oil fields in South America. Imperial Oil was thus reborn as a corporate entity, albeit still part of the wider US-owned multinational (Taylor and Baskerville 1994).

Multinational subsidiaries developed competences based on specific market or cultural circumstances in their host economies. During the 1960s and 1970s, for example, Unilever's South African affiliate was responsible for a number of innovative new personal care products. In 1967 it launched Unilever's first male deodorant, which was inspired by the combination of South Africa's sporting culture and the cultural preference in that country for a high degree of cleanliness. Four years later a perfumed deodorant was launched, inspired by a product just launched in Scandinavia by Bristol-Myers, a US company which was Unilever's largest competitor in South Africa. In 1970 Bristol-Myers invented the perfume deodorant concept and launched it, initially in Scandinavia, as *Mum 21*, in a package rather than the traditional can. Unilever's new brand, *Impulse*, was subsequently transferred throughout Unilever, using the original South African marketing and advertising concept, and became one of the world's largest-selling deodorants (Jones 2005).

Host government policies sometimes influenced the evolution of subsidiaries. The Australian subsidiary of Ericsson played a leading role in that Swedish company's ascendancy in the telecommunications switching business by developing the AXE digital switch in 1982. This importance was far greater than the relative size of the affiliate would suggest. The Australian affiliate had good management leadership. As important was the government's insistence on strong local technological capability as a precondition for market access. The government obliged Ericsson to cross-license its technology to two other local manufacturers, both multinational subsidiaries, and then required that the company maintain an Australian R & D team to service the licensing obligations and promote local development (Bartlett and Ghoshal 1989).

From the 1980s, as many multinationals began to establish global business units, it became harder to define subsidiary roles. In emerging markets national subsidiaries remained strong, often for political reasons, but in developed markets national subsidiaries were replaced by discrete activities—such as R & D and manufacturing—which reported through their own business units or functional lines (Birkinshaw 2001). Yet large multinationals increasingly sought to use subsidiaries as centers of excellence for functional activities, including R & D (Frost, Birkinshaw, and Ensign 2002). Firms sought to access geographically-based knowledge to develop technologies which are distinct from, but complementary to, those created by their parent companies. A study based on patents granted in the US to the world's largest firms from 1969 to 1995 which examined inward investment into geographical regions in Britain, Italy and Germany showed that multinationals located research centers in sites with good local infrastructure and a good science base (Cantwell and Piscitello 2002). The widespread use of acquisitions as an entry mode gave multinationals 'instant embeddedness' in local markets (Zander 1999).

As subsidiaries adapted to local conditions and developed specific competences, they became 'hybrids'. This phenomenon was as old as multinational investment itself, but the term was first used to describe the Japanese transplants built in the US automobile and electronics industries during the 1980s. The Japanese producers transferred parts of their production system, including work teams, limited job classifications, and open plan offices. Quality circles and Japanese-style employee suggestion schemes were also employed, although less widely than in Japan. However, other Japanese practices, such as consensus-decision-making and seniority systems, were not used, creating a kind of 'hybrid' factory which was neither fully Japanese nor American in its organization (Abo 1994). Subsequent studies of the international automobile industry demonstrated how factory management systems were adapted in different contexts. The newly adapted processes were sometimes diffused back to the parent firm, which was enriched as a result (Boyer et al. 1998; Freyssenet et al. 1998).

The importance of considering subsidiaries as quasi-independent actors emerges strongly from a case study of a British engineering multinational, Aluminium Plant & Vessel Company Ltd (APV), which became the world's largest manufacturer of food and drink processing equipment through a series of mergers and acquisitions in the 1980s, before being acquired itself in 1997. The study examined the British, Danish, and US affiliates of this company, each of which had been a long-established firm before its acquisition. Each subsidiary joined APV as a result in part of its own strategic effort. The US firm had wanted to expand its presence in foreign markets, for example, while the Danish firm opted for APV after considering how its factories and markets would fare under several different alternative owners. After the acquisition, each subsidiary continued to pursue its own agenda. The national subsidiaries introduced their own innovations in productive organization and new product development. From this perspective, subsidiaries can be seen pursuing their own strategies of survival and expansion in a corporate context where production entities are bought and sold, integrated into, and divested from, multinationals (Kristensen and Zeitlin 2004).

A major challenge for the head offices of the twenty-first-century multinationals was to mobilize the dispersed and fragmented knowledge located in subsidiaries within their own boundaries. The organizational responses to this challenge will be discussed in Chapter 7.

■ SUMMARY

Multinationals have employed multiple strategies to enter and grow in foreign markets. The growth of affiliates was often achieved by some combination of greenfield investment and acquisition, although the latter became the main vehicle for multinational investment in developed markets during the second global economy. Both strategies encountered the 'liability of foreignness'. Numerous cross-border acquisitions failed in every generation. Divestments were a constant feature of multinational enterprise. Many firms, especially outside the United States, collaborated when they crossed borders. Collaborative strategies were particularly prominent at times of rapid technological change, and during eras of fast globalization in the late nineteenth and late twentieth centuries. However, the management of international collaborative agreements was difficult, partly for cultural reasons. International joint ventures and strategic alliances had high dissolution rates, although this did not always signify that they had failed.

Multinationals constantly evolved over time. Typically, they grew incrementally in host economies. During this process, affiliates often became large business enterprises in their own rights. They became 'hybrids' which contained characteristics of their parent and the local environment. This enhanced their value to the organization as a whole, but it was no easy matter to retain that value.

7 Managing multinationals

7.1 The challenge of distance

The explanations for the existence of multinationals assume the capability to build effective organizations. If multinationals exist to overcome transactions costs, their organization must offer advantages over markets. If the rationale of multinationals is that they provide superior means to transfer knowledge across borders, then their organizations must be capable of performing such a function.

The challenges posed by distance meant that building such effective cross-border organizations was not easy. They needed to be effective in different political, legal and cultural environments separated by geographical distance. There needed to be cohesion in overall corporate strategy yet a firm needed to be responsive to its local environment. The potential benefits of operating across borders had to be translated into commercial realities. People from different languages and cultures had to be managed. The difficulties of limiting opportunism were made more difficult because bounded rationality and asymmetric information were magnified by distance and culture. Organizational design had also to fit the prevailing environment, including the state of technology and the political context, and also change as that environment evolves.

An influential study by Bartlett and Ghoshal (1989) argued that the organization of a multinational needed to 'fit' the dominant strategic requirements of an industry in terms of efficiency, responsiveness to local conditions, and transfer of knowledge and competencies. The relative importance of these characteristics for competitive success varied by industry. The authors illustrated their argument by examining nine companies in three industries: branded packaged goods, which traditionally demanded a high degree of national responsiveness; consumer electronics, where there was a need for global efficiency; and telecommunications switching, where the ability to develop innovations and transfer them around the world was essential.

Bartlett and Ghoshal identified three types of organizational form which 'fitted' these strategic requirements. In the multinational model, companies managed a portfolio of national entities which had considerable autonomy. This provided a high level of local responsiveness. Philips in electronics, Unilever in packaged goods, and ITT in telecommunications, were taken as examples in this study. The international model was a coordinated federation in which a parent company transferred knowledge and expertise to foreign affiliates, and exercised quite tight control. General Electric, P&G, and Ericsson fitted into that category. Thirdly, there was a global model based on scale economies in which most decisions were centralized. This produced a high level of global efficiency.

The authors identified Matsushita, NEC and Kao as representative of this type. Bartlett and Ghoshal maintained that the complex environment of the late twentieth century required firms to move towards a fourth, transnational form which could simultaneously achieve responsiveness, efficiency and innovation. While the first three types of organization were 'hub and spoke' models, the transnational was an integrated network of interdependent subsidiaries.

Bartlett and Ghoshal were concerned with the late twentieth century, and with manufacturing industries of the second industrial revolution. This book covers a much longer chronological period and a far wider range of industries. Yet they identified a set of key generic issues which had to be addressed when managing a multinational in contrast.

7.2 Hierarchies, clans, and business groups in the first global economy

As firms began to make greenfield investments or acquisitions across borders during the nineteenth century, the problems of managing distance were enormous. The slow speed and poor reliability of communications made close monitoring of distant operations impractical. The search for minerals or trade often took firms into remote regions entirely lacking a modern business infrastructure or basic communications system. Tropical and other diseases were widespread, and often fatal. Indigenous people sometimes were able to mount effective resistance to threats to their way of life.

Nevertheless, the reasons why multinational investment occured at all was that the once overwhelming obstacles posed by geography were being eroded by telegraph, railroads and steamships. Moreover, nongeographical barriers to cross-border business were low. Governments imposed few restrictions on foreign-owned firms. People could move across borders without passports or work visas. Capital, although not trade, could flow freely across borders. The City of London served as a global information hub. Colonialism and informal imperialism imposed Western institutions and legal systems widely. 'Regime changes' could be enforced on countries which opposed globalization. If firms could build the administrative structures, there were few exogenous obstacles to their organization in a coordinated or even 'global' fashion.

The organizations built by the first multinationals reflected their experiences at home, the countries in which they invested, and the industries in which they operated. The most widespread organizational form in the first global economy was the free-standing company. This organizational form worked well for the industries in which it predominated, including mining, plantations, trade-related services including banking and shipping, and utilities. Compared to the complex organizations examined by Bartlett and Ghoshal, the strategic requirements faced by free-standing firms in these industries were simpler. They needed to transfer abroad start-up capital, a number of skilled personnel and knowledge about mining or banking, but not complex technologies. There were lots of efficient markets in resources so extensive vertical integration was not a requirement. Most of their industries did not have large economies of scale compared to mechanical processes in manufacturing. In most cases, subsidiaries were established in only one geographical region.

The tiny head offices and fragile or non-existent managerial hierarchies which were characteristic of free-standing companies were sufficient for the primary functions of raising finances, distributing dividends and monitoring foreign operations. The problem of distance and the unpredictable and non-routine nature of many tasks, meant that managerial hierarchies and large bureaucracy were not the most efficient way of regulating effort. Instead these firms controlled managers at distant offices by creating strong corporate cultures based on the recruitment of a homogenous managerial corps. Managers were always nationals of the home country, except in countries settled by European colonists, such as Australia and Canada. Typically they belonged to particular social groups. In the British case, they were normally the products of that country's fee-paying 'public' schools. Head offices devoted great attention to the recruitment of staff with the right character and background, who would be trusted to function honestly and in accordance with overall corporate norms without close bureaucratic supervision. Head offices retained a monitoring role by deciding on matters such as individual salary levels, awarding or denying permission to marry, vetting prospective wives, and congratulating or admonishing individual performance (Munro 1988; Jones 1993).

The 'clan'—whose members are heavily socialized and share common goals and understandings—offered a superior organizational form in situations in which there are considerable problems of measurement, and too great uncertainty existed for prices or rule systems to be able to function well. The clan form has less need for formalized and sophisticated flows of information, because common ideas, beliefs and values function as information carriers and provide sufficient guidance for management action (Ouchi 1980; Alvesson and Lindkvist 1993). This type of organization worked well where mining companies were searching for minerals on distant frontiers. Managers on the spot needed to be given autonomy in day-to-day operations because close monitoring was implausible. In activities such as trading, which involved numerous non-routine transactions, the best defence against opportunism in the form of speculative or unauthorized dealing lay in the creation of 'moral' cultures rather than bureaucratic monitoring which at best could be retrospective (Jones 2000).

The use of clan methods of control rested in part on nation-specific characteristics. The British preference for socialization strategies rested on that country's homogeneous culture, as well as Victorian cultural norms including notions of service and imperial mission. There were regional dimensions also. British-owned enterprises in Asia were often managed by Scots, and sometimes headquartered in Scotland. Jardine Matheson for several generations recruited managers almost entirely from Scotland, and largely from one region, the county of Dumsfriesshire (Jardine Matheson 1947). Japanese companies later also made extensive use of socialization methods of control, again made possible by a homogeneous culture. The heterogeneous nature of the United States, even in the nineteenth century, helps to explain that country's greater preference for bureaucratic methods.

Free-standing companies operated in many countries where local organizational and technological capabilities were low. As a result, they possessed far better managerial competences than almost any local firm in Latin America, Asia, and Africa. They often secured first mover advantages in the shape of mining concessions or customer franchises which were hard to overcome. Their organizational advantages in the United States were more transient. This provided one reason why many European free-standing companies had passed into American ownership by 1914 (Wilkins 1988a).

The free-standing organization was not static. This was a trend for many head offices to exercise stronger management control over foreign affiliates towards the end of the nineteenth century. This reflected improved communications, but was also in response to perceived managerial failings. In the case of the British overseas banks, a number of banking crises in Australia and elsewhere in the early 1890s, which led to the collapse of some banks, prompted London head offices to exert greater control over their overseas branches. Quite extensive reporting systems were developed to monitor lending at branches (Jones 1993).

The linking of free-standing firms into business groups centered on British, and to a lesser extent Dutch, trading and mining companies who created extensive businesses in Asia, Latin America, and Africa. These groups used different modes for different business streams. Wholly owned branches were responsible for trading and shipping and insurance agency businesses. Plantations and mines were placed in independent firms which were floated on the London or other capital markets. Typically the parent company would retain equity in the venture, but sometimes as low as 1 percent, and would place some directors on the board. It would also hold a management contract with the firm. Some parents functioned as in-house banks which made loans to affiliates, and received deposits from them. There was extensive intragroup trade flows. A commodity such as tea would be produced by a partly-owned plantation company, sold and moved by a wholly owned branch, and then warehoused, packed, blended and distributed through other affiliates. Each would make a profit on the transaction (Jones 2000).

These business groups organized around British trading companies grew to a considerable size and geographical spread (see Box 7.1). Before 1914 Balfour Williamson had extensive trading, land, investment, oil production and refining, and flour milling businesses along the West Coast of the Americas stretching from the states of Washington and Oregon in the United States to Chile and Peru. Jardine Matheson employed over 110 000 workers in China in the interwar years. James Finlay, which had extensive plantation and manufacturing operations in India, as well as tea plantations in East Africa and cotton textile manufacturing in Scotland, employed around 160 000 in 1945 (Jones 2000).

Such business groups do not fit easily into the Bartlett and Ghoshal organizational typology. They served as venture capitalists in countries where capital markets were highly undeveloped, identifying opportunities, financing them, and ultimately bringing them to market. They performed a wide range of market intermediation functions in the face of an equally wide range of market imperfections. The location of much decision-making at the level of the affiliated company facilitated a high degree of local responsiveness. However the parent company provided strong strategic direction for the group as a whole, and coordinated the business. They recruited the management for all the affiliated companies, and facilitated the international marketing of products. There was considerable diffusion of information and knowledge within groups (Jones 2000). They might be regarded as precursors of the transnational organizational form.

Box 7.1 Harrisons & Crosfield as a business group

Harrisons & Crosfield (H & C) was founded as a Liverpool-based partnership engaged in tea trading, buying tea in India and China and selling it in Britain. From the 1890s the firm opened overseas branches in Sri Lanka, India, Malaya, the Dutch East Indies, the United States, Canada, Australia and New Zealand. These branches were usually established to trade in tea, but soon diversified into other trading and acted as agents for insurance and shipping companies. In 1899 the firm began buying tea estates in South Asia, and established tea distribution companies in Britain and North America. In 1903 the firm began buying rubber plantations, and it became one of the largest plantation companies in Southeast Asia. During the interwar years, H & C invested in logging in Sabah (British Borneo). In Malaya H & C diversified from rubber plantations to rubber manufacture. The Canadian branch diversified into chemicals distribution during the 1930s. This led to investments into specialty chemical manufacturing in Europe from the 1950s.

The London head office of H & C presided over a network of wholly-owned branches which traded in tea and other commodities, acted as agents for shipping and insurance companies, and provided plantation management services. The plantation and timber ventures were placed into separate companies. H & C floated around 40 rubber plantation companies on the London Stock Exchange between 1903 and 1914. H & C retained a share in the equity of between 1 percent and 70 percent, and had 1 or 2 directors on each board. H & C acted as secretaries or agents to the plantation companies. The secretarial function included the provision of management support to the board of plantation companies in return for a fixed fee. H & C also recruited expatriates as plantation managers. The agency function, which involved the provision of plantation management services, and the collecting and transmitting of data to individual company boards. Agency fees were charged per planted acre, not on profits. H & C provided specialist technical services for affiliated companies.

(*Source*: Jones and Wale 1999; Jones 2000.)

During the nineteenth century many other large European businesses functioned as business groups. From the 1870s the Paris branch of the Rothschild banking family invested in and managed railroads in Spain and elsewhere; built a large-scale international metals processing and marketing business; and developed the second largest oil producing company in Russia. These were run as independent businesses registered in the various host economies, yet they were supervised closely by the Rothschild family and a few trusted advisers (McKay 1990).

In Latin America, the large German electrical firms developed new organizational forms to manage the companies they promoted as part of the *Unternehmergeschäft* strategy to develop a market for their products (see Chapter 5). AEG and Siemens formed financial holding companies jointly with German, Swiss and other banks. These *Finanzierungsgesellschaften*—such as AEG's Bank für elektrische Unternehmunger established in 1895—acquired the equity of utility companies, which were held during the development period, and then sold to the public, but with a minority equity stake retained.

The financial holding companies were typically headquartered in Belgium or in Switzerland which were politically 'neutral' countries with well-organized financial markets and favorable company legislation. They developed sub-holding companies to control regional groupings of utility operations. The AEG group had a cluster of such sub-holding companies, including the Deutsche Überseeische Elektricitäts-Gesellschaft (DUEG) for Argentina, Chile and Uruguay (Hertner 1986, 1987b, 1993). DUEG's shareholders included AEG and Deutsche Bank, which held 16 percent of the equity each, together with eight German and Swiss banks. With assets of $73 million in 1914, this holding company was the biggest German FDI before World War I (Jacob-Wendler 1982; Schröter 1993a).

Organizational forms differed even within the same industry. Before 1914 the three large German companies, Metallgesellschaft, Aron Hirsch, and Beer, Sondheimer were leading participants in the international trading and processing of metals (Becker 1998). They were all family-owned and -managed firms, but they organized their businesses in different fashions. Metallgesellschaft founded multiple legally separate companies, such as the American Metal Company, established in New York in 1887. It sought to provide cohesion by means of interlocking shareholdings, market-sharing agreements, and cross-directorships. This type of organization was employed in some other large German domestic companies, including the steel company Thyssen (Fear 2004), and Metallgesellschaft's owner explicitly maintained that the local autonomy achieved by this structure was essential given the problems of geographical distance. Aron Hirsch followed the same organizational form. However the third German metals trader, Beer, Sondheimer, opened foreign branches of its firm in preference to establishing separate companies. Its only attempt to found a separate company, in Belgium in 1897, proved a failure (Becker 1998).

The place of family firms in the growth of multinationals is controversial. Chandler (1990) suggested that the separation of ownership and control in the United States facilitated the growth of multinationals, while the family owners in Britain and elsewhere often preferred to pay out earnings in dividends rather than invest in new products or foreign markets. However the sheer scale of British multinational investment during the first global economy makes it hard to sustain this argument. Small Dutch family firms have also been shown to have competed successfully in international markets. In margarine and other foods, a leading sector for Dutch firms, the Jewish firms of Van den Bergh, Van Zwanenberg, and Hartog settled close relatives in London to take advantage of the much larger British market, creating Dutch and British branches of the family (Arnoldus 2002). Family ownership and management, albeit combined with the use of professional managers, also characterized many of Germany's largest multinationals before 1914, including Siemens, Bayer, and Stollwerck, the chocolate manufacturer. It is not even evident that Britain had more family firms than Germany before 1914 or later (Church 1993).

There are many conceptual problems with the use of 'family firm' as a generic term. The scale, scope, boundaries, organization and legal status of family firms has varied widely historically, between sectors and between countries. The definition of a family business is problematic. In many countries families have been able to use special classes of shares to control companies with a small share of the equity. There is a case for splitting the definition into family-owned and family-controlled firms (Casson 2000). One recent study has defined a family firm as '(partly) owned by a family and includes the characteristic that at least one important management position is held by the family' (Arnoldus 2002).

The organizational forms employed by manufacturing companies, and by US-owned firms more generally, were quite different from that seen in many resources and services. They were characterized more by hierarchy than networks. As US manufacturing and oil companies invested abroad, they typically sought to extend the borders of their managerial hierarchies in the same fashion as they had grown within the United States. The problems of monitoring employees were addressed by rules and other policing methods. The large integrated US corporations which grew during the last nineteenth century were organized as centralized, functionally departmentalized operating structures. A hierarchy of managers coordinated and monitored operations. Parent companies were closely involved with the establishment of the foreign subsidiary. The products manufactured by foreign affiliates would normally be identical to those produced by the parent. They would have close links in terms of finance, technology and staffing.

Larger companies had elaborate organizations. By the 1900s Standard Oil, the largest corporation in the world, had an extensive hierarchy in New York which supervised and coordinated its businesses. Many other companies had few international operations, and often only in Canada, and rudimentary structures. The problems of distance meant that monitoring in all companies was often ad hoc. Systematic standardized reporting procedures were basic. Control was often exercised by personal visits from headquarters (Wilkins 1970). These US firms might be seen as striving towards an international model even if geography dictated that in practice a high level of local autonomy was permitted.

A number of US companies, including Standard Oil and Kodak, sought to overcome some of the costs of distance by using British affiliates to supervise European and other international businesses. The Singer Sewing Machine Company used offices in London and Hamburg as regional head offices for Europe and Asia, although in practice Singer's New Jersey factory supervised manufacturing worldwide, while sales organizations reported directly to the New York offices (Carstensen 1984).

The European companies which invested across borders similarly reflected systems of management which prevailed in their home countries. Family ownership remained strong in German business, although they often employed professional managers. German firms often cooperated with each other. In Britain, 'personal capitalism' meant that manufacturing firms were smaller and management systems less systematic. There was often a lack of systematic controls by parents, and a high degree of operational autonomy by foreign subsidiaries. However this may have been the most appropriate organizational design in many of the branded consumer goods industries in which British firms were especially prominent, including food, soap, and cotton thread. Local market knowledge and responsiveness were key drivers of competitive success in such industries.

There was no single model of a 'global firm' during the first global economy. The varied institutional forms taken by capitalism in different countries, as well as the wide range of opportunities and challenges, meant that multiple different types of organizations were employed. The upshot was a striking biodiversity in organizational forms in which elements of the multinational, international and transnational forms coexisted.

7.3 **The growth of local autonomy**

During the interwar years there was a growth of large companies in many advanced economies as firms engaged in horizontal and vertical integration, and expanded in new products and countries. As these giant industrial enterprises came to dominate their home markets, they sought to penetrate foreign markets either through trade or FDI. Unlike the free-standing firms, they transferred to their subsidiaries both technological capabilities and marketing knowledge. This involved more capital, and the knowledge needed constant updating.

A number of large US (and German) firms pioneered the development of the multi-divisional structure (or M-form) which offered a solution to diseconomies of scale by de-centralizing decision-making to product or geographical operating divisions. During the interwar years large corporations managed by professional managers became pre-eminent in capital-intensive industries and in branded consumer products in the United States. These firms were the major sources of US multinational investment (see Chapter 2).

In other countries the growth of large corporations meant that they also accounted for an increasing percentage of multinational investment. However there was limited con-vergence towards the US organizational model. In Germany the growth of large corpor-ations in industries such as chemicals and steel coincided with more cartelization. Families remained more important as owners of firms. In Britain, the growth of large corporations as a result of a major merger wave during the 1920s did not end family ownership or lead to the widespread adaption of M-form. In Britain, holding companies were created to manage federations to operating subsidiaries, whose businesses often overlapped. However, such organizational forms did not prevent considerable new multinational investment. The leading British chocolate manufacturers Rowntree and Cadbury, both family-owned, established factories in the developed markets of the British Empire and although some affiliates made substantial losses, others were quite successful (Jones 1986a).

The organizational ecology of international business continued to be diverse. There were few new free-standing companies or business groups created in Europe, and this organizational form declined in relative importance. However ITT grew as a giant, US-based, free-standing company. The European-owned business groups and overseas banks in Asia, Africa, Latin America and Australia also retained their organizational forms created before 1914. They proved robust during the turbulent economic and political conditions of the interwar years. The *Finanzierungsgesellschaften* controlling utilities in Latin America and elsewhere passed out of German control as a result of World War I, but the organizational form persisted under the new ownership of Swiss banks (see Chapter 5).

In some cases there was an incremental shift towards modification of the free-standing form. In a number of instances domestic companies took equity holdings in British free-standing companies. Over a fifteen-year period following Lever Brothers' initial invest-ment in West Africa (see Chapter 3), all of the British trading companies in West Africa were acquired and merged into the United Africa Company (UAC), which became the largest modern business organization in the region. UAC was wholly owned by Unilever. However it was retained as organizationally distinct from its parent, with its own Board of

Directors and distinctive operating procedures and culture. This arrangement continued until 1986 (Fieldhouse 1994).

A similar phenonomenon occurred in British overseas banking. The previous sharp division between domestic and overseas banks was partly modified when two of Britain's largest domestic banks acquired shares in overseas banks. Between 1918 and 1936 Lloyds Bank acquired most of the equity of all the British overseas banks which operated in Latin America, and purchased another bank which had branches in India and Egypt. Barclays Bank fully acquired banks with branches in the West Indies, West Africa and Egypt, as well as a local South African bank, which in 1925 were merged into a separate affiliate called Barclays DCO which had over 450 branches outside Britain. However in both cases the overseas banking business was retained in separate organizations. In the case of Lloyds, in particular, little attempt was made to exert managerial control (Jones 1993).

The geopolitical environment of the interwar years provided strong incentives for firms to make local responsiveness a higher priority than efficiency or knowledge transfer. Paradoxically this happened just as communications and travel became easier and faster than ever before. The growth of nationalism and the adoption of nationalistic policies by many governments obliged firms to emphasize local identities. Trade barriers and exchange controls discouraged the flow of trade between countries. Barriers to emigration hindered the transfer of people inside firms.

There was a trend towards growing local autonomy within many multinationals. Within US manufacturing firms, many foreign units during the interwar years developed their own separate histories and their own satellite activities. They sometimes undertook their own R & D and made their own (third country) investments. A number of US firms sold part of the equity of European affiliates, often because of liquidity problems in the United States, which further enhanced their quasi-independent status. Exchange controls encouraged or forced firms to retain profits in host economies. These were often used to diversify along the value chain, undertaking within one country activities which had previously been shared between countries (Wilkins 1974a).

During the interwar years some US companies formed separate international divisions. In 1919 General Electric's wholly owned International General Electric took over a large and complex foreign business which included wholly-owned manufacturing subsidiaries, joint ventures, and small equity stakes in some European firms (Wilkins, 1974a). In many instances, and this was to remain a characteristic of US firms, international operations were seen as peripheral. This often led them to be given considerable autonomy by default. However even within the same industry there was considerable diversity in the levels of autonomy given to foreign affiliates (see Box 7.2 for the cases of Ford and GM).

In most multinationals, 'local' business became more important. European overseas banks, faced by the decline in international trade, responded by extending their lending to 'local' businesses not related directly to international trade and exchange. Trading companies, adversely affected by falling commodities prices and trade barriers, responded by deepening their involvement in local economies. Dutch trading companies began manufacturing textiles and other products in their principal host region, the Dutch East Indies (Sluyterman 1998). In Latin America, British trading companies responded to rising tariffs and the growth of local industries by distributing local products instead of foreign imports (Jones 2000).

Box 7.2 The organization of Ford and General Motors in Europe, 1920–60

During the interwar years Ford pursued rigid centralization and the direct transfer of US product, production and organization to its major European subsidiaries. During the 1920s Ford insisted on the local production of the Model T, and refused to permit local managers in Britain and Germany to adapt the design to local tastes. A massive factory constructed at Dagenham, near London, in 1928 sought to replicate the American mass production system, even though it was located in a much smaller market. During the 1930s there was a half-hearted attempt to develop a small car for the British market, but the application of a new US engine technology, which was overpowered for British conditions, resulted in a large loss of market share. Ford pursued the same standardization policies in Germany. Only belatedly was there an attempt to improve performance by building trucks for the Nazi militarization program.

GM's international organization was wholly different. Its major European subsidiaries, Vauxhall in Britain and Opel in Germany, were acquired during the 1920s. GM devolved control and accepted local initiative, although at times it transferred some US practices to its subsidiaries. Senior management consisted of nationals. During the 1930s GM pioneered the technique of unitary construction for its European cars, which was not to be utilized in the US for the following two decades. Opel was allowed to develop a close relationship with the Nazi regime, building a new truck factory to supply military demand.

After World War II, GM's Opel remained autonomous, and consolidated its strong position within Germany. Vauxhall was also left autonomous, but lacked sufficient capabilities to sustain innovation, and became a technical backwater. It was only from the late 1950s that GM began to integrate its European companies more closely, both with its US business and with other affiliates. Ford remained more centralized. The poorly performing German subsidiary was largely neglected. Ford declined to Americanize the management, yet distrusted the local management. The situation only changed with a project in 1960 to built a small car for the US market. Although the project was ultimately aborted, there was a huge investment in the German technical and production capabilities. In Britain, where Ford was a large and more successful company, the local management began to acquire more autonomy from the 1950s.

(*Source:* Tolliday 2000.)

European-owned multinationals were typically decentralized, either by default or by design. Case studies of large British manufacturing multinationals suggest a lack of systematic management—often control and monitoring continued to be achieved by chief executives or directors making personal visits—and a high degree of operational autonomy. However there was no single uniform pattern. During the 1930s improved management accounting at British companies, including the rubber manufacturer Dunlop, enabled more effective monitoring of affiliates (Jones 1986a). While in a number of the British overseas banks there was a shift in the locus of decision-making away from London to management located in host regions, in other cases head offices remained powerful (Jones 1993).

The search for a greater local identity raised issues of race and culture for European companies active in developing countries. The socialization strategies and strong corporate cultures which had been successfully used to control expatriate managers were difficult to extend to Asians, Africans and other non-nationals. Firms found it harder to 'trust' people from other national cultures, and there remained strong elements of racism in the colonial environment. During the interwar years a number of British banks, trading and other companies began to appoint a few Indian nationals to management posts. There were similar developments in West Africa. However this proved a difficult process which was not advanced by the outbreak of World War II (Jones 1993, 2000).

Organizations which facilitated local responsiveness often seemed to perform best in the interwar years. The decentralized organization of GM in Europe permitted its German affiliate Opel to grow as a center of innovation, while Ford's centralization handicapped its European affiliates. Yet local autonomy was no guarantee of competitive success. Two of the largest British-owned affiliates in the United States, Courtaulds' American Viscose Corporation (AVC) and Unilever's Lever Brothers, had considerable autonomy in the interwar years, although with different outcomes. AVC became technologically stagnant until the late 1930s, when the British parent intervened to install a new management, albeit it one largely consisting of American nationals (Coleman 1969). In contrast, Lever Brothers, which enjoyed a high degree of autonomy under an American manager, mounted a successful competitive assault on the incumbent P&G (Jones 2002).

7.4 Multinational, international, and global organizations

By the 1950s there were a number of very large multinationals which faced complex management challenges. The Shell Group employed at least a quarter of a million people worldwide by that decade. Nestlé had over 125 manufacturing plants spread across most of the world. As such firms resumed multinational investment, the exogenous constraints which had encouraged an emphasis on local responsiveness were progressively relaxed. Organizational choices again reflected industry characteristics. However, the 'administrative heritage' of firms exercised a major constraint on the choices made, as firms which had owned substantial multinational operations in the interwar years often had a high level of decentralization which was not easy to change. New entrants to multinational investment were freer to choose their organizational structure, but had to learn about the complexities of cross-border investment (Bartlett and Ghoshal 1989).

The organizational choices made by firms continued to reflect their home countries. In the United States, the large, vertically integrated, horizontally diversified, managerial corporation was dominant. The M-form was widely used to administer the foreign operations of US multinationals. US companies stressed structure and systems as a means of exerting management control. They exercised strong central influence over affiliates through the use of formalized reporting and written guidelines, and the use of expatriates in key positions. Most companies placed a strong emphasis on quarterly financial performance (Humes 1993; Child, Faulkner, and Pitkethly 2000). However US firms also created wholly different organizational forms to operate abroad. Coca-Cola built and managed the world's largest soft drink brand using a franchise operation. It franchised independent 'bottlers' who produced the drink, while the company owned and ran the marketing side (Giebelhaus 1994).

In Bartlett and Ghoshal's terminology, many US companies might be described as fitting into the international model, although they classified one of their three US cases—ITT—as multinational. Yet there appears to have been a wide spectrum of organizational types employed by US firms after World War II. Many US multinationals were closer to GM than Ford in their preference for local autonomy. In 1949 IBM placed its international affiliates under a new wholly owned subsidiary. IBM's founder, T. J. Watson, appointed his younger son to become the effective head of the new IBM World Trade. Within a decade World Trade operated in eighty-six countries and had a non-US workforce of 33 000. National companies were autonomous, staffed largely by nationals, and with little coordination between them. In the United States, IBM had an infamously strong homogeneous 'blue suit' corporate culture, but this was not rigidly applied to World Trade. It was only from the mid-1960s, with the introduction of System 360, that IBM sought a greater degree of international coordination (see Chapter 4). The domestic company took overall responsibility for development engineering and manufacturing. A regional production network was developed, with responsibility for the development of specific processors or peripherals in the 360 line assigned to different laboratories in Europe and the United States (Dassbach 1989; Olegario 1995).

The new US-based entrants to multinational investment often experimented with appropriate organizational structures. Typically they would begin by founding autonomous foreign subsidiaries. In time, an international division would be formed, headed by a senior executive, although the control systems used varied widely depending on the number of foreign subsidiaries and the nature of the transactions among the subsidiaries. While in some companies each subsidiary served a single national market and had little contact with other companies, in other cases a few large foreign manufacturing subsidiaries acted as supply points for marketing subsidiaries in other countries. As the numbers and spread of subsidiaries grew, some US firms responded by appointing regional general managers, each responsible for the performance of one group of the foreign subsidiaries, and each reporting to divisional headquarters (Stopford and Wells 1972).

European companies often opted for the multinational rather than international organizational model. Bartlett and Ghoshal placed two of their three European cases—Philips and Unilever—in this category. Typically, European companies employed a 'mother–daughter' organization. The heads of foreign subsidiaries reported directly to the head of the parent. They were often left relatively autonomous, with control generally exercised by informal, personalized relationships (Franko 1976). European companies often placed more emphasis on personal relations than formal structures. Job descriptions were less clearly defined than in the United States. Unilever recruited people from similar backgrounds, whose subsequent careers passed through common rituals and shared experiences. Managers from many countries and product areas met on courses at Unilever's in-house training center in Britain, where long-lasting contacts were forged. There were annual conferences of senior managers which were used as a means of policy making, and policy dissemination. Unilever's rotation of its 'high flying' managers through various jobs in different product groups and countries built webs of personal contacts. It was the strength of relationships which permitted the decentralized nature of this company to function as a collective whole. Despite the appearance of a bureaucratic organization with formal rules and procedures to cover every eventuality, important decisions were taken on the basis of relationships and 'know-who' (Maljers 1992; Goffee and Jones 1996).

Bartlett and Ghoshal (1989) emphasized the historical advantages of Unilever's multinational organization in providing national responsiveness in contrast to the international organization of P&G and the global organization of Japanese competitor Kao (see Box 7.3).

Unilever's decentralized model was not exceptional in Europe. Nestlé, the Swiss foods company, expanded rapidly internationally after 1945. Its product range included dairy products, chocolate, frozen food, instant food, and pet food. This was managed by Nestlé headquarters in Vevey, Switzerland in an 'arm's-length' fashion, in which cohesion was achieved by personal relationships (Humes 1993; Heer 1966). Shell managed a vast international petroleum business largely by coordinating and monitoring. Following a major reorganization undertaken after a McKinsey investigation in 1959, four new central service companies were created based in the head offices in Britain and the Netherlands. Control was decentralized to geographic regions which operated autonomously within broad lines of policy. Shell's operating companies in each country had a great deal of autonomy (Channon 1973; Humes 1993).

European multinationals often allowed their US affiliates great autonomy in the immediate postwar decades. This was partly due to concerns about the extent and unpredictability of US antitrust laws. There was a particular concern that close managerial control over US affiliates might result in worldwide businesses being investigated. Shell, which only partly owned its US affiliate Shell Oil between 1922 and 1985, also felt constrained by concerns about law suits from minority shareholders (Priest 2001). It was also widely believed that the size and income levels of the American market made it unique, with characteristics only American managers could understand. Such was the prestige of the United States and the belief that its companies were the exemplar of the best management practice, that foreign managers were reluctant to exert control over US affiliates. US managers themselves tended to have a strong emphasis on autonomy and independence which made them resistant to control from abroad. It was only from the late 1970s that many European-owned firms moved to exercise tighter managerial control over US affiliates. Unilever replaced the highly autonomous American management of its Lever Brothers affiliate, and started to integrate its American business into its worldwide operations. In 1985 Shell took the same route, and acquired full ownership of its US affiliate (Priest 2001; Jones and Gálvez-Muñoz 2001; Jones 2002).

As Japanese companies expanded internationally from the 1960s, they displayed a number of distinctive organizational features. Typically they used a large number of expatriate managers, and had a loose control system and a strong local market orientation in the Asian markets where much of the original investment went. However the electronics and automobile manufacturers which invested abroad subsequently took advantage of falling trade barriers to integrate their investments globally. All three of the global firms identified by Bartlett and Ghoshal (1989) were Japanese-owned. Kao, the Japanese competitor to Unilever and P&G in packaged consumer goods, considered its foreign subsidiaries primarily as delivery pipelines for standardized products. The company had a strong headquarters with a full range of functional capabilities.

Box 7.3 Procter & Gamble and Unilever: centralization versus decentralization, 1945–80

During the postwar decades Unilever and P&G were the two largest companies in the world soap and detergents market, and engaged in fierce oligopolistic rivalry. While the former was highly decentralized, the latter was more centralized. During World War II, many of Unilever's affiliates were isolated from each other, and from head offices. Subsequently, the need to reconstruct Unilever businesses quickly in post-war Europe led to a reliance on local initiative and autonomy. Responsibilities were largely delegated to national managements. The importance of local decision-making became a key component of corporate culture. P&G was characterized by strong central direction from its Cincinnati headquarters. Its managers were sometimes described as 'Proctoids'.

Unilever's extensive business in Latin America, Asia and Africa was facilitated by decentralization and local decision-making. The organization was less effective elsewhere. In the United States, the European head offices exercised little managerial control over the two local subsidiaries, despite a long-term failure to compete successfully against P&G which, by the mid-1970s, had resulted in Lever Brothers becoming unprofitable in the United States. Unilever also experienced excessive brand proliferation. During the 1950s Unilever began to experiment with product management—known as Coordination—designed to rationalize brands and functions, but there was great internal resistance. It was not until 1966 that product groups were given profit responsibility. Five years later a McKinsey investigation confirmed the organization. Thereafter European-wide rationalization proceeded slowly. Unilever still had over 180 European factories in 1988. Organizational design was complicated by Unilever's product range which spanned foods such as margarine and ice cream as well as home and personal care. In foods, markets and competitors remained more local than in detergents.

P&G had a less extensive international business than Unilever. Before the 1980s P&G had few operations beyond developed markets. Its centralized systems made the firm uncomfortable with the unstable and unpredictable conditions in many emerging markets. In Europe, it began manufacturing in interwar Britain, but only entered other countries from the 1950s. As a new entrant, P&G did not have Unilever's inheritance of national brands and factories. It transferred technologies and brands from the United States, and was able to capture large market shares in key markets such as Germany. It also integrated European operations. As early as 1963 it established a European Technical Center in Brussels to serve its European affiliates in product research, engineering and manufacturing.

P&G implemented a regionalization strategy following the oil price rises in 1987 and 1974 which raised raw material costs. This began with a closer coordination of R&D followed by manufacturing and marketing. By 1980 P&G had a European headquarters that exercised considerable control over national subsidiaries and sought to rationalize manufacturing, centralize research and coordinate marketing on a European-wide basis, although country managers retained profit responsibilities within P&G's European organization. P&G evolved a matrix structure which enabled senior executives to double subsidiary heads and category managers for the region. By the late 1980s Europe was one of P&G's strongest and most profitable units.

(*Source*: Bartlett and Ghoshal 1989; Dyer, Dalzel, and Olegario 2004; Jones and Miskell 2005; Jones 2005.)

The large number of expatriates used by Japanese firms indicated their use of clan forms of organization. Like the earlier experience of European companies, this raised difficult issues concerning the incorporation of foreigners into senior management. A 'rice paper ceiling' was often identified (Beamish and Inkpen 2001). In this sense, US firms such as P&G and IBM, which had strong corporate cultures and understood the power of common values and beliefs, were potentially better equipped to incorporate non-Americans into their systems.

7.5 Matrixes, heterarchies, and convergence?

The organizational challenges faced by large multinationals intensified with the growth of the second global economy. There were new opportunities and challenges arising from regional economic integration, and the melding of industries and capital markets with the globalization of products. As European and Japanese companies invested abroad, there was an intensified competitive environment. The upshot was a renewed search for organizational structures that would enable effective management in a complex environment.

During the 1970s US companies began to replace international divisions with new types of global structures: initially worldwide product divisions, or geographic divisions, and then a combination of both in the form of a global matrix. Dow Chemical, which had implemented a multifunctional business team approach for product management as early as 1958, was a pioneer. A matrix structure attempted to balance and integrate the roles and responsibilities of business, geographical and functional units. Stopford and Wells (1972) saw the regional managements which had been adopted earlier as transitional to a global matrix structure. However many firms struggled to implement matrix systems. These included Cargill, the commodity trader whose international operations from the 1950s had been managed by the highly autonomous Tradax subsidiary in Switzerland (see Chapter 5). The tensions between the international and domestic management which rose to a high level during the 1960s led to experiments with a matrix based on geography, product and function, but this proved hard to implement during the following decade (Broehl 1978).

There were major disadvantages arising from the overlapping of the authority and responsibility of the product, geographic, and functional matrix managers. Interpersonal clashes occurred because of the heterogeneity of managers within large multinationals, and the physical distances which separated them. The difficulties of reconciling product complexity, marketplace diversity and functional specialization also slowed down decision-making (Kramer 1994).

Although some form of matrix organization balancing product and geographical functions continued to be employed, many matrix structures were modified during the 1980s, and there continued to be a search for more efficient structures. Many firms continued to employ regional rather than global management structures (Morrison, Ricks, and Kendall 1991). For example, many US and Japanese firms created European regional managements. These reduced the problems caused by distance, and facilitated understanding of common features in a region (Sullivan 1992; Lehrer and Asakawa 1999). A study of the role of the European head offices of Japanese automobile and pharmaceutical companies during the 1990s showed that their importance in different functions varied. They were closely involved in production and sales management, but less so in R & D, whose links with the parent companies in Japan were closer (Ando 2004).

Bartlett and Ghoshal's (1989) argument that successful firms needed to adopt a national responsiveness and the ability to develop and transfer knowledge worldwide was supported by the perceived poor performance of three of their sample firms—General Electric, ITT, and Kao—which was ascribed to their retention of an organization based on responding to only one strategic demand. The other sample firms were seen as moving towards the new transnational model in which firms functioned as an integrated network in which subsidiaries had differentiated and specialized roles, and were participants in global sharing and development of knowledge.

The view that multinationals needed to adopt more flexible organizational forms which could achieve the mobilization of the dispersed and fragmented knowledge contained within the borders of corporations was widely shared. One study described a heterarchy involving the dispersal of traditional head office functions as foreign subsidiaries assumed strategic roles. The organization would be held together by normative mechanisms, including shared cultural values (Hedlund 1986; Hedlund and Rolander 1990). Another study proposed that multinationals needed to be organized as a differentiated network. National affiliates would vary greatly in size, power and internal organization. The goal was an organizational structure which would be internally differentiated to respond to different environments, yet at the same time being bound by a common purpose (Nohria and Ghoshal 1997).

These idealized organizations had many resemblances to the business groups which had developed in the nineteenth century, especially in respect to their use of networks rather than hierarchy, employment of multiple modes, and use of shared cultural norms as binding agents. It is unclear how many, if any, contemporary multinationals have become 'differentiated networks'. A number of firms based in small European economies were often cited as examples. ABB, the electrical engineering multinational created through the merger of Swedish-owned Asia and Swiss-owned Brown Boveri in 1987, attracted considerable interest because of a flat hierarchy and 'multidomestic' matrix organization. During the 1990s ABB was restructured as a global network of profit centers in an attempt to leverage the group's core technologies and provide global economies of scale without damaging its local market presence and responsiveness (Bartlett and Ghoshal 1993).

In practice, ABB's organization may have been less radical. A detailed case study of ABB's power transformers business showed the standardization of subsidiary operations through the adoption of American-influenced versions of Japanese management. The author described the company as 'an Americanized cosmopolitan multinational' (Bélanger 1999). This organization appeared closer to an international or global form rather than a transnational (Kristensen and Zeitlin 2004). Subsequently ABB's position as a role model was severely tarnished by corporate governance scandals and financial problems following litigation concerning asbestos sales against a US affiliate.

There were powerful forces for convergence of national management systems during the second global economy. After World War II, and sometimes earlier, US management principles were diffused internationally. The Allied occupation of Germany and Japan resulted in aspects of the US business system, including antitrust legislation, being imposed on those countries. Subsequently US multinationals, business schools and management consultants served as 'carriers' of the US model. The process was not continuous. The impact of 'Americanization' was especially strong during the post-war decades. During the 1970s and 1980s the competitiveness problems of US industries made German and Japanese capitalism appear more attractive models. During the following decade the rapid growth of the 'new economy' in the United States again made US corporate models, and concepts such as 'shareholder value', attractive for a time, at least before the corporate scandals and economic downturns at the end of the century (Kipping and Engwall 2002; Kudo, Kipping, and Schroter 2004).

By the new century there were far more similarities between large US and European multinationals in their management styles and structures than half a century earlier. British capitalism, formerly characteristically family or personal capitalism, became characterized by large firms, professional managers, and the M-form (Jones 1997). A study of large British, French and German corporations confirmed a striking convergence towards the M-form, albeit a flatter more cooperative version than that seen earlier which could be described as a 'network' M-form (Whittington and Mayer 2000). Nowhere was the US or any other model adopted in its entirety. Adaptations were usually transposed over earlier structures, creating another form of hybrid organization (Kogut and Parkinson 1993).

The extent of true organizational convergence was difficult to establish. Most companies worldwide sought to adopt the latest fashions and concepts taught at leading US business schools and management consultancies. Almost certainly, the behavior of managers and the 'way things were done' remained more divergent between countries than organizational structures and the terminology used to describe them. European and US firms continued to reflect national differences. Japanese multinationals continued to feature close coordination from parent companies, greater use of expatriates, and the retention of more of their innovation and higher value-added manufacturing in Japan (Westney 2001). The Japanese experience provides a major discontinuity to any convergence hypothesis.

As most research focused on large existing firms, especially US-based ones, the organizational forms of the tens of thousands of smaller multinationals were largely unknown. The evidence pointed towards continuing diversity. A number of East Asian newcomer multinationals, including Acer and Li & Fung, developed a 'cellular' organization which devolved as much responsibility as possible to semi-autonomous business entities which related with one another through contracting and subcontracting (Mathews 2002). These might be seen as concrete manifestations of 'differentiated networks'.

Finding the most appropriate balance between central direction and local autonomy remained difficult. The correct balance continued to differ according to products and markets, as it always had. Nor was the impact of new technologies clear. While new communication and information technologies were initially seen as facilitating 'differentiated networks', there was evidence that their effect might be the opposite, as they had the potential to increase central co-ordination (Westney 2001). Although much management literature regarded the issue of 'control' as unfashionable in a world of 'differentiated networks', it had not disappeared as an issue. In 1995 the 233-year-old

British investment bank Barings lost over $1 billion through the illicit trading of one of its Singapore-based traders. Barings was subsequently sold to the ING Bank of the Netherlands for less than $2.

7.6 The persistence of 'older' forms of organization

It is noteworthy that organizational firms characteristic of the first global economy remained vibrant during the second global economy. Family-owned and often -managed business remained widespread in most countries. In 2000, seventeen of the top 100 companies in Germany and the United States were family-owned, and so were forty-two of the top Italian firms (Colli 2003). In Italy, the largest industrial groups were controlled by families such as the Agnellis at Fiat. After World War II a cluster of medium-sized family firms in Italy also grew to dominate international market niches in clothing, luxury goods, and machinery. These included the Benetton group, which was founded in 1950s by four brothers and sisters who started a small subcontracting activity in hosiery. By 2000 Benetton employed 30 000 persons, and had textile and restaurant businesses in Europe and the United States. Although listed on the Stock Exchange in 1986, the family retained ownership, and the four founders and their descendants continued to hold managerial responsibilities in the group's subsidiaries (Colli 2003).

Family ownership and management remained important in France. The early French multinational automobile industry was led by Peugot and Renault, both family firms. Although Renault was nationalized after World War II, the Peugot family regained control of their firm after the war, and rejuvenated it. Peugot remained a stronghold of family capitalism (Chadeau 1993). Family-owned Michelin grew from the world's seventh largest rubber company in 1960 to the largest, and came to control around 20 percent of the world tire market. Michelin's growth rested on a technological lead in the production of radial tires which was patented in 1946. From the late 1950s Michelin opened factories throughout Europe. Factories in North America followed in the 1970s, and the Uniroyal Goodrich Tire Company was acquired in the United States in 1990. Michelin invested in Latin America during the 1970s, and Asia, beginning in Thailand and Japan, a decade later. Michelin remained managed, as well as owned, by the founding family. A family-controlled holding company in Switzerland owned the firm, while tire production worldwide was coordinated from France. Those inheriting shares were required to sign an undertaking that family members would have preference should the shares be sold later. Young family members were trained as engineers (Chadeau 1993; Fridenson 1997; Lottman 2003).

In the highly internationalized Dutch business system, family ownership and management remained important throughout the interwar years and beyond (Sluyterman 2003). During the 1920s the family firms of Van den Bergh, Hartog and Jurgens came together in the Margarine Unit, but this remained under family control. The merger with Lever Brothers to create Unilever did not eliminate family influence. Members of the founding families remained influential for several decades. A Hartog served as chairman of

Unilever NV between 1966 and 1971 (Arnoldus 2002). Philips remained family-managed until the 1970s (Sluyterman and Winkelman 1993). Heineken, the brewer, has remained family-owned and -managed since its foundation in 1863. The company, which began its international expansion in 1937 when it granted a license to a foreign brewer, became the world's second largest brewer in the 1990s. It held 5 percent of world beer production, and was the largest imported brand in the United States.

The persistence of family ownership was noteworthy elsewhere in Europe. They were often found in capital and scale-intensive industries. During the 1980s half of the largest 20 Swedish multinational manufacturing firms were part of Sweden's largest business group, which was owned and managed by the Wallenberg family (Jones and Schroter 1993). In Germany, leading multinationals with substantial family ownership included BMW and Porsche in automobiles, and Henkel in detergents. The Siemens family continued to control 14 percent of the voting shares in Siemens (Whittington and Mayer 2000). Roche, the Swiss pharmaceuticals successor to Hoffman La Roche, remained controlled by the founding families Oeri and Hoffman.

In Britain family ownership was seen in some of Britain's most successful postwar multinationals. Pilkington's growth as one of the world's largest glass manufacturers, based on the invention of the float glass process in the 1950s, occurred during the ownership of the family which had founded it in 1826 (Barker 1986). Although Pilkington became a public company in 1970, a family member was chairman until 1995. Cadbury, founded in 1824, remained family-owned until its merger with Schweppes in 1969. There was a family chairman or chief executive until the 1990s, by which time the company was one of the world's largest confectionary companies. However Britain moved closer to the US model of corporate capitalism than most European countries, and over time capitalism family ownership and management was largely eliminated in large British corporations.

In industries such as shipping, family-owned firms remained the organizational norm. Both liner and tramp shipping in the nineteenth century was characterized by family-owned firms operating in networks based on trust and reputation (Boyce 1995; Valdaliso 2000). However over time the organization of the two branches of the industry diverged. In liner shipping there was extensive cartelization, while tramp shipping remained optimistic and competitive (see Chapter 5). During the 1970s containerization, which involved radically new designs for vessels and cargo handling facilities, encouraged the growth of large managerial corporations such as Danish-owned Maersk which offered global services to clients. During the same decade traditional tramp ships were also replaced by specialized ships built according to bulk cargoes and the specialized bulk shipping markets. However it was relationships—for example, with charter and insurance brokers and agents at foreign ports—rather than size which continued to determine success. Trust and reputation continued to provide the basis on which these relationships operated.

Tramp shipping remained dominated by groups of family enterprises which both competed and collaborated with other firms on the basis of common national cultures of traditional maritime countries, especially Greece, Norway, and Japan (see Box 7.4). Even within countries the shipping business was geographically clustered around a number of home ports. In Britain, before the collapse of its shipping industry after World War II, the

Box 7.4 Families and networks in Greek shipping

Greek-owned shipping development was almost exclusively in the tramp sector of the industry. During the nineteenth century Greek ships carried bulk cargoes, particularly grain from the Black Sea and coal from north-west Europe, along the routes of the Mediterranean and accounted for 2 percent of world shipping tonnage by 1914. Many Greek firms had offices in London as well as the major Greek port of Piraeus. During the 1950s and 1960s New York also became a major operational center, but changes in US taxation led Greek firms to shift back thereafter to London and Piraeus as the main operational centers.

The Greek shipping industry was a family business. In 1900 about 200 families owned some 250 shipping firms. In 2000 there were about 700 families owning and managing over 1,000 firms. Before 1914 the largest ship-owning groups came from the Ionian islands of Cephalonia and Ithaca. During the interwar years family groups from the Aegean islands, largely Chios, became pre-eminent. In 1958 Chiots owned almost one-third of the Greek fleet.

The shipping companies operated within close networks based on kinship, islands and ethnicity. Intermarriages were used to keep businesses within closed circles. Although the firms competed with one another, network ties provided a flow of information about markets, chartering, shipbuilding, repairing, financing and insurance. The ship owners employed seamen from their islands of origin. Before World War II at least two-thirds of Greek seamen came from the islands.

After World War II a number of 'outsiders', including Aristotle Onassis, rose in importance in the industry, but they married into traditional ship-owning families. From the 1970s, as the Greek fleet grew, a new generation of non-traditional ship owners rose to prominence. They were Peloponnese or from the Athens/Piraeus area, and these areas also provided the main sources of seamen. By the 1990s Greek ship owners accounted for 15 percent of world tonnage, making it the largest fleet in the world.

(*Source*: Harlaftis 1993.)

most important included the ports in the northeast of England, including Hull, and the Clyde region of Scotland (Boyce 1995; Munro and Slaven 2001). In Norway, the town of Bergen was the location of the traditional ship owning families, and provided the home of large tanker owners such as Wilemsen (Harlaftis and Theotokas 2004).

Family business was also prominent in a number of other industries. In alcoholic beverages, the largest worldwide firms included family-owned Anheuser Busch (US), Pernot Ricard (France), and Heineken. Bahamas-based Bacardi was largely owned and controlled by the Sardinias family, originally from Cuba and resident in Florida after the advent of the Castro regime in 1959 (Lopes 2002). Family ownership remained strong in multinational trading companies. Swire and Jardine Matheson remain owned and managed by the fifth generation of their British families. Similarly, Sweden's Johnson group remain family-owned (de Geer 1995, 1998). Cargill, the giant US commodity trader, remained owned by the sixth generation of the Cargill and MacMillan families, whose members were also active in the management. Cargill, which had annual revenues of

$60 billion in 2003, was the largest family- and privately-held company in the United States (Broehl 1998).

Family ownership and management remained the predominant form of business in all of the 'late industrializing' countries of Asia and Latin America (Amsden 2003). Even in the United States the family influence in Cargill was not exceptional. The Ford family continued to hold a considerable share of Ford's equity. In 2002 the chief executive was replaced by a family member. Mars, the confectionary company, remained family-owned and managed from its foundation in 1911 until the present day.

Family firms, therefore, remained an important component of international business. The new generation of multinationals from emerging markets were overwhelmingly family-owned. There was evidence that they were less able than managerial firms to operate internationally, although they did have distinctive advantages and disadvantages. The latter included issues relating to the raising capital for further expansion, problems of succession, and the complexities arising from the extension of family conflicts into business. On the other hand, family firms often developed strong corporate cultures which yielded powerful competitive advantages. In some instances, they were willing also to adopt longer-term perspectives on their businesses than managerial firms.

The business groups which had featured extensively in the first global economy also proved a resilient organizational form, although their relative importance in the world economy shrank. They survived the radical improvements in the information environment which occurred in stages with the progressive introduction of the telegraph, telephones, faxes, and internet. They also survived radical shifts in the political environment—associated with the end of Empire and widespread nationalizations as in China—and in technological paradigms. They frequently 'reinvented' themselves to suit the evolution of context.

Harrisons & Crosfield retained its organizational form as a business group until 1978, when a takeover bid for one of the largest plantation companies led H & C to acquire the outstanding equity of its major affiliates. During the 1980s H & C responded to political pressures in its host region by selling its plantations, while its Borneo timber concession ended, and the firm became for a time a diversified conglomerate spanning chemicals, timber and foods businesses, primarily in Europe. In 1998 the business was re-organized as the specialty chemicals company, Elementis (Jones and Wale 1999).

The longevity of Harrisons & Crosfield was not unique. Swire's and Jardine Matheson survived the total elimination of their vast China businesses in 1949, and were reborn as diversified business groups active in Hong Kong and elsewhere. As sea transportation gave way to air travel after World War II, Swire's—which had owned a large commercial shipping fleet—established Cathay Pacific in the late 1940s, which became one of Asia's leading airlines. During the 1970s Swire's used the land from its former dockyards and sugar refinery in Hong Kong to develop a private housing estate, laying the basis of a large real estate business. It also became a Coca-Cola bottler first in Hong Kong and from the late 1970s in the United States. During the 1980s and 1990s both Swire's and Jardine Matheson entered numerous joint ventures in China. Both firms retained the business group organization with numerous partly-owned and publicly quoted affiliates. The parents of both companies were family-owned (Jones 2000).

Business groups also featured prominently in many emerging countries. This organizational form was variously known as business houses in India, chaebol in Korea and *grupos económicos* throughout Latin America. Like the earlier European groups, they were structured as loose constellations of legally independent firms spanning a wide variety of manufacturing and service industries. Equity holdings were only one of the modes linking them, and often not the most important. They were typically family-owned. As in the nineteenth century, these business groups compensated for the poorly functioning markets within which they typically operated. They were also very resilient. Studies of contemporary Chilean and Indian groups have shown how they have responded to improvements in ambient information and higher levels of competition by 're-invention' rather then disbanding (Khanna and Palepu 1997, 2000; Khanna 2000; Fisman and Khanna 2004).

Business groups were often the most active multinational investors from emerging markets. In South Korea four large chaebol—Samsung, Hyundai, Daewoo and Lucky-Goldstar (LG)—grew as family-owned conglomerates which were used by the government to promote economic development. Typically the founding family or family holding company controlled all the operating units, but some of the largest companies such as Hyundai Motors and Samsung Electronics were publicly traded (Amsden 1997). The chaebol were the principal forces behind South Korean direct investment in electronics and automobiles. In Latin America, the *grupos económicos* with substantial multinational investments included Grupo Alfa, a Mexican group active in steel, petrochemicals, telecommunications, and food, Argentina's Technit in steel, and the Venezuelan-owned Cisneros group, a food and beverages company which diversified into media and telecommunications from the early 1990s (Grosse 2001). Section 9.4 discusses the multinationals based in emerging markets in greater detail.

7.7 Creating and leveraging knowledge

7.7.1 Knowledge creation

A central organizational challenge for multinationals was to create and transfer knowledge. From the nineteenth century the world's largest multinationals included its largest innovators. In the capital-intensive manufacturing industries, US, European and later other corporations drove innovation through the establishment of their own research laboratories.

Multinationals were initially seen as vehicles for transferring the knowledge of the parent companies to subsidiaries in the 'hub and spoke' mode. Bartlett and Ghoshal's (1989) *international* organization seemed particularly effectively in arranging this transfer. However quite early on affiliates began developing their own innovatory capabilities. By the interwar years customer demand for locally adjusted products and rapid service led firms to develop research and development in affiliates.

The larger foreign-owned chemical, pharmaceutical and petroleum firms engaged in R & D in the United States during the interwar years. Swiss-owned Hoffmann-LaRoche confined itself to pharmaceuticals, where it undertook substantial research by the end of the 1930s, but its counterparts Ciba, Sandoz, and Geigy developed broader research interests and were more broadly engaged (Wilkins 2004). Shell probably had the greatest research capacity of any foreign-owned company in the United States at this time. In 1927 Shell established a special affiliate near Berkeley in California designed to undertake fundamental research. Shell's chemical company also undertook research in the United States, and Shell refineries conducted applied research. During World War II Shell Oil became the center of innovation within the Group, pioneering new types of aviation fuel and synthetic rubber (Beaton 1957).

Foreign firms invested in R & D in other developed countries also. In 1935 over 30 of the 300 foreign-owned manufacturing companies in Britain were engaged in research. This was particularly found in the chemicals and electrical engineering industries. Most of this research was adaptive or development-related rather than basic. It often originated as technical support for manufacturing or marketing. In individual instances it grew to a considerable size. Kodak, the US-owned photographic film manufacturer, established a research laboratory in 1928 which undertook fundamental research work, spending more than its locally-owned competitor (Bostock and Jones 1994).

There is aggregate evidence from patent data that the internationalization of techno-logical activity by large manufacturing firms was quite extensive by the interwar years. It is likely that protectionist policies encouraged the building of technological capabilities in local markets. Figure 7.1 measures the share of patenting that was attributable to research outside the home country of firms.

There were wide variations in corporate strategies between countries, as well as over time. The patent data suggests that German and French firms in aggregate conducted little research outside their home economies in the interwar years, and the share only increased slowly afterwards. British and Dutch-owned firms were much more heavily internationalized during the interwar years. Swedish and US firms formed a third category. Their internationalization of research was greater in the interwar years than subsequently. US electrical equipment firms including GE and RCA saw a particularly high degree of internationalization of technological activity in the interwar years. In Sweden, it was mechanical engineering companies such as Alfa-Laval which internation-alized their research (Cantwell 1995).

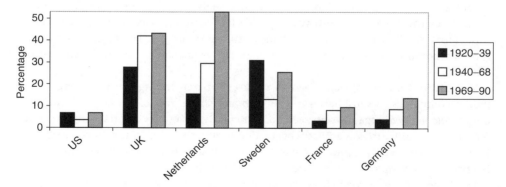

Fig. 7.1 Share of US patenting of the largest US and European industrial firms due to research located abroad, 1920–90.

Source: Based on Cantwell (1995).

Large manufacturing companies were not the only firms that dispersed their innovation. In developing countries, foreign-owned plantation companies often sought to improve crop performance. In interwar Malaya, the large British-owned companies undertook considerable research in raising the yields of rubber crops, and developing palm oil. As experimental techniques were developed, they were transferred between the companies within each group (Jones 2000). Smaller foreign-owned companies, including one Danish-owned firm, were also successful innovators in palm oil (Martin 2003). After World War II foreign plantation companies continued to innovate, and transfer innovations between countries. During the 1950s Unilever's Congo subsidiary developed new processing technology tailored to the characteristics of the Tenera oil palm, which was then transferred to its subsidiary in Malaya. During the following decade Unilever in Nigeria bred oil palms with resistance to a chronic disease known as Vascular Wilt, enabling a great increase in the yields from palm oils in Southeast Asia (Unilever 1984).

There is some evidence to support the case that the largest US and Swedish industrials lost interest in internationalizing their research after World War II. In 1954 the Swedish electronics company Ericsson established a laboratory in Darmstadt, Germany to access a surplus of engineers at a time of shortage in Sweden, yet this was closed in 1963 as it became easier to recruit at home. Ericsson's share of R & D spent abroad declined during that decade, despite the development of marine radio in Norway and work on switching technology in Australia (Attman and Olsson 1977). There was, however, considerable variation between industries. US electrical firms seem to have reduced their international innovation. GE focused most of its research, as opposed to product and process development, on its laboratories in the United States after 1945. However US pharmaceutical companies expanded their overseas laboratories. During the 1950s a number of the largest US firms, including Pfizer, established research laboratories in Europe (Bostock and Jones 1994). A study in 1980 indicated that overall about 15 percent of US corporate R & D spending was spent abroad, almost entirely by large corporations (Behrman and Fischer 1980).

A large share of the foreign R & D undertaken between the 1950s and the 1970s was adaptive or development-oriented. In consumer products, such research was essential because of variations in local tastes and national legislation. Foreign research affiliates were often granted considerable responsibility for new product research (Behrman and Fischer 1980). However even the large consumer products companies typically confined adaptive research to the larger markets in Western Europe and North America. The foreign-owned corporate sector in post-war Australia largely relied on importing innovation undertaken elsewhere. One estimate is that over four-fifths of the firms responsible for major innovations in Australia between 1939 and 1953 had foreign affiliations. At the end of the 1980s four-fifths of payments for technical know-how went to related foreign enterprises (Fleming, Merrett, and Ville 2004).

Few multinationals undertook much basic R & D in developing countries, although there were occasional exceptions. Unilever's Indian affiliate opened a research laboratory in Mumbai (Bombay) in three rooms on the top floor of the engineering building of Hindustan Lever's factory in the 1950s. New buildings were opened in 1967. By 1980 the laboratory employed over 30 scientists and over 200 staff in total. This became one of the largest corporate research laboratories in India. It was noteworthy for research on the use of indigenous materials. During the 1970s significant advances were made in the use of unconventional oils for soap-making, including castor, of which India was the world's second largest producer, rice bran—a by-product of rice milling, and tree-borne oilseeds. This research enabled Hindustan Lever to continue to produce products even when import restrictions made supplies of raw materials uncertain (Behrman and Fischer 1980).

The dispersion of research in different countries often raised management challenges. It was sometimes resisted within firms on the grounds that it diluted or duplicated existing research. In the early 1980s such considerations delayed proposals that Glaxo's fast-growing US affiliate should include research laboratories, although a facility was finally opened in 1986 (Jones 2001). It was often difficult to identify the optimal strategy. Corning, the innovative upstate New York company which made a transition from glassware to fiber optics, began to considering globalizing its innovation during the 1970s, a period when the firm as a whole lost momentum. A joint venture with the French glassmaker Saint-Gobain included a small French laboratory, but even after acquiring full ownership in 1972, Corning struggled to identify an international research strategy. There was one proposal for an 'international' (but English-speaking) laboratory on a neutral site which could attract the best researchers from several countries. However it was eventually decided to retain the French laboratory, and to better integrate it by appointing a senior Corning researcher to head it. The French laboratory turned out to be more flexible than Corning's much larger facility in the United States. It was in closer contact with consumers, more open to novel ideas, and produced a series of innovations. This success led in time to the establishment of new laboratories in Japan, Russia and Britain (Graham and Shuldiner 2001).

A study of the overseas R & D of large US and European multinationals in 1980 identified an equal division between firms favoring a decentralized form of control over R & D and those favoring a decentralized form. Both had drawbacks. In the former case there were time delays as research proposals passed through the corporate hierarchy. In the latter case, there were problems of duplication and redundancy (Behrman and Fischer 1980).

As noted in earlier chapters, there was much evidence of disappointing innovation performance by large corporations in recent decades, although it was noteworthy that during the 1990s the world's 700 largest industrial firms still accounted for around one half of the world's commercial inventions as measured by patent counts (Patel and Pavitt 1991). However, it was generally accepted that large corporations faced obstacles to innovation from technological and resource lock-ins, and routine and cultural rigidities.

There were a number of organizational responses. In some high technology industries, corporations remained innovative by buying creative venture capital start-ups, mostly in the United States. In telecoms and other industries there was some outsourcing of innovation to cheaper and possibly more creative locations, such as India's software cluster around Bangalore. Another response was the geographical dispersion of technological capabilities within firms which provided a means to access the continuing variations in the nature and scope of innovation between countries, regions and localities caused by the nature of the educational system and the business culture, and relations between firms and public policy (Nelson 1993; Cantwell 1989). Multinationals could enhance their innovatory capabilities by drawing on research conducted in different localities, and so capture 'home base augmenting effects' (Kuemmerle 1999).

There were wide variations between multinationals in their willingness to disperse research. Patent data showed that US—and Japanese—firms remained more reluctant than European firms to decentralize R & D facilities abroad. Within Europe, British and Dutch large firms had more than half their patents in overseas subsidiaries by the 1990s, whilst French and German firms conducted more innovation at home. Large European companies divided their R & D facilities among their home country, other European countries and the United States. The firms with the most dispersed innovatory technology also continued to be in 'traditional' industries such as food, drink and tobacco, building materials and petroleum. In computers, aerospace, and motor vehicles, there was a strong propensity to concentrate technological activities at home (Archibugi and Iammarino 2000).

Few firms seemed to actively take strategic decisions to access foreign research expertise. International mergers and acquisitions lay behind much of the observed trend of dispersion of technological capabilities (Patel 1995). Moreover, a study based on the US patenting of 24 leading Swedish multinational firms between 1946 and 1990 concluded that there was no clear link between such dispersion and the competitiveness of firms. In some cases, firms had reduced their international innovation network without apparent effects on their competitiveness (Zander 1999).

7.7.2 Knowledge transfer

In internalization theory, the existence of multinationals is explained by their ability to transfer knowledge across borders more efficiently than markets. However the efficient transfer of knowledge within the borders of a firm has never been automatic. Tacit knowledge or 'know-how' is complex, difficult to codify, and 'sticky' (Kogut and Zander 1992; von Hippel 1994). As a result, as Bartlett and Ghoshal stressed, the transfer of knowledge within multinationals posed a major organizational challenge.

Knowledge transfer featured widely in the growth of multinationals during the first global economy. Utility companies transferred across borders the knowledge about manufacturing and generating gas and electricity; banks transferred the skills needed to lend and take deposits; mining companies transferred the capabilities to search for and exploit minerals. As chemicals, pharmaceuticals, cotton thread and other companies built factories in foreign countries they patented inventions, and registered trade marks, in the United States and elsewhere (Wilkins 1989). Both large and small companies transferred knowledge. One study of small family-owned specialty steel firms from Sheffield (Britain) demonstrated their considerable transfer of technologies to US affiliates before 1914, even though most of these companies were not commercial successes, and ultimately passed out of British ownership (Tweedale 1986).

Although there were numerous engineering manuals and texts which codified existing technologies in the nineteenth century, tacit knowledge or 'know-how' was transferred physically by people. The Sheffield steel companies despatched technicians and managers to their US plants, some of whom remained long after they had passed into US ownership (Tweedale 1986). When International Harvester, the US grain harvester company, established factories in Sweden, France, and Germany during the 1900s, it sent experienced workers from its American plants to get production started. An attempt to start manufacturing in Russia at a fast pace and without skilled American workers ran into serious problems (Carstensen 1984).

As the first US companies began to establish manufacturing businesses in Japan after 1899, the role of people in transferring technologies was crucial. Western Electric, which acquired majority control of Nippon Electric Co. (NEC) on the day that Japanese law was changed to permit direct investment by foreign firms in July 1899, began production of telephones a few years later. The new plant layout was designed and the construction supervised by Western Electric's engineers, and a complete set of production machinery was transported from its American factory. Even pencils and erasers were sent from the parent in the United States. American foremen supervised production, while Japanese workers were sent for training in the United States (Uchida 1991).

The role of people in transferring tacit knowledge remained crucial as multinational organizations grew in size. Despite the availability of instantaneous communications, multinationals continued to use expatriates not only to control foreign affiliates, but also to transfer tacit knowledge (Bonache and Brewster 2001). As innovative knowledge was held by individuals, mobility both between firms and within firms is essential for knowledge transfer (Almeida and Kogut 1999). It was, therefore, not surprising that as Japanese automobile and electronics firms made large-scale multinational investments in the United States and Europe they made extensive use of expatriates. The flexible and team-based characteristics of the Japanese production system involved a high degree of tacit information which was not codifiable. Although aspects of Japanese management practices were unusual—for example, the appointment of nationals to formal positions whilst Japanese expatriates served as 'shadow' advisers—the principle was as old as multinational enterprise itself (Abo 1994).

As multinationals grew in size and complexity, so did the organizational obstacles to knowledge diffusion. It became a matter of negotiation between the multiple actors within firms, and it faced problems arising from incongruent incentives within organizations. There were often motivational barriers to such transfers. The knowledge possessed by an affiliate represented bargaining power. The extent and effectiveness of intrafirm knowledge transfer depended on the nature and efficiency of transmission channels within firms, including the willingness of head office to coerce, and also the nature of the knowledge, especially the extent to which it was tacit or ambiguous (Gupta and Govindarajan 2000; Foss and Pedersen 2002).

The large theoretical literature discussing intrafirm knowledge flows and the learning opportunities for firms opened up by internationalization is not matched by a wealth of empirical evidence concerning these processes (Kristensen and Zeitlin 2004). There is strong evidence from many of the historical examples discussed in this and earlier chapters that intrafirm knowledge transfers have not been smooth. The Ford cars sold in Britain and Germany in the 1930s were based on US designs, but these were developed in wholly different ways, and subsequently designs and technologies diverged even more. During the 1960s Ford opened research and development centers in both Germany and Britain, but with little coordination between them as they were embedded in their respective national organizations (Bonin, Lung, and Tolliday 2003). The deteriorating competitive performance of the US subsidiary of Courtaulds in the 1930s was due to manufacturing methods and organization that were much worse than those in the British parent. Yet the US-based managers withheld information, and opposed knowledge transfer, from the British parent (Coleman 1969).

Knowledge diffusion within multinationals was shaped by organizational context. A study of foreign-owned affiliates active in Canada between the 1880s and the 1950s showed that among the major features affecting decisions involving transfers of technology were the role played by managers in the affiliated firm in negotiating for these transfers, and the degree of control exercised by the parent company over the Canadian enterprise (Taylor 1994). In the case of Shell's US affiliate, Shell Oil, this was allowed considerable operational autonomy after World War II, but was constrained from undertaking its own FDI by its position within the wider group. This stimulated the American management to seek alternative growth opportunities by investing heavily in research. The affiliate developed technological competences which were superior to those of its parent. However, Shell could only fully access these competences by buying out the minority shareholders in the US affiliate in 1985 (Priest 2001). The multinational organization described in Bartlett and Ghoshal (1989) seems to have had particular problems achieving fast knowledge diffusion within its boundaries (see Box 7.5).

There is sufficient historical evidence to suggest that the view that multinationals provide a superior means to transfer knowledge across borders is more a supposition than a proven reality. International, global or transnational organizations might be more efficient than multinational organizations in this regard, but there is no reason to assume that they did not also confront obstacles to knowledge transfers. Despite the use of expatriates, there was limited international job mobility within multinationals, and given the importance of individuals in the spatial diffusion of knowledge, this is a major constraint. Indeed, a recent study concluded that multinationals are not particularly well equipped to continuously transfer technological knowledge across national borders and that its contribution to the international diffusion of knowledge has been 'overestimated' (Solvell and Zander 1998).

7.8 International marketing

As firms invested abroad they faced multiple marketing challenges. These included establishing how far products, brands, and prices needed to be different in different markets; how to create distribution channels or access existing channels abroad; and how far to adjust to local circumstances advertising, promotions, packaging and services. These issues have remained constants in international business.

International marketing preceded international production. Josiah Wedgwood, the eighteenth-century British potter who pioneered modern branding strategies, gave early attention to foreign markets, using celebrity marketing to persuade aristocrats and nobility to buy his products. By the 1780s Wedgwood exported almost 80 percent of his production (Koehn 2001). However, he did not establish his own selling organization abroad. Nor did British textile manufacturers whose exports rose dramatically after

Box 7.5 Creating and transferring knowledge at Unilever, 1950–90

From the 1950s Unilever dispersed its innovation across a large number of sites. Initially there was one central research laboratory in Port Sunlight (near Liverpool, Britain). Subsequently new laboratories were opened elsewhere. By 1970 Unilever had nine central research laboratories in four European countries, each with a distinctive competence. Port Sunlight was focused on soap and detergents. The Dutch laboratory at Vlaardingen was strongly oriented towards basic research in biochemistry and nutrition. There were also research laboratories in New Jersey and Mumbai, India. In addition, half of Unilever's worldwide research spending was conducted in local operating companies. This was largely concerned with product development, but also involved basic research. By 1980, 7,000 people were employed in Unilever's research laboratories.

The Unilever laboratories were responsible for many innovations in foods and household and personal care products, but there was concern about the apparent inability of high levels of research spending to translate into commercial products. Unilever's decentralized structure and a culture based on consensus slowed the commercialization and diffusion of research. New products and brands were typically transferred using personal relationships more than formal channels. A separation of research and marketing functions compounded the situation.

There were serious problems with the transfer of knowledge across the Atlantic because of the autonomous status of its US affiliates. There was no transfer of personnel over the Atlantic, and even visits by European executives to the United States were regulated by the affiliates. The degree of autonomy was striking in particular because of the poor performance of Lever in the US soap and detergents market, where it progressively lost market share. During the 1960s and 1970s Unilever could not transfer its considerable manufacturing and marketing knowledge in margarine, shampoo, and detergents from Europe to the United States, although capabilities in tea, soup, and toothpaste were transferred the other way.

Unilever's traditional reliance on personal networks to transfer information and knowledge worked especially badly because of the low level of socialization between the US affiliates and those elsewhere. In addition, Unilever's greater familiarity with European markets influenced the direction of knowledge flows as managers were better able to perceive opportunities in Europe than the other way round.

From the 1970s Unilever sought to improve its innovation performance. By 1980 many of the smaller European research laboratories were closed. Research was concentrated at sites in Britain and the Netherlands. During the 1990s continued concerns about under-performance in the commercialization of research led to a new regional strategy. Beginning in 1992, ten 'innovation centers' were established in personal care across the world, each with its own specialization, and each in contact with the Unilever central research laboratories.

(*Source*: Jones 2002; Jones and Kraft 2004; Unilever Annual Reports 1970–2000.)

the Industrial Revolution. They sold their products to wholesale merchants in other European countries or the United States. In the developing markets of Asia and Latin America, they used British merchants and trading companies as trade intermediaries (Jones 2000).

The branded and mechanized products of the Second Industrial Revolution required greater investment in international marketing. The competitive success of Singer in foreign markets rested heavily on marketing. During the 1870s Singer's British company expanded on Singer's domestic US strategy of selling on installment by introducing the concept of door-to-door salesmen (or canvassers) and collectors. These well-dressed and carefully trained agents went from home to home demonstrating sewing machines and selling installment plans, providing after-sales service, and collecting payments. This worked extremely successfully, and Singer adopted the strategy elsewhere. There was further adaptation as Singer expanded geographically. The British-style split between canvassers and collectors was inappropriate in more rural and sparsely populated Russia. Singer's managers in Russia innovated by merging the two positions and devising incentives to prevent opportunism (Carstensen 1984).

In some developing countries multinationals used local merchant networks to access markets. In late-nineteenth-century China, Standard Oil's products were sold through relatively autonomous networks of merchants, although by 1914 the US company had established its own distribution organization. The Japanese trading company Mitsui also replaced Chinese merchants with a hierarchy, and went further by replacing Chinese in the marketing function with Japanese nationals trained in the Chinese language. The cigarette company BAT employed both its own hierarchy and employed Chinese merchants. However the latter worked better, and during the interwar years were given primary responsibility for BAT's distribution (Cochran 2000).

During the late nineteenth century, as national markets replaced local markets, brands grew in importance as means to inform consumers about products and to provide guarantees of quality. Products which had been homogeneous began to be differentiated by brands (Wilkins 1994b). This raised the issue about the extent to which both products and brands were transferable across borders given variations in tastes and habits, and languages.

It was quickly realized that some product adaptation to local markets was critical. As William Lever began selling soap in foreign markets, he soon perceived that people in different countries liked to smell differently. Lever and other consumer products manufacturers needed to change the chemical compositions of their products, and change the packaging, to suit local conditions (Wilson 1954). As the Gramophone Company expanded to Russia, India, and elsewhere, it made numerous recordings of local artists and music before 1914 (Jones 1985). Even in the case of Ford, which made few modifications to local conditions as it expanded abroad, the British management of the company was able to secure permission for cars to be manufactured with right-hand drive. A nonexclusive dealer system also allowed dealers to make further modifications to the vehicles for local tastes (Bonin, Lung, and Tolliday 2003).

There were relatively few international brands. Local and regional brands were common in many industries. Manufacturers often translated brand names into local languages. Companies which used their own corporate names as brands were exceptions to this generalization. Ford initially used both the parent name and product names—such as Model T—in foreign markets. US branded food manufacturers such as Campbell and Heinz also used their names in international markets. Coca-Cola, which made its first foreign sale in 1899 and registered its trade market in its first foreign country—Canada—in 1905 and used its brand name abroad from the beginning (Giebelhaus 1994).

The situation was more complicated for companies which did not use their names as brands, and those which grew by merger and acquisition. Unilever owned hundreds of brands by the 1930s, many with strong national identities built up over the years. P&G's famous development of brand management system was said to have derived from watching the chaos of Unilever brands competing with one another in Europe in the 1930s. In neither case was the parent company's name used as a brand.

After World War II multinationals faced worldwide changes to both advertising medium and distribution channels, but their nature varied considerably between countries. In the United States there were six commercial television stations in 1945, and over 400 a decade later. Television advertising became a crucial component of marketing strategies (Tedlow 1993). Commercial television spread more slowly elsewhere. The first channel opened in Britain in 1955, and even later elsewhere in Europe. For many years there were restrictions on what could be advertised.

After World War II, consumer products multinationals faced increasing challenges as retailers grew in bargaining power, and in some case developed private labels. However, companies faced very different situations in different markets. European retailing became concentrated earlier than American, and private labels became much more important. Large European retailers increasingly promoted their own brands as part of their corporate image, and employed increasingly sophisticated advertising and promotions and favored in-store merchandizing to support their brands. US retailers were much slower to invest in quality brands and were less able to secure the image of good value and quality seen in Europe. While in some European markets retailer brands took one-third of packaged grocery sales by the 1990s, in the United States the percentage remained under one-fifth (Hoch and Banerji 1993; Williams 1994).

The use of different formulations and packaging for different countries was the norm rather than the exception. This often reflected local legislation, and cultural preferences were also important. In Asia, for example, the color red was associated with good luck and white with mourning, but in Western countries white was associated with purity and black with mourning. Consumer tastes remained highly specific. In foods, national taste preferences have continued to be diverse. Although Nestlé successfully developed *Nescafe* as a global brand, it had two hundred blends world-wide for this product in 2004 (*The Economist*, 7 August 2004). Climatic differences were important also. The formulation of petrol had to be changed to cope with extremes of temperature.

National legislation varied considerably even for a product such as ice cream. In Britain cheap vegetable substitutes and sugar were used instead of milk fat for making ice cream during World War II, and this usage has persisted. Almost all British ice cream remains non-dairy, and national legislation did not require a milk fat content. However in Germany 'ice cream' was required by law to contain at least 10 percent milk fat. The equivalent figure in France was 7 percent. French legislation even defined the minimum levels of natural flavors which could be used in ice cream (Reindeers 1999).

It remained a frequent occurrence for even the largest multinationals to misjudge foreign marketing (see Box 7.6). During 2004 Coca-Cola, which owned more than 20 water brands in more than 100 markets, had a disastrous launch in Europe of its *Dasani* bottled water brand. *Dasani* had become the second largest water brand in the United States following its launch in 1999, but this did not prevent multiple marketing problems. There was public outcry in Britain, where it was initially launched, after it was revealed that Dasani would use treated and purified tap water, while in France and Germany it would have been sourced from a spring in Belgium. The brand was finally recalled in Britain altogether within months after it was discovered that the purified water contained high levels of a non-metallic salt linked to a high risk of cancer (*Financial Times*, 25 March 2004).

After World War II US companies were more active in building 'global' brands than their European counterparts. They accounted for some of the best known global brand names including Coca-Cola, Avis, American Express, and McDonald's. There was a striking contrast between the branding strategies of P&G and Unilever. In 1975 Unilever marketed 665 detergents brands in the forty-two countries in which it operated, while P&G had 186 brands in the twenty-one countries in which it operated (Jones and Miskell

---

Box 7.6 Procter and Gamble and the Japanese market in the 1970s and 1980s

In 1972 P&G entered Japan through a joint venture with a small Japanese company which it bought out five years later. US brands, including Cheer laundry detergent, were transferred from the United States. Cheer could clean clothes at three different temperatures—hot, warm and cold. However as most Japanese washed their clothes in cold tap water, this advantage had no relevance. The product failed in the test market. P&G's introduction of the US practice of seeking good relationship with retailers had the effect of alienating small retailers and Japan's powerful wholesalers. P&G reintroduced *Cheer* in a high density formula in compact packages with appealing new lemon fragrance, but early gains were lost after 1977 as local competitors Kao and Lion launched products including new technologies. Cheer stabilized at less than 5 percent of the market.

When P&G introduced Pampers disposable baby diapers in Japan, it offered the US product without any modification. At that time 98 percent of the market was held by cloth diapers. Japanese babies were smaller than American babies and the American-sized products did not fit. Pampers met American standards for quality, but not the higher expectations in Japan. A Japanese competitor soon launched a better fitting and absorbing diaper.

By 1983 P&G had lost $300 million in Japan. The company responded with a set of initiatives labeled 'A Fresh Start'. This involved a greater awareness of the differences between Japan and the United States. In 1985 P&G put its best worldwide technology into new diaper products launched first in Japan rather than the United States. P&G collaborated with wholesalers and retailers to revise their terms of trade. P&G's sales in Japan increased from $132 million to $566 million between 1985 and 1988, and the company made its first profit in 1987.

(*Source*: Dyer, Dalzell, and Olegario 2004.)

2005). In industries such as alcoholic beverages, consistent brand positioning of 'global' brands came very late. Among many examples given by Lopes (2005), was the leading Scotch whisky brand *Glenfiddich*. This brand originated in 1886, but was not sold outside Scotland until the 1960s. When it was launched elsewhere, the brand image varied widely. In England it was associated with authenticity and tradition. In France and Italy, the brand image was of luxury and 'jet setting' lifestyles. It was only in the 1990s that a strategy was developed to create a global image for the brand.

In 1983 the American marketing professor Ted Levitt published a famous article on 'The Globalization of Markets' which predicted that world consumers would become homogenized (Levitt 1983). It became a classic in the marketing literature, but its predictions remained to be realized. Two decades later numerous local and regional markets remained. Ghemawat's (2001) cultural, political, geographic and economic distance framework demonstrated the continuing impact of distance on different products and industries. Cultural distance affected products with a high linguistic content or national identity, including foods. Administrative or political distance impacted demand for national champions or national security. Geographic distance impacted products which were perishable or fragile. Differences in the wealth and income of consumers, and disparities in supply chains and distribution channels, remained major barriers. However it was not merely a matter of obstacles. By the new century it was evident that the globalization of markets could produce a violent reaction in certain places and cultures (Tedlow and Abdelal 2004).

■ **SUMMARY**

The organizational history of multinationals was one of a constant search for the most effective means to control and benefit from cross-border operations. Geographical and cultural distance posed an enormous challenge to managers. The process of building organizations that were more efficient than markets that achieved the right balance between central direction and local responsiveness, and which could transfer knowledge more effectively, was neither automatic nor easy. Shifting technologies and political conditions meant that the organizational solutions of one generation easily became an organizational burden for the next. This meant that organizational learning was far from straightforward.

The past two centuries saw multiple forms of organization at any one time. Variants of the multinational, international, global and even transnational forms coexisted as firms experimented with ways to achieve efficiency, local responsiveness, and knowledge transfer. Biodiversity has been the norm. Organizational forms varied widely between industries, and within industries. Firms from different countries have organized cross-border business in different ways. Family firms have coexisted with managerial firms, and business groups with hierarchical firms.

PART IV

External Environment

8 | **Public policy**

8.1 **Multinationals and governments**

The relationship between firms and governments has been central to the history of multinationals. The tensions in this relationship derive from the fact that the borders of multinationals and nation states are not, by definition, identical. As a result, governments are confronted by economic entities whose ultimate control and ownership lies beyond their borders, while firms face multiple jurisdictions rooted in different political systems. The problem of jurisdictional asymmetry lies at the heart of the tensions between multinationals and governments.

This chapter reviews the historical evidence on relationship between multinationals and governments. Why have government policies towards multinationals oscillated over time? Why have different countries pursued different policies? How have firms influenced these policies? Which side has been the more powerful? Have firms undermined the sovereignty of nation states? How should the multinational firm be regulated?

8.2 **Governments as hosts**

8.2.1 **Developed economies**

During the eighteenth and nineteenth centuries European nation states, and the countries founded by their colonists such as the United States, grew in their capability to regulate, tax, and monitor individuals and firms within their borders. However, the national ownership of firms was rarely identified as an issue of importance by policy-makers. During the nineteenth century there were few barriers to the entry of foreign firms either by greenfield or acquisition; virtually no controls over the behavior of foreign firms; and only selected cases of official discrimination in favor of locally-owned firms against foreign firms.

During the second half of the nineteenth century there was a striking divergence between the trade and investment policies of many governments. The United States adopted one of the highest levels of protection in the world, but foreign firms could enter and operate there almost without restriction. The major exception was banking. Historically this was a politically sensitive industry for Americans. After the American Revolution, the two attempts to create nationwide banks, the Bank of the United States (1791–1811) and the Second Bank of the United States (1866–1941) attracted considerable foreign investment, but strong political opposition to the concentration of power resulted in the cancellation of their charters (Wilkins 1990). The United States developed a regulatory system designed to prevent banks from opening across state lines or over wide geographical distances.

Within this context, foreign ownership of banks was made progressively more difficult. Banks operated under either federal or state regulation. At federal level, the National Bank Act of 1864 restricted national banks from branching and specified that bank directors had to be US citizens resident in the area in which the bank did business. Foreign banks were also subject to state regulations which became increasingly restrictive. New York prevented foreign banks from receiving deposits or issuing bank notes. By 1914 Illinois was almost alone among states in permitting foreign banks to operate. From the late nineteenth century US state governments introduced wide-ranging restrictions on foreign participation in insurance companies and mortgage lenders. There were also laws restricting foreign land ownership, and foreign investors were barred from coastal shipping. In 1920 the Mineral Leasing Law excluded from leases on public land the citizens of any country whose laws, regulations or customs similarly denied such privileges to US citizens or corporations. This was used to threaten European governments which blocked US entry to oilfields in their colonies (Wilkins 1989; Venn 1986).

In nineteenth-century Europe, there were few restrictions on foreign companies. London flourished as the world's largest financial and trading center in which foreign bankers and firms could locate and operate without restrictions. Almost all of the merchant banks were founded by foreign emigrants. The Baring family were of Dutch origins. During the French Revolution and Napoleonic Wars between 1792 and 1815 German merchants such as the Schröders, Hambros and Rothschilds moved to London, establishing in time large international banking houses. Rothschilds, which became one of the biggest, functioned throughout the century in association with other branches of the Rothschild family living elsewhere in Europe (Ferguson 1998; Michie 1992).

Although London was wholly exceptional in the degree of cosmopolitanism in the nineteenth century, the lack of concern about the nationality of ownership was general. This policy stance did not shift with the intensification of nationalistic rivalries within Europe before World War I. The uniforms of British and French soldiers were dyed by the products made by the local affiliates of the German dyestuffs companies. Indeed, patent legislation requiring local production to secure patent rights was one factor in the establishment of these subsidiaries before 1914 (Hagen 1997a, b).

It was only in the petroleum industry that nationality had emerged as an issue before 1914. In the nineteenth century the use of petroleum for heating and lighting meant that it was regarded like any other commodity, but the use of the product in internal combustion engines and, especially, in warships, made it a strategic commodity. The location of most of the world's oil production in the United States and Russia, and the presence in the industry of the giant Standard Oil Company, was sufficient to alarm even British governments, the most laissez-faire in Europe. A policy of preventing Standard Oil and other foreign companies from searching for oil in British colonies was combined with support for British-owned oil companies searching for oil overseas. This trend culminated in the British government's acquisition of 51 percent of the equity of the Anglo-Persian Oil Company in 1914 (see Chapter 3).

World War I represented a major discontinuity in policy towards foreign ownership of companies on both sides of the Atlantic. Governments investigated the national ownership of firms, and expropriated without compensation the assets owned by enemy countries. This was a radical departure from the policy environment of the nineteenth century (see Box 8.1). There has yet to be a restoration of the laissez-faire policy towards foreign multinationals.

During the interwar years foreign ownership of companies was far more of an issue than previously. Several European countries, including France, Italy, and Spain, followed the British precedent of creating national oil companies. Nevertheless European governments had relatively few restrictions against foreign firms. In Britain, there was no formal legislation, although in practice, public policy excluded foreign ownership of banks and defense-related industries (Jones 1990a). In Germany there was much discussion about foreign influence over German business, but this did not translate into policy. GM was

---

Box 8.1 The impact of World War I on host government policies

Following the outbreak of World War I in Europe in July 1914, both sides began to investigate the ownership of firms on their territories. Enemy-owned firms were taken over by governments, and their assets sold in due course to local firms. Wartime expropriations of German corporate assets in Britain reached nearly $8 million (around $100 million in 2003). These assets included German-owned chemicals companies which were used to create the basis of a British-owned dyestuffs industry. In 1915 German-owned oil distribution and transport companies, including the British Petroleum Company, were taken over. Two years later they were transferred to the ownership of the Anglo-Persian Oil Company.

US firms such as Kodak, GE, Singer, Standard Oil of New Jersey and American Express continued to operate on both sides of the conflict. However, following the US entry into the war in April 1917, both sides took control of each other's business assets. In the United States, German assets were placed under the control of the Alien Property Trustee. After the end of the war, the sequestrated affiliates of German companies in the United States were sold to local firms with the intention of strengthening indigenous companies in sectors such as chemicals and electricals. Both physical assets and intellectual property, such as patents, were taken. The Bayer brand, Aspirin, and its registered trademark were sold to Sterling Drug. It was only in 1986 that Bayer recovered the right to use its own name in the United States. In 1994 it paid $1 billion to reacquire the right to use its trademark.

The largest expropriation of foreign business during the war occurred following the Communist Revolution in Russia in November 1917. The new government issued decrees that declared banking a state monopoly, repudiated government loans, abolished private ownership of land and natural resources, and confiscated the property of foreign firms. The total amount of FDI in Russia, which amounted to $1,150 million, was taken. In 1921 the Soviet Union acknowledged a legal obligation to compensate foreign claims for their expropriated investments, but it demanded that Western nations pay for the damage they had inflicted following their invasion of the country during the civil war which had followed the Revolution. Ultimately, few foreign companies received compensation.

(*Source*: Lipson 1985; Jones 1988.)

allowed to acquire Opel, Germany's leading automobile manufacturer in 1929, and GE purchased one-third of the equity of AEG, one of Germany's largest electrical companies (Feldman 1989). The tolerance of foreign firms continued even in Nazi Germany, provided they followed government policies, including the dismissal of Jewish employees. A number of US business leaders, including IBM's Thomas J. Watson, developed a close relationship with Nazi leaders (Tedlow 2003).

Paradoxically, it was the United States which saw the sharpest policy shift towards restricting foreign firms. Although the United States shifted from being the world's largest debtor nation to being a net creditor over the course of World War I, this was accompanied by a growing nationalism which resulted in major restrictions in a range of industries.

Box 8.2 The growth of US government restrictions on foreign firms 1914–40

During World War I there was a growing conviction among Americans that their economy should be under national control. A Shipping Act in 1916 further tightened restrictions on foreign participation in US shipping, and provided means to encourage American shipping. The share of US international trade carried on American flagships rose from 14 percent to 40 percent between 1913 and 1918. Following US entry into the war in April 1917, German and other enemy-owned firms was sequestrated.

Between 1919 and 1923 there was a surge of nationalist and anti-foreign (especially anti-British) feelings. Federal government policies restricted foreign firms in four industries. First, foreign (principally British) domination of international cables and radio was overturned. In 1918 the US Navy purchased 45 control stations and 330 ship stations from the Marconi Wireless Telegraph Company. The Navy also orchestrated the transfer of Marconi's radio stations to the newly created Radio Corporation of America (RCA), whose charter included the stipulation that no more than 20 percent of the voting could be held by foreigners. Second, the Merchant Marine Act (1920), excluded from coastal shipping, extended the definition of US citizens to corporations which were not at least 75 percent owned by citizens of the United States. Third, the Mineral Lands Leasing Law (1920) excluded from leases on public land the citizens of any country whose laws, regulations or customs denied such privileges to US citizens. Fourth, the Edge Act (1919) prohibited foreign investors from taking advantage of newly available (to domestic banks) forms of international banking. In addition, the Prohibition in 1919 of the manufacture, sale, and transport of alcoholic beverages to and within the United States had the effect of eliminating $150 million of British brewing assets in the country.

Following the Great Depression, restrictive legislation towards foreign multinationals was intensified. The Communications Act of 1934 expanded rules originally established in 1927 that forbade the granting of broadcasting licenses to foreign owners. The Civil Aeronautics Act (1938) expanded a 1926 law which specified that only a domestic business could carry air passengers from one place to the next within the United States. While the 1926 Act required a majority US ownership of domestic airlines, the new Act defined a domestic company as 75 percent owned by US citizens. The Revenue Act (1936) taxed the US income of foreign banks at a higher rate than that of domestic banks.

(*Source:* Wilkins 2004.)

During World War II both sides again sequestrated without compensation the business assets of the enemy. In Nazi Germany, all enemy-owned companies were taken under control (Linder 1991). In some cases, local managers continued to retain the firm's autonomy even though relations with the parent were cut off. After 1933, for example, the German subsidiary of US-owned Norton Company, a manufacturer of the bonded abrasives used in machine tool manufacture, had cooperated with the industrial policy of the Nazi regime, and was able to blunt hostility by appointing German nationals to the senior management. This management protected Norton's interests even after the United States entered the war against Germany, and even worked to protect Norton's assets in occupied France (Cheape 1988).

The conclusion of World War II restored democratic, liberal regimes in most of Western Europe, but not in other parts of that continent. The extension of Soviet influence in central and eastern Europe led to the nationalization of all foreign-owned businesses in these countries by the end of the 1940s. In Spain and Portugal, fascist regimes remained in place which disliked large firms, and especially foreign ones. These regimes imposed tight restrictions on multinationals, and sought a high level of focal participation in the equity of subsidiaries. As a result, telephone utility ITT, the mining company Rio Tinto and the automobile manufacturer Ford all divested from Spain between 1944 and 1954 (Mendoza 1994; Estape-Triay 2003).

Elsewhere in Europe, there was more intervention in business in general, and this included relations with multinationals. In France, Britain and elsewhere, nationalization closed most utilities and some other industries to private enterprise altogether. Exchange controls and import controls prompted US firms to establish local manufacturing, but were also used to 'screen' inward FDI proposals so they met desired policy goals regarding the balance of payments, and they were also used to prompt foreign companies to locate factories in regions of high unemployment. Although some US firms were blocked by such 'screening' in Britain and elsewhere, the actual number was not great (Jones 1990a; Rooth and Scott 2002).

During the 1960s policies became more restrictive. In France, growing alarm at foreign control over high technology industries was crystallized by a bid by GE to take over Machines Bull, France's largest computer firm. During 1965 the government virtually banned all foreign takeovers of French firms, and for a time blocked all applications for approval of new investments. Over the following decade the government screened inward investments, a process often involving lengthy delays. When foreign takeovers of French firms were proposed, such delays were used to find French purchasers instead (Safarian 1993). French national champions were also promoted in industries including electronics and computers, but with little long-term success. However, French policy was constrained by membership of the EU: a foreign investor barred from France could build a plant in another member country, and have unrestricted access to the French market. Moreover, the importance attached to attracting foreign technology led the government to acquiesce in takeovers of local firms which had been technologically outpaced by foreign competitors (Caron 1984).

There were echoes of the French policies elsewhere. In Britain, the Labour government between 1964 and 1970 sought 'assurances' from new foreign investors about their employment, capital investment and exports strategies, though little attempt was made to monitor the outcome (Jones 1990a). National champions were promoted in strategic industries including ball-bearings, automobiles, and computers, but again with no sustained success. In computers the government encouraged a merger of British firms to form ICL, and acquired 10 percent of the equity, but despite heavy R&D spending, it proved impossible to create a British competitor to IBM. ICL became dependent on the technology of Fujitsu during the 1980s, and was acquired by that Japanese company in 1990 (Campbell-Kelly 1989; Chandler 2001).

West German government policies were among the most liberal in Europe. There was no authorization or screening of firms on entry, or of foreign takeovers, except insofar as they affected antitrust policies. This tolerance only waned when it seemed that the governments of OPEC countries might use their oil wealth to buy up German companies. Iran's acquisition of 25 percent of Krupp, and the Kuwaiti government's purchase of a 14 percent interest in Daimler-Benz, led the government to ask banks and major companies to report impending sales of companies or large blocks of shares to foreigners, especially OPEC governments. In a few cases the government encouraged German investors to buy equity being offered for sale (Safarian 1993).

Japan and the United States represented different ends of the policy spectrum between the 1940s and 1980s. In Japan, government policies were highly restrictive (see Box 8.3). Even the largest foreign companies faced formidable obstruction. In 1956 IBM applied for the permission required to import the technology and other assets necessary to manufacture computers at its existing subsidiary in Japan, and to remit earnings from this activity. It was only four years later, after a threat to abandon any plan to manufacture in Japan, that IBM was finally given the permission it required. In return the US company had to license its basic computer patents to Japanese companies, including all seven major domestic computer manufacturers (Mason 1992).

In the United States, there were no limits on percentage ownership by foreign firms, nor on methods of market entry. The US regulations on foreign firms were virtually identical to the rules facing domestic US firms, but all the restrictions put in place in the interwar years remained. Federal law barred or limited foreign ownership in coastal shipping, radio and television broadcasting, operation of nuclear power facilities, and domestic air travel. Foreign-controlled firms were also not eligible for the facility security clearance required to bid on US defense contracts. At the state level, there were widespread restrictions on foreign companies in banking and insurance, and limitations on land use and ownership. Some states discriminated against foreign-owned firms in their public procurement (Safarian 1993). Although antitrust laws did not discriminate against foreign firms, they were sometimes employed as a protectionist device. Domestic firms threatened by foreign predators were able to use litigation—or else direct appeals to Federal or state agencies—to create lengthy delays and difficulties for foreign investors (Safarian 1993).

During the 1980s there was a worldwide public policy shift away from monitoring and restricting foreign firms. The globalization of the capital and money markets systematically undermined national controls over banking and financial systems, and over the ability of governments to influence the financial strategies of multinationals. The case for restrictions was undermined by their ineffectiveness. Governments proved unable to monitor multinational behavior effectively. In Europe, the national champion strategy

Box 8.3 Japanese policy towards multinationals before 1980

Between the 'opening' of Japan in the 1850s and 1899 foreigners were allowed to operate only within designated port areas, known as the 'Treaty Settlements'. However, for the next three decades policy became much more liberal. The acquisition of foreign technology was regarded as essential for the rapid modernization of the economy. Governments preferred foreign companies to form joint ventures with local companies, but wholly owned investments were permitted. Foreign companies were excluded from utilities, shipping, financial services, mining, and dyestuffs.

Japanese policy became highly restrictive after 1931. In the context of the increasing militarization of the Japanese economy, foreign ownership in strategic industries including petroleum, automobiles, machine tools, and aircraft manufacturing was strictly limited, and foreign-owned firms were discriminated against. After 1945 the Allied Occupation authorities retained a restrictionist policy. Foreign companies, it was feared, might complicate Japan's economic recovery. It was only in 1949 that inward FDI was again permitted, subject to approval of new investment proposals.

The key laws restricting multinationals were introduced during the Occupation, and retained after Japan recovered sovereignty. The Foreign Investment Law of 1950 regulated the acquisition by foreign investors of corporate stocks and proprietary interests. Each individual investment proposal was screened. Typically foreign investors were pressured to abandon FDI, and license their technology to Japanese companies; if the foreign investor refused to license, then a joint venture with a Japanese firm was proposed. Typically, the government would consult extensively with the local firms most directly affected by a proposed foreign entry. Foreign companies not approved under the Foreign Investment Law were subject to the Foreign Exchange Control Law, promulgated in 1949, which made every international transaction subject to official approval.

Public policy was not wholly responsible for the low inward FDI into Japan. It was not until the late 1950s that high economic growth rates began to make the country's economic prospects look attractive. The problems of operating in Japan ranged from the complex national language which took Western people a long time to master, to complex distribution channels. The widespread use of cross-shareholdings in keiretsu and kigyo shudan business groups also made acquisitions of local firms virtually impossible. These factors help to explain why inward FDI remained low even after liberalization policy began in 1967. The initial measures provided for automatic government approval for up to 100 percent FDI to establish new corporations in some industries, and for up to 50 percent FDI in others. The initial industries selected for liberalization included soy sauce, where substantial inward FDI was unlikely. In 1980 the Foreign Investment Law was abolished altogether, although restrictions remained longer in financial services and agriculture.

(*Source*: Mason 1992; Encarnation 1992.)

accumulated a record of costly failures (Moran 1993). The Reagan administration in the United States and the Thatcher government in Britain led the trend towards economic liberalism. In Britain, the election of Thatcher in 1979 was followed by the suspension of exchange controls, the progressive privatization of the state-owned sector, and the abandonment of the national champion strategy.

In the United States, the general trend towards removing restrictions, deregulation, and a much laxer enforcement of antitrust laws was usually only tempered by security concerns. In 1988 the Exon-Florio Amendment to the Defense Production Act gave the President powers to block foreign acquisitions of US firms which were held to be a threat to national security. In 1993 a Chinese state-owned firm was required to direct its holdings in a Seattle-based aircraft parts manufacturer (Wilkins 2001). Foreign ownership in broadcasting and aviation continued to be blocked.

In general, however, the most striking trend in all developed countries was the progressive dismantling of restrictions on entry, ownership, and dividend transfers. Manufacturing became fully open to FDI, although restrictions lasted longer in natural resources and services such as telecommunications, transportation, and media activities. An important element in this process was regional integration. In the European Union in particular, the Single Market program launched in 1986 was designed in part to facilitate regional integration by European companies by harmonizing national legislation and removing regulatory barriers to trade and factor flows. During the 1990s the liberalization process intensified (see Table 8.1).

The attraction rather than restriction of inward investment emerged as the primary policy concern. This reflected the rapid growth of unemployment following the oil shocks of the 1970s. A number of European countries and regions, particularly ones with high unemployment, had already sought to attract foreign firms during the 1950s and 1960s, including the Republic of Ireland which developed an extensive range of incentives for new industries. Subsequently most European governments began to offer incentives to inward investors. Canada and many states of the United States followed with tax concessions, subsidized sites and other infrastructure facilitation. By the 1990s even the Japanese government was providing incentives for foreign investors.

The level of subsidy was sometimes high. Daimler's Mercedes plant was attracted to Tuscaloosa, Alabama with incentives of $250 million. The total investment in the plant was $300 million, and the incentives were the equivalent of $167 000 per employee (Wilkins 2001). In both developed and developing countries, governments offered tax incentives and capital grants, infrastructure investment, and much else to attract multinationals. There was no return to the 'free markets' seen in the first global economy.

The relationships between companies and governments also became more complex. The sovereignty of national governments, especially in Europe, passed in part to regional

Table 8.1 Changes in national regulations of FDI, 1991–2002

	1991	1992	1993	1994	1995	1996	1997	1998	1999	2000	2001	2002
Number of countries that introduced changes in their investment regimes	35	43	57	49	64	65	76	60	63	69	71	70
Number of regulatory changes of which:	82	79	102	110	112	114	151	145	410	150	208	248
More favorable to FDI[a]	80	79	101	108	106	98	135	136	131	147	197	236
Less favorable to FDI[b]	2	—	1	2	6	16	16	9	9	3	14	12

[a]Including liberalizing changes or changes aimed at strengthening market functioning as well as increased incentives.
[b]Including changes aimed at increasing control as well as reducing incentives.
Source: United Nations (2003).

jurisdictions and regional blocks. This meant that companies, which were themselves often active in a range of strategic alliances or other cooperative arrangements with other companies, had to negotiate with several different layers of government. In Belgium, the authority of the national government was devolved to regional governments representing the two main language groups. Even FDI statistics were no longer collected nationally. Although national governments in Europe retained their own competition regulators, there was a striking growth in the power of EU competition regulators. EU competition regulators seemed stricter than their counterparts in the United States. In 2001 EU regulators blocked a proposed merger between General Electric and Honeywell, both US-based firms, which had been provisionally approved by US regulators. Three years later they sought to impose a $600 million fine on Microsoft for competition violations.

8.2.2 **Developing economies**

There were few restrictions on MNEs in the developing world before the interwar years. The colonial governments which controlled much of Asia and Africa generally followed the same open policies towards inward FDI as their home governments. In some instances colonial governments discriminated against the firms of other nationalities, especially in strategic sectors. In the 1900s Standard Oil found its attempt to obtain oil concessions in both the Dutch East Indies and British-controlled Burma blocked by their colonial governments (Reed 1958; Wilkins 1970; Jones 1981). There were major tensions again at the end of the 1920s when the British government sought to block US companies securing concessions in the British 'protected' Gulf sheikhdoms of Bahrain and Kuwait, both suspected of possessing rich oil resources. However, Standard Oil of California was eventually able to secure a concession in Bahrain by forming a Canadian subsidiary, which was regarded as 'British', while Gulf Oil formed a 50/50 joint venture in Kuwait with the Anglo-Persian Oil Company (Wilkins 1974a; Ferrier 1982).

In general, colonial governments did not restrict inward FDI. There were US manufacturing and distribution investments in India and other parts of the British Empire which operated without restriction (Wilkins 1970, 1974a). Swedish Match established a multiplant business in India which, by 1932, accounted for half of all Indian match production (Modig 1979). British-owned Lever Brothers was awarded some amount of land in the Belgian Congo, which it managed using a Belgian-registered, but wholly owned, subsidiary (Wilson 1954; Fieldhouse 1978).

Countries which remained outside Western imperial control, including China, Thailand, and Iran, had more autonomy in dealing with foreign companies. Yet their acceptance of international property law, a perceived need for foreign entrepreneurship and technology, the weaknesses of state structures, and the diplomatic and military hegemony of the West seldom left their governments with much room for maneuver. Thailand, surrounded by either French or British colonies, sought to retain some autonomy by awarding concessions to firms of different nationalities.

In Latin America during the second half of the nineteenth century, there was a widespread belief in liberal economic policies, including free trade, and a strong conviction that economic modernization would be facilitated by foreign business (Abel and

Lewis 1985). Insofar as government restrictions against FDI existed, they were largely found in the financial sector. In Argentina between the mid-1880s and the mid-1890s, there was an attempt to develop a state-owned venture as a quasi state or development bank, and to subject the British banks to taxation. This strategy faltered when it and other local banks collapsed during the Baring Crisis of 1890, and from the mid-1890s there were few government attempts to restrict the activities of the British banks (Jones 1993).

The interwar years witnessed a reaction against foreign firms, especially in the petroleum industry, and in a number of countries in the Middle East and Latin America. In Iran there was the cancellation and subsequent renegotiation of the Anglo-Persian Oil Company's concession in 1932 (see Box 10.6). In Argentina, a state oil company—YPF—had coexisted with foreign companies since 1907, but in the mid-1930s the government reserved for YPF the areas most likely to have petroleum deposits. Subsequently the government forbade both oil imports and exports, and placed oil distribution under strict government regulation. In Venezuela, which had been a haven for foreign oil companies until the death of the dictator Gómez in 1935, legislation obliged the companies to provide a wide range of social benefits for their workers, and in 1938 a new law authorized the Venezuelan government to enter the oil industry (Wilkins 1974a).

In 1937 Latin American policies towards foreign oil companies took a new turn when the Bolivian government expropriated Jersey Standard's properties in that country. The US company had found oil in Bolivia in the 1920s, but relations with the government had deteriorated at the end of the decade, when Jersey had cut production and stopped exporting in response to an increase in tax rates and the lack of a cheap means of oil transportation. The most noted Latin American nationalization occurred a year later in 1938, in Mexico. There had been continuing tension between the foreign oil companies and the Mexican government since the adoption of the 1917 constitution, which had vested direct ownership of all subsoil rights in the Mexican nation. A serious area of contention was the Mexican insistence that foreign oil companies obey Mexican labor laws. Finally, in 1938 the government expropriated most of the foreign oil industry, which was dominated by Shell and Jersey Standard (Wilkins 1974a; Venn 1986). This assertion of national sovereignty over natural resources was of enormous significance, as was the fact that the Mexicans succeeded in their goals without retaliation from Western governments, thanks in part to the fortuitous outbreak of World War II.

These specific measures against oil companies formed part of wider regional propensities to restrict inward FDI. In the Middle East, Turkey and Iran's interwar modernization programs involved the use of state-owned or sponsored enterprises which challenged existing foreign firms, and left no room for new entrants. Latin American governments introduced new controls over foreign mining companies, obliging them to hire indigenous personnel and to provide welfare benefits. Much FDI in agricultural properties was nationalized, especially in Mexico in the 1930s. Foreign-owned transport and energy utilities, as highly visible 'natural' monopolies producers of essential services and large employers of labor, proved easy targets for nationalistic politicians. They were subjected to new government controls, which added to the burdens they faced from depreciating local currencies, and rate structures fixed and controlled by host governments.

The environment for international business changed markedly in Latin America as a result of government policies. Utilities became highly regulated, and foreign firms were excluded from activities. In 1937 a new Brazilian constitution forbade any company with foreign stockholders from obtaining new hydroelectrical concessions (Wilkins 1974a). Yet at this stage foreign companies more often faced a deteriorating business environment in Latin America rather than total exclusion. Companies were often able to negotiate to mitigate the impact of some legislation to find ways to get round new laws (Eakin 1989). The potential for negotiation, evasion, and compromise was considerable.

World War II and its aftermath intensified pressures against foreign firms. The Communist Revolution in China in 1949 was followed by the withdrawal of all privileges from foreign enterprises and the establishment of total state control over foreign trade. Over the following few years the government took control of all foreign companies in China (Shai 1996). The spread of Communism to North Korea and North Vietnam, and to Cuba after 1961, further closed countries to foreign companies.

Elsewhere, the end of colonial empires usually moved policy in a more restrictive direction. During the last years of colonial role in countries such as Nigeria and Kenya, British colonial administrators preferred to promote political tranquillity rather than support British or other foreign firms. In Nigeria, the colonial government created marketing boards in the late 1940s which undermined the international trading business of the incumbent large European trading companies, including Unilever's United Africa Company (Tignor 1998). After independence, the new governments were anxious to establish their national identities, and this often involved seeking to curtail or limit foreign investment in their economies. The association of foreign companies with former colonial powers, their employment of expatriates in senior positions, their past history (real or imagined) of discrimination against local workers, and their embodiment of alien cultural values all contributed to the suspicion with which foreign companies were regarded. (The case of India is discussed in Box 8.4.)

Foreign control over resources and utilities aroused the greatest sensitivities. Mining and petroleum often dominated economic activity—and especially exports—in developing economies, and foreign ownership was regarded as incompatible with national control over such vital resources. Reactions against multinationals were particularly strong in countries where a handful of companies dominated the key industries.

The Middle East became a particular focus of hostility to Western business in the early 1950s. In 1951 Iran nationalized its oil industry. The subsequent boycott of Iranian oil by Western oil companies and a British- and American-inspired coup which overthrew the government in 1953 secured the reversal of this policy, though at a cost. The monopoly of the Anglo-Persian Oil Company (renamed British Petroleum in 1954) was broken and it returned to Iran with only a 40 percent stake in a new oil consortium, with the residual shared between other major oil companies (Bamberg 1994).

In Egypt, the overthrow of the former monarchy in 1952 and the advent the more nationalist government of Colonel Nasser led in 1956 to the nationalization of the Suez Canal Company, a French concessionary company which operated the Suez Canal. The nationalization led to a violent reaction by France and Britain, whose armies invaded Egypt in collusion with Israel. Their subsequent withdrawal, under US pressure, was followed by the nationalization of all British and French FDI in 1957. Subsequently Egyptian-style 'Arab socialism' exercised a strong influence on a number of neighboring countries, especially Syria and Iraq, which nationalized foreign assets in the early 1960s (Jones 1987).

Box 8.4 India's policy towards foreign firms after 1947

On independence from Britain in 1947, India was a large host economy. The official policy of the ruling Congress Party was to limit foreign enterprise's role in India and, ultimately, see its transfer into indigenous hands, but no specific legislation was introduced initially to achieve these goals. There were no restrictions on the 100 percent ownership of Indian subsidiaries, but the authorities exerted informed pressure on foreign companies to sell part of their equity to local investors. The policy environment was sufficiently unpredictable to discourage new entrants into India, while some companies, including Ford, withdrew rather than permit local capital participation.

There was a shift towards a more liberal policy in 1957. A major foreign exchange crisis threatened access to the foreign technologies which the government sought to facilitate its import substitution policies. If multinationals brought technology and finance into India, they were permitted to retain full managerial control. The new policy regime encouraged a considerable flow of new FDI in India. While in 1957 foreign firms controlled one-tenth of India's corporate assets, ten years later the proportion had risen to one-fifth.

During the early 1970s, policy became very restrictive. Enterprises with over 40 percent foreign ownership were classified as tightly-regulated FERA (Foreign Exchange Regulation Act) firms. Companies including IBM and Coca-Cola divested, while there were few entrants. Most companies reduced their shareholdings in Indian affiliates to 40 percent or less. A rare exception was the Indian affiliate of Unilever, which was able to remain majority-owned through the skilful bargaining of its management—which was headed by Indian nationals after 1956—the company's investment in heavy chemicals, and a high profile commitment to rural development. Hindustan Lever grew as one of India's largest private sector companies.

India became an unusual developing economy. It had a fairly large industrial sector, which was largely locally owned, and achieved considerable self-reliance in technology. Yet, export performance was poor. Between 1960 and 1980 India's per capita income grew by only 1.4 percent per annum.

During the 1990s Indian policies towards foreign multinationals began to be radically revised. The first liberalization in 1991 provided automatic approval of FDI project proposals with up to 51 percent foreign equity ownership in 34 priority industries. In 1993 full ownership was allowed for foreign firms on a case by case basis. This liberalization resulted in the re-entry of prominent multinationals such as IBM and Coca-Cola which had disinvested in the 1970s and 1980s, though India's complex web of regulatory controls, bureaucratic corruption, and lack of adequate infrastructure, continued to act as major constraints on the attraction of FDI.

(*Source*: Fieldhouse 1978; Encarnation 1989; Balasubramanyan and Mahambare 2003.)

The growth of more restrictive policies towards foreign firms took place in the context of an increase in state intervention in many developing countries as governments pursued import substitution strategies. This was often combined with extensive controls over the private sector, including industrial licensing and import restrictions. These policies had the result of both closing off some activities to foreign participation, as well as controlling the behavior of foreign firms in the remaining ones. However, the outcomes were not always negative for multinationals, especially in manufacturing. In Brazil, high tariffs and on imports of manufactured goods during the 1950s were combined with incentives, such as subsidies on imports of machinery and equipment, to attract multinationals. They were allowed to serve the Brazilian market through wholly owned subsidiaries, and to acquire Brazilian firms. By the beginning of the 1970s multinationals held about half of the assets of the largest manufacturing firms in Brazil (Encarnation 1989; Fritsch and Franco 1991).

For governments seeking to control their national economies, the ability of multinationals to move resources across borders was perceived as much as a threat as an opportunity. The importance of intrafirm trade in natural resources and, later, manufacturing raised questions about the prices—transfer prices—charged to affiliates within companies. The ability to set prices in such a way as to maximize overall profits within the group as a whole suggested that multinationals were well-placed to avoid taxation and distort prices. The limited administrative resources of most developing countries rendered counter-strategies hard to sustain. An investigation of the transfer pricing issue by the Colombian government for the period 1967–70 estimated that import prices for pharmaceuticals were 87 percent greater than the world price. In that case, government action against the multinationals involved resulted in an annual saving of $3.3 million out of an import bill of $15 million (Lall 1973).

There were only a limited number of expropriations without compensation before the late 1960s. Given the American domination of the world economy outside the Communist block, the threat of economic sanctions—and the American capacity for military intervention—were major deterrents. However, Western countries were unable to get international bodies such as the United Nations to guarantee the property rights of international investors. A series of United Nations resolutions affirmed the right of member states to nationalize natural resources. The Charter of Economic Rights and Duties of States, passed by the General Assembly in December 1974, provided a wide-ranging endorsement of national efforts to control foreign companies, by expropriation, contract abrogation and other tactics (Lipson 1985).

During the 1970s the number of expropriations rose rapidly (see Figure 8.1). These expropriations demonstrated that the West, and the United States in particular, was no longer able nor willing to use its power to protect foreign investments. Nonetheless, less than 5 percent of all foreign-owned firms in developing countries were expropriated between 1960 and 1976. Less than thirty countries, mostly in Africa and the Middle East, accounted for nearly two-thirds of all expropriation acts. The expropriations were also heavily concentrated in petroleum, mining, other natural resources, and public utilities. By 1976 the nationalization of large-scale mining and petroleum ventures was virtually complete throughout the entire developing world (Kobrin 1984; Kennedy 1992).

In many instances, foreign participation continued by means of management and other contracts. Multinationals sometimes used nationalization as a strategy for strengthening relationships with host governments. The Kenyan government in the late 1960s and early 1970s introduced a range of policy instruments to constrain the operations of foreign companies, and partially nationalized some industries including banking, cement manufacturing, and bus transport. These nationalizations were often

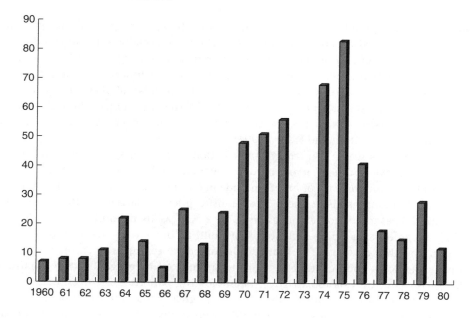

Fig. 8.1 Number of expropriations in developing countries, 1960–80.
Source: Kennedy 1992.

undertaken at the initiative of the companies, which desired government partners to ensure access to the machinery of government, or to facilitate repatriation of capital back to head offices. The reality of relations between the multinationals and the Kenyan government was, thus, quite different than that suggested by the public image of expropriation (Langdon 1981).

Many governments which did not seek to exclude foreign companies altogether nonetheless insisted that they should form joint ventures with local partners. Government policies were a major reason why so many MNEs used joint ventures in developing countries. As host government policies liberalized in the 1980s, there was a sharp fall in the formation of joint ventures (Contractor 1990).

The lack of a correlation between government policies and economic performance was demonstrated in the case of the fast-growing Asian NIC economies. Both South Korea and Taiwan pursued restrictive policies towards foreign companies. They operated Japanese-style restrictions on inward FDI, restricted foreign participation in many sectors, and encouraged it to take the form of joint ventures or licensing in others. Both governments sought to combine the acquisition of foreign technology with the development of local innovative capabilities. In contrast, the British colonial administration in Hong Kong pursued a laissez-faire policy with open access to firms of all nationalities. Singapore combined an open policy towards foreign firms with extensive state intervention to promote economic development (see Box 8.5).

As in developed economies, hostility towards multinationals waned during the 1980s. The nationalization of the sensitive natural resource industries was virtually complete by the mid-1970s. The passage of time reduced previous sensitivities about colonial

Box 8.5 Singapore as an open economy after 1965

Virtually from the state's full independence in the mid-1960s, Singapore had one of the most open policy regimes towards foreign multinationals anywhere in the world. During its long history as a British colony, Singapore had always been an entrepôt, but trade patterns changed as the European empires were dismantled and neighboring countries began to raise tariff barriers. For a short period, Singapore planned a strategy of mild import substitution based on access to the larger market of Malaya, which had become independent in 1957. Singapore joined the Federation of Malaysia in 1963, but political tensions led to separation only two years later. As a small island lacking in resources, an import substitution strategy was not practical. The result was the adoption of an export-led growth strategy.

The government introduced one of the world's most liberal policies towards inward investors. Trade barriers were sharply reduced. Investment incentives were offered in the form of low taxes and minimum control over operations. There were almost no controls on foreign exchange and licensing, the extent of foreign ownership, imports of machinery, local content requirements, employment of foreign personnel, ownership of real estate or acquisitions. There were no laws regulating competition or market dominance.

The Singaporean policy coincided with the new strategies of multinationals in electronics and other industries to embark on policies of worldwide sourcing. Singapore's cheap and flexible labor force made it an attractive location for manufacturing for world markets. However, the government also invested extensively in communications, education and other infrastructure facilities. State-owned companies, which included Singapore Airlines, and the Development Bank of Singapore, facilitated the government's strategy to create an attractive environment for international business, and to constantly upgrade it. There were also tight controls over wages, working conditions and labor-management relations.

The investment climate was facilitated by a high level of stability. The country was a democracy, but control has remained in the hands of a single party since Independence. The Prime Minister between 1959 and 1990, Lee Kuan Yew, paid special attention to the creation of a highly professional and honest bureaucracy. Singapore grew as one of the least corrupt countries in the world. Between 1960 and 1980 Singapore's per capita income grew by 7 percent per annum. By 2004 the country had one of the world's highest per capita incomes.

(*Source*: Mirza 1986; Huff 1997.)

dependencies. Over time the administrative capabilities of some countries increased sufficiently to make regulatory control—rather than simple expropriation—a viable policy option. There was evidence of the growth of host country capabilities over time, though the mass expropriation undertaken by the new Islamic Republic of Iran in 1979–80 occurred in a country which had achieved a high level of regulatory control over multinationals (Kennedy 1992; Kobrin 1984).

A further influence on the changed policy emphasis was the relative lack of success of earlier strategies. Many countries experienced disappointing results from the nationalization of their natural resource industries. Productivity fell sharply, new technologies were not introduced, companies were used as employment devices, and managerial inefficiency proliferated. There was sometimes a painful recognition that host government policies were constrained by their ability to implement them. In many sub-Saharan countries state-owned firms became keywords for incompetence.

From the 1980s many developing hosts liberalized their policies towards inward investment. There was a widespread adoption of policies designed to attract export-oriented manufacturing industries or projects involving advanced technology. Rather more slowly, access to service industries which had been closed to foreign companies began to be opened, and restrictions on the natural resource sector were lifted. Privatization reopened access to natural resource industries which had been nationalized in earlier decades. There was also a widespread abandonment of compulsory joint ventures with government or local private participation.

The policy environment faced by foreign companies changed radically as a result. In Latin America a catalyst for change was the outbreak of the world debt crisis in 1982 following Mexico's declaration of the government's inability to service its foreign bank debt. In 1986 Mexico joined GATT, and began reducing tariff and other trade barriers. Within a decade restrictions on ownership, prohibition of remittances and local content had been swept away in most of Latin America. During the 1990s the privatization of state-owned airlines, telephone companies, utilities, and banks opened up formerly closed sectors to multinationals.

Regional integration added to the forces behind policy liberalization. Mexico's membership of NAFTA in 1994 introduced national treatment standards for foreign investors. Although the NAFTA agreement incorporated existing restrictions, and Mexico reserved the right to legislate in entertainment, telecommunications, and social services, it was prohibited from introducing new discriminatory measures, especially against American and Canadian investors, without breaking the agreement (Grosse 2001; United Nations 2003).

The sharpest policy changes occurred in the Communist or former Communist countries which were reopened to FDI. The most dramatic consequences were seen in China, where the gradual opening of the domestic market to FDI in the 1980s and the extension of the liberalization program to services in the following decade, facilitated China's sudden emergence as the single largest host economy among the developing countries (see Box 8.6).

The Chinese experience was mirrored, on a less dramatic scale, in the transition economies of central and eastern Europe. Beginning in 1989, these formerly closed economies opened their industries to inward FDI. By 1992 wholly owned FDI was permitted in most of the region. The accession of many of these countries to the European Union in 2004 completed the harmonization of their investment regimes with the rest of Europe. The Russian Federation also substantially liberalized its regulation on FDI, but foreign ownership faced other restrictions, especially in natural resources. Foreign investors also faced serious issues related to the rule of law and the protection of intellectual property rights. Consequently flows of inward FDI into Russia remained subdued.

During the 1990s most sub-Saharan African countries also underwent a widespread liberalization of their inward FDI policies, which had become some of the most restrictive in the world. Many countries abolished requirements for government or local

---

Box 8.6 The liberalization of FDI policy in China since 1979

The Communist Revolution in China in 1949 resulted in the elimination of all inward FDI within a few years. Foreign companies were not allowed to invest in the country until 1978. In that year, a policy of liberalization began to facilitate the goal of modernization and development sought by the country's leader, Deng Xiaoping. Although China remained a Communist dictatorship, which ruthlessly suppressed political dissent, Deng opened the economy to market forces, arguing that it did not matter whether a 'white cat' or a 'black cat' was used to catch a mouse, or achieve economic prosperity.

In 1979 China formally opened itself to FDI by establishing the Equity Joint Venture Law, which explicitly outlawed the nationalization of foreign investor assets without due cause and compensation. FDI was limited to certain economic sectors. Although the Law allowed unlimited foreign investment in joint ventures, it required a Chinese citizen to be the venture's board chairman, no matter how much foreign equity was contributed. Over the next two decades, FDI controls were liberalized. In 1980, Special Economic Zones (SEZ), which offered a wide range of economic benefits and tax advantages, were created near major industrial hubs. From 1986 to 1991, China began actively promoting FDI across the country. Many joint ventures and wholly-owned foreign enterprises received more favorable economic benefits than did many State Owned Enterprises (SOEs) and private domestic firms. In 1992, restrictions on FDI were lifted in several economic sectors: distribution, transportation, and finance. Foreign power companies were allowed to build and operate plants for the first time. Joint ventures in transportation, port development, oil exploration, and financial services were permitted, though they all faced significant limitations.

China's accession to the WTO in 2001 led to the introduction of more favorable FDI legislation. General commitments included nondiscriminatory treatment of foreign and domestic enterprises, adherence to WTO rules on intellectual property rights, and the elimination of various restrictions on foreign exchange, local content and technology transfer. WTO membership also began the liberalization of the tight restrictions on foreign participation in services, infrastructure and high-technology industries. Foreign companies continued to experience problems related to the degree of official corruption and the lack of a strong legal environment. Foreign companies had little confidence in the willingness of Chinese courts to enforce contracts.

(*Source*: Huang 2003; Tseng and Zebregs 2003.)

---

participation in business ventures, although there were often restrictions in utilities, resources and services. However, it was less the regulatory framework which deterred foreign investors, than wider concerns related to physical infrastructure, access to global markets, and lack of transparency in legal and administrative processes. Above all, sub-Saharan Africa suffered from a severe 'image' problem (United Nations 2000).

8.2.3 Explaining long-term national differences in policies

Within the broad chronological shifts in host government policies towards foreign firms, there were evidently variations between countries in the extent to which they have been identified as entries which needed to be restricted or controlled. These differences in policy orientation have not simply mirrored differences between 'rich' and 'poor' countries, a number of other factors seem to be important.

First, there was a correlation between open policies and the extent of a country's outward FDI. Countries with large amounts of multinational investment, including the United States and Britain, had to consider the danger of retaliation against their own firms if restrictive policies were pursued against other nation's companies. Conversely, countries with low outward FDI have been more often found with restrictive policy stances.

Second, policies towards foreign firms reflected the wider industrial policy background of each country. Governments which followed liberal, market-oriented economic policies have generally not sought to restrict or tightly control foreign business. Governments which had more active industrial policies were more inclined to regulate foreign companies, as they threatened their control over the economy.

Third, the industrial distribution of inward FDI has been a factor. Foreign control over politically sensitive or strategic industries such as resources, banks and airlines aroused considerable concern in many countries. Inward investment in manufacturing industries has tended to be less controversial, although certain sectors, including defense, computers and automobiles, were often seen as sensitive for prestige or security reasons.

Fourth, the nationality of investing firms has affected policy. In developing economies, governments were often hostile to multinationals from former imperial powers. In contrast, linguistic and cultural similarities between home and host countries tended to reduce tensions. During the 1970s and 1980s public opinion in the United States was far more alarmed by Japanese multinational investment than by the much larger amount of FDI from Britain.

Fifth, large economies have often been more restrictive than small ones. The list of the most restrictive countries in the twentieth century included Russia, China, and India. In contrast, Switzerland, Belgium, and the Netherlands, and, in more recent decades, Singapore and Hong Kong, have been consistently liberal. These countries had small national markets, and a high degree of trade dependency.

A final influence on host government policies has been the cultural and historical inheritance of the country. Japan's self-imposed isolation from the rest of the world during the Edo period from the seventeenth to the nineteenth century both reflected a strong resistance to foreign cultural influence, and re-enforced such sentiments. Conversely, countries with a long tradition of being open trading economies were usually less concerned about foreign participation in their economies.

8.3 Governments as homes

From the nineteenth century, governments were aware that national diplomatic influence and national economic influence were related. This led European and US governments to support their nationals generally—by seeking to secure their access to, and safety in, foreign markets—and more specifically, when military interventions were made in developing countries to protect business interests. In countries of great strategic interest, such as China before World War I, European governments and their business interests worked closely with one another. Certain natural resources, notably petroleum, were of such strategic interest that the industry became thoroughly political. The inter-war Middle Eastern oil industry was a prominent example of a situation in which diplomatic and corporate rivalries overlapped and reinforced one another. The use of subsidies and other forms of assistance to support shipping companies, airlines and other symbols or sources of influence in foreign countries was also widespread before World War II.

By the interwar years, governments were also aware of possible negative consequences from outward investment by their firms. In the United States, the Republican administration of the 1920s generally encouraged US firms to move abroad, but also expressed concerns about the consequences, including the export of jobs and technology, and of the dangers of creating competition abroad to US exports. However, these concerns did not translate into policies to restrict US outward FDI. Instead, some positive inducement was given to US firms in the form of tax concessions to invest in less developed areas, especially in Latin America and China (Wilkins 1974a).

The spread of exchange controls extended the ability of home governments to control foreign investment permits by their firms. After the Nazi regime came into power in 1933, all new FDI had to be approved officially. As the regime wanted to retain investment in Germany, only exceptional investments were permitted (Schröter 1993a). In contrast, Britain's exchange controls were designed to curb flows of portfolio investment rather than FDI. However they may have limited the creation of new free-standing firms, because the former method of financing new ventures overseas by subscription and issue of fresh capital was made difficult.

During the 1930s Japanese governments promoted Japanese overseas business activities in the wake of its military aggression against China. Many of the investments made by Japanese firms in China in the 1930s were Chinese plants occupied by the Japanese Army, and turned over to Japanese companies for their management. After the outbreak of full-scale war with China in 1937, Japanese enterprises were progressively integrated into the tightly controlled war economy (Yasumuro 1984; Maeda 1990).

After World War II, home country policies towards outward investment continued on a rather low-key basis. The US government generally sought to provide a supportive environment for US FDI, which was seen as making an important contribution to world economic welfare. At times guarantees were offered against currency devaluation and expropriations (Behrman and Grosse 1990). The thrust of US policy in the 1950s and 1960s was to encourage US companies to invest in less developed countries through guarantees and soft and hard currency loans. In 1962 Congress also passed a measure—the Hickenlooper Amendment—that threatened the withdrawal of US foreign aid to a country if expropriation of US properties was not followed by prompt and adequate compensation (Wilkins 1974a). In practice, this threat was rarely implemented, at least till before the end of the Cold War.

Home governments typically supported their firms in foreign countries if they encountered difficulties, but the nature of that support varied enormously with the size and strategic importance of the investment, the nature of the host economy, and the prevailing circumstances. In the immediate postwar decades, this sometimes led to military intervention. The more prominent examples included the overthrow of the Iranian government in 1953, in a coup orchestrated by the British and American secret services, and the British and French invasion of Egypt in 1956 following the nationalization of the Suez Canal. In Central America, the US military intervention in Guatemala in 1954 to stop that government from taking unused lands of the United Fruit Company for redistribution to peasants became notorious. These episodes were exceptional, and more generally home governments used a mixture of diplomatic persuasion and coercion to support their firms abroad.

Concerns about the economic impact of outward investment sometimes resulted in government action. European governments used exchange controls to monitor, and sometimes restrict, capital flows. The regulations usually covered fresh capital funded by parent companies or raised for acquisitions, as distinct from overseas profits reinvestment, and their main impact may have been to influence the method of financing FDI by encouraging the use of overseas borrowing and retained earnings. In 1965 US firms were also asked voluntarily to limit the outflow of capital to their affiliates in developed countries, and also to increase the inflow of their dividends. However, the ability of firms to borrow abroad to finance their foreign operations meant that the overall effect on US multinationals was small, beyond increasing such foreign borrowings. The capital controls were liberalized in 1969 and removed five years later (Safarian 1993; Wilkins 1974a).

The only country which sought to restrict outward FDI on a large scale was Japan. Under the terms of the Foreign Exchange and Foreign Trade Control Law of 1949, the Japanese authorities regulated all overseas investments. Over the following two decades, the government scrutinized every potential Japanese FDI abroad, and denied requisite foreign exchange to those investment proposals that did not gain their approval. The main policy aim was to retain scarce capital in Japan to reindustrialize the country. FDI was not completely suppressed by these controls, but it was heavily dampened. Generally, the policy-makers favored investment applications that either promoted Japanese exports of manufactured goods or secured Japanese imports of initial raw materials. Proposed investments that threatened Japanese producers at home were unwelcome. It was only in the late 1960s, as Japanese trade surpluses rose, that these capital controls began to be liberalized. In 1972 all remaining restrictions on manufacturers were removed, and by 1980 banks had also been largely freed from such controls (Encarnation 1992).

Home governments sometimes introduced laws to regulate the behavior of their firms. During the 1970s the corporate use of bribery raised widespread concern. The most prominent cases included payments by United Fruit to Honduran government officials in an attempt to bring down the export tax on bananas, and evidence of widespread bribery by Lockheed, then a leading US aerospace manufacturer, of senior individuals in Japan and Europe. These kinds of incidents led to US legislation on corporate bribery, which obliged disclosure of illegal or improper payments to government officials. The Foreign Corrupt Practices Act of 1976, however, was not emulated by other home economies (Safarian 1993). In Europe, bribes were sometimes tax deductible.

During the 1980s there were also legislative moves in the United States, but not elsewhere, to restrict US investment in South Africa because of its apartheid policies.

In 1986 the US Congress passed the Comprehensive Anti-Apartheid Act banning all US investment, exports and imports from South Africa. However this did not oblige US firms with existing investments to leave (Kline 1997).

National attempts to develop and legislate standards for multinationals ran the risk of jurisdictional conflicts due to differences in policies or legal approaches. The United States in particular has sought to extend its jurisdictional reach extraterritorially. An early example came in the early 1950s when US courts sought to apply antitrust laws to the British chemicals company ICI with respect to its cartel agreements with the US company Du Pont outside the United States (see Chapter 3). This resulted in the US courts requiring action which the British courts then prohibited. Subsequently the United States regularly sought to enforce its laws against trading with China, Cuba, and other proscribed countries on the foreign affiliates of US corporations. As those affiliates were under the jurisdiction of European, Canadian, and other countries which opposed the US laws, this gave rise to serious jurisdictional conflicts (Kobrin 2001).

In this respect, multinationals restrict the sovereignty of their home governments as much as they do host governments. Each multinational corporation is headquartered in a single country—with the idiosyncratic exception of the handful of companies organized with two parent companies in different countries—because a firm can only register its existence in a nation state. However, no single jurisdiction has sufficient authority or information to understand and control a firm operating in multiple jurisdictions. In the contemporary global economy, multinationals can be seen as one of the forces which have diminished the authority of national governments. The center of gravity in world markets, one political scientist argued in 1996, had moved from 'states to markets and market operators' (Strange 1996).

8.4 Multilateral regulation

The expropriation of foreign property by the Soviet Union in 1917, stimulated the first attempts by home countries to establish an international code regulating the conduct of host countries. In the 1930 Hague Conference on the Codification of International Law, an attempt was made to include the subject of the responsibility of states for damage caused in their territory to foreign persons and their property. However, many developing countries refused to accept the international minimum standards of treatment which Western nations insisted upon. The Latin American countries asserted the Calvo Doctrine, proposed by an Argentine diplomat in the 1860s, which asserted that an investor's home country should not intervene to support its investor abroad (Lipson 1985; Muchlinski 1995).

During and after World War II the issue was raised again in proposals to form the International Trade Organization (ITO), which was intended to function as a third leg to the International Monetary Fund and the World Bank in an attempt to manage the international economy. The primary purpose of the ITO was to facilitate trade, but it also sought to promote FDI by encouraging 'the international flow of capital for productive investment'. However developing countries insisted on numerous qualifying provisions. The whole proposal floundered when the US Congress refused to ratify the ITO

Charter. However, one piece of the ITO proposal survived, the GATT, which over the following decades drove the liberalization of world trade through successive multilateral negotiations.

In the 1970s the wave of nationalizations of multinationals by developing countries led the Organisation for Economic Cooperation and Development (OECD) to establish guidelines for the behavior of international firms. These committed firms to uphold good corporate governance principles in host economies, to contribute to development by training employees, to avoid improper involvement in local politics, to abstain from bribery, and a range of other general principles. However, there was no consensus on the enforcement of these guidelines. While some member countries sought legally binding codes of conduct, the business community lobbied for a voluntary code, as well as stressing the need for the removal of obstacles to FDI. The OECD Guidelines did not become a legally binding law (Muchlinski 1995).

From the 1970s there were a growing number of attempts to develop international codes of one sort or another by international organizations, NGOs and companies themselves (see Figure 8.2). During the same decade an extended dialogue began at the United Nations concerning the formulation of a code of conduct for multinationals and governments. Newly independent and developing country member states, termed the 'Group of 77', saw the Code as a means to facilitate economic development, and restrict the political ambitions of large firms. As a result, there were proposals obliging firms to transfer technology, to take local shareholdings, and to reveal information about their operations. In contrast, developed countries continued to seek commitments to protect their investments, and to prevent discriminatory behavior. The result was a deadlock. Every attempt to develop a mandatory code was blocked by the United States. Ultimately a draft code was produced in 1986. By then, following the world debt crisis in 1982, many developing countries had begun to attract foreign firms rather than restrict them. In 1992 negotiations about the Code were suspended, and remained so.

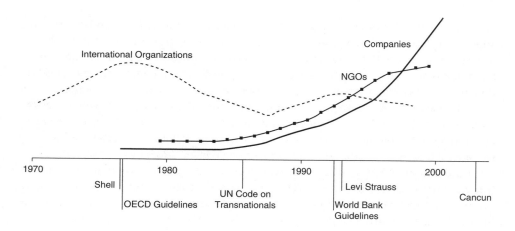

Fig. 8.2 Multinational codes of conduct, 1970–2004.

Source: Adapted from Kolk and van Tulder (2002).

In 1991 the IMF and the World Bank proposed a legal framework to promote FDI which they argued would enhance the efficiencies of host economies 'through greater competition, transfer of capital, technology, and managerial skills and enhancement of market access and in terms of the expansion of international trade'. The World Bank Guidelines, adopted in 1992, were proposed as a statement of policy and good practice, and were again not mandatory. They covered the policies of host governments towards FDI which, it was hoped, would permit FDI, and once admitted, that foreign companies would be subject to 'fair and equitable treatment' (Shihata 1993). The Guidelines specified that disputes should be settled through negotiations, national courts, or some other agreed method.

The lack of a codified international law on the relations between host governments and multinationals led to a growing use of bilateral, subregional, or regional investment treaties. The first Bilateral Investment Treaty was signed in 1959. By 2002 almost 2,200 treaties had been signed encompassing 176 countries. These agreements committed governments, on a reciprocal basis, to observe the standards of treatment laid down by the treaty in its dealings with investors from the other contracting state. They focused on protection, treatment and dispute settlement, and did not attempt to govern the conduct of companies (United Nations 2003; Kolk and van Tulder 2002).

The contrast between the regulation of multinationals (or the lack of it) and that of trade was highlighted by the transformation of the GATT into the World Trade Organisation (WTO) in 1995. The WTO considerably expanded the role of GATT, and many of its provisions directly affected multinationals. It included, on American insistence, new provisions on intellectual property and services. The General Agreement on Trade in Services (GATS) established a variety of obligations such as transparency and nondiscrimination for both trade and investment in services. The agreement on Trade-Related Aspects of Intellectual Property Rights (TRIPs) included new rules on protection standards across countries, and obliged governments to provide transparent processes to enforce them. The WTO also had greatly strengthened dispute settlement mechanisms. This power in turn highlighted the primary influence of developed countries in WTO decisions, and the lack of transparency in the governance structure. This provided a powerful stimulus for the growth of the antiglobalization movement, and the public protests which often accompanied WTO meetings, most notoriously in Seattle in 1999 (Ostry 2001; Brewer and Young 2001).

In the absence of agreement about an international legal code for investment, from the 1970s companies began to commit themselves to global codes, norms and values. Shell was a pioneer, and announced its first code in 1976, which was revised and extended on several occasions. In 1997, after public criticism over its role in the Brent Spar environmental disaster and the exploitation of Nigerian oilfields, Shell became the first multinational to embrace the United Nations Universal Declaration of Human Rights.

During the 1990s there was a proliferation in corporate codes of conduct covering issues such as child labor and the environment. In the sporting goods industry, Levi Strauss was the first firm to adopt a supplier code in 1992. Nike followed a few months later with its Nike Code of Conduct. The Nike Code was noteworthy for an exceptionally high minimum age for employment (16 for apparel, accessories and equipment, and 18 for footwear). Like many corporate codes, the compliance mechanism was left unclear.

It was followed by Reebok, which had been severely criticized for its labor practices in Indonesia in the early 1990s, with a 'human rights production standard' (Kolk and van Tulder 2002). Most large multinationals also engaged in extensive environmental reporting, although it was not always easy to judge how these translated into performance (Lundan 2004). Some critics talked of 'green washing'. In general, skeptics believed that voluntary codes provided little more than a smokescreen to give a false impression that corporations were practicing responsible social behavior, and to prevent governments and organizations from establishing a binding international law (Christian Aid 2004).

In the 2000s the world seems no nearer to a multilateral legally enforceable code for multinational investment than in 1930. This lack of a global governance framework was reflected in the use of an obscure US law, the Alien Tort Claims Act, to seek restitution from companies, worldwide, accused of wrong-doing (see Box 8.7). There was, however, a patchwork of laws and codes which governed aspects of multinational behavior. These included a web of bilateral investment treaties between countries, and the voluntary codes proposed by the OECD, World Bank and companies themselves. The WTO was also an increasing influence on investment as well as trade.

8.5 Lobbying

Multinationals have never been merely the recipients of government policies. While, typically, companies have always sought to influence policy formation in both home and host countries, their ability to influence outcomes has varied enormously from rare cases of extreme subversion to the kind of routine lobbying which is a feature of every capitalist system.

From the moment governments became important for corporate strategies, companies have sought to influence their policies. Typically, firms sought to persuade their home governments to support them abroad. Oil companies and their governments were closely entwined from the early twentieth century. Foreign firms were disadvantaged in lobbying host governments compared to their local competitors. However, by appointing nationals to head local affiliates, multinationals could sometimes access governments. During the 1930s, the head of a British firm's huge Mississippi cotton plantations was a well-connected US national who also served in senior positions on government cotton agencies. The British-owned Fine Cotton Spinners' and Doublers' Association became the recipient of large government subsidies (Wilkins 2004). After World War II, the appointment of nationals to head affiliates in developing countries provided one means for multinationals to mitigate the worst excesses of antiforeign policies. The lobbying abilities of the Indian chief executives of Unilever's Indian business played an important role in enabling that firm to survive the hostile government policies during the 1970s (see Box 8.4).

It has been shown that Japanese government policies towards foreign firms were shaped by powerful local firms. When foreign firms attempted to make investments in industries in which Japanese firms were already powerful, domestic companies were

Box 8.7 The Alien Tort Claims Act and multinationals

The 33-word Alien Tort Claims Act (ATCA) of 1789 specified that 'The district courts shall have original jurisdiction of any civil action by an alien for a tort (civil wrong) only, committed in violation of the law of nations or a treaty of the United States.' The Act lay dormant for two centuries. The first modern ATCA case was filed in 1979, when a Paraguayan police inspector living in the United States was accused of torturing and killing the son of a Paraguayan dissident in Paraguay. The victim's relatives won a $10 million judgment, which was never paid. During the 1990s, the ATCA was used to bring claims of torture, murder and human rights violations against government officials including Ferdinand Marcos of the Philippines.

In the early 1990s, ATCA was used by a New York lawyer Edward Fagan to win a $1.2 billion settlement against Swiss, German, and Austrian firms that used forced or slave labor during the Nazi regime. This set a precedent for the use of the law against multinational corporations for alleged abuses. In 1996, Burmese citizens filed a class action suit against Unocal for abuses committed by the Burmese military against citizens during the construction of the Yadana Gas Pipeline. In 1999, a class action suit was filed against Chevron for its role in helping the Nigerian military shoot protesters at a company offshore platform in the Niger Delta. Two villages that offered support to the protesters were destroyed. In 2003 lawsuits were filed in US federal courts on behalf of victims of apartheid in South Africa including a number of multinational corporations, including IBM, GM, and Shell, accused of supporting the white South African government during the years of apartheid before 1994. In 2004 DaimlerChrysler AG was sued over its role in Argentina following a military coup in 1976 which resulted in an estimated 300 000 people being killed before the Army gave up power in 1983. The lawsuit, filed by the victims' relatives in federal court in San Francisco, sought an undisclosed amount for DaimlerChrysler's alleged responsibility in the disappearance and presumed death of nine workers and the torture of eight others who worked at its Mercedes Benz plant on the outskirts of Buenos Aires.

Both the US Government and major business groups opposed the use of the ATCA in this fashion. In 2004 the International Chamber of Commerce, the US Chamber of Commerce, the National Foreign Trade Council, and the National Association of Manufacturers filed an amicus brief with the United States Supreme Court calling for the clarification of the statute. They argued the law increasingly interfered with international investment flows and US foreign relations. The Supreme Court ruled that lawsuits would be permitted for violations of international law that have "definite content and acceptance among civilized nations".

(*Source: Financial Times*, 30 June 2004.)

often able to influence the government to block or impede the unworked foreign investors. However, in industries where Japanese investors did not hold powerful positions, they had much less or no influence over policy. It was in these areas that foreign companies were able to build successful businesses in Japan after World War II (Mason 1992).

There were many parallels in the United States, where corporate lobbying of policy-makers has been extensive for many decades, and highly influential in trade policy. As US firms faced growing international competition from the 1960s, they frequently lobbied Washington for protection from imports. However, they rarely lobbied the US government to prohibit FDI, even though it was generally stimulated as a result of protectionism. US firms did often seek a range of indirect measures designed to discriminate against foreign-owned firms. These included local content requirements, treating foreign-owned firms differently from locally owned firms, the attachment of conditions to foreign acquisitions, and the classification of local production by foreign-owned firms as 'foreign' for the purpose of implementing trade legislation. This lobbying tended to be less consistent than that for trade protection. While US firms had long experience on the latter issue, the institutional framework for seeking protection from FDI was much less developed, unless there was a clear threat to national security or breach of antitrust laws. It was also much harder to win public support as foreign investors were widely seen as creating employment. A further complication was that most large US firms had multinational investments of their own (Crystal 2003).

The nature of such lobbying in the United States varied greatly between firms and industries, and over time. During the 1970s US color television producers responded in different ways to foreign firms. Firms which were active internationally favored liberal policies, while domestically oriented firms sought greater protection. In the airline industry, the large US carriers sought tight government restrictions over foreign competitors as a strategy to use US market access to open foreign markets. As regulation prohibited foreign ownership and control of domestic airlines, they were able to make highly protectionist demands.

The situation was more complicated in automobiles. The 'Big Three' US domestic companies—GM, Ford, and Chrysler—put enormous pressure on Washington for protection against foreign imports during the 1970s. As part of that campaign included demands that Japanese firms relocate production to the United States, the automakers did not seek discriminatory measures when transplants were erected. However, as production from the transplants gained market share, the industry made demands during the early 1990s for limiting transplant output, labeling their products as 'foreign', and especially raising the local content of transplant cars. GM took a more liberal stance than the domestically-oriented Chrysler, but Ford—despite its vast presence in foreign markets—also lobbied for restrictive measures. Lobbying strategies usually reflect a mixture of economic interest, appreciation of political realities, and firm-specific concerns (Crystal 2003).

The lobbying by multinationals was not confined to national policies. Following the formation of the European Economic Community in 1958, policies set in Brussels began to have a growing influence on multinationals, initially in trade policy, but also over time in consumer protection, competition, and other matters. Europe functioned through constant consultation, discussion, and compromise between interest groups, and firms needed to address multiple layers of decision-making and jurisdiction including national governments, the European Commission, and the European Parliament.

Multinationals sought to influence European policy-making through all the channels. The larger firms typically had influential contacts with national governments. In the Netherlands, for example, Shell, Unilever, and Philips belonged to a select group of large firms which shaped the collective views of the business community, and transmitted those views to the government through an organization known as ABUP, which had been established before World War II. This body agreed to the policies of Dutch business towards European legislation, and transmitted those views to the Dutch government. Shell and Unilever had second home governments in Britain through which they sought to voice their policies.

At the European level, while many US multinationals established representative offices in Brussels, European-based companies often preferred to lobby indirectly, through associations, third parties and networking. The European Commission sought to deal with Community-wide associations only, with the result that from the late 1950s there was a proliferation of European federations of professional associations such as IMACE (margarine) and EUROGLACE (ice cream). Similarly there was a confederation of European employers associations (UNICE). All these organizations were engaged in a constant dialog as legislation was formulated and promulgated. The views of large companies were well-represented as each of their affiliates would belong to its respective national organization, which in turn was represented in the European-wide body (Jones and Miskell 2005).

Firms were active participants also in WTO processes. Although WTO disputes were technically between governments, typically, governments acted in response to political pressures from firms. A prominent example during the 1990s included the dispute between the United States and the European Union over the latter's banana regime, which provided preferential access to bananas from former European colonies in Africa, the Caribbean, and Pacific over those from Latin America. The US government's intervention arose from its support of Chiquita which sought to export more bananas from its Central American plantations (Brewer and Young 2001).

An extreme variant of corporate lobbying has occurred when firms have chosen to relocate their domicile and consequently change their home governments. Although the phenomenon of firms choosing their own governments has been rare, it has not been unknown. The most well-known example of firms engaging in regulatory arbitrage has occurred in the shipping industry after 1945. Much of the world's tonnage became registered in 'flags of convenience', such as Panama and Liberia, which had low registration fees and no employment registrations. In other cases, large corporations have shifted domicile because of concerns about political stability, or to seek a more favorable regulatory regime. In advance of the reversion of Hong Kong to China, HSBC shifted domicile to Britain in 1993. A decade earlier Jardine Matheson had shifted domicile from Hong Kong to Bermuda, a jurisdiction which also made hostile acquisitions more difficult. In both cases, this included a relocation of the parent company, while the very large local businesses have remained under the ownership of locally-registered affiliates (Jones 2000). During the 1990s several large South African corporations, including Anglo-American and Gencor, shifted domicile to Britain primarily to facilitate capital-raising in the context of the depreciating South African currency.

■ SUMMARY

Government policies towards multinationals have evolved in a circular direction over the last century. Before 1930, host governments had few restrictions, except in a number of strategic sectors. Thereafter, there was a worldwide growth in restrictions, and some countries excluded multinationals altogether. From the 1980s there was a worldwide trend towards liberalization. There were national differences within these general patterns. The nationality of ownership mattered more in some countries than others.

During the twentieth century the nation state secured a degree of power and an ability to control affairs far greater than in previous centuries. Governments which sought and gained the ability to control and influence their national economies did not share an identity of interests with business enterprises which coordinated economic activities across national borders. For much of the twentieth century, national governments sought—in varying degrees—to restrict, control, or ban multinationals as a solution to this conflict. The difficulty was the lack of alternatives to gain access to the latest technologies and organizational skills, and to markets. As the pace of global integration and technological change accelerated, policies shifted from restricting international firms to seeking to attract them.

| PART V | **Outcomes** |

9 Multinationals and home economies

9.1 Multinationals and nations

This chapter explores the relationship between multinationals and their home economies. The organization of knowledge by firms is forged by the interplay of national institutions and entrepreneurship. As a result the firms of different countries developed distinct capabilities and organizational forms. This was reflected in the strategies and organization of firms from different countries. This chapter examines the long-term differences between the firms of different nationalities in their propensities to invest, and the geographical and sectoral distribution of their investments. It then turns to examine the impact of multinationals on their home economies. Finally the issue of whether nationality still matters is discussed.

9.2 Home economies over time

9.2.1 The geographical distribution of multinationals

The number of major home economies has always been small. As Chapter 2 showed, before World War I at least four-fifths of world FDI came from a handful of countries in Western Europe. Britain alone accounted for nearly one half of world FDI. The United States held another 14 percent. Thereafter ownership became more rather than less concentrated. Between World War I and 1980 the United States, the United Kingdom and the Netherlands accounted for between two-thirds and three-fourths of total world FDI. From the 1980s the number of major home economies rose again, but the six large home economies shown in Box 9.1 accounted for two-thirds of world FDI in 2002.

This ownership pattern reflects strong national differences in the timing of international business activities. In a historical perspective, three categories of home economy can be identified: persistent, erratic, and latecomer. The persistent investors began to invest in the nineteenth century, and continued on a substantial scale despite shifts in the political and economic environment. The United States belongs firmly to this category. Even more striking was the propensity of British companies to invest abroad which persisted in the face of relative economic decline and the end of the Empire. In 2002 its stock of world FDI was proportionately much larger compared to its domestic

Box 9.1 The six largest home economies in 2002

Country	Amount (US $ Million)	% World Total FDI	% Gross Domestic Product
United States	1 501 415	22	14.4
United Kingdom	1 033 003	15	66.1
France	652 105	9	45.8
Germany	577 849	8	29.0
Netherlands	355 652	5	84.7
Japan	331 596	5	8.3
All other developed countries	5,987 746	87	24.4
World Total	6 866 362	100	21.6

(*Source*: United Nations 2003.)

economy and also compared to other large economies. This was likely to have been the case since the late nineteenth century.

Three smaller European economies—the Netherlands, Sweden, and Switzerland—have also been persistent foreign investors (see Box 9.2 for the Netherlands). These countries are now amongst the world's richest in terms of GDP per head, but their firms emerged as prolific direct investors in the nineteenth century, when these countries were relatively less wealthy. During the twentieth century their stock of FDI remained large relative to their size, and much larger than their immediate small-economy neighbors. In 2002 Switzerland's outward FDI amounted to 110 percent of its GDP, compared to neighboring Austria's 20 percent. The equivalent figures for Sweden and Norway were 60 percent and 20 percent respectively (Jones and Schröter 1993; United Nations 2003).

A second category of countries were erratic investors. France and Germany were major capital exporters before 1914, and their firms were active direct investors. Thereafter, both countries experienced fifty years of subdued multinational investment, as their firms opted for exporting or other strategies in foreign markets. French and German multinational investment only began to increase substantially from the 1970s.

Japan has also been an erratic category. Despite Japan's late industrialization and low incomes, by the interwar years the worldwide activities of Japanese trading and other service sector companies, as well as investments by Japanese cotton textile and mining companies in the markets and resources of Asia—especially China—resulted in the creation of a complex international business system. Although the stock of Japanese FDI probably never reached 3 percent of the world total, in 1930 it was almost 14 percent of Japan's GDP (Kuwahara 1990). After World War II, Japanese outward FDI remained at low levels until international growth resumed from the 1970s. The stock of Japanese FDI grew spectacularly from $20 billion in 1980 to over $200 billion in 1990, at which point it was the world's largest foreign direct investor in terms of flows. However, thereafter the collapse of the bubble economy and the acute difficulties of the banking system led to

Box 9.2 The Netherlands as a home economy

The Netherlands has been one of the world's largest multinational investors since the nineteenth century despite its relatively small size. In 1914 the Netherlands accounted for around 5 percent of total world FDI. By 1938 the Dutch share had reached 10 percent. During the 1960s it was equal to that of Germany, France, and Italy combined. It was only around 1980 that the stock of Dutch FDI—about 8 percent of the world total—was surpassed by that of Germany. In 2002 the Netherlands, with a population of 15 million, accounted for 5 percent of world FDI.

The Dutch economy was heavily dependent on international trade and investment since the days of the Dutch East India Company in the seventeenth century. During the late nineteenth century hundreds of 'free-standing' companies were formed to invest in the resources of the Dutch East Indies, including the Royal Dutch Petroleum Company, whose merger with the British-owned Shell Transport and Trading Company in 1907 created Shell, 60 percent owned by the Netherlands. Dutch FDI survived World War I intact as the Netherlands remained neutral. During the interwar years Philips (electricals) and AKU (chemicals) became large direct investors. A cluster of margarine and foods companies merged to form the Margarine Unie in 1927, which two years later merged with the British-owned Lever Brothers to form Unilever. In quantitative terms, most Dutch FDI came from a small number of large firms, including the Anglo-Dutch Unilever and Shell.

After World War II, Dutch FDI remained substantial despite the decolonization of the Dutch East Indies. It was largely reoriented towards developed economies. Prominent Dutch multinationals included Heineken (beverages), Ahold (retailing), ING and Aegon (insurance and banking) and ABN-AMRO (banking). Banking and financial services accounted for a growing share of Dutch FDI. During the 1990s Dutch firms were also involved in cross-border mergers, creating the Anglo-Dutch Reed Elsevier (publishing) and Corus (steel), and the Dutch-Belgian Fortis (insurance). In 2003 the Dutch airline KLM was acquired by Air France.

(*Source*: Gales and Sluyterman 1993; Hoesel and Narula 1999; Sluyterman 2003.)

much slower growth and even at times stagnation (Westney 2001). Although Japan's outward investment remained far in excess of inward investment, it was less important compared to its overall size than the United States, let alone the Western European countries.

Finally, there are a group of latecomer investors. In Europe, this category includes southern European countries such as Italy and Spain. Although Italy had a small number of long-standing multinationals, including Pirelli and Fiat, in aggregate the country's FDI as a share of GDP was only 1.6 percent in 1980. The Spanish equivalent was less than 1 percent. During the nineteenth century there had been some Spanish direct investment in the Spanish colonies of Cuba, Puerto Rico, and the Philippines, but little after their loss to the United States in 1898. Spanish firms rarely invested abroad during the Fascist dictatorship between 1939 and 1975, and it was not until 1992 that the Spanish government fully liberalized capital movements. Spanish FDI, which had only been $1.9 billion in 1980 and $16 billion a decade later, reached $216 billion in 2002, or the equivalent of 33 percent of GDP (Toral 2001). The stock of Italian FDI, which had grown to $194 billion in that year, remained a modest 16 percent of GDP.

The latecomer category included firms from the emerging economies of Asia and Latin America, particularly Hong Kong, Singapore, South Korea, Taiwan and Brazil, whose outward FDI began on a small scale in the 1960s, and then grew rapidly from the 1980s. Taiwan and South Korea became net outward investors in 1988 and 1990 respectively. By the 2000s China-based firms had also begun to make direct investments. Section 9.3 considers multinationals from emerging markets in greater detail.

9.2.2 Sectoral and locational patterns

There have been persistent national differences in the sectoral distribution of multinational investment. In terms of broad economic sectors, the United States, the United Kingdom, France, and the Netherlands made large investments in resources during the nineteenth century. Before 1914 as much as a half of US and British multinational investment may have been in resources (Wilkins 1970; Corley 1994). Although German-based companies were large investors in petroleum and metals before World War I, thereafter manufacturing was the main sector of German FDI. Swedish and Swiss FDI was also concentrated in manufacturing before the 1970s. In services, Britain may have had around one-third of its total FDI in 1914 in utilities, railroads, and financial services. The international expansion of utility companies in the 1920s resulted in over one-fifth of the total stock of US FDI being in that industry by 1940. After World War II, this proportion fell rapidly, but the internalization of US banks raised the relative importance of finance in total US FDI from 4 percent to 14 percent between 1957 and 1982 (Lipsey 1988). However, it was Japanese FDI which was most skewed towards services, reflecting in particular the importance of the sogo shosha. From the late nineteenth century until the 1970s services were the most important sector in Japanese FDI.

Within manufacturing, strong national differences are apparent. In the case of the United States, the machinery and electrical industries were the most active outward investors before 1914, followed by the food and automobile industries in the interwar years, the chemical industry from the 1950s, and the computer and electronics industries subsequently. These industries have remained the main areas of US multinational manufacturing (Mataloni and Goldberg 1994). The British had a bias towards branded consumer goods from the late nineteenth century. This grew in relative importance until during the 1950s and 1960s one half of all British overseas assets in manufacturing were in food, drink, and tobacco. This bias remained strong—in the 1980s these industries represented 30 percent of Britain's stock of manufacturing FDI although chemicals, pharmaceuticals, and engineering became increasingly more important (Balasubramanyam 1993).

Among other home economies, similar long-term patterns of specialization were apparent. From the nineteenth century the chemicals and electricals industries were the most prominent in German FDI—accounting for one-fifth and one-tenth of the total stock in the mid-1970s. German FDI in automobiles also became significant from the 1950s. In the Dutch case, food and, from the interwar years, chemicals and electrical engineering have been the most important manufacturing sectors. Swedish manufacturing FDI was heavily concentrated in engineering and machinery. Swiss manufacturing FDI first occurred in textiles, and later textile machinery, followed from the late nineteenth century by branded food products, chemicals, and pharmaceuticals (Jones and Schröter 1993a). Japanese manufacturing FDI was heavily concentrated in textiles until the international expansion of the electronics and automobile industries began in the 1970s.

From the 1980s all countries except Japan have seen a shift towards services which has resulted in a convergence of sectoral distribution of the outward FDI of leading home economies (see Figure 9.1). The shift towards services was particularly fast in the case of the United States.

The shifting geographical location over time of the multinational investments of different countries reflected overall trends in international business. Those economies which undertook extensive FDI in natural resources and related services had a considerable proportion of this investment in developing countries before World War II. Subsequently this proportion fell as multinational investment became more focused on manufacturing and services in the developed economies.

Within this general trend, multinational investment has been skewed by geographical, political, and language influences. This can readily be explained in terms of risk aversion. It has been shown that, especially when firms first invest abroad, they prefer countries which are geographically or culturally close to their own. US companies, for example, often invested first in Canada and then used Britain as an entry point to Europe (Davidson 1980). This pattern was repeated again and again for many countries, as their firms sought to make investments, especially initial ones, in countries with low information costs for themselves. Scandinavian researchers used the concept of 'psychic distance' to explain the empirical observation that firms from that region began their internationalization in proximate neighboring countries before moving on to more culturally distant markets (Johanson and Vahlne 1977, 1990).

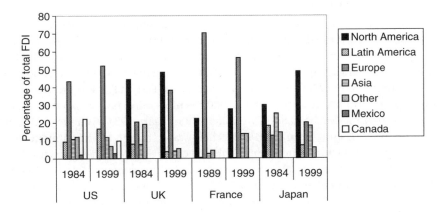

Fig. 9.1 Sectoral distribution of US, UK, French, and Japanese outward FDI, 1984–99.
Source: OECD (1993; 2000).

This perception of risk-reduction has not always translated into reality. There have been many instances of catastrophic or unsatisfactory British investments in the United States, including most of the large acquisitions made in the banking sector in the 1970s and 1980s (Wilkins 2001; Jones 1993). A common language alone has never provided a firm with sufficient competitive advantage in a foreign market.

The influence of geography is evident in the skewing of US FDI towards elsewhere in the Americas. In 1914 Canada and Mexico held over one-fifth each of total US FDI. Cuba and the West Indies accounted for a further tenth. Subsequently, Mexico and Central America generally became much less important for American investors. Latin America as a whole accounted for 40 percent of total US FDI in 1950, though this ratio fell sharply thereafter. Canada's share of US FDI was between 25 percent and 30 percent until the 1970s, while Britain was, and remained, the largest European host for US FDI (Wilkins 1970, 1974a). Canada alternated with the United Kingdom into the 1980s as the single most important recipient of US FDI.

In case of Japan, the amount of FDI in East Asia—primarily China—far exceeded that elsewhere before World War II, even though significant service sector investments were made in the United States (Wilkins 1990). During the postwar decades Japanese FDI was heavily skewed towards Southeast Asia as well as other developing regions, notably Latin America. This remained the case until the growth of Japanese manufacturing FDI in the United States and Europe from the 1970s.

The geographical distribution of European FDI was also heavily influenced by a tendency to make manufacturing investments in neighboring countries. This was the primary destination for manufacturing investments over a long period, apart from some investments in the United States. The main deviation from this pattern occurred in the countries which had colonial empires, which resulted in political and language ties that proved more compelling than those of physical distance. Before World War I around two-fifths of total British FDI was located in the Empire. The remainder was widely spread over Latin America, the United States and elsewhere in Europe (Corley 1994). The share invested in the Empire grew during the interwar years, and by 1962, 55 percent of the stock of British FDI was in the former empire, compared to 13 percent in Western Europe and under 10 percent in the United States. It was only from the 1970s that British multinationals shifted rapidly elsewhere in Europe and the United States (Jones 1994).

Among the other European colonial powers, almost three-fourths of Dutch FDI was located in the Dutch East Indies in 1914, and around one half in 1947 (Gales and Sluyterman 1993). In the early 1970s around 30 percent of total French FDI was located in former colonies—primarily in Africa—though by 1980 the proportion had dropped dramatically to less than 5 percent (Michalet and Chevallier 1985: Savary 1984). When Spanish multinational investment grew from the 1980s, there was considerable investment in Latin America, despite the fact that the Spanish colonial empire had ended earlier (see Box 9.3).

From the 1980s there was also a convergence in the geographical destination of multinational investment (see Figure 9.2). Over the more recent decades, US multinational investment shifted to Europe, while European and Japanese firms invested in North America, primarily the United States. Yet each country retained distinctive patterns. Canada and Latin America attracted much US FDI, while Asia still accounted for a quarter of Japanese FDI. British multinationals had almost half of their FDI in North

---

Box 9.3 The influence of language and culture on Spanish multinational strategies since 1980

Spanish FDI began to grow during the 1980s following capital market liberalization in 1979. Initially over half of Spanish FDI went to Latin America, especially in industrial machinery, bus and truck manufacturing, shipyards and fishing, but following Spain's accession to the European Union in 1986 the share of Spanish FDI in Europe rose sharply. During the second half of the 1990s Latin America again became the largest destination, and over three-fourths of Spanish FDI was located there by 1999. Spanish firms were anxious to find new markets as other European firms invested in their domestic market, while profitable opportunities were perceived in Latin America as market-oriented reforms were implemented, including privatization. Linguistic, historical, and cultural similarities encouraged Spanish firms to consider that the risks were lower than elsewhere. Latin America's transition from closed to open markets and widespread privatizations appeared to be a repeat of their experiences in their home economy a decade earlier.

During the 1990s the largest Spanish investors in Latin America were Telefónica (telecommunications), Endesa España (electricity), Repsol (oil and natural gas), Iberdola (electricity), Banco Bilbao Viscaya and Banco Santander (banking) and Iberia (air transport). This entry was closely related to the region's privatization programmes. In 1999, for example, Repsol acquired Argentina's state-owned oil company YPF to become the largest petroleum company in that country.

A number of the Spanish investors found that linguistic and cultural similarities were insufficient to sustain competitive advantage. This proved to be the case with Iberia. In 1990 the Spanish state-owned airline participated in the privatization of Aerolineas Argentininas, in the following year in that of Venezeula's Viasa, and in 1993 it acquired equity in Ladeco, a Chilean privately-owned airline. These acquisitions gave Iberia a one-third share of the Latin American passenger market. However, none of the acquisitions were profitable. Iberia itself was also loss-making. In 1996 it was saved from bankruptcy by the Spanish government, but the EU imposed as a condition the sale of the Latin American investments. Viasa was closed and Ladeco was sold, while Iberia's stake in Aerolineas Argentininas was also sold.

(*Source*: Toral 2001; United Nations 2000.)

America, and another two-fifths elsewhere in Europe. France, like Germany, the Netherlands and most other Continental European countries, had over one half of its FDI elsewhere in Europe, and a smaller proportion in North America.

9.3 The home country impact on multinationals

As companies grew across borders they were transformed from national firms to international producers. However, the national origins of firms shaped strategies and

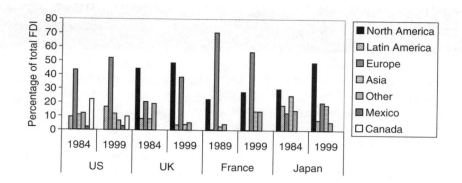

Fig. 9.2 Geographical distribution of US, UK, French, and Japanese outward FDI, 1984–99.
Source: OECD (1993; 2000).

organization. There were also persistent variations between countries in multinational propensities and timing, and industrial and geographical distribution.

9.3.1 Evolutionary models

A number of models have related the national differences in multinational investment to the stage of a country's economic development. In the investment development path model, a country's international investment position is related to its level of development as measured by its GNP per capita. A developing economy passes through four stages. In stage 1 of pre-industrialization there is no inward or outward FDI. In stage 2, if the economy has developed, the country will begin to attract inward FDI as domestic markets increase and the variable costs of servicing those markets are reduced. In stage 3, a country's net inward investment per capita begins to fall. This may be because the original ownership advantages of foreign firms has declined, or because local firms have begun to improve their competitive capacity, or because local firms have developed their own comparative ownership advantages which they have begun to exploit through FDI. In stage 4, a country is a net outward investor, with its investment flows abroad exceeding those of foreign-owned firms in its own country. This reflects the development of strong ownership advantages by its firms and/or an increasing propensity to exploit these advantages internally from a foreign rather than a domestic location (Dunning 1981).

This investment development path model provides a dynamic link between economic development and FDI flows. Historically, the surges of economic development first in Western Europe, then in the United States, then in Japan, and most recently in NICs, have been followed by accelerating FDI flows from those regions. Yet the historical experience of individual countries has not uniformly followed this pattern. Different countries have displayed different FDI propensities at similar stages of their development path. Nor have net FDI positions always matched the stage model. From World War II until the present, US FDI abroad has exceeded foreign FDI in the United States, but during the 1970s and 1980s the two amounts almost matched before US outward FDI again increased rapidly in the 1990s (Wilkins 2001).

The influence of country-specific factors features in the product cycle model first proposed as an explanation for the large flows of US manufacturing FDI into postwar Europe. It was argued that firms based in the United States had a greater propensity to develop new products because of high per capita incomes and high unit labor costs in their home economy. The model suggested that when a new product was developed in the United States, a firm normally chose a domestic production location, partly because of the need for close contact with customers and suppliers. As a product matured, long-run production with established technology became possible. When it became economic to invest abroad, Western Europe was the preferred choice of location since demand patterns were close to the US and (at that time) labor costs were relatively low. When the product entered its standardized phase, the lowest cost supply point became a priority, and production could be transferred to developing countries (Vernon 1966). In later formulations, the role of the United States as a source of new products was reduced to take account of the increased importance of Europe and Japan, but the modified model continued to stress the role of home economies in innovatory activities of their firms (Vernon 1979).

The view that manufacturing FDI is associated with technology leaders is supported by considerable historical evidence. There has been a strong correlation between the innovatory competitiveness of countries in particular sectors and the propensity of their firms to engage in multinational activity. Since the nineteenth century, new waves of multinational investment in manufacturing have originated from technologically leading firms clustered in specific home economies which were either present or former world technology leaders (such as the United States and the United Kingdom), or else highly technologically developed (such as the Netherlands, Switzerland, and Sweden). The home country distribution of outward FDI has reflected the fact that countries differ in their technological capabilities, and that these differences—and differences in the patterns of technological specialization among countries—have been stable over long periods of time (Pavitt and Soete 1982; Cantwell 1989).

These technological differences in turn have to be understood in a wider institutional context. Chandler has provided the most powerful historical model relating shifts in technological leadership and innovatory capability in the new capital-intensive industries which developed in the late nineteenth century to the adoption (or otherwise) of managerial capitalism (Chandler 1990). Kogut (1991) specifically related national differences in FDI and trade patterns to a country's technological and, especially, organizing abilities. The evidence that technological specialization among developed countries is stable over long periods of time can be explained by persistent variations in such abilities between countries. The 'stickiness' of knowledge and institutional inertia means that these capabilities diffuse more slowly than technologies across borders. Within a broad sweep of history, the international importance of Britain in the nineteenth century can be regarded as resting on the expansion of organized industrial production. The subsequent US pre-eminence was built on mass production and the principles of scientific management. In turn, the growth of Japanese multinational manufacturing from the 1970s rested on lean or flexible production.

These evolutionary models work best at explaining patterns of multinational investment over the very long period, especially in the capital goods manufacturing sector employing frontier technologies. They have little to contribute towards understanding the impact of exogenous shocks, whether wars or regime changes, which have resulted in major shifts in investment patterns.

9.3.2 **The diamond model of international competitive advantage**

The continuing significance of the home country environment in even the most global-ized of industries was the theme of Porter's 'diamond' model of the sources of inter-national competitive advantage (Porter 1990). Porter argued that four sets of attributes of a home economy are critical for the competitiveness of its firms: the level and compos-ition of natural and created resources; the quantity and quality of demand by domestic consumers; the extent to which its firms are able to benefit from agglomerations or external economies by being grouped in clusters of related activities; and firm strategy, structure and rivalry. These four sets of attributes are interlinked and interact with one another in a 'diamond'. Government and chance are two other determinants which may affect the primary four attributes.

This model does not seek to explain patterns of multinational investment. The inter-national activities of firms are seen as primarily exporting rather than investment. However, the model can provide a powerful means to identify factors behind national strengths in particular industries (Dunning 1993). It is evident in broad terms how factor endowments have influenced the historical evolution of multinational activities. Capital availability was important. The leading European capital exporters of the late nineteenth century—the United Kingdom, Germany, and France—were also leading homes to multi-nationals, while the development of the United States as the world's largest creditor after World War I was accompanied by that country's emergence as the largest home economy in terms of FDI flows. However, the United States, Sweden, and Japan grew as direct investors before 1914 while their economies were net capital importers. Britain remained a major outward investor long after it ceased to be a net capital exporter.

The existence of natural resources in home economies helps to explain national variations in the sectoral distribution of the FDI. The existence of natural resources provided companies with access to skills which could be exploited abroad in mining or agriculture, and sometimes in manufacturing. Examples included the Swedish multi-nationals which grew out of that country's raw material base of iron ore and forest products, and the Swiss companies which reflected the importance of that country's dairy products industry.

Created resource endowments became progressively more so over time. The origins of Sweden's international competitiveness in advanced engineering products rested on the heavy investment in technical schools and literacy in that country even when—in the nineteenth century—it was still a poor country. The combination of human capital and institutional arrangements which facilitated knowledge acquisition from abroad seem to have given that country a high 'absorptive capacity' (Lundgren 1995). During the second half of the twentieth century US leadership in computer and information technology industries reflected not only the size of the US market and US defense spending in particular, but the web of relationships and information flows between companies and universities, and between venture capitalists and entrepreneurs, which provided a unique environment for creativity and innovation.

The size and nature of demand of home economies was important also. The growth of the United States as a large, mass consumption society by the late nineteenth century provided the environment for US firms to pioneer the introduction of low-cost, standardized, mass-marketed products in many industries. Their position in the world's largest and richest home market continued to provide many advantages to US-owned firms. The relative importance of the Netherlands, Switzerland, and Sweden as home countries raises the possibility that a 'small economy' effect is significant in explaining FDI propensities. Enterprises from those countries were often driven abroad from the nineteenth century onwards because their home markets were so small (Gales and Sluyterman 1993; Olsson 1993). However, the coexistence of these cases with neighboring small countries with low propensities to invest suggest that variables other than size need to be considered.

The industrial structures of the economies was probably among the most important such variable. Small countries have more 'unbalanced' industrial structures than large ones—some industries proportionately large, others missing. Depending on its particular complement of industries, it can therefore be predicted that a small nation will have either a very large amount of FDI or a very small one (Caves 1996). The industrial structure in turn resulted in differences in concentration levels. It was the small economies with high concentration levels which were the most active in outward FDI. In contrast, low European investors such as Denmark and Norway were the ones where the role of small and medium-sized companies was considerable (Jones and Schröter 1993).

The significance of concentration levels is not limited to the small economies. The United Kingdom's continued prominence as an outward investor may be in part explained by the growing importance of large firms in its economy. Beginning in the interwar years, and gathering pace in the 1950s and 1960s, concentration levels in British industry rose rapidly. By 1970 the share of the 100 largest enterprises in manufacturing net output was considerably higher in the United Kingdom than in the United States, while the small or medium-sized enterprise sector had shrunk (Channon 1973). British companies may have possessed advantages in capital-raising derived from their large size, as well as the large size of the British capital market (Clegg 1987). In contrast concentration levels remained lower in Germany, France, and especially Italy.

The influence of both governments and chance was much more pervasive than the diamond model might suggest. Home country laws exercised important influences on international business. US antitrust laws discouraged over a long period much of the collaborative behavior which was frequently seen in the international operations of both European and Japanese firms. On a number of occasions, antitrust rulings reshaped the corporate landscape of US multinationals. Examples included the shift of control over the tobacco company BAT from the United States to Britain before 1920, and Alcoa's loss of ownership of its Canadian affiliate, Alcan, after World War II (see Chapters 3 and 4).

Government regulations and trade barriers have shaped outward multinational investment. After 1945 the considerable advantages derived by US firms from the US defense budget were bolstered by the fact that foreign-controlled firms were not eligible for the security clearance required to bid on US defense contracts (Safarian 1993). Japanese consumer electronics and automobile industries grew to a large scale within a Japanese market protected by import controls and strict limits on inward FDI.

The diamond framework needs some modification to explain firm-level competitiveness in the second global economy. The reason is that multinationals, especially but not only those from small economies, derive characteristics and advantages from multiple locations rather than merely their home economies. By 2003 Honda, the Japanese automobile manufacturer, sold over 50 percent of its total world production in North America, and less than 30 percent in Japan. This raises the issue whether Honda had one home base or two (Porter 1998; Rugman and Verbeke 2001). As a result, a 'double diamond' approach has been proposed which suggests that firms now build upon both domestic and foreign diamonds to become globally competitive (Moon, Rugman, and Verbeke 1998).

The relevance of the 'double diamond' framework may not be confined to the contemporary global economy. The competitiveness of the Anglo-Dutch firms Shell and Unilever was based on two home economies from their foundation in 1907 and 1930 respectively. Within these companies, managers were able to make choices between the different 'diamonds' in which they were based. Over many years Shell located research and technical functions in the Netherlands, and marketing and shipping functions in Britain. Within Unilever, expertise in margarine and edible fats was centered in the Netherlands, and in personal care and detergents in Britain. However, these patterns fluctuated over time. During the 1950s and 1960s the British side of Unilever appeared to carry the greatest weight in decision-making, but from the 1970s there was a steady growth of Dutch influence. Although the Anglo-Dutch companies were exceptional, many Swiss, Swedish, and other small economy firms already had high proportions of the sales and output outside their home economies by the interwar years.

9.3.3 The role of culture

The strong differences between countries in the organization of their firms and the behavior of their managers can be said to derive in part from national cultural values. However, because the influence of culture is diffuse and hard to demonstrate, analysis of the home-country cultural influence on multinationals remains difficult.

The impact of culture was seen in several different areas. Differences in levels of outward investment may have reflected wider differences between outward- and inward-looking cultural orientations. The colonial and mercantile traditions of Britain and the Netherlands resulted in a strong outward-looking commercial tradition in their business cultures. Switzerland and Sweden were not colonial, but had a long tradition of international trade and exposure to foreign cultures. Both countries became noteworthy for their multilingual abilities. Switzerland was composed of three language groups—German, French, and Italian—while in Sweden, German and later English were widely understood. Outward orientation was often reflected in migration flows. Britain (including Ireland at that time), the Netherlands, Switzerland, and Sweden were major sources of emigrants in the nineteenth century. The United States—to which most of these people emigrated—was a country of immigrants.

The pre-eminence of the English-speaking economies in the development of international business was a continuation of the expansive drive which led to the settlement of large tracts of lands in earlier centuries, but this was also a self-reinforcing process. The fact that English was the common language of the United States, the United Kingdom, and a large number of countries which came under British colonial influence, encouraged cross-investments by reducing the perceived risks of international investments. This was perhaps the most important example of the 'nearby' phenomenon. Cultures developed more inward-looking orientations also. Japan emerged from the long Edo era of national seclusion with little knowledge of the rest of the world, and a strong sense of the uniqueness of Japanese culture. Modern Japan developed as outward-looking in some respects—for example, in the acquisition of foreign technology—but with a distinctly arm's-length attitude to the people and firms of foreign countries.

It is not difficult to make very broad generalizations about the link between national cultures and multinational investment. The ownership of world FDI has historically been correlated with cultures identified by Hofstede as being individualistic, a preference for equality and a willingness to tolerate uncertainty. The United States, Britain, and the Netherlands shared these characteristics. It might be hypothesized that international business, as it is more risky than domestic business, would be favored by cultures which were more individualistic and less risk-averse than others. The particularly prominent role of English-speaking countries as sources of FDI in natural resources might be explained in such cultural terms. Mining and petroleum were high-risk businesses. Cultures in which entrepreneurs were willing to act independently and take risks provided a competitive advantage in such an environment.

A study of US, Japanese, Taiwanese, and Korean direct investment in the European microcomputer industry during the 1980s and 1990s suggested a strong correlation between national culture and corporate strategy. These were major differences between firms in backward linkages strategies concerning the organization of hardware components in the same industry. These differences appeared to reflect the national culture of the parent company, as well as the age of the firm. The study found that older established US firms, such as IBM, followed the entrenched industry practice of organizing component productive activities internally. The Asia Pacific entrants followed this practice, but 'youthful' US firms, including Dell and Gateway, opted for contracting relationships with specialist component suppliers. The study suggested that Asia Pacific firms coming from cultures with 'collective values' were inclined towards the integrated linkage strategy, while youthful US firms from the 'individualistic' US culture pioneered the disintegrated linkage strategy (Tsang 2002).

The attempts to build specific linkages between culture and international business face serious methodological and empirical challenges. It is difficult to isolate the impact of national culture from other variables. Firms are influenced by several different types of culture—corporate, industry, and national—which overlap. Further complexities arise from 'cultural shift'. It is unlikely that the values of twenty-first-century Americans and their nineteenth-century predecessors were identical, even though there is much evidence that underlying cultural orientations change rather slowly, unless subject to major external manipulation.

9.3.4 Wars and chance

Major exogenous upheavals have been shown to have exercised a major long-term influence on the development of international business. The low level of German FDI between

World War I and the 1970s, and the low Japanese FDI between 1945 and the 1970s, can only be understood in the context of the sequestrations of those countries' foreign assets as a result of the world wars, even if other important variables were also at work. It would appear that a rise in risk aversion was more important than the loss of capital in explaining such long-term consequences. The high perceived risk of FDI encouraged entrepreneurs to consider alternative modes and locations for operating abroad.

In contrast, the high propensity of Sweden and Switzerland to invest abroad can be related to their neutral status during both the world wars. The Netherlands was neutral in World War I. Neutrality left foreign assets intact—although Swedish firms suffered from the destruction and loss of property in Russia following the Communist Revolution and in eastern Europe following World War II—while their business at home was spared from the destruction seen elsewhere in Europe.

British and Dutch firms remained persistent foreign investors despite momentous changes in their environment. World War II, decolonization, and the growth of nationalism in developing countries had a serious impact on both countries. Britain may have lost 40 percent of its total overseas business assets between 1938 and 1956 through sequestration, wartime destruction of property, and obligatory sales. The latter included the enforced wartime sale of the largest British-owned manufacturing asset in the United States—the American Viscose subsidiary of Courtaulds (Coleman 1969; Wilkins 2004). The end of the Dutch colonial empire in Indonesia in 1949, followed by the nationalization of Dutch property a decade later, was a climactic event for Dutch FDI. Yet, in both the British and Dutch cases, such massive external shocks did not result in a diminution of their desire to invest abroad. This probably reflected the strength of the international investment horizon which had become embedded in their firms and entrepreneurs

9.3.5 Firms, nations, and time

Home country characteristics provide only a partial explanation of the dynamics of multinationals. There are strong country commonalities in the strategies pursued by firms from the same country, but firms of a particular nationality do not share equally the resources of their home countries. There has always been a wide range in performance among firms headquartered in the same country. During the 1980s and 1990s the Japanese automobile industry as a whole was very internationally competitive, but there was a wide divergence between the three leading firms, Toyota, Honda, and Nissan. The latter performed so poorly that it was ultimately acquired by France's Renault.

The growth of the largest multinationals of the twentieth century—Shell and Exxon, Ford and GM, Unilever and Nestlé, Matsushita and Sony—reflected idiosyncratic firm-specific experiences which differentiated them from numerous less successful national competitors. These experiences ranged from individual entrepreneurial decisions at crucial moments, to the development of a particular management or production system which turned out to be very effective. The growth of these global giants can be regarded as resting on certain aspects of their home economies, but their individual histories demonstrate great diversity in management, strategy, culture, and performance.

The stock of multinational investment of a country was also a cumulative process. It reflects past factor endowments, laws, and national 'diamonds', and cultural values at least as much as contemporary ones. Firms sometimes remained prominent in an industry long after their home country lost the comparative advantage which stimulated their growth initially. First-mover and incumbency advantages proved very strong in many industries.

9.4 Multinationals from emerging markets

The growth of multinationals based in emerging markets raises a further set of issues regarding the home economy impact on multinationals. The first Taiwanese direct investment was in a Malaysian cement factory in 1959, while the first Korean direct investment was in a forestry project in Indonesia in 1968. These 'first wave' of emerging market multinationals were usually small-scale and involved labor-intensive technology. These characteristics reflected home markets which were small and lacked a strong innovation base, but which possessed abundant supplies of low-cost labor. It was logical to follow a low-cost, low-price strategy employing borrowed technology adapted to local factor conditions. While some researchers at the time argued that such competitive advantages were not sustainable over the long term (Wells 1983), others proposed that the advantages of these firms rested on special knowledge of developing country markets and widely diffused technologies which would prove more durable (Lall 1983).

Whatever the constraints faced by multinationals from emerging markets, they were insufficient to prevent a sustained growth of outward FDI from the second half of the 1980s. South Korea and Taiwan were joined by firms from other Asian and Latin American countries. These 'second wave' firms were less restricted to neighboring developing countries, and began to invest in developed markets also. They invested in assembly-based and knowledge-based industries such as electronics, automobiles, and telecommunications, and pursued strategies which not only had access to resources and markets, but also to new strategic assets and efficiency gains.

The electronics industry figured prominently in this second wave. The Korean industry, developed from the 1960s, was dominated by a small number of large companies. By 2000, Samsung Electronics had become the world's largest manufacturer of memory chips for computers. In Taiwan, a domestically owned personal computer industry grew from the late 1970s. Acer was the largest firm, but there was also a large number of smaller companies. Both Korean and Taiwanese firms invested extensively elsewhere in Asia, but also more widely, including in the United States and Europe. Acer, which was established in 1976, opened a small sales office in North America in the following year, and a full sales subsidiary in Germany in 1985. Over the following decade it established a network of sales subsidiaries in North America, Europe and Japan, followed by an assembly plant in Malaysia in 1992. By 2000, Acer had sales of nearly $10 billion, and operated twenty-one manufacturing sites and twenty assembly plants in twenty-one countries (Mathews 2002). The Korean and Taiwanese electronics companies accumulated technology in an incremental fashion, starting at the production level. As their home economies were not at the technological frontier, these firms began learning technologies from the shop floor, and then over time shifted their focus to developing skills in marketing and R & D (Tolentino 1993; Hoesel 1999).

Multinational investments often originated from firms embedded in the business groups which characterized many emerging markets (see Section 9.6). By the mid-1990s the Samsung chaebol, which included Samsung Electronics, had almost 400 foreign subsidiaries in over sixty countries. Daewoo, which was established in 1967 as a small textile exporter, became Korea's second largest exporter within five years, and by the 1980s owned hundreds of overseas subsidiaries including heavy machinery, consumer electronics and telecommunications. This chaebol grew further internationally as Daewoo Motors erected motor vehicle assembly plants in emerging markets during the 1990s.

In many other Asian emerging economies, business groups were the mainstay of multinational growth. The CP Group, which became the largest Thai-owned multinational, was founded in 1921 by recent emigrants from China as a small venture selling imported vegetable seeds. It became a major animal feeds manufacturer after World War II. In 1971 a joint venture with Arbor Acres, a leading US poultry breeding firm, became the basis for the creation of a modern integrated chicken business in Thailand. Further diversification followed into real estate and retailing, often through joint ventures with Western firms. During the 1990s CP's close contacts with leading politicians enabled it to secure contracts to build and operate phone lines.

CP expanded internationally first in trading in neighboring Asian countries, and established an animal feed mill in Indonesia in 1969. Thereafter CP expanded its agribusiness elsewhere in Asia, in Turkey, the United States, and especially in China. CP made its first investment in China in 1979, and subsequently CP's agribusiness activities were extended to most provinces in that country. It also invested in automotives, real estate, telecommunications, brewing, and retailing. In 1997 CP operated over a hundred subsidiaries in China, and was ranked as one of the largest inward investors (Brown 1998; Pananond 2001).

The role of diversified business groups suggested that the growth of multinationals from emerging markets rested on factors other than technology. These have sometimes been described as networking or contact capabilities (Kock and Guillen 2001). Business organizations in Asia were rooted in cultures where business networks and social relationships are closely linked. The Chinese phenomenon of *guanxi* reflected a very long tradition of building social networks which could be exploited for commercial or political purposes. In many countries successful business groups had extensive connections with governments and politicians. Arguably, such firms could exploit such networking skills in other countries, especially emerging markets although this raises the question whether the ability to influence and/or bribe is a generic skill or a nation-specific one.

The ethnic Chinese firms spread over East and Southeast Asia provided powerful networks to facilitate international expansion. Embedded networks of personal and business relationships were one of the factors behind the competitive advantage of Hong Kong-based firms (Yeung 1998). The ethnic Chinese origins of Thailand's CP facilitated close relations between that company and the Chinese government. During the 1990s CP's chairman and his brother served as economic advisers to the Chinese government, and sat on the advisory board overseeing Hong Kong's handover to China in 1997 (Brown 1998).

Latin American multinationals were also often parts of wider business groups. They typically emerged from markets which had seen high levels of protection and monopoly in the past, and often benefited from close ties with governments. Typically, they began their international growth in culturally or linguistically proximate countries (see Box 9.4 for the case of Technit).

Whatever the influence of the home economy context on the initial growth of these firms, sustained international competitiveness rested on the creation of organizational capabilities. Cemex, which became Mexico's largest multinational and the third largest cement company in the world, was founded in 1906, and grew to be one of the largest cement producers inside its highly protected home market. It also diversified into mining, hotels, and petrochemicals. It began exporting from Mexico in 1976, and it was only from the late 1980s, after Mexico had begun to liberalize its economy, that acquisitions of cement companies began elsewhere in Latin America and Spain. In the late 1990s Cemex started acquiring cement plants in Asia also, and in 2000 purchased the second largest US cement producer. By 2000 Cemex operated fifty cement plants in ten countries, and it was also established as leading cement trading company in the world. This growth was sustained by a distinctive use of advanced technology in an industry generally regarded as low-technology. In 1988 Cemex was the first private Mexican company to invest in a satellite communications system to allow data and voice transmission between its local plants. This established a tradition of investing in IT infrastructure and advanced technologies. In 2000 the company launched a wide-ranging e-commerce business (Mathews 2002; Chung, Paddack, and Marchand 2003).

Box 9.4 Multinationals from emerging markets: Argentina's Technit Group

Technit was founded in Argentina by the Italian engineer Agostino Rocca in 1945. He had previously managed Dalmine, during the fascist dictatorship of Mussolini. Initially Technit provided engineering and construction services. In 1954 seamless steel tube plants were opened in Argentina (Siderca) and Mexico (Tamsa). In the late 1960s Technit established a flat steel cold rolling plant in Argentina. It diversified into multiple activities, often on the basis of contracts from the government, and behind high protectionist tariffs. By 1983, it consisted of nearly fifty companies. Technit's largest international business is manufacturing seamless pipes, which are used for drilling and transporting oil and gas. In 1993 it acquired full control of Tamsa, Mexico's only seamless steel pipe maker, and in 1996 it acquired the Italian steel tube manufacturer Dalmine after it was privatized. Subsequently steel tube manufacturing plants were built or acquired in Brazil, Venezuela, Japan, and Canada. In 2002 these operations were grouped together under the brand name Tenaris, which gained the world's largest market share in seamless pipes.

During the 1990s Technit acquired the Argentinian oil and gas exploration company Tecpetrol, which subsequently invested in Venezuela, Bolivia, Brazil, Ecuador, and Peru. In Italy Technit built and managed a hospital near Milan. In 2003 the Technit Group had over 100 companies, a combined turnover of $7.8 billion, a workforce of 42 000 and offices in nearly thirty countries

(*Source*: Kock and Guillen 2001; www.technitgroup.com)

The issue of the sustainability, or otherwise, of emerging market multinationals reappeared with the Asian financial crisis in 1997. The rapid multinational growth of Thai companies was abruptly halted. CP divested most of its non-agribusiness stakes in China, and sold its agribusiness in the United States. In South Korea, about a dozen chaebol, including Daewoo—once the second largest business group—collapsed. Hyundai, formerly the largest chaebol, had to spin off its car-making and shipbuilding arms. There was restructuring among the survivors. In 2003 LG, which had become the second largest chaebol, reorganized its affiliates under a holding company, dismantling its complex web of cross-shareholdings, with the result that the founding families lost control of it. The pace of change was slower at the highly diversified Samsung, which accounted for one-fifth of South Korea's total exports. Samsung Electronics remained the world's top maker of dynamic random-access memory (DRAM) and other memory chips, as well as a major global manufacturer of LCD panels, DVD players, and cellular phones. It had production facilities on four continents.

The Asian financial crisis demonstrated some of the organizational constraints faced by firms from emerging markets as they internationalized. It was not easy for firms to create the governance structures and achieve the level of professional management required to sustain foreign businesses, especially when they encountered exogenous economic or political shocks. The 'crony capitalism' which often provided the dynamics behind their rapid growth provided a fragile long-term basis for sustained competitive advantage.

Nevertheless there were new waves of multinationals from other emerging countries, including China (see Box 9.5). The dynamics of the global economy may have lowered the barriers for new entrants because of the growing disintegration of production systems and their replacement by networks of interfirm linkages. The rapid growth of outsourcing to contract manufacturers created new opportunities. In China, networks of small and medium-sized enterprises flourished as OEMs, establishing influential positions in world supply chains in fields of low or mid-level technology. By 2004, the China-based Galanz had become the world's largest microwave manufacturer as a result of this process. In electronics, outsourcing to contract manufacturers created new multinationals. The Singapore-based Flextronics, which experienced a growth in revenues from $450 million to $13 billion between 1995 and 2002, established manufacturing operations in multiple countries. The most sophisticated processes were conducted in the United States and Sweden, while labor-intensive operations were located in low-cost economies, including Mexico, Brazil, Hungary, Poland, and especially China (United Nations 2002).

Within a network-type global economy, firms from emerging markets were able to piggyback on incumbent Western or Japanese firms as customers through subcontracting, linkages, and leverages. Although they lacked the size and technological capabilities of incumbents, there was the potential to grow through leveraging resources from others through joint ventures and contract relationships (Mathews 2002). Yet in terms of overall world FDI, the role of emerging countries as home economies remained extremely modest. The outward FDI of Brazil, the largest Latin American home economy, was less than 1 percent of the world total in 2004. The share of Taiwan and South Korea combined was only 1.5 percent. Even these very small figures were exaggerated by financial transactions and other factors. Although official figures reported Hong Kong's outward FDI

Box 9.5 The growth of China-based multinationals

Although overseas Chinese-owned companies from East and Southeast Asia have been active internationally since the 1960s, the international growth of China-based companies is a recent phenomenon which only began in 1989. However by 1995 it was estimated that over 900 Chinese companies had established 4,600 overseas affiliates in 130 countries, though the majority of the investment was made in Hong Kong and Macao in anticipation of their integration with China in 1997 and 1999 respectively. In 2004 China only accounted for less than 0.5 percent of world outward FDI.

Among the most active initial investors were state-owned resource companies. By 2004 the three largest oil companies, Sinopec, Petrochina, and China National Offshore Oil Corporation had invested in fourteen countries. Among manufacturing companies, Huawei Technologies, established in 1988, grew rapidly after it began to make telecom equipment in the mid-1990s, becoming a leading supplier of digital switches and routers in China. In 1997 Huawei made its first overseas investment. By 2003 the firm employed 15 000 people worldwide, and had secured 3 percent of the world market for routers. Huawei had research centers in Silicon Valley, Bangalore, and Russia.

The leading Chinese multinationals often had a mix of public and private shareholding, which enabled them to access capital markets while retaining strong connections with the government. Haier, China's largest electrical appliance manufacturer, was jointly owned by the Qingdao municipal government, local investors and the firm's management. It was able to grow rapidly within China by acquiring many unprofitable state-owned enterprises in the early 1990s. It entered the compact refrigerator market in the US in 1994, and the wine cooler market three years later. In 2000 Haier established a design center in Los Angeles and opened a factory in South Carolina. By 2004 Haier had thirteen sites abroad, including factories in Iran and Indonesia, as well as the United States.

(*Source: The Economist*, 6 September 2003; Zeng and Williamson 2003.)

stock as $370 billion in 2002—or larger than that of the Netherlands, a breakdown of this amount showed one half was invested in the British Virgin Islands, a small British colony in the Caribbean which was not even a significant offshore financial center (United Nations 2003; Hong Kong Census 2003).

9.5 Multinationals and competitiveness

9.5.1 Multinationals as measures of competitiveness

In a general sense, both the ability and the incentive of firms to produce outside their national boundaries is related to the competitive advantages held by their home economies. However, the correlation between the amount of FDI possessed by a country and its competitiveness is not straightforward. This is partly because of the cumulative nature of FDI. And it is partly because countries can exploit international competitive advantage as much by exporting as by direct investment. Historically, the amount of FDI owned by a country is not a good indicator of national competitiveness. The era of fast economic growth experienced by Western Europe and Japan during the 1950s and 1960s coincided with low levels of FDI from those countries as their firms opted for exporting rather than investment.

The link between international business and home country competitiveness can work in several ways. While home economies can provide competitive advantages for their firms, multinationals may also seek to escape from unattractive homes and relocate production in more attractive economies. The high levels of British multinational investment after World War II might be partly explained by firms seeking to escape from the relatively slow growing British economy by investing in more dynamic markets overseas (Jones 1994).

The essential point is that firms have comparative advantages separate from those of their home economies. The significance of this issue can be seen in the case of the United States. The US share of world export of manufactured goods fell from 18 percent to 12 percent between 1996 and 1990. The emergence of trade deficits prompted a national debate whether the country was becoming less internationally competitive (Porter 1990; Chandler 1994). Yet a calculation of the world market export shares of US-based multinationals including both parent companies and their overseas affiliates demonstrated almost no decline (Lipsey 1994). This did not mean that the United States was not becoming less competitive as a production base, but it did mean that explanations alleging managerial failures in US firms were misplaced.

A similar phenomenon can be observed in other countries. While Swedish shares in world manufactured exports fell by almost one-third between 1965 and 1990, the share of world exports held by Swedish-owned firms marginally increased (Blomström 1990; Lipsey 2004). A broader study covering the period between the middle of the nineteenth century and the 1990s also suggested that British-based multinationals were more competitive than the British economy for much of the period, at least until the British economic performance began to improve from the 1980s (Nachum, Jones, and Dunning 2001).

9.5.2 Multinational impact on home economies

Outward investment by multinationals has an impact on the competitiveness of their home economies. The remittance of dividends, royalties, and income generated abroad should have a positive impact on a home country's per capita income, but there are also potential 'losses' arising from the ability of MNEs to transfer resources from their home economies to other economies.

The fact that multinationals operate abroad through FDI might suggest a mechanism under which foreign investment 'crowds out' domestic investment. The huge British capital exports before 1914 aroused such concerns at the time, and some later historians identified this as a possible explanation for the slowing of British domestic economic growth. The London Stock Exchange served as a highly effective channel for investing British savings abroad, often in 'free-standing companies'. In 1914 around one half of total British savings were invested abroad. It has been suggested that 'inefficiencies' in the British capital markets may have led to a bias towards foreign rather than domestic investments (Kennedy 1987). The main drawback to this argument has been that it has proved hard to find evidence of domestic British entrepreneurs facing a shortage of finance. Although they made less use of the capital markets, entrepreneurs financed their businesses through retained earnings or the use of informal channels (Davis and Gallman 2001).

Nonetheless, some case study evidence points to the possibilities at times of a trade-off between domestic and foreign investment. An examination of the domestic and foreign fixed investment expenditures of seven US multinationals between 1960 and 1980 found a considerable interdependence between foreign and domestic investment. A 1 percent exogenous rise in foreign demand or in a firm's overseas output reduced the parent firm's US fixed investment by amounts ranging from 0.3 percent to 0.8 percent in most of the firms (Stevens and Lipsey 1992). A study of Dutch multinationals in the food and metal/electronics industries between 1978 and 1984 also found that there was an interdependence between domestic investment and FDI. If the Netherlands became less advantageous relative to foreign locations, Dutch MNEs allocated more capital abroad and invested less domestically, and vice versa (Belderbos 1992).

A second major area of debate concerning the impact of multinationals on the home economies concerns their effects on trade. The central issue concerns the extent, if any, that foreign production was a substitute for home-country exports. However, a series of aggregate studies over the last forty years, particularly on data for the US, Sweden, and Japan, have been unable to establish a general relationship between production abroad and exporting. In the minority of cases when a relationship has been found, it was positive (Lipsey, Ramstetter, and Blomström 2000).

A more controversial matter was the extent to which foreign production affects the level of demand for labor in home economies. In crude terms, multinationals might appear to 'export jobs'. In practice, this depends on the type of investment being undertaken. The extensive resource and service sector investments before the 1950s generated substantial employment in head offices, as well as distribution and processing facilities, located in the home economy. Moreover, during the course of the twentieth century it has been seen that many manufacturing affiliates were established in response to tariffs. Insofar as exporting was no longer feasible, home economy employment may have been lost anyway.

The growing integration of international production has increased the relevance of this issue, which began to be widely debated in the United States when the NAFTA agreement was negotiated. The reallocation of production to countries with lower wages can be expected to impact employment in the home economy. Between 1977 and 1999, US multinational manufacturers shed around two million jobs in the United States, and increased their employment elsewhere by about the same number. Over this period, the share of employment accounted for by overseas affiliates increased from 15 percent to 26 percent. The real wages of US workers employed by these firms remained flat over the same period (Harrison and McMillan 2004). Multinational investment also had an impact on the skill-mix within investing industries with a shift in demand favoring white-collar employees at the expense of blue-collar workers. This was because multinationals tend to export production activities, while concentrating management, marketing, and R & D at home (Lipsey 2004).

Within individual firms, the transfer of value-added activities across borders could certainly impact domestic employment. This issue has been highlighted by the outsourcing of jobs to India from the 1990s (see Box 9.6).

Multinationals can have a major impact on the innovatory capabilities of their home economies. In theory, by investing abroad, a firm gains access to tangible and intangible resources—not only technology, but also management systems and natural resources. When it transfers these resources back to its home economy, it may improve the latter's competitiveness. In practice, a number of outcomes are possible. In highly concentrated industries, corporate strategies had the potential to cause major shifts in national innovating capabilities. In the pharmaceutical industry, for example, although European-based companies such as GSK and Novartis remained among the industry leaders, they increasingly shifted the research capabilities of their companies to the United States to be closer to its large and more profitable market for drugs, better universities, and greater public funding of medical research. Novartis moved its global research base to Cambridge, Massachusetts in 2002, while the chief executive of GSK was based in Philadelphia. There was at least the potential for long-term negative implications for the levels of research conducted in Europe.

These issues can be framed in terms of the benefits of 'economic restructuring' versus the threat posed by 'hollowing out'. Multinationals contributed to the restructuring of economies by shifting low value-adding activities abroad out of their home economies, permitting the upgrading of the use of domestic resources. During the 1950s and 1960s Japan's manufacturing investments in Taiwan and other Asian economies were in labor-intensive activities in which it was losing its comparative advantage, such as textiles and

---

Box 9.6 The growth of outsourcing to India since the 1990s

During the 1990s US and British companies began to shift services to India. India offered a combination of low wages and an almost wholly non-unionized workforce. More than half of India's population of 1.05 billion was under the age of 25. There was a large number of English-speaking graduates in the labor force.

While British companies transferred back office and call center jobs, US firms outsourced software contracts on a substantial scale. During the late 1980s US firms began to outsource software development to firms located in Bangalore, which worked on mainframes located in the United States via high speed satellite links. Indian software exports grew from $24 million in 1985 to $850 million in 1996. By 2004 it was estimated that around 470 000 US jobs may have been reallocated to India. Most analysts predicted a fast growth of outsourcing to India in professions such as chartered accounting, legal services, medical consultations, and publishing.

The growth of outsourcing raised political concerns, especially in the United States. At the state level, several states prohibited offshore companies from doing government contract work. Some US politicians called for a 'right to know' law to oblige call centers to disclose their location. However, large US companies emphasized the enormous cost savings available from outsourcing to India, which would permit the upgrading of skills of their domestic workforces.

(*Source*: McKinsey Global Institute 2003.)

toys. These investments facilitated the industrialization of those economies, and assisted them to capture large shares of world markets for their products. The subsequent rising wage rates and trade surpluses in Taiwan and elsewhere undermined their comparative advantage in labor-intensive sectors, which they transferred through FDI to less-developed neighboring countries. At the same time, Japan continued to transfer higher-value manufacturing goods and services to the Asian NICs as the dynamic restructuring process continued (Ozawa 1992). A similar process began during the 1990s as German and other Western European companies transferred production activities to central and eastern Europe following the collapse of Communism. It might at some stage be replicated by South African firms investing in sub-Saharan Africa.

The alternative to a virtuous circle of regional upgrading is a 'hollowing out' process whereby innovatory capabilities and manufacturing capacity are transferred out of a home country without any compensatory upgrading of the remaining resources. This mechanism might lead to a country losing key components of its competitiveness. However, a long time frame is necessary to observe the full extent of any such impact. During the postwar decades, British companies shifted an increasing proportion of their more sophisticated or higher value-added products, and their R & D, to the United States and elsewhere in Europe where income levels were higher. In a country with a high level of outward FDI such as the United Kingdom, this process has the potential to become self-reinforcing, and lead to a spiral of downgrading rather than upgrading (Panić 1982).

However, there were trade-offs. One of the consequences of outward FDI was that exposure to international competition could prompt firms to increase their efficiency, which can in time lead to an upgrading in the use of their domestic resources. In the early 1960s US MNEs were considerably more profitable in their foreign operations than British firms, but over the following two decades the profitability of British firms abroad rose sharply relative to those of other nations, as well as compared with British firms operating only in the United Kingdom (Dunning 1970, 1988b). The enhanced competitiveness of internationally active British firms may have contributed to the improved performance of the British economy at the end of the twentieth century.

9.6 Global firms?

During the 1990s influential studies suggested that multinational firms were in the process of being denationalized (Ohmae 1990). It was noted that the world's largest companies had a considerable percentage of their output outside their home economies, and have their stock quoted on numerous equity markets. Important headquarters functions—such as R & D, finance, and marketing—were being dispersed geographically within large MNEs, and were no longer confined to their home countries. In global firms organized as hierarchies or differentiated networks, nationality would be a legacy of the past rather than a living reality.

This analysis had major policy implications. An influential book by Robert Reich, later to become Secretary of Labor in the Clinton Administration, argued that issues of ownership, control, and national origin were of diminishing importance for policies concerned with the competitive performance of the US economy. The US economy benefited far more from the operations of a foreign-owned company, which undertook R & D and product design and manufacturing in the United States, than it did from a US company which performed most of these functions beyond the national borders. The policy implication was that the US government should facilitate the entry of foreign companies in the United States, while avoiding protection of US companies, simply because they were American-owned. 'The old notion of national boundaries is becoming obsolete' (Reich 1990).

In practice, the influence of nationality continues to be more persuasive than this analysis suggests. The sources of multinational investment and the direction of investment flows continued to show strong national differences. The boards of directors of even the largest firms, especially those based in the United States and Japan, continued to be predominantly of home country origin. There was no strong evidence that organizational markets were converging even between large companies while the behavior of managers with them continues to show persistent national or cultural differences (Laurent 1983; Child and Kieser 1979).

■ **SUMMARY**

The persistent influence of nationality on international firms is one of the paradoxes of multinationals. The ownership of international business has always been concentrated in a small number of home economies, whose firms have differed considerably in the industries and countries in which they invested, and how they organized their businesses. The factor endowments, the size regulatory system, and cultural values of their home economies shaped the nature of their multinational firms. In these ways, geography and culture have shaped the dynamics of international business.

The world's richest economies have always been the home for multinationals. As countries have developed, their firms have sought markets and knowledge across borders. Yet, beyond this generation, the relationship between multinationals and national competitiveness has been shown to have been more complex. In some cases, firms have sometimes chosen to exploit their competitive advantages through exporting rather than FDI. In other cases, firms have sought to use FDI to escape from unsatisfactory home economies. Nor have the gains to home economies of multinational investment been universally positive. Although the historical evidence is elusive, the possibility of asymmetry between the interests of multinationals and their home economy is evident.

10 Engines of growth?

10.1 Assessing the impact

Since the nineteenth century multinationals have discovered and exploited world resources, created transportation and information infrastructures, and moved production processes across borders. They have built and rebuilt the webs of the global economy. This chapter reviews the historical evidence on the long-run impact of multinationals on their host economies. The past provides rich and compelling data, but because multinationals have such a long and heterogeneous history, it also cautions against overgeneralization. It will be shown that multinationals have often served as 'engines of growth', but that negative outcomes have also been evident. This empirical evidence also needs to be framed within the wider context. The spread of multinationals since the nineteenth century has coincided both with an extraordinary growth in world incomes, and with the growing gap between the rich and the poor, the North and the South.

10.2 Host economies over time

10.2.1 The geographical distribution of multinational investment

As earlier chapters showed, in the nineteenth century and the interwar years, the majority of multinational investment was located in the developing world, especially Latin America and Asia, primarily in natural resource and services. Box 10.1 provides the only available estimates of the distribution of FDI by host economy.

These figures provide at best orders of magnitude—Wilkins is unable to quantify her ranking in 1914—but they make three important points. Firstly, multinational investment has never been randomly scattered around the globe, but has clustered in certain locations. Secondly, the United States, Canada, Britain, and Germany were among the world's largest host economies even in the period when the largest share of FDI went to developing countries. Thirdly, it is striking that a number of developing economies, including Brazil, India, and China, have been at various times major recipients of FDI, yet they have remained poor countries.

The shift of FDI to the developed world after World War II, and the reasons for it, were reviewed in Chapter 2. By 1960 the world's three largest hosts were Canada (24 percent of the world total), the United States (14 percent) and the United Kingdom (9 percent)

Box 10.1 Leading host economies in 1914 and 1929

Box Table 10.1 Inward stock of foreign direct investment in 1914 (Ranking of hosts)

	Country
1	United States
2	Russia
3	Canada
4	Argentina
5	Brazil
6	South Africa
7	Austria-Hungary
8–9	India
	China
10–12	Egypt
	Mexico
	United Kingdom

(*Source*: Wilkins 1994a.)

Box Table 10.2 Inward stock of foreign direct investment in 1929 (Ranking of hosts)

Country	Amount (US $ million)
	2,400–1,400
1 Canada	
2 United States	
	1,200–800
3 India	
4 Cuba	
5 Mexico	
	800–500
6 Argentina	
7 Chile	
8 United Kingdom	
9 Malaya	
	500–350
10 Venezuela	
11 Brazil	
12 Australia	
13 South Africa	
14 Netherlands East Indies (Indonesia)	
15 Egypt	
16 China	
	350–200
17 Germany	
18 Spain	

(*Source*: Wilkins 1994a.)

Box 10.2 Inward stock of Foreign Direct Investment in 2002 (Top 20 hosts)

Country	Amount (US $ million)	% World total FDI	% Gross domestic product
United States	1 351 093	18.9	12.9
United Kingdom	638 561	10.0	40.8
Germany	451 589	6.3	22.7
China	447 892	6.3	36.2
Hong Kong, China	433 065	6.1	265.7
France	401 305	5.6	28.2
Netherlands	314 569	4.4	74.9
Brazil	235 908	3.3	52.1
Canada	221 468	3.1	30.4
Spain	217 769	3.1	33.2
Ireland	157 298	2.2	1,210.1
Mexico	154 003	2.2	24.0
Australia	128 696	1.8	32.2
Italy	126 481	1.8	10.6
Singapore	124 083	1.7	137.5
Switzerland	118 139	1.6	44.2
Sweden	110 482	1.5	46.0
Bermuda	78 070	1.1	3,015.0
Argentina	76 992	1.1	74.7
Japan	59 646	0.8	1.5
World Total	**7 122 506**	**100.0**	**22.3**

(*Source*: United Nations 2003.)

(Stopford and Dunning 1983). Among former large hosts, there was no FDI in Russia and China, and very little in India. From the 1980s there was a partial reversal of these trends. The United States became the world's largest host economy, while Western Europe, led by Britain, absorbed an even greater share of world FDI. The most extraordinary development was the emergence of China as a major host economy. Combined with the former British colony of Hong Kong, it had become the world's second largest host economy by the new century (see Box 10.2).

Box 10.2 demonstrates the limited correlation between the amount of inward investment and the overall size of the economy. Singapore, a city-state of 3 million people, had double the stock of inward FDI of Japan in 2002. The relative importance of FDI to countries also differed greatly. Inward FDI was hugely important in small economies such as Hong Kong, Singapore, and Bermuda, and even in the United Kingdom, the world's fourth or fifth largest economy. In contrast, despite the absolute size of FDI in the United States, its relative importance was much smaller.

Box 10.3 The World's Least Favorite Hosts for FDI in 2002

Country/Region	Amount (US $ million)	% World Total FDI	% Gross Domestic Product
Africa (except South Africa)[1]	119 878	1.7	n.a.
India	25 768	0.4	5.1
Russia	22 563	0.3	6.5
Latin America and Caribbean (except major hosts)[2]	508 924	7.1	n.a.
All Developing Countries	2 339 632	32.8	36.0

[1]Stock of South Africa FDI in 2002 was $50 998 million.
[2]Excludes Brazil, Argentina, Mexico, Bermuda, Cayman Islands.
n.a. = not available
(*Source*: United Nations 2003)

As the twenty-first century began, FDI continued to be clustered in a relatively small number of countries. Emerging country hosts accounted for one-third of the stock of world FDI, but one-third of this amount was located in China and Hong Kong. Most of Africa and Latin America, as well as India, held little FDI in absolute terms (see Box 10.3).

10.2.2 Regions and cities

A focus on national economies as hosts can be seriously misleading because multinational investment has rarely been spread evenly in host economies. Multinational investment in mines and oilfields was, almost by definition, concentrated in particular geographical regions. The geographical concentration of FDI may have intensified in recent decades. Japanese automobile transplants in the United States were heavily concentrated in the industrial Midwest and upper South (Kenney and Florida 1993). Foreign affiliates in China were heavily clustered in the coastal regions of that country since the 1980s. The impact of multinationals was experienced most strongly at this regional rather than national level. The attractiveness of countries as hosts was in part the attractiveness of particular regions.

Cities played an increasing role in this schema. As early chapters made clear, international financial and mercantile activities have clustered in a few cities for centuries. These were typically ports, such as Amsterdam, London, and New York. Economies of agglomeration often meant that these cities continued to flourish despite great shifts in the environment. Paradoxically, given the widespread view that new technologies permitted the 'death of distance', the global economy which took hold during the late twentieth century saw an enhanced role of cities. Sassen (2000, 2001) described the enhanced role of 'global cities' such as London, New York, and Tokyo. These cities retained their traditional roles in international trade and banking, but also assumed a new importance as the command centers for the geographically dispersed activities of corporations, and as the homes of specialized service firms. The mixture of firms and talents in such 'global cities' created a giant information center.

Alongside these 'global cities', there was the growth of regional hierarchies of cities where most multinational and other business activity was clustered, such as Paris, Zurich, Mexico City, and Mumbai. Globalization often resulted in rapid shifts in the relative importance of such cities. Over the recent past, São Paulo grew rapidly as a business and financial center in Brazil compared to Rio de Janeiro and Brasilia, while Shanghai grew very fast compared to Hong Kong.

10.2.3 Explaining the relative importance of hosts

A number of factors help to explain the relative importance of countries as hosts.

First, there is the distribution of natural and created resource endowments. The availability of natural resources was a major influence in pre-World War II investment flows. It was the major locational determinant for developing host countries, and also accounted for a significant share of investment in the United States and Canada. National resource endowments continued to influence multinational investment after 1945, but the growth in importance of manufacturing and service sector investments made created resource endowments of growing significance. Foreign companies were attracted to economies such as Singapore and Switzerland because of high levels of investment in human capital and infrastructure.

Second, market size has been extremely important. From the nineteenth century, multinationals sought access to the United States because of its size and income levels. The major Latin American hosts, Brazil, Mexico, and Argentina, were large markets which companies wanted to serve. However, some smaller countries, including Singapore and Ireland, served as export platforms to serve other markets.

Third, geographical location has been important. Both Canada and Mexico owed much of their position as major hosts to their geographical proximity to the United States.

Fourth, there is the influence of national culture. The high risks involved in international business have meant that firms often preferred culturally and/or linguistically similar locations to make investments. Throughout the last 100 years the United States and the United Kingdom have been the single largest inward investor in the other country. The perceived lower risk made the United Kingdom the preferred first location for many US companies investing in Europe. A similar mechanism explains why a high proportion of inward FDI into China initially came from overseas Chinese.

Fifth, corporate governance systems have been important. The position of the United States, Britain, and other English-speaking countries as major host economies has reflected in part the ease of acquiring firms in those countries. This became increasingly important as acquisition grew in importance as the main mode of entry over the last thirty years. Conversely, countries in which corporate governance systems made acquisitions, especially contested ones, difficult, were less important as hosts. Japan and Italy were two examples.

Sixth, influence has been host government policies. Major shifts in the historical rankings of hosts—such as the disappearance of once-major hosts such as Russia and

India—have typically been due to policy shifts. The location of international financial centers, or international insurance centers such as Bermuda, has been closely related to the light as well as competent regulation in those locations (See Chapter 8).

Seventh, there is the issue whether FDI is attracted by strengths or weaknesses in a host economy. In general, especially in recent years, substantial inward FDI has been taken to demonstrate the 'competitiveness' of a host economy. Yet it might also indicate that an economy lacked strong incumbent firms. The foreign multinationals which invested in Britain typically located industries in which British-owned firms (for whatever the reason) were weak, whether it was pharmaceuticals or chemicals before 1914, or automobiles and consumer electronics in the 1980s and 1990s (Bostock and Jones 1994). This is also the case in contemporary China, where many state-owned firms are highly inefficient (Huang 2003).

10.3 The impact on host economies

There are at least seven major areas in which the impact of multinationals needs to be disaggregated.

First, the conditions under which multinationals operated have changed markedly with time. This is particularly evident in the natural resource sector, where the distribution of rents between firms and host governments experienced rapid change (to the benefit of the latter) from the 1950s. While the impact of multinationals can be compared over time, the nature of the comparison needs to be carefully specified. The element of time is also extremely important for assessing the impact of individual investments. The contribution of a foreign enterprise may look greatest at the initial stage of an investment, when it introduces new products or processes into a host economy, and may look negative at later stages, when dividends are flowing out to the parent.

Second, outcomes have varied between industries. Multinationals in manufacturing, services and resources can all bring benefits, or impose costs, on host economies. But the nature of the benefits or costs varies because of inter-industry variations in technology, skill, size, and export-orientation. A stereotyped contrast might be drawn between FDI directed towards natural resources and to labor-intensive manufacturing sectors supplying relatively simple consumer goods, and FDI in a highly innovatory sector or producing high quality differentiated products. The latter type of investment cannot be automatically regarded as more 'beneficial' than the former, but its impact on a host economy will be different. A crucial question for assessing the impact on a host economy is the kind of value-added activities performed by a foreign firm. If an economy is a host for a large quantity of low value-added assembly operations, it may experience rapid economic growth, but its developmental prospects in the long term may be less good. The quality of FDI, rather than its quantity, may well be the crucial determinant of its impact.

Third, the impact of international business on a host economy has varied between enterprises. Because each MNE has a unique combination of skills and resources, it will have a discrete, firm-specific impact on a host economy. Nationality of investing firm may also influence the distinctive package of resources transferred.

Fourth, the mode of entry of foreign firms into a host economy may be an important influence. Entry by a greenfield investment or by the acquisition of an existing domestic firm may have different effects on concentration ratios and on technology transfer. A greenfield investment might result in new products and process being introduced. However, the consequences of greenfield and acquisition modes of entry are often not clear-cut. Multinationals have frequently combined acquisition and greenfield strategies as they grow in a foreign market (Wilkins 1974a; Bostock and Jones 1994).

Fifth, the use of different institutional and contractual forms to operate in foreign countries may have had different consequences. The willingness of an MNE to transfer technology or brands to a foreign subsidiary might be influenced by whether that subsidiary is wholly owned or a joint venture, although the reasons why the firm entered such an arrangement will be a significant factor. Licensing, franchising, and direct investment strategies can be expected to differ in their impact on host economies.

Sixth, the impact of multinationals depends on the nature of the host economy, especially the level of human capital development, and the quality of infrastructure and institutions. The host country response will also be partly conditioned by the policies of its government. Host governments can improve the ability of their enterprises to absorb foreign technologies by investing in education and infrastructure. They can set the conditions under which foreign firms enter and operate in their country. They provide the overall macroeconomic framework under which foreign-owned affiliates function.

A broad distinction might be made between the impact of multinationals on developed and developing economies. In the former, it could be expected that local enterprises would have more capacity to absorb foreign technologies, or to offer competition to foreign multinationals. Governments are more likely to be better placed than their developing country equivalents to negotiate with large foreign companies. The cultural differences between multinationals and developed hosts are likely to be much less than between multinationals and developing countries (Buckley and Casson 1989).

Seventh, it is difficult to generalize about the overall impact of international business because of the difficulty of defining the 'counterfactual' position. What would have happened if the multinational investment had not been made? There are major methodological problems involved in reaching a conclusion. It is possible to make a calculation on a case-by-case basis. Lall and Streeten (1977), in a classic study of the impact of 159 multinationals on six developing countries in the 1960s, compared actual foreign investments with their most likely local replacements using local technology or easily purchased foreign technology. The problem with such studies is that the crucial variable is the availability of entrepreneurship rather than technology. It is usually a matter of speculation whether a particular FDI introduced an activity a local firm would never have done, or alternatively 'crowded out' local firms from engaging in such activity.

10.4 Transferring and creating resources

10.4.1 Knowledge

Multinationals transfer products and processes, and technologies and organizations, across borders. Given the central role of innovation in economic growth, such knowledge transfers might provide one of the most important ways in which firms act as engines of growth. Since they transfer capabilities across borders, they have the capability to function as Schumpeterian-style entrepreneurs in disrupting established practices and introducing innovations (Wilkins 1974a).

History provides rich evidence on these transfers. Manufacturing multinationals have been important transferors of technology between industrialized economies from the nineteenth century onwards. Before 1914 European enterprises in the United States transferred new products, processes and technologies in such industries as chemicals (Wilkins 1989). US multinationals transferred technologies in electricals, and later automobiles, to Europe (Wilkins 1974a, 1974b). However, the existence of technology transfers by multinationals does not automatically imply that it had growth-inducing impact. Transferred technologies across borders within a multinational were not always absorbed and utilized by locally owned firms. In an interwar context, Ford's Dagenham factory in Britain was enormous, but it was physically located away from the principle centers of British car production, which limited technological 'spin-off' to domestic firms (Church 1986).

The establishment and maintenance of mines, oil fields, plantations, shipping depots, and railroad systems also involved the transfer of packages of knowledge to developing economies in the nineteenth century. The foreign-owned enterprises which introduced modern transportation systems, power utilities, and telephones into host economies provided technologies which radically changed the lifestyles of those affected by them. Given the absence of appropriate infrastructure in developing countries, foreign enterprises frequently not only introduced technologies specific to their activities, but social technologies such as police, postal, and education systems. The impact of plantation agriculture on lifestyles and even the physical appearance of countries was enormous (see Box 10.4).

Technological diffusion from plantations and mines was often limited because they functioned as enclaves in their host economies (see Section 10.7). An even greater constraint was local capabilities. In nineteenth-century China, the system of political economy and the attitudes of its officials have been identified as major obstacles to technology transfer. Foreign firms were restricted in the activities they could undertake, and the government sought to confine them geographically to coastal ports (Brown 1979). In many countries high illiteracy rates, undeveloped infrastructures and alien business cultures proved to be formidable obstacles. It has remained constant that successful technology transfer by multinationals rests on the absorptive capacity of host economies (Borensztein, De Gregorio, and Lee 1998). Japan was one country which demonstrated a considerable amount of absorptive capacity as it sought to create a modern economy from the late nineteenth century onwards (see Box 10.5).

Box 10.4 Banana plantations in Central America

By 1914 United Fruit controlled a vast acreage of plantations in Central America, justifying its local name of 'El Pulpo', or the Octopus. The creation of plantations involved cutting down jungle forests. Drainage and water systems were built. Company towns were built in former jungle areas, and a social infrastructure put in place. The Central American Atlantic coastline was transformed from a sparsely populated location for scattered Indian tribes and exiled American fortune seekers, into a well-organized plantation economy. There was a great change in the composition of the population also, as labor was imported from Jamaica and elsewhere to work on the plantations of Costa Rica, Panama, Guatemala and Honduras. The plantations had few inputs of local origin, and much of the value-added occurred after the product had left the exporting country. Workers were paid in vouchers which could only be used in the company stores.

United Fruit invested heavily in medical provisions in order to counter the high mortality rates endemic to the tropical lowlands of Central America. The first hospital was opened in Panama in 1899. Initially, company hospitals served only white, North American employees, but later the whole labor force was treated in order to counter both high labor turnover and labor inefficiency caused by ill health. In the mid-1920s the company launched a concerted effort against malaria, involving improved sanitation and the extensive use of insecticides, which caused a sharp fall in infection rates. Little attention was paid to respiratory diseases such as pneumonia and tuberculosis that caused the highest mortality among the largely malnourished labor force. Pneumonia victims died soon after entering the hospital, and it was believed to be cheaper to allow the disease to run its course.

Bananas were highly susceptible to disease and rapidly depleted soils, and before the 1960s could not be cultivated on the same land for more than about ten years. When United Fruit left disease-infested lands for newer terrain, it removed infrastructure which had any value. In Costa Rica, United Fruit switched from the Atlantic to the Pacific coast in 1938, leaving behind both the Jamaican workers and the small producers from whom it had purchased bananas. It moved back to the Atlantic in the 1960s.

United Fruit held a very strong position in its host economies. Its interests were protected by the US government, which intervened regularly in the region. The US Army invaded Honduras in 1903, 1912, and 1919, the Dominican Republic in 1903 and 1916, Nicaragua in 1907 and 1909, and Panama in 1912 and 1918. The ownership of multiple sites in different countries, as well as contracts with local producers, gave United Fruit considerable power in dealing with the labor unrest which grew in the interwar years. In 1934 a strike at Limón, in Costa Rica, included 10 000 workers, and involved the Communist Party. The export taxes paid by the company were a tiny proportion of the total volume of the fruit it shipped abroad. If taxes were raised, United Fruit was able to pay lower wages to its workers or lower prices to independent producers.

United Fruit continued to dominate Central America till after the end of World War II. It was the single largest private sector company in Honduras and Guatemala, and one of the largest elsewhere. During the 1950s it accounted for 75 percent of the banana exports in Guatemala, 93 percent in Panama and 98 percent in Costa Rica.

(*Source*: Chomsky 1996; Facio 1972; Seligson 1980.)

Box 10.5 Technology transfer and absorptive capacity in Japan, 1899–1940

Despite the low amount of inward FDI received by Japan, foreign firms played an important part in that country's early modernization. Between 1899, when FDI was permitted by the government, and the 1930s Western multinationals made direct investments in Japan in technologically advanced industries, especially machine equipment and electric machinery, in which Japanese business was weak or nonexistent. US companies such as Western Electric and General Electric were among the pre-1914 investors, while the US automobile companies invested in the 1920s. In many cases, foreign firms formed joint ventures with Japanese partners, several of which later became leading Japanese enterprises. The first of these joint ventures was the Nippon Electric Company (NEC), established in 1899 with Western Electric as a 54 percent shareholder.

There were considerable technological and managerial transfers from these foreign affiliates. Mitsubishi Electric, founded in 1921, rapidly became a major manufacturer of heavy electric apparatus as a result of an affiliation with Westinghouse, through which a large transfer of production and management techniques was made to the Japanese company. There was dissemination of techniques learned from foreign affiliates as companies emulated one another, and as workers changed companies. This can be seen in the case of the Japanese rubber industry, which owed its origins to the British-owned Dunlop's factory in Kobe which opened in 1909. Bridgestone, the first Japanese-owned rubber company to make automobile tyres, was dependent on former Dunlop engineers and skilled workers for its production technology in its early stages.

The Japanese business system both absorbed new technologies and adapted them to local conditions. The Japanese automobile industry originated in the 1920s entirely through the operations of Ford and GM, which established assembly operations. The US firms bought parts locally, and a network of suppliers grew around them. These included Nissan, which started in the motor vehicle industry as a Ford parts supplier. In the same period Toyota's sales organization was formulated by personnel who had learned American marketing methods while working with the GM affiliate. In the 1930s, when the Japanese government introduced restrictions on Ford and GM which led them to divest from Japan, Nissan and Toyota took over many former Ford and GM suppliers and dealers, as well as key personnel.

(*Source*: Mason 1992; Udagawa 1990; Wilkins 1990a.)

Research on technology transfer by multinationals to developing countries from the 1960s has highlighted some of the problems which arise in this area. It was sometimes found that the profits, royalties and fees were high. Multinationals often imposed restrictive conditions as a condition of technology transfer, which limited the export capacities of affiliates, and restrained the expansion of technology capacity (Hood and Young 1979; Chen 1994). There is conflicting evidence on the consequences of foreign acquisition of firms in developing countries during the 1990s. There have been cases of both reduction and expansion of R & D in acquired firms. Innovative activity could be downgraded by acquisitions in countries in which it is lagging behind world frontiers (United Nations 2000). This might stimulate a spiral of decline rather than growth in a developing country. Indeed, the shift of pharmaceutical research to the United States over the last two decades suggests that globalization has the potential to concentrate innovative activity in a limited number of favored locations.

Multinationals sometimes used overly capital-intensive technologies in developing countries, which were used to produce inappropriate products. However, there were wide variations between countries, industries, and firms in outcomes. Research in the 1970s and 1980s into whether foreign affiliates used more capital-intensive technologies than domestic firms, found that they indeed did, for example in India, Brazil, and Ghana, but did not in the Philippines, Mexico, and Malaysia (Chen 1994). There is strong evidence that multinationals always make some adjustment of technology to local conditions. The initial engineering of a plant is virtually always geared to the characteristics of each site. Once a facility is established, there is often further adaption in ancillary activities, though not in the core technology (Lall 1993).

A more crucial issue than both the cost and the appropriateness of transferred technology is the extent to which it is utilized and diffused in the host economy, and thus contributes to that economy's own technological capability. The fact that multinationals have undertaken technological development mostly in their home economies has limited their impact in this area, especially in developing economies, where little R & D has even been undertaken (United Nations 2000). Developed host economies have faced a different problem that most R & D undertaken by the foreign affiliates of multinationals has been directed to the adaptation of particular products and processes rather than to basic or fundamental research (Casson 1991b). The location of R & D has also been a regional issue within host economies. Since World War II a number of European regions, such as Scotland, suffered from 'branch plant syndrome', or a concentration of low skill and low value-added activities, while foreign multinationals located their R & D either at home or in more attractive regions of the host economy.

The transfer of soft technologies, especially management and organizational practices, was an important component of knowledge transfers by multinationals. The technologies which were transferred by the service and natural resource investors of the nineteenth and early twentieth centuries were embodied in discrete managerial and organizational systems. In the twentieth century, multinationals have facilitated the partial transfer of management systems between countries. US affiliates transferred a range of marketing, accounting, and other managerial techniques to Western Europe after 1945. From the 1970s Japanese multinationals transferred 'lean production' internationally. This was achieved partly by the opening of Japanese transplants in the United States and elsewhere as discussed in Chapter 4, which in turn stimulated US firms to find ways to learn the new methods. Ford purchased 24 percent of the Japanese car maker Mazda in 1979, while GM secured access to Toyota's technology through the NUMMI joint venture. US companies used these links to import Japanese models—relabeled with American names—to supplement their domestically produced models, and gain access to Japanese-style manufacturing methods (Kenney and Florida 1993).

There is little doubt, both that the international transfer of knowledge by multinationals has considerable potential to promote economic growth, and that historically much of this potential has not been realized. During the 1990s, for example, the Spanish airline, telecommunication, banks, and other firms that invested extensively in Latin America were almost always technologically more sophisticated and efficient than the local firms they acquired, but many investments experienced management problems, and some failed entirely, and the amount of successful knowledge diffusion was probably much less than might have been anticipated (Toral 2001). Knowledge transfer and diffusion across borders is difficult. New organizational practices, institutional structures and work methods take longer to diffuse across national boundaries than do narrowly defined technological innovations, because they are embedded in past historical traditions and are 'culture bound' (Hofstede 1980). As shown in Chapter 7, the ability of large corporations to transfer knowledge even within their own boundaries may have been significantly less than once thought.

10.4.2 Capital

The transfer of capital by multinationals can supplement domestic savings and contribute to domestic capital formation. For countries that are capital-constrained, this can bring large incremental benefits by providing an addition to domestic investment. In the nineteenth century this was quite important. The European 'free-standing' companies provided the institutional means to transfer large amounts of capital to develop and exploit the resources and markets beyond Western Europe. Although fraud and failure were commonplace, and it would seem that a good proportion of the capital raised in Britain and elsewhere never left those countries, the significance of large capital flows was considerable. They financed the building of the infrastructure of the first global economy, and the development of the minerals and foodstuffs which fueled its growth.

Research on multinationals since World War II has tended to downplay the significance of capital flows. Firms made extensive use of local borrowing and reinvested earnings. A study of Brazil and Mexico between 1967 and 1989 showed that reinvested earnings by multinationals accounted for between 15 percent and 90 percent of annual inflows of FDI (United Nations 1992). However, during the 1990s FDI was the largest source of external finance for developing countries as a whole. It was also more stable than portfolio flows, which proved highly volatile during the financial crises of that decade (United Nations 2000).

Historically, foreign enterprises have sometimes contributed considerably to more efficient financial intermediation. In the nineteenth century European overseas banks introduced the entire concept and infrastructure of modern banking into some developing countries. In other cases they comprised the most stable element of the banking system, as in late nineteenth-century Latin America. By financing their lending through locally raised deposits and the issue of bank notes, they contributed to the financial deepening of their host economies, even if they did not transfer large amounts of capital to them (see Chapter 5). Later generations of multinational banks made important contributions to financial intermediation. From the 1960s US banks were important in extending banking services, strengthening markets for foreign exchanges, and reducing the risks of financial services. The American banks which opened branches in Europe in this period often exercised a dynamic role on local banking systems by introducing new lending instruments and more aggressive marketing practices (Kelly 1977).

Financial deepening by foreign enterprises involved costs as well as bringing benefits. The European overseas banks in the nineteenth century had lending policies which favored international trade finance. They focused their lending on European businesses or large-scale indigenous commercial enterprises, and did not lend to the peasant agriculture which was so important in many of their host regions. In Asia (and elsewhere) lending to locally owned businesses was channeled through intermediaries—such as the *comprador* in Chinese-speaking regions—which increased their cost of borrowing. These practices continued into the 1950s and, although they reduced risks for the banks, they may well have hindered the development of entrepreneurship in these host economies (Jones 1993a). More recently, multinational banks in developing countries have often specialized in serving other multinationals or large domestic clients. While host government restrictions have often encouraged or even obliged such strategies, it has meant that foreign banks have assumed little role in the domestic intermediation process.

10.4.3 Employment

It seems likely that the importance of multinationals in terms of world employment was relatively greater historically than more recently today because of the vast numbers of workers which were employed in labor-intensive plantation and mining. US mining and smelting properties in Mexico are estimated to have employed more than 500 000 Mexicans in 1915. At the end of the 1920s the Guggenheims employed 100 000 workers in their Chilean nitrate operations (Wilkins 1974a).

However, the large numbers of jobs in mining, plantations, and utilities offered few opportunities for the upgrading of human skills. In colonial and other developing countries, expatriates were used to handle the newest technologies and install and manage complex systems. Training was provided to local employees to enable them to fill unskilled or semiskilled jobs (Headrick 1988). This issue has been examined in detail in the case of the French-controlled Suez Company, which built and operated the Suez Canal in Egypt between 1854 and 1956 under the terms of a concession. The Canal had a major stimulus on the Egyptian economy, but the company had no interest in developing a qualified local workforce or a local elite of technicians. Until 1936 the Egyptian staff were almost exclusively unskilled workers. The company became widely regarded as a symbol of foreign exploitation, and was nationalized in 1956 (Piquet 2004).

Manufacturing multinationals were significant employers in developed countries by the 1920s, during which ITT's workforce in Europe reached almost 35 000 (Wilkins 1974a). The overall significance of foreign affiliates in total employment remained small until the postwar decades. While in 1932 the British manufacturing subsidiaries of US multinationals employed around 65 000 people, thirty years later British employment in US manufacturing affiliates had reached around 450 000, or 5 percent of the manufacturing workforce (Bostock and Jones 1994; Jones 1988).

The expansion of the second global economy led to a growth in the worldwide employment by foreign affiliates from 19 million to 53 million between 1982 and 2002 (United Nations 2003). This was a small share of the world's total workforce, and a negligible proportion of employment in developing countries, though multinationals also created indirect employment through linkages with subcontractors and suppliers. Typically the low-skill assembly jobs in developing economies provided opportunities and incomes which are marginally higher than those available in the indigenous sector. Many studies have shown that the affiliates of foreign firms typically pay higher wages than locally owned firms (Lipsey 2004).

The creation of employment by multinationals was not a linear process. It may have become more volatile during the second global economy. Cross-border acquisitions were often followed by job losses. In Latin America, central and eastern Europe, and elsewhere, cross-border acquisitions of privatized services typically led to sharp falls in employment. In developed countries, cross-border mergers and acquisitions in financial services, automobiles, and other industries also resulted in large redundancies as a result of restructuring (United Nations 2003).

As trade barriers fell and investment restrictions were reduced in many countries, it also became easier for firms to move low-skill jobs between countries. Between 1979 and 1991 US automobile companies reduced their American workforce by around 300 000, in part by shifting production offshore. The growth of China as a host economy had a disruptive effect on other low-cost manufacturing locations. It lay behind the sharp fall in employment in Mexico's *maquiladores* after 2000 (see Box 4.6). Nor was volatility restricted to low skill manufacturing jobs, as companies began to 'outsource' accounting, IT, and other professional jobs to lower wage countries.

It was often argued that multinationals were more 'footloose' than purely domestic firms. There is almost no systematic historical data to support or counter this view, but some research on the recent past provides some support. A study of manufacturing plant closures in Indonesia between 1975 and 1989 showed that closure rates were significantly lower for foreign-owned plants than for locally-owned ones. However, the plants of foreign companies were larger and more efficient than local ones. When the study compared factories owned by foreign firms with factories of the same size and efficiency, the probability of closure was 20 percent higher for multinationals (Bernard and Sjoholm 2003). A similar result was derived from a comparison of plant closures within the United States by US-owned firms with multinational operations and purely domestic businesses (Bernard and Jensen 2003).

The quality rather than the quantity of employment provided by multinationals was also an important issue. Since World War II US multinationals have exhibited a much greater propensity to employ nationals in senior positions than Japanese multinationals. However, in all cases there was a correlation between the number of expatriates and the age of the investment—new ventures typically began with nationals from the parent firm in senior positions—and its condition, as multinationals typically made a greater use of expatriates if an affiliate had difficulties. There are industry differences also. Multinational banks typically appoint their own nationals to senior positions in foreign branches. This reflects the importance of personal contacts in banking services, but it has made a distinct impact on the skill-mix of the employees available in major international financial centers such as London and New York (Daniels 1986).

In recent decades, the role of multinationals as employers of women has become important. A large proportion of the labor force employed by multinationals in export processing and free trade zones were young females. In many cases this has provided employment opportunities for women who had previously had low levels of participation in paid economic activity because of sociocultural traditions and overt discrimination. However, most jobs were overwhelmingly low-paid and low-skilled, and might be regarded as confirming rather than challenging the lowly status of women in certain countries. Gender stereotyping is often reinforced. Often the payment of low wages is justified by claims that female earnings are only 'supplemental'. Almost invariably, these jobs have little or no labor protection, while the growing use of subcontracting and other devices has further weakened employee rights (Collins 2003).

Multinationals from a number of Western countries, especially the United States, have for decades had a growing proportion of women in managerial positions. Exposure to women in senior managerial positions in multinationals might be expected to break down stereotypes and social restrictions on the employment of women in senior positions in host economies where female emancipation is less advanced. However, in practice, multinationals have not yet assumed a dynamic role in lessening gender discrimination. Few multinationals have sent female managers abroad, especially to host countries where the representation of women in management is small, on the grounds that foreign prejudice renders them ineffective (United Nations 1992). Moreover, while US firms have been in the forefront of equal employment opportunities, Japanese companies have been among the most extreme in their discrimination against female managers. As a result, there remains no correlation between multinational activities and enhanced female career opportunities.

Foreign-owned companies have often used different employment terms, conditions, and practices from those prevailing in the host economy. When US manufacturers invested in Europe in the first half of the twentieth century, they were often disinclined to negotiate with trade unions (Jones 1988). After World War II US multinationals introduced important innovatory practices into their European affiliates, especially bargaining at the level of the enterprise or plant and productivity bargaining. A number of prominent companies, including IBM and the confectionary company Mars, would not permit trade unions. US firms were often uneasy with regulations governing worker participation in European companies. They had clear preferences for performance-related pay and formalized performance appraisal systems (Edwards and Ferner 2002).

Although the country-of-origin effect in multinational employment policies appears strong, foreign firms adjusted their policies to take account of the laws and customary practice of host countries. In postwar Germany, statutory provision was made requiring employment representation on the boards of firms above a certain size. Foreign companies had to meet these legal requirements for co-determination. US companies investing in Scotland between the 1940s and 1970s were only partially able to resist the strong trade unions in that country (Knox and Mckinlay 1999). In many European countries, as well as in Japan, the 'hire-and-fire' policies often favored by US firms were either not socially acceptable, or else constrained by extensive requirements to make redundancy payments. Foreign affiliates often followed local practices in the United States, whose weak employee protection laws provided no strong incentive to transfer more expensive home country practices (Rosenzweig and Nohria 1994). Multinationals did not transfer more expensive human resource policies from their home economies if they were not required to do so by hosts. German firms, for example, have not implemented co-determination (or high welfare payments) in foreign affiliates, and often adopted elements of the American model in their international business (Ferner and Varul 2000).

10.5 Trade

Almost by definition, multinationals have a greater involvement in the international economy than purely domestic firms. Before the 1930s the trade effects of international business on developing hosts were highly significant given that so much was concerned with primary commodities. Petroleum and mining firms, trading companies, overseas banks and other service companies provided a business infrastructure to exploit and export commodities. The consequences were sometimes, as in the case of petroleum, dramatic. The international oil companies turned one economy after another—Russia and Mexico before 1914, Iran and Venezuela in the interwar years, Kuwait and Saudi Arabia subsequently—into major export economies. Multinationals turned other countries into major exporters of bananas, sugar, rubber, and other commodities. Some countries became heavily dependent on one or a few commodities for almost all of their export earnings. The sharp contraction in the value and volume of world commodity trade in the 1930s highlighted the risks and limitations of this specialization (see Box 10.6).

It is not very productive to speculate whether developing host economies would have been 'better-off' if their mineral or agricultural resources had not been developed, or developed by local rather than foreign firms. However, certain corporate strategies reduced the advantages derived from host economies from their exports. The fact that most minerals and agricultural commodities were exported with only the minimum of processing meant that most value was added to the product in the developed economies, which was usually the MNE home economy. Complex patterns of vertical and horizontal integration resulted in the transfer pricing between the various stages of mining/growing and processing not taking place at arm's length.

The literature on the strategies of manufacturing affiliates since the 1960s generally shows that they have a high propensity to export, and tend to tilt the industrial structures of host economies towards internationalization. The historical development of this pattern is still in the process of being established. Insofar as a considerable amount of manufacturing FDI before World War II took place as a response to protectionism, it is reasonable to assume that the bulk of the output of subsidiaries was for host country consumption. However, the exporting activities of some affiliates were considerable even in the interwar years. By the 1930s at least one-third of foreign-owned manufacturing subsidiaries in Britain were engaged in exporting (Wilkins 1974a; Bostock and Jones 1994).

From the 1960s, multinationals were major drivers of exports in electronics, garments, and other assembly industries from Southeast Asia and elsewhere, and later from China. In 2002 they accounted for nearly one half of China's exports. Over 90 percent of these exports were manufactured goods, especially machinery and equipment.

Box 10.6 Oil in Iran before the 1950s

Before 1914 Iran was one of the poorest and least developed economies on earth. The great majority of the population were employed in subsistence agriculture and had extremely low incomes, and there was a dearth of modern infrastructure from education to transport. The economy was dominated by foreign enterprises. The most important was the Anglo-Persian Oil Company (later British Petroleum) which discovered oil in the southwest of the country in 1908. By 1914 it had built a pipeline to the coast and a refinery at Abadan.

Iran emerged as a major world oil exporter, and oil was the country's largest export in the interwar years. The Anglo-Persian Oil Company operated on the basis of a concession which awarded a monopoly for petroleum exploitation and development over virtually all of Iran. Exports and imports were free of all taxes, though the government possessed an ill-defined right to receive a proportion of the annual profit of companies formed to work the concession.

Because of the geographical isolation of the oilfields, as well as the decentralization of government before the mid-1920s, the oil company had to provide its own economic and social infrastructure. In southern Iran, it constructed and operated roads, electricity and water supplies, telephone lines, transportation, education, and security. Abadan, where the refinery was located, was a self-sufficient industrial complex with few local contractors or other contacts with the local economy. By the end of the 1930s only about 5 percent of Anglo-Persian's total production was consumed in Iran.

There were some linkages with the domestic economy. The royalties paid by the company to the government, together with its sales of foreign exchange to secure the local currency needed for its operations, provided Iran's largest single source of foreign exchange. The company employed 27 000 Iranians in 1930, and was the largest employer in the modern industrial sector. A special training school at Abadan took school-leavers and put them through an apprenticeship course. Though most workers stayed with the company, a minority left, and Iranian industrial occupations became full of persons who had been trained by the oil company.

To most Iranians, Anglo-Persian became the symbol of British imperialism. In 1907 Iran was divided into 'spheres of influence' which recognized Russia's 'interest' in the north and Britain's 'interest' in the south. During World War I it became a battleground for competing armies, and the British and the Soviets occupied it again in World War II. Iran's focal position as a center of diplomatic rivalries forced home governments and their business interests into a close, if not always harmonious, relationship. Anglo-Persian had close contacts with the British government. The relationship became closer still when the British government acquired its shareholding in the oil company in 1914.

The symbolic role of British business provoked a violent reaction from modernizing Iranian governments from the 1920s. The government became determined to maximize both its control over, and its revenue from, Anglo-Persian, as part of a strategy to develop the Iranian economy and to reverse foreign political and economic domination. Oil, as the major source of foreign exchange, became regarded as a vital resource for national progress. When the onset of the Great Depression reduced demand in the world oil industry, and cut state oil revenues, company–government relations deteriorated. In 1932, the company's concession was unilaterally cancelled. A new concession was finally

continues

> **Box 10.6 Oil in Iran before the 1950s (*continued*)**
>
> agreed in the following year, which reduced the concession area and improved the financial terms for the Iranian government, but the episode proved a curtain-raiser for the nationalization of the British company in 1951.
>
> (*Source*: Ferrier 1982; Bamberg 1994.)

The presence of foreign affiliates also affects the volume and composition of host country imports. During the initial establishment of foreign affiliates, multinationals can have high import propensities because of limited knowledge of market conditions in host countries and locally available inputs. Over time, foreign affiliates may switch to a greater use of domestic goods and services. However, multinationals often also favor foreign sources of supply in order to maintain greater control over quality and reliability of supply, or take advantage of bulk purchases for the firm as a whole. A high import propensity will limit the net balance-of-payments effect of multinationals on a host economy even if they are very active in exporting, though the importing activities of multinationals can serve as an engine of growth. For example, by importing capital and intermediate goods, multinationals can relieve supply constraints in developing countries.

The role of multinationals in setting up integrated production systems across countries has major implications for host economies. By the 2000s, multinationals were responsible for an estimated two-thirds of world trade, about half of which took place inside the boundaries of firms (United Nations 2000). The creation of such production systems opened trade and distribution channels, but it did mean that corporate strategies were the decisive influence on trade flows, and with them the international location of value-added activities. While multinationals can provide the marketing channels which enable access to international markets, affiliates assigned to the lower end of production value-added chains might stagnate.

10.6 Market structure

Multinationals influence the structure of markets in host economies. Multinationals became particularly pronounced in manufacturing sectors characterized by market imperfections, such as oligopolistic competition, extensive product differentiation and entry barriers. This might suggest that the effect of multinationals will be to increase concentration levels. The alternative possibility is that multinationals might increase competition and reduce industrial concentration by their entry into existing markets. The empirical testing of either hypothesis is difficult, partly because concentration ratios are affected by many other factors than FDI, and partly because it is difficult to arrive at a dynamic model of cause and effect. The broad conclusion of the research which has been undertaken is that (once again) the nature of the impact on market structure will depend on industry- and host country-specific factors (Caves 1996).

Historically, the entry of multinationals has often increased competition, and may have reduced concentration levels, although during the interwar years the widespread use of cartels rendered this outcome unlikely. It has also been quite common for foreign multinationals in the past to hold dominant market positions at certain times in developed host economies. Ford, whose first British assembly plant opened in 1911, accounted for almost a quarter of British automobile production a decade later. The dominant market positions held by such multinationals was fully explicable by their possession of technological, managerial, and other ownership advantage, but these positions were almost never a stable long-term phenomenon. Most dominant positions tend to be eroded by new competitors or the loss of competitive vigor, as in the case of Ford in interwar Europe (Church 1994). In more recent decades competition policy has limited the impact of multinationals on concentration levels. The United States, European Union, and other developed countries all scrutinize cross-border mergers and acquisitions for negative impact on competition, which tends to further diminish the impact on concentration.

The entry of multinationals into small emerging markets may have a more significant impact on concentration levels. The growth of multinationals in Malaysia, Mexico and a number of other developing countries in the 1960s and 1970s appeared to raise concentration levels by introducing new capital-intensive processes and differentiated products (Lall 1979: Blomström 1986). As many emerging markets deregulated and privatized industries, large foreign firms were able to assume dominant positions, especially as many countries had only weak regulatory frameworks (United Nations 2003).

10.7 Linkages and spillovers

Many of the potential benefits which multinationals bring to their host economies arise from spillovers and linkages. There is a considerable body of research showing that, at least for recent decades and the manufacturing sector, foreign-owned plants have higher productivity than locally owned ones in the same sector. This phenomenon was first explored in a comparison between US and local companies in Britain during the 1950s (Dunning 1958). The productivity differential has persisted in Britain, and similar evidence has been found for the United States. There are many studies showing the superior productivity of foreign-owned companies in the manufacturing sectors of developing countries over the last three decades. The higher capital intensity or larger scale of production in foreign-owned plants often accounts for at least some of this productivity difference (Lipsey 2004).

In theory there can be substantial 'knowledge spillovers' to the local economy from multinationals. Workers and managers trained by foreign companies may change jobs and transfer to local companies the skills and attitudes learned with foreign employers. Pecuniary spillovers arise when the foreign affiliate pays higher wages to prevent such workers from leaving. However, research on the experience of recent decades has found little or no aggregate evidence of spillovers from multinational firms to local firms in the same sector, especially in developing countries. One explanation is that multinationals have an incentive to minimize technology leakages to competitors (Alfaro and Rodriguez-Clare 2004).

The presence of multinationals can exercise a 'demonstration effect' on locally-owned firms. Greater competition has forced them to adopt more efficient products methods, or else driven weaker firms out of business. The historical evidence suggests that both outcomes have been frequent in developed markets. This was shown in a study of the impact of US machinery firms such as Singer, National Cash Register (NCR), and Otis Elevator on the German industry before 1914. NCR sought to eliminate its German cash register competitors by price cutting and patent suits. Two out of the three local competitors went out of business. In sewing machines, some local companies reacted to Singer by reducing their production costs and adopting American manufacturing methods. Others diversified away from sewing machines. Opel became Germany's largest automobile manufacturer (Blaich 1984).

In many developing countries local firms have lacked the capabilities to compete with large multinationals, and the greater the technology gap, the more difficult this gap was to fill. In branded consumer goods, such as cosmetics, foreign entry has often resulted in local firms retreating into the lower end of the market, competing on cost. However, there have been major exceptions to this trend. In postwar India, for example, the fabrics wash market was dominated by Unilever's long-established affiliate Hindustan Lever, which sold hard soap—which accounted for over 90 percent of the total Indian market—as well as premium detergent powder. The market was transformed from the late 1970s by an entrepreneurial firm which sold little packets of detergent powder called Nirma, initially made in the owner's shed, which was the same price as hard soaps, but had much better washing power. Poorer urban and later rural consumers switched from hard soap. Later, the Indian company moved up-market with products which directly competed with Unilever's premium customer base. From the mid-1980s, Hindustan Lever responded with the launch of several low-cost products, but Nirma was firmly established as one of the largest selling detergent brands in the world, and the Indian company held 35 percent of the overall detergents market compared to Hindustan Lever's 30 percent (Butler and Ghoshal 2002).

There is convincing evidence of the positive linkages between multinationals and suppliers in many developing countries over recent decades. Foreign affiliates are often more demanding in their specifications and delivery targets, while more willing to provide assistance and advice to local firms (Alfaro and Rodriguez-Clare 2004). In the interwar years and later, US affiliates in Europe and elsewhere had a similar effect (Dunning, 1958, 1986).

The impact on local firms is lessened if foreign investors are accompanied by suppliers from their own country. This has a long history in the automobile industry. When US automobile companies invested in Europe in the interwar years, they were accompanied by US car body builders, tire companies, manufacturers of wheels, batteries, spark plugs, and window glass (Wilkins, 1974a). In some cases, their factories were physically located in host countries next to the main automobile assembly plant (Bostock and Jones 1994). The same phenomenon occurred when the Japanese automobile firms invested in the United States in the 1980s. If foreign-owned suppliers completely replaced local suppliers, the linkage effect might be regarded as weak. Wilkins distinguishes between technology transfer and technology absorption: 'only when nationals on their own (or virtually on their own) are able to produce the product does true diffusion—in contrast with mere geographical transfer—of the technology occur' (Wilkins, 1974b).

Spill-over effects were limited in the case of the enclavist-type investments which were common in the natural resource sector. The linkage effects of banana production were slight. There were few inputs of local origin, and much of the value added occured after the product had left the exporting country. In interwar Latin America, US mining operations were often centered on self-sufficient company towns. Oil company towns in particular were often 'closed towns' which strictly regulated those who lived or entered there (Wilkins 1974a). However, there were wide variations between minerals and crops in their forward and backward linkages. Tin, rubber, and tea production in Asian economies stimulated transport facilities and engineering capacity, which could be turned to other uses (Thoburn 1977).

Similar issues arose in export processing zones. In countries where export-oriented FDI was concentrated within such zones, linkages with local firms had often been weak. Multinationals needed to cross the 'border' in order to source locally, and they often preferred to source in neighboring countries (see Box 10.7 for the case of Malaysia).

Box 10.7 Multinationals and the Malaysian electronics industry after 1970

Foreign firms created a large electronics industry in Malaysia. They were attracted by good infrastructure, political stability, low wages, and the widespread use of English. In the early 1970s US electronics companies began to locate their labor-intensive assembly operations in Malaysia, and Japanese firms followed. By the 1980s, Malaysia had become the world's largest single exporter of electronic components.

Initially most exports went to the United States, reflecting the tight links between the US parents and the affiliates in semiconductors. Wafers manufactured in the United States were airfreighted to Malaysia, where they were assembled into circuits, and then airfreighted back to the parent firm. The entry of Japanese companies created more diverse trade patterns. By the late 1980s the United States only accounted for 30 percent of semiconductor imports, with Singapore, Japan, and Korea as large sources of supply.

The industry was overwhelmingly concentrated in export processing zones. The initial impetus for the first of these zones, established in Penang in 1971, came from the state government, faced by rising unemployment following the slow withdrawal of the island's free port status. The promotion of manufacturing was also an important feature of the Malaysian government's New Economic Policy. After severe riots in 1969 between the majority Malays and minority Chinese, employment creation became a major goal, but the Malay-dominated government was also determined to increase the participation of the Malays in business and to reduce the domination by Chinese, who represented around two-fifths of the population, but who dominated business.

These government policies influenced the strategy towards the zones. Products could be shipped in and out without customs duties. Goods purchased by firms in the zones from within Malaysia were treated as exports from Malaysia. Companies were exempted from income tax for periods of up to ten years. The government, concerned that foreign multinationals should not strengthen local Chinese business interests, allowed foreign

continues

Box 10.7 Multinationals and the Malaysian electronics industry after 1970 (*continued*)

companies to have 100 percent ownership of their subsidiaries provided they exported their entire output, thus tacitly discouraging joint ventures with local firms.

The upshot was that 80 percent of the intermediate products used in electronics manufacturing in the export processing zones were imported. This meant that the industry imported almost as much as it exported in the 1980s. Local firms supplied basic items such as cardboard boxes. The industry was heavily concentrated in the component subsector with an absence of forward linkages from components to the manufacturer of consumer and industrial products. The government provided no incentives for local firms to become involved in products such as television receivers and keyboards. Low value-added components—where Malaysian factories usually added only about 30 percent of the value of the product—accounted for around 80 percent of the country's electronics sector in the 1980s. Little design and R & D was undertaken in Malaysia, partly because of a shortage of graduate scientists and skilled technicians.

As multinationals integrated their operations within the region, linkages were created regionally rather than locally. Firms chose Singapore to locate knowledge-intensive activities, due to its excellent infrastructure, communication and transport facilities, while Malaysia was seen as a place for cheap assembly. From the late 1980s, the local state of Penang, where ethnic Chinese were in the majority, did adopt policies to encourage foreign multinationals to outsource parts of their value chain to local firms, and there was a significant growth in small- and medium-sized components businesses. Beyond Penang, few links were forged between foreign and local firms.

Malaysian employment in electronics grew from 600 in the mid-1970s to 300 000 in 1995. By 2000, electronics accounted for over a quarter of Malaysia's manufacturing employment. The jobs were overwhelmingly low skilled. In 2000, women contributed 80 percent of the labor force. The electronics firms preferred to hire women between the ages of 16 and 23, who were more manually dexterous than males, and more easily disciplined. Vertical mobility within the firms was low because there were few skilled and higher-level jobs available in the offshore manufacturing plants, and supervisory jobs were held by males. Employees took on women workers in the expectation that they would only remain for around three years. The nature and pace of the work in the electronic factories—which involved looking through a highly magnified microscope for eight hours a day—led to numerous health problems. In the early years of the industry, mass hysteria was a frequent occurrence on the late-night shifts.

(*Source*: Lim 1980; Warr 1987; Jesudason 1990; Phongpaichit 1991; Rasiah 2001.)

10.8 Sovereignty, culture, and globalization

10.8.1 Political influence

Multinationals had an impact on sovereignty. Because ultimate decision-making in a multinational resides with the parent rather than the subsidiary, host governments have less control over foreign-owned firms than over local firms. Multinationals may also use the international nature of their organization to circumvent host government policies or, in extreme cases, attempt to subvert governments.

The most extreme form of loss of sovereignty has occurred when companies exercised direct political influence on countries or even became quasi-governmental institutions. This phenonomenon occurred not infrequently in the colonial area. The English East India Company's political control over the Indian subcontinent in the eighteenth century was an extreme example. In late nineteenth- and early twentieth-century colonial West Africa, trading companies such as the Niger Company functioned almost as the local government. In countries where the size of a single company dwarfed the remainder of the economy, such as United Fruit in Central America, business was in a position to dictate to governments. If such firms were supported by powerful home governments, their position was all but unassailable.

In the postcolonial era, the challenge to sovereignty did not go away. Many developing countries had weak insititutional structures, and their governments had limited bargaining power against large multinationals with access to advanced technology, organization skills and finance. During the 1950s and 1960s some developing countries exercised an option to opt out of the capitalist system altogether, and sought technology and military support from the Soviet Union or Communist China. However, the attractiveness of this option declined over time, and disappeared altogether during the 1980s.

The balance of power between multinationals and host governments always rested on a number of factors. The more valuable and unique the firm-specific assets possessed by a company, such as technology and management skills, the more leverage it had to challenge or modify government policies. A host government's leverage was a function of its possession of resources required by the multinational such as a large domestic market or natural resources; the degree of competition between different firms for access to these resources; and a host country's ability to develop resources capable of substituting for those controlled by foreign companies. In low technology extractive industries, it has been widely argued that a multinational's power was greatest at the beginning of a project, when its capital and technology was badly needed. Over time, the foreign firm's investment was sunk and knowledge about its techniques spread, providing more leverage to the host government. This has been termed the 'obsolescing bargain' process (Vernon 1971). In import-substituting manufacturing industries, host governments could use the promise of access to the local market as a bargaining advantage. The foreign investor was, therefore, weakest at the point of entry. Once manufacturing firms were established, networks of suppliers, distributors, joint-venture partners, and consumers can provide a tacit political base of support for multinationals (Haggard 1989).

The balance of power between host governments and foreign firms was considerably influenced by the domestic politics of policy formation towards multinationals, including the ability of governments to pursue coherent policies, which might be undermined by divisions of opinion or by corruption. The role of local firms in shaping policies was often extremely significant. They have sometimes cooperated with multinationals, and helped influence host governments in their favor. In other cases, they resisted foreign companies and encouraged governments to restrict their activities (Moran 1993).

The number of extreme examples of political interference in host government affairs have been few if highly publicized. A cause célèbre was ITT's intervention in Chilean politics in the early 1970s, when it collaborated with the US government to overthrow the democratically elected government and replace it by a military dictatorship. However, such incidents have been rare, if only because of the catastrophic public relations consequences for the firms involved. Many large multinationals adopted strict rules against any participation in local political matters, partly in order to protect themselves from requests for political donations.

In the second global economy, multinationals were not implicated in overthrowing governments, but this did not mean that sovereignty was not constrained. Insofar as governments competed to attract multinational firms, many saw their ability to pursue welfarist or nonmarket economy policies as constrained. Critics believed that globalization exercised a strong downward pressure on government spending for redistribution and welfare, despite the heavy social costs arising from open economies (Rodrik 1997). In a wider sense, the abilities of governments to forecast the future, and to plan, were constrained by the growing integration of capital and trade flows, and international markets. During the 1990s the series of major financial crises in Mexico, Asia, and Russia disrupted the flows of capital to all developing countries regardless of their specific policies and achievements.

10.8.2 Dependency and cultural imperialism

During the decades after World War II, radical critics of multinationals in Latin America developed the *dependencia* critique which regarded large foreign corporations as major obstacles to economic growth. They were seen as transferring technologies which caused mass unemployment and displaced local businesses. This critique was later modified to take account of Latin America's rapid industrialization from the 1960s. Multinationals were accepted as potential engines of growth, but of a lop-sided development, the costs of which included too great an emphasis on luxury consumer durables and widening income disparaties (Cardoso and Faleto 1979).

In this literature, writers such as Fernando Henrique Cardoso, who later became President of Brazil in the 1990s, regarded the role of multinationals in the growth of Brazil, Mexico, and elsewhere as 'dependent development'. They baulked at the limitations on national policies required to maintain 'good investment climates'. These dependency relations were solidified by a 'triple alliance' between multinationals, host country governments, and externally oriented segments of the local business community. Local firms provided the skills in political maneuvering, multinationals provided the technology, while governments provided the institutional framework and established a common set of goals (Evans 1979; Gereffi and Evans 1981).

It turned out that the relations between the three elements in the 'triple alliance' has varied widely between countries. In Malaysia, the government was suspicious of local—ethnic Chinese—business rather than wanting to form an alliance with it. In Brazil, the creation of an automobile industry showed that the government was more effective against the multinationals, and the economy less structurally constrained, than the 'dependent development' model suggests. However, Brazil's enormous size, large urban middle class, and relatively effective administrative structures, gave it options that most other countries did not possess (see Box 10.8).

Box 10.8 Multinationals and the Brazilian automobile industry, 1956–80

In the early 1950s Brazil had only the beginnings of an industrial base. Virtually all the vehicles used in Brazil were imported as knock-down kits. By 1968 eight foreign firms manufactured 280 000 vehicles in the country. A further surge of growth resulted in annual production of over one million vehicles by 1980, giving Brazil the tenth largest automobile industry in the world.

In 1956 the Brazilian government began a comprehensive program to develop a local industry when it set up the Grupo Ejectivo de la Industria Automovilistica (GEIA) responsible for promoting the industry. The Brazilians—and later other Latin American governments—saw automobiles as a vital element in their import substitution strategies. In the early 1950s, the industry accounted for around 14 percent of total imports, causing a considerable drain on foreign exchange.

It was the threat of market closure in 1956 when prohibitively high tariffs were imposed which attracted and set the timing of foreign investment. Even more critical was state policy towards the level of local content. GEIA established local content targets for the industry which were to rise from between 35 percent and 50 percent of vehicle weight in 1956 to 90–95 percent by 1961. These high domestic-content levels meant that firms were forced to produce the 'technological heart' of their vehicles in Brazil, which was definitely not on their agenda. Participating firms were offered fiscal incentives such as exemption from duties and taxes on imports of parts and machinery, and special credit machinery. GEIA enforced domestic content requirements by withholding foreign exchange allocations from those firms that were not in compliance. Within five years, eleven firms had initiated vehicle production. By 1961 Brazilian total vehicle production had reached 145 000 units, with an average domestic content share of 93 percent by weight.

The GEIA plan coincided with the internationalization of motor vehicle production. The emergence of European competitors in the 1950s also loosened the power of the US automobile multinationals, and so increased Brazil's bargaining power. Competition for foreign markets was intensifying in the industry, especially in Europe, and firms responded by following each other to these markets. The automobile multinationals did not want to manufacture in Brazil and constantly tested the resolve of the government. The credibility of GEIA's threats rested on its possession of sufficient authority and coherence to make it costly for firms not to follow its program. It was assisted by the large size of the Brazilian market, which made a domestic industry viable and offered considerable growth potential.

The most positive response to the government's plans came from Germany's Volkswagen, which at that time had no foreign manufacturing plants and was anxious to expand abroad. It established production facilities to make its 'Beetle' cars in Brazil, establishing a commanding position in the Brazilian passenger car market. The US multinationals opted out of the passenger car market, and it was only after 1968 that Ford and GM entered the passenger car market, becoming the second and third largest automobile producers after Volkswagen. The Italian company Fiat entered Brazil later still, beginning production in 1976, but by virtue of extensive subsidies from a state government, was able to establish a large business.

During the 1970s the government focused on providing export promotion incentives. In 1972 the BEFIEX (Export Fiscal Benefits) programme was established. This allowed for tax

continues

> **Box 10.8 Multinationals and the Brazilian automobile industry, 1956–80 (*continued*)**
>
> exemptions against export performance commitments. Following the first oil shock in 1974, all incentives for local production were removed except those available under BEFIEX. In 1970 none of the total production of over 300 000 units were exported; by 1980 around 15 percent of the production in excess of 900 000 units were exported. This outcome again was facilitated by a coincidence of policy aims and wider trends in the world automobile industry, especially the increased resort to offshore sourcing for parts and components, and the growing integration of plants in countries with lower labor costs.
>
> The industry had high linkage effects, stimulating the development of new sectors to produce its intermediate inputs, particularly in the metallurgical industry. Linkages were fostered by a high domestic content requirement combined with policies that banned the importation of components and parts for which there were domestically produced similars. This resulted in Brazil acquiring a large supplier network—larger than in the case of Mexico, which had lower domestic content requirements. On the other hand, firms were reluctant to change models frequently because of tooling costs, and as a result the country's streets became full of antiquated car models.
>
> (*Source*: Shapiro 1991, 1993, 1994; Fritsch and Franco 1991.)

Local firms have not been invariably subordinate to multinationals in developing countries. In Asia and Latin America, local firms were sometimes able to leverage their contacts with multinationals to acquire and enhance their capabilities, as Thailand's CP Group did through its joint venture, a US poultry breeding firm (see Section 9.4). In certain conditions, local firms experienced considerable organizational learning as a result of their associations with foreign firms in areas such as corporate governance, production quality and international market knowledge. During the 1990s Chinese firms in relationships with foreign companies may have benefited from such organizational learning (Guthrie 2001).

In some cases, particular firms came to be seen as so symbolic of their home countries that their business was seen as a quasi-threat to national sovereignty. Anglo-Persian and United Fruit became symbolic of British and American imperialism in Iran and Central America, but the phenonomen was not confined to developing countries. After World War II Coca-Cola was closely associated with the United States, a connection reinforced as the US Government had partially financed the opening of the company's plants in overseas markets during the war. In France, there was uproar in the late 1940s when Coca-Cola arrived. Critics of 'Coca-Colonization', who spanned a spectrum from the Communist Party to wine and mineral water producers, regarded the brand as a symbol of US imperialism. There were moves in France's National Assembly to ban the importation, manufacture, and sale of Coca-Cola, which some argued was a health risk. Eventually the company was able to overcome its critics, although per capita consumption of the drink remained subdued in France for decades thereafter (Kuisel 1993; Giebelhaus 1994). McDonald's later became regarded in the same fashion. Its restaurants were sometimes targeted—in France and elsewhere—by anti-American protestors.

Foreign firms have sometimes been able to assume a local identity even in the most nationalistic environments. Before 1914 the Bell telephone company expanded from the United States over the border to Canada. Despite Canada's nationalistic aversion to the United States, Bell was successfully able to present itself as serving the goals of Canadian nationalism by helping to unite the country by providing telephone services (McDougall 2004). In 1947 Sears, the US department store chain, started a successful business in Mexico, a country which had only a decade earlier expelled foreign oil companies and was widely regarded as highly nationalistic. Sears carefully crafted its marketing and strategy to appeal to Mexicans, representing policies such as profit-sharing, pensions and low priced meals—some of which it employed in its operations at home—as in the traditions of the Mexican Revolution (Moreno 2003). In these ways, foreign companies served not to undermine local identities and cultures, but even to reinforce them. Although particular national images can enhance the attractiveness of brands—French perfumes or German engineering, for example—it has rarely been in a company's interest to stress that it was a foreign rather than a local company.

The impact of multinationals on consumption patterns has sometimes been regarded as cultural imperialism. Large corporations have the marketing capabilities, including powerful brands, to make a significant impact on consumption preferences, especially in developing countries. This might widen consumer choice, but negative outcomes are not unknown. During the 1970s and 1980s the marketing of baby food by Nestlé was widely criticized for making mothers in developing countries so eager to use the formula that they used it any way they could. This often resulted in mixing the formula with polluted water or trying to make the expensive supplies last longer by using an insufficient amount of formula, thereby starving their infants. The marketing of baby foods in developing countries may have contributed to sharp declines in breastfeeding by mothers which posed serious health risks given the environmental and economic conditions of many countries (Bader 1980). The marketing of cigarettes provides another example. As consumption faltered in the developed countries through health concerns and legislative action, the major tobacco companies increasingly marketed their products in developing countries and, from the late 1980s, in eastern Europe and China.

In consumer goods products, brand images influence identities and aspirations. As US cosmetic firms such as Max Factor and Ponds expanded internationally in the interwar years, their advertising endorsed white European and American concepts of beauty, which became the standards to which women in other contexts and ethnic backgrounds were encouraged to aspire. The impact of Hollywood films reinforced corporate advertising in shaping idealized views of beauty. After World War II, the US dominance in the personal care market—accounting for at least one half of world sales in the 1950s—made that country the center of innovation in new products such as deodorants which in turn became the standards to which consumers aspired elsewhere.

Although multinational firms were able to utilize their capabilities in branding and marketing to diffuse internationally Western or American concepts of beauty, the process was nuanced. A study of cosmetic advertising in Mexico in the 1930s and the 1940s showed considerable variations between corporate strategies. Among the leading US companies, while Ponds insisted that beauty was a universal phenomenon, and used internationally famous US and European figures in its advertising, Palmolive employed subjects and ideals more in line with the daily experience of Mexican women (Moreno 2003).

In China more recently, P&G, Unilever and L'Oréal and other large multinational personal care companies introduced international brands with considerable success. L'Oréal's Maybelline, which had only been acquired in the United States in 1996, held one-third of the Chinese lipstick market in 2004. Yet such brands were usually advertised with local models, product formulations were changed to suit Chinese hair, skin and tradition, and local preferences continued to shape the market. The Chinese skin care market was dominated by skin whiteners rather than the tanning products popular in the West, reflecting the Chinese preference for pale rather than dark skin. Moreover the Japanese-owned cosmetics company Shiseido developed a high margin business by developing specifically Chinese brands alongside international ones. In 1994 Shiseido launched an *Aupres* skincare brand manufactured and sold exclusively in China. Ten years later this was adopted as the official cosmetic of the Chinese team participating in the Athens Olympics. However, Shiseido also imported and marketed its international brands, including *Revital* and the exclusive *Clé de Peau Beauté*. (*Financial Times*, 1 April 2004.)

10.9 The consequences of being left out

There remains the issue of the consequences of not having multinational investment. As Section 10.2 made evident, most developing countries have received little FDI over the past thirty years, including almost all of Africa, the world's poorest continent, whose share of global FDI flows was less than 2 percent in 2002 (United Nations 2003). Given the importance of multinationals in both knowledge creation and diffusion, and in international trade flows, a low level of FDI has potentially devastating consequences for a country in the second global economy. Whatever the possible negative consequences of multinationals, the consequences of not receiving multinational investment seem even bleaker.

The historical evidence lends only a partial qualification to this overall conclusion. In the past the correlation between a country's importance as a host economy and its economic performance has not been especially close. Before 1914 India and China were much larger host economies than Japan, but it was in the latter country that modern economic growth took strongest hold. After World War II, Britain has consistently attracted more multinational investment than France and Germany, let alone Japan, yet it was the latter countries that had the far stronger growth performance, at least before the 1990s.

Foreign multinationals also played only a limited role in the East Asian 'economic miracles' from the 1960s. Taiwan and South Korea, although not Singapore and Hong Kong, followed the Japanese policy regime of blocking wholly-owned foreign affiliates in favor of joint ventures and licensing agreements with local firms. South Korea's chaebol grew on the basis of privileged government support and behind restrictive trade barriers (Amsden 1989). There was a striking contrast between the growth of the automobile industry in South Korea and that in Brazil. During the 1960s the government banned the import of built-up vehicles as a strategy to develop a domestic automobile industry under the control of the chaebol. Hyundai began producing motor vehicles in 1967, followed by Daewoo in 1978. Kia, a third vehicle producer, evolved from making bicycles in 1944, to motorcycles in 1961, to passenger cars in 1974. Hyundai and Kia were active in developing technological capacity and their own distribution networks, while Daewoo—partly owned by GM—did little to develop domestic technological capacity and relied on GM's sales network, which would not sell its products in North America. South Korean production surpassed that of Brazil in the second half of the 1980s.

The interpretation of this historical evidence is not straightforward. The most important caveat is that economic performance rests on multiple factors beyond multinational investment. Korean growth might have been faster still with significant inward FDI, while a similar restriction of FDI in country lacking the corporate capabilities, level of human capital and institutional structure of Korea was likely to have had different consequences. Contemporary sub-Saharan Africa has multiple factors that restrict development, including disease, civil war and weak governance structures. The historical experience would suggest that neither a large flow of multinational investment nor purposely keeping the economy closed to FDI will, alone, achieve economic development.

In addition, the kind of policy regime seen in East Asia between the 1960s and 1980s is no longer an option in the more integrated global economy in the new century, which made more apparent the drawbacks rather than the benefits of such a model. This was vividly shown in South Korea after the outbreak of the Asian financial crisis in 1997. Within a few years most of the country's leading automobile companies had been bought by foreign companies, including Daewoo and Samsung, which were acquired by GM and Renault respectively. Hyundai remained in Korean ownership.

The consequences of not depending on multinationals might well differ between generations. Between the 1950s and the 1980s the low level of inward investment in India was widely seen as growth constraining, limiting flows of new technology and contributing to India's only partial engagement with the world economy. Yet strong domestic business developed with considerable capabilities in industries such as pharmaceuticals. India's far greater reliance than China on domestic rather than foreign-owned companies might have laid the basis for greater growth potential in the future (Huang and Khanna 2003).

■ SUMMARY

If there is one lesson of history, it is that multinationals are not the panacea for economic growth. Since the nineteenth century they have transferred resources between countries, especially intangibles such as knowledge, and facilitated trade. They have developed natural resources, opened export markets, introduced new products, transferred management methods, created jobs, trained workers, and increased the efficiency of local suppliers.

However, there have been strict limits to the transforming power of multinationals. Their contribution to the transfer and diffusion of knowledge has been limited. Corporate strategies contributed to negative outcomes. The knowledge transfers arising from the huge FDI in developing countries during the first global economy were limited by the enclavist nature of many investments, and by the reluctance to train local workforces to perform complex tasks. The concession system may have facilitated flows of FDI, but also severely limited its linkage effects. However, both during the first and second global economies, the nature of the host economy and host government policies were also important influences on outcomes contributed. The most positive outcomes were seen when multinational investment was combined with effective policies and institutions, as in the case of Singapore from the 1960s.

Multinationals have not made the whole world rich. Their emergence and growth over the last 150 years has coincided with growing income disparity between countries, and within them. Business enterprises have built the webs of the first and second global economies, but those webs have not always been strong, and they have not always enhanced the incomes or the security of those joined by them. Indeed, the progressive integration of the world economy in the new century may have left even its richer citizens more insecure about their futures than for many decades.

11 | Conclusions

11.1 Multinationals in the two global economies

Globalization is one of the most important themes in history. A world that was once totally fragmented by geography, culture, language, and politics has become deeply interconnected. Although this process occurred over a very long time period, it accelerated radically from the nineteenth century. While governments provided the legal and administrative framework and technology defined the parameters of strategic and organizational options, business enterprises were the principal orchestrators of the flows of trade, capital, and knowledge across borders.

11.1.1 The first global economy

The nineteenth century saw the creation of the first real global economy. It was firms rather than markets or governments that drove the enormous cross-border flows of capital and trade. International investment was spurred by the spread of imperialism, which reduced the risks of multinational investment in many regions, and by the emergence of modern industrial growth, which encouraged firms to cross borders in search for markets, raw materials, and foodstuffs. The submarine telegraph cable made transcontinental business organization a feasible proposition, and firms developed new competences to sustain cross-border organizations. Legal and other reforms created more stable corporate structures and widened the possibilities of capital-raising. As firms grew, they became multifunctional and multiproduct, both domestically and internationally.

The role of firms in building the first global economy was remarkable. Multinationals developed new supplies of minerals and oil, and built rubber, tea, and tropical fruit plantations. By 1914 the production or the marketing of most of the world's resources outside the United States was controlled by multinationals, in some instances by only a handful of firms. The global reach of service multinationals was also striking. During the nineteenth century, business enterprises put in place the banking, trading, and informational infrastructure of the first global economy. A global transportation and communications network was built by cable and later wireless telegraph companies. Shipping companies cut the costs and speed of oceanic transport by building global networks of steamship lines which handled the exchange of commodities for manufactured goods which characterized the first global economy, and they transported the millions of emigrants which were such a distinctive feature of it.

Multinational manufacturing appeared for the first time in the nineteenth century. Beginning with the electricals company Siemens and Singer Sewing Machine, companies in industries characterized by proprietary technologies, brand names, and other intangible assets increasingly established factories in foreign countries as an alternative to exporting. By their investments in marketing and production, they transferred concepts such as branding and technological inventions across borders.

As in natural resources, the international scale of a handful of manufacturing firms was formidable. Nine out of ten sewing machines in the world were made by Singer on the eve of World War I. However, many of the thousands of firms crossed borders during the first global economy were small. There were numerous failures, and most firms disappeared over time, especially in high-risk industries such as mining. Yet some firms established before World War I grew to become giants. The list includes manufacturers such as Ford, Nestlé, Siemens, BASF, and Ericsson; oil companies such as Exxon, Shell, and BP; and banks such as Citibank, HSBC, and Deutsche Bank. These firms developed competences and routines which, combined with first-mover and incumbency advantages, enabled them to survive momentous political and economic shocks, and to continue to be major forces in the second global economy.

11.1.2 The backlash against globalization 1914–1970s

Between the interwar years and the 1970s many of the key components of the first global economy were destroyed, dismantled or diminished by shocks including wars and revolutions, trade protectionism, decolonization, and the spread of Communism.

Wars and revolutions led to the sequestration for the first time of huge amounts of multinational investment. German firms, which had been amongst the most active multinational investors, lost almost all their international assets as a result of World War I. The Communist Revolution in Russia eliminated two-thirds of French and Belgian FDI. The result was long-term shifts in investment patterns. French firms became less active internationally, and shifted their focus to French colonies. During the interwar years German chemical and other firms did seek to use their limited resources to rebuild international distribution networks and even foreign production subsidiaries, but all German overseas assets were lost again as a result of World War II. Between the 1950s and the 1970s German firms opted for exporting rather than FDI.

World War I was characterized by wartime inflation and the suspension of the Gold Standard. The severe disruption of the international monetary system induced governments to erect exchange controls and restrictions on foreign ownership of firms and industries, and to further increase barriers against international trade. By the 1920s, as a result, the international mobility of capital and goods began to falter. Visas and immigration controls blocked the movement of people across borders.

The dynamic growth of cross-border business was halted. During the 1930s many manufacturing and resource multinationals responded to the restrictions and increased risks by forming international cartels as an alternative to FDI, although in automobiles and many consumer products, large corporations continued to make new cross-border investments. In addition, the developments of the 1930s made multinationals more national. Trade barriers and exchange controls led to the increased autonomy of national affiliates, which increasingly became responsible for most of the value-added chain of their products. Nationalism encouraged firms to strengthen their 'local' identities. European overseas banks, faced by the decline in international trade, responded by extending their lending to businesses not related directly to trade and exchange.

The end of European colonial empires and growing state intervention made many regions in the developing world inhospitable to multinationals. Decolonization was often followed by the imposition of regulatory controls on foreign firms. In India high taxes and increasing control and regulations reduced inward FDI to tiny levels. During the 1970s expropriations eliminated a large share of multinational ownership of mining, petroleum, and plantation assets in Asia, Africa, and Latin America. As a result, vertical integration down to the production level was weakened or eliminated in most commodities. In China, one of the world's largest host economies before World War II, the Communist Revolution in 1949 was followed by the total exclusion of foreign companies for three decades.

Between the 1950s and the 1970s multinational investment became progressively marginalized in much of the world. In many developing countries the natural resource and service sectors became the preserve of locally owned firms. Local participation in manufacturing investments was often required. The fast-growing Japanese economy was largely closed to foreign multinationals. Even in North America and Western Europe, many service and other industries were closed to multinationals.

11.1.3 Towards a second global economy

The multinational as a form of business organization survived the meltdown of the global economy. Although the creation of new entrepreneurial firms such as free-standing companies became a rarity, the business groups which linked clusters of such firms retained large shares of the international trade in commodities. In retrospect, new entrants to multinational business began to lay the basis for the rebuilding of a global economy in the decades after World War II. In services, although foreign firms were progressively blocked from activities reserved for nationals, including telecommunications and utilities, new types of multinational service firms became conduits of US management practices and, more generally, values and lifestyles. Management consultants followed their US clients abroad, and diffused US (and later Japanese) management practices and structures. Advertising agencies 'globalized' aspects of US management practice. Hotels and fast food retailers spread lifestyle and consumption patterns. Multinationals began to create 'global' brands on an unprecedented scale.

Multinational banks rebuilt a global financial infrastructure following the development of the Eurodollar markets in London from the late 1950s. The new markets, which were geographically concentrated in a handful of international financial centers, became powerful forces for the integration of financial markets worldwide. Trading companies were also major forces in the building of the new global economy. The sogo shosha were the primary drivers of Japanese international trade. They were among the world's largest multinationals in terms of revenues. Giant commodity trading companies held dominant positions in the market for commodities such as cereals. Their market power was sufficient to significantly influence world market prices.

As in the past, manufacturing multinationals transferred the latest production processes and knowledge across borders. In particular, large US corporations made many investments during the postwar decades, especially in Western Europe. However, although there was considerable multinational manufacturing, it was far from 'global'. Affiliates remained primarily 'national' in their business strategies. There was little rationalized production and intrafirm trade was low.

The globalization process intensified from the 1970s. Technological innovation in communications and transport widened the options for firms, making it possible to transfer assembly work to low wage economies. By the 1980s liberalization and deregulation had begun to open up countries and sectors which had been closed to foreign firms for decades. Multinationals became powerful drivers of economic integration in the new global economy because of their importance in both trade and knowledge flows.

As the new global economy expanded, the firms of more countries participated in it through FDI as well as exporting. Although most multinational investment continued to be located in developed markets, there were striking shifts in the relative importance of host economies. The increased integration of the United States in the world economy was facilitated by a surge of inward multinational investment from the 1970s. A second major change was the re-entry of foreign firms in China from the late 1970s. Beginning with investments by overseas Chinese firms, massive investments by foreign firms drove the integration of the Chinese economy into the global economy, along with spectacular double digit growth. By the new century, China and Hong Kong combined were the world's second largest host economy.

As in the first global economy, large numbers of firms crossed borders in pursuit of profitable opportunities. However, and far more than before 1914, a small number of global giants held dominant positions in many industries. Although multinationals owned fewer of the world's natural resources, their control over transportation, processing and marketing stages gave them enormous market power in commodities ranging from coffee and bananas to aluminum and gold. While financial services had been fragmented before 1914, a century later a small number of very large commercial and investment banks wielded enormous global financial power. In high technology and consumer products, corporate giants allocated resources worldwide. Nokia accounted for over one-third of sales of cellphone handsets; Cisco Systems was responsible for a large share of the world's Internet networking; L'Oréal accounted for one-tenth of world cosmetics sales; Unilever and Nestlé sold between them at least one third of the world's ice cream.

In spite of this increased globalization, strong evidence remained that supported the arguments of those who stressed that the world remained far from 'borderless'. Multinational investment was extremely unevenly spread around the globe. The strategies of even the largest multinational corporations were 'regional' rather than global. In industries as important as banking, air travel, and the media, the liability of foreignness and government regulations greatly constrained the extent of 'globalization'. The international mobility of labor remained strikingly restricted compared to the nineteenth century.

11.2 Explaining multinationals

11.2.1 Theory and history

The recognition that multinationals are profoundly heterogeneous is one of the most important lessons from history. Business enterprises which crossed borders over the last two centuries represented an enormous diversity, and included firms of all sizes and many nationalities, which were engaged in most types of business activity. There was no inherent and single logic behind the growth of multinationals beyond the capitalist search for profitable opportunities. Nevertheless, the theories that have been developed over past decades to explain the growth and organization of international business do find support from the historical evidence.

The possession of ownership advantages was one of the elements that theory has deemed important for FDI to take place. The historical evidence supports theories which suggest that knowledge and entrepreneurial ability often lay at the heart of sustained advantages. Access to capital was also important. It was the size and depth of Britain's capital market before 1914 which enabled the creation of thousands of free-standing companies. However, the ownership advantages of firms were often different from those conceived by Hymer and other early theorists of the multinational, who were concerned to explain the importance of large US manufacturing corporations in the world economy of the 1960s and 1970s. The advantages of many firms lay less in proprietary technologies or sheer scale than in soft and tacit knowledge, relationships, and networks.

The resource-based theory of the firm would support such a view, yet the argument that multinationals possess a superior efficiency as an organizational vehicle to transfer knowledge across borders rests on fragile empirical evidence. Even the largest and most internationalized corporations seemed to face obstacles in achieving efficient intrafirm knowledge flows. While from the outside, and especially to critics of global capitalism, large multinationals appeared as all-powerful monoliths, in practice knowledge and other resources were often fragmented inside them. Moreover, the numerous failed multinational investments in every generation demonstrated that the ownership advantages possessed by many firms were insufficient to sustain their business. The histories of many of the largest and longest established multinationals has, and continues, to feature misjudgements and sometimes catastrophes in foreign markets.

Another explanation emphasized in theory to explain multinational investment is the concept of transactions costs. The historical evidence confirms that high transactions costs arising from bounded rationality, opportunism, and asset-specificity have provided incentives to replace markets with hierarchies, even if the precise measurement of such transactions costs is elusive. Transactions costs combined with the capital intensity of operations provided systematic factors behind the growth of large integrated multi-nationals in mining. Multinational manufacturing was stimulated in part by the desire of firms to exploit and protect the proprietary technologies and brands which became important in the late nineteenth century. The complexity of writing contracts for com-plex technologies made it difficult to exploit such brands and technologies in foreign countries through alternative market-based transactions. Transactions cost considerations are less relevant to explain the continued existence of multinationals. Foreign firms often became embedded in their host countries, accumulating knowledge about markets, local business networks, and political systems.

11.2.2 Geography and location

Any explanation of the determinants of multinationals needs to incorporate the influence of location and geography. Terms such as 'multinational' or 'transnational' suggest that multinational firms transcended national influence on their ownership and management. In fact, multinational investment has been concentrated both by source and destination during both global economies. Despite rhetoric on 'stateless' multinationals, the international strategies and organization of firms have continued to reflect their different home country characteristics.

Multinational investment has always originated almost entirely from rich countries. During the first global economy, firms from a wide range of western European countries as well as the United States invested internationally, but Britain alone had accounted for almost one half of all world FDI. Between 1914 and 1980 about two-thirds to three-fourths of world FDI came from the United States, Britain and the Netherlands. Between 1945 and the mid-1960s, the United States alone accounted for 85 percent of total new FDI outflows.

During the second global economy, the sources of multinational investment broadened. Continental European and Japanese firms switched from exporting to multinational strategies. French automobile, pharmaceutical, and personal care companies, and Japanese automobile and electronics companies, were among the largest multinationals in their industries. There was a growth of multinationals from emerging markets. Korean and Taiwanese electronics companies and Mexican cement companies became leaders in world industries. There was evidence that the dynamics of the global economy lowered barriers for new entrants through the disintegration of production systems and their replacement of networks of interfirm linkages. Yet at the beginning of the new century two-thirds of total world FDI originated from just six home economies.

Geography and culture were also important in determining the destination of multinational investment. Information and knowledge-related market imperfections increased as the distance between market participants increased. As firms first crossed borders, they reduced the risks of operating abroad by investing in geographically or culturally close countries. US firms built their first factories in Canada and Britain, and searched for natural resources in Canada, Mexico or the Caribbean. Firms based in French-speaking Switzerland invested first in France, whilst those from German-speaking Switzerland invested in Germany. The biases caused by geography and culture have persisted until today. The United States and Britain have been the single largest inward investor in the other country for over a century. During the 1980s overseas Chinese firms accounted for a high proportion of inward FDI into China. As Spanish companies internationalized during the same period, they looked to Latin America as a host region. Cultural similarities, real or imagined, were perceived as reducing risks, although in practice they were no guarantor of competitive success.

In spite of a concentration of investment in countries that were geographically close, before 1914 multinational investment was still widely dispersed. Entrepreneurs based in Western countries pursued resources almost everywhere without restrictions. Formal and informal imperialism significantly reduced the distance between countries. Thereafter the geographical flows of multinational investment was progressively circumscribed. European companies responded to political risk by shifting much investment towards colonies. Subsequent decolonization and the spread of restrictions against foreign companies led to multinational investment being transformed into primarily consisting of cross-investment between developed countries.

Although the second global economy saw the harmonization and liberalization of developing country policies towards foreign firms, multinational investment remained highly unevenly distributed. Most of the world's FDI went to developed countries. Although from the 1980s FDI became the largest source of capital flows to developing countries, these flows were highly concentrated in a small number of emerging countries, led by China. Most of Africa, Latin America, and South Asia received little FDI. Even in developed countries, the distribution of FDI was skewed. Britain was disproportionately important as a host economy within Europe. Natural and created resource endowments, market size, geographical location, and cultural and linguistic ties, all contributed to these geographical patterns. In developing countries, the quality of domestic institutions, broadly defined, was important in explaining the wide geographical differences in flows of multinational investments.

Within countries, multinational investment was typically concentrated in particular locations rather than evenly spread. Before 1914 foreign banks and merchants were clustered in London rather than Britain. The global money and capital markets which developed from the 1960s were again physically concentrated in a limited number of international financial centers. Location and ownership were largely divorced. The same phenomenon was observable in many other industries. 'Global cities' developed a new importance. In knowledge-intensive industries the importance of tacit knowledge similarly encouraged a clustering of innovative activities in specific locations. The computer software industry became largely clustered in a handful of the world's cities, especially San Francisco, San Jose, Boston, and Bangalore.

In the new global economy, as in the first, no multinational was 'stateless' in a meaningful sense. As global competition intensified, the home country influence on the propensity of firms to invest abroad, and on the composition of these investments, remained striking. Multinationals evolved by different trajectories depending upon their national origins. British firms remained persistent multinational investors long after their country ceased to be the world's largest capital exporter. British FDI represented a much larger proportion of national GDP than comparable-sized economies throughout the twentieth century. Dutch, Swedish, and Swiss firms were disproportionately active as multinational investors, compared to neighboring small economies. German multinationals have been heavily concentrated in manufacturing, especially after 1914. The service sector held a long-run importance in Japanese FDI.

A combination of trading or colonial heritages (or lack of them), concentration levels, industrial structures, and entrepreneurial orientations helped explain such biases. Multinationals remained embedded in the business systems of their countries of origin. The

Boards and senior managements of most large multinationals were heavily dominated by nationals of their home countries. Despite much academic discussion of the benefits of dispersal of innovation, most US and Japanese corporations have continued to conduct most of their research at home, especially in such technology industries as computers, aerospace, and automobiles. Only a handful of large corporations had sales spread evenly between North America, Europe, and Asia. Most firms pursued regional rather than global strategies. Insofar as multinationals were primary drivers of trade and knowledge flows, they contributed to the 'semi-globalized' state of the world economy in the new century.

11.3 Building organizations

Managing a cross-border business has always been difficult. Political, geographical, economic, and cultural distance pose enduring managerial challenges. While firms which operate domestically face a constantly shifting environment, as political and economic circumstances change and technologies evolve, firms which operate in multiple countries face multiple environments changing in different ways and at different speeds.

In each generation of multinationals, there was a struggle to create and sustain organizations which could operate efficiently, find the appropriate balance between centralization and local responsiveness, and which were able to transfer knowledge and competencies inside their boundaries. Organizational solutions have been heavily contingent on the industry, the state of technology, the home economy of the firm, and public policy, as well as the specific competences and routines of each firm. As a result, there was never a single model of a multinational towards which all firms have been converging.

However, general historical patterns in the organization of multinationals can be discerned. In the first global economy in the nineteenth century, a crude distinction can be made between 'informal' or 'network' forms of organization, and 'formal' or 'hierarchical' forms. European, and also later, Japanese firms placed much emphasis on personal relations and socialization, although this did not prevent the development of quite bureaucratic structures in some cases. This was built on earlier traditions of international business in the past centuries when prevailing technologies had left managers with little choice but to rely on trust to control and monitor cross-border operations.

Subsequently, socialization methods of control remained important in European and Asian companies even as transportation and communication improved. They worked effectively especially in industries such as international trading which involved numerous non-routine transactions, and in managing operations in developing countries where political and economic conditions were unpredictable. Interfirm collaboration provided a means to share competencies and spread risks. As a result, large business groups were built around European trading companies, French banks, and German electrical companies.

In contrast, US-based firms developed an early preference for formal organization and bureaucratic procedures. They expanded within the United States using hierarchies and rules, creating many of the world's largest corporations by the early twentieth century. When they expanded abroad, they typically used hierarchies rather than networks to manage complex processes in manufacturing and processing. Rules and standardized reporting procedures became the norm in US multinationals.

During the interwar years multinationals became more national in their organization. National affiliates grew in autonomy. Trade barriers and exchange controls made cross-border flows of trade within affiliates more difficult, and obliged firms to retain profits in host economies which were often used to diversify along the value chain. However, there remained a wide diversity of practice even among competing firms of the same nationality, as exemplified by the contrast between the decentralization seen in GM and the centralization of Ford in the interwar years.

In the decades after World War II, a variety of organizations coexisted which at least partly continued to resemble those seen previously. Many large US corporations were organized as coordinated federations in which the parent company exercised quite a close control on overall strategy, and transferred knowledge to foreign affiliates. This model contrasted with the preference of European companies for leaving national entities possessing considerable autonomy. These preferences were in part influenced by the different periods firms had expanded abroad. Many of the larger European companies had a large number of affiliates in the interwar years which had grown accustomed to autonomy. In contrast, the US companies which expanded abroad after 1945 had no organizational legacy, and could take advantage of the falling trade barriers within Europe and elsewhere to coordinate national subsidiaries. The Japanese companies which went multinational from the 1970s could benefit from even lower tariffs and faster communications to achieve greater centralization.

As the process of globalization intensified in the late twentieth century, there was a search for more flexible forms of organization. Increased global competition, combined with the growing importance of continuous technological innovation, meant that firms had to increasingly take advantage of the global division of labor. This meant using subsidiaries to take advantage of the specific factor endowments of countries, and seeking to transfer knowledge more widely and smoothly within the organization. As a result, multinationals sought organizational forms that could meet all three strategic requirements of efficiency, local responsiveness and internal knowledge transfers. These forms of organization were variously described as hierarchies, transnationals, or differentiated networks. Few corporations seem to have achieved such goals. Knowledge and information remained 'sticky' inside firms.

Despite such general tendencies, the periods of fast globalization seen in both the late nineteenth and late twentieth centuries, witnessed an enormous diversity in the organizational forms employed by firms to operate across borders. The boundaries of firms showed a persistent tendency to blur when they crossed borders. Networks and alliances, joint ventures and other equity and nonequity modes were widely used. In the second global economy, 'older' forms of multinational organization persisted in the form of the new multinationals from emerging markets (and many others), which were often family-owned and organized as business groups.

11.4 **Multinationals and the wealth of nations**

In each generation multinationals have played an important role in the world economy. They have been major facilitators of trade flows. By the early twenty-first century, around one half of total world trade took place inside the boundaries of firms. They have transferred technologies and organizational skills across borders. Multinational strategies have featured in nearly all of the world's most dynamic manufacturing industries since the late nineteenth century. In each generation they have spread innovations across borders, and transformed lifestyles in the process. Both service and resource multinationals have been important as transferors of organizational and technological systems across borders. There are, however, no easy generalizations about the consequences of multinational investment for both home and host economies. The historical record remains full of uncertainties and under-researched topics, but it points to a diversity of outcomes.

The historical evidence on the long-term impact of multinationals on the competitiveness of their home economies is highly nuanced. Countries have gained from the receipt of dividends and income from the foreign operations of their multinationals, but many have lost if multinationals transferred resources from their home economies to other economies. Multinationals have assisted in the economic restructuring of economies by shifting low value-added activities abroad and permitting the upgrading of the use of domestic resources. But they might also 'hollow out' an economy by transferring out innovatory capabilities and manufacturing capacity without any compensatory upgrading of the remaining resources. In concentrated industries, such as automobiles and pharmaceuticals, decisions taken by a small number of corporations have a major impact on the value-added activities performed in even a large, mature, industrial economy. The historical evidence confirms that the possession of a large stock of outward FDI does not necessarily either reflect or sustain a country's overall competitive situation.

Historical evidence has also been mixed regarding the impact of multinationals on host economies. The difficulties of assessing the impact of multinationals on host economies arise from the many ways in which they can make an impact. They create employment, but many drive out local competitors. They can expand exports, but also increase imports. The new technologies which they introduce may be accompanied by a package of cultural values which may or may not be welcome or desired. Multinationals may not be efficient transferors of technologies in all cases. Indeed, concerns to prevent leakage of knowledge beyond their boundaries provided a major constraint on the extent of knowledge transfer by multinational firms. For this and other reasons, knowledge spillovers to host economies were often very limited. The employment and promotion of women by foreign multinationals in a socially conservative society may be welcome to many females in a host economy, and unwelcome to some males. An entrepreneurial and risk-taking investment in one generation might appear as a rapacious foreign investor draining profits out of a country in the next.

The impact of multinationals on individual host economies has depended on the type of investment undertaken, its quality as well as its quantity, the source of the investment, the mode of entry, the type of institutional and contractual form employed, and the alternative at any one time. In addition, the nature of the host economy—including its stage of development, the quality of domestic institutions, and the availability of entrepreneurship—and its culture have exercised a decisive influence on the impact of multinational investment.

The policies of governments were often a major influence on outcomes. The Brazilian government from the 1950s used a mixture of threats and incentives to encourage foreign firms to build an automobile manufacturing industry. The Singaporean government combined an open policy regime towards multinationals with extensive investments in infrastructure to persuade these firms to constantly upgrade their value-adding activities in the country. However, most developing countries lacked both large and attractive domestic markets and high levels of administrative competence. Moreover, the worldwide integration of capital and trade flows towards the end of the twentieth century appeared to leave governments with few policy options beyond providing incentives for multinationals to invest in their economies.

These complexities are evident when assessing the impact of the huge flows of multinational investment to developing countries. During the first global economy, foreign firms created vast mineral and commodity export sectors, transferred technologies, and created employment for hundreds of thousands of people. However, typically, processing was carried out elsewhere; mines and plantations often functioned as enclaves; higher skill jobs were reserved for expatriates; and concession agreements meant that foreign firms made little or no fiscal contribution. Multinational firms also functioned as one component of formal or informal imperialism. In the second global economy, the international supply chain in commodities such as coffee worked in such a fashion that large multinational firms captured most of the value while producers were often impoverished. However, as industries such as electronics outsourced much of their supply chains, firms from emerging markets were also able to piggyback on incumbent multinationals as customers through subcontracting, linkages, and leveraging.

Multinationals have, in appropriate institutional and public policy contexts, served as powerful drivers of wealth creation. Moreover, the twentieth-century experiments in socialist or autarkic policy regimes failed to deliver alternative successful economic models. Yet global capitalism has been a disruptive process which has involved winners and losers. While in the long run the world has become a far richer and healthier place as a result of globalization, the process has included at various times the enslavement of Africans, colonialism, the displacement of workers through technological change and shifts in competitive advantage, and the employment of millions in mind-numbing, labor-intensive tasks in plantations, and later in assembly factories. The growing concentration of knowledge within large multinational corporations has meant that their strategies can exercise a self-reinforcing effect on existing patterns of wealth and poverty.

11.5 The past and the future

The twenty-first century started as a semiglobalized or regionalized world rather than a global one. It remained less 'global' by most measures than in 1914. The influence of nationality, geography, and culture proved remarkably strong despite extraordinary technological advances. Even the largest global corporations were not 'stateless'. The liability of foreignness persisted. The power of national governments had not been undermined by firms. Government policies regulated, controlled, and restricted multinationals in ways unthinkable during the first global economy.

The past provides no basis on which to predict the future. In twenty or fifty years, the world economy might be dominated by a handful of truly 'global' giants regulated by world government. However, it is not fanciful to imagine alternative scenarios under which the current level of economic integration will have been reversed. The ideology of liberal capitalism which sustains the global economy was unsuccessfully challenged by Communism in the twentieth century, but there are other religious (and nonreligious) ideologies which might seek to challenge it in the twenty-first century. The history of multinationals and the creation of global capitalism have been distinctly nonlinear. Periods of global integration have alternated with periods of global disintegration. Public policy and prevailing ideologies have fluctuated widely. There is nothing inevitable about global capitalism or global firms.

The possibility of a new major backlash against globalization will always remain strong so long as so much of the world's population is so poor. There is widespread insecurity and poverty even in the countries which have grown, by historical standards, immensely rich as a result of two centuries of global capitalism. Multinationals can be agents of development, but liberalization policies based on assumptions that they will provide a guaranteed panacea to a country's poverty rest on illusions. The package of resources that multinationals can transfer across borders has great potential to increase welfare and incomes, but history shows clearly the costs as well as benefits in multinational investment. Both the exact nature of the package and, above all, the institutions and policies of the host economy will be crucial determinants of the final outcome.

Appendices

APPENDIX I

The world's top fifty nonfinancial multinationals, ranked by foreign assets, 2001

Ranking Foreign assets	Corporation	Country	Industry	Assets (Millions of dollars and number of employees) Foreign	Assets Total	Sales Foreign	Sales Total	Employment Foreign	Employment Total
1	Vodafone	United Kingdom	Telecommunications	187 792	207 458	24 602	32 744	56 430	67 178
2	General Electric	United States	Electrical and electronic equipment	180 031	495 210	39 914	125 913	152 000	310 000
3	British Petroleum	United Kingdom	Petroleum exploration/refining/distribution	111 207	141 158	141 225	175 389	90 500	110 150
4	Vivendi Universal	France	Diversified	91 120	123 156	29 652	51 423	256 725	381 504
5	Deutsche Telekom	Germany	Telecommunications	90 657	145 802	11 836	43 309	78 722	257 058
6	ExxonMobil Corporation	United States	Petroleum exploration/refining/distribution	89 426	143 174	145 814	209 417	61 148	97 900
7	Ford Motor Co	United States	Motor vehicles	81 169	276 543	52 983	162 412	188 919	354 431
8	General Motors	United States	Motor vehicles	75 379	323 969	45 256	177 260	148 000	365 000
9	Royal Dutch/Shell Group	United Kingdom/Netherlands	Petroleum exploration/refining/distribution	73 492	111 543	72 952	135 211	52 109	89 939
10	TotalFinaElf	France	Petroleum exploration/refining/distribution	70 030	78 500	74 647	94 418	69 037	122 025
11	Suez	France	Electricity, gas and water	69 345	79 280	29 919	37 975	128 750	188 050
12	Toyota Motor Corporation	Japan	Motor vehicles	68 400	144 793	59 880	108 808	186 911	246 702
13	Fiat	Italy	Motor vehicles	48 749	89 264	24 860	52 002	103 565	198 764

continues

(continued)

Ranking Foreign assets	Corporation	Country	Industry	Assets (Millions of dollars and number of employees)		Sales		Employment	
				Foreign	Total	Foreign	Total	Foreign	Total
14	Telefonica	Spain	Telecommunications	48 122	77 011	14 303	27 775	93 517	161 527
15	Volkswagen Group	Germany	Motor vehicles	47 480	92 520	57 426	79 376	157 579	324 413
16	ChevronTexaco Corp.	United States	Petroleum exploration/refining/distribution	44 943	77 572	57 673	104 409	35 569	67 569
17	Hutchison Whampoa	Hong Kong, China	Diversified	40 989	55 281	6 092	11 415	53 478	77 253
18	News Corporation	Australia	Media	35 650	40 007	13 880	15 087	24 700	33 800
19	Honda Motor Co.	Japan	Motor vehicles	35 257	52 056	40 088	55 955	59 000	120 600
20	E.On	Germany	Electricity, gas and water	33 990	87 755	22 744	71 419	64 285	151 953
21	Nestlé	Switzerland	Food and beverages	33 065	55 821	34 704	50 717	223 324	229 765
22	RWE Group	Germany	Electricity, gas and water	32 809	81 024	23 151	58 039	65 609	155 634
23	IBM	United States	Electrical and electronic equipment	32 800	88 313	50 651	85 866	173 969	319 876
24	ABB	Switzerland	Machinery and equipment	30 586	32 305	18 876	19 382	148 486	156 865
25	Unilever	United Kingdom/Netherlands	Diversified	30 529	46 922	28 675	46 803	204 000	279 000
26	ENI Group	Italy	Petroleum exploration/refining/distribution	29 935	55 584	19 437	43 861	26 570	80 178
27	BMW	Germany	Motor vehicles	29 901	45 415	25 304	34 482	23 338	97 275
28	Philips Electronics	Netherlands	Electrical and electronic equipment	29 416	34 070	27 598	28 992	157 661	188 643
29	Carrefour	France	Retail	29 342	41 172	31 513	62 294	235 894	358 501
30	Electricité De France	France	Electricity, gas and water	28 141	120 124	12 468	36 502	38 066	162 491
31	Repsol YPF	Spain	Petroleum exploration/refining/distribution	27 028	45 575	13 752	39 135	16 455	35 452
32	Sony Corporation	Japan	Electrical and electronic equipment	26 930	61 393	38 605	57 595	99 300	168 000
33	Aventis	France	Pharmaceuticals	26 368	34 761	13 377	20 567	47 968	91 729
34	Wal-Mart Stores	United States	Retail	26 324	83 451	35 485	217 799	303 000	1 383 000

35	DaimlerChrysler	Germany	Motor vehicles	25 795	183 765	43 556	137 051	76 441	372 470
36	Lafarge	France	Construction materials	24 906	26 493	10 537	12 280	73 940	82 892
37	Nissan Motor Co.	Japan	Motor vehicles	24 382	54 113	29 078	47 091	37 417	125 099
38	AES Corporation	United States	Electricity, gas and water	23 902	36 736	5 809	9 327	35 000	38 000
39	Roche Group	Switzerland	Pharmaceuticals	22 794	25 289	17 156	17 463	55 451	63 717
40	BASF	Germany	Retail	20 872	32 671	17 108	29 136	41 606	92 545
41	Deutsche Post	Germany	Transport and storage	20 840	138 837	9 844	29 924	52 680	276 235
42	Bayer	Germany	Pharmaceuticals/chemicals	20 297	32 817	15 778	27 142	52 300	116 900
43	GlaxoSmithKline	United Kingdom	Pharmaceuticals	20 295	31 758	27 319	29 689	60 962	107 470
44	Royal Ahold	Netherlands	Retail	19 967	28 562	40 150	59 701	183 851	270 739
45	Compagnie de Saint-Gobain	France	Construction materials	19 961	28 478	19 091	27 245	130 000	173 329
46	BHP Billiton Group	United Kingdom/Australia	Mining and quarrying	19 898	29 552	14 821	17 778	33 070	51 037
47	Diageo	United Kingdom	Food and beverages	19 731	26 260	13 747	16 020	59 868	62 124
48	Conoco Inc.	United States	Petroleum exploration/refining/distribution	19 383	27 904	17 530	38 737	10 362	20 033
49	Philip Morris Companies Inc.	United States	Diversified	19 339	84 968	33 944	89 924	39 831	175 000
50	National Grid Transco	United Kingdom	Electricity, gas and water	19 080	24 839	3 829	6 3008	10 154	13 236

Source: United Nations (2003).

APPENDIX 2

Glossary

Antitrust	Laws against monopolies or restrictive practices in uncompetitive market conditions.
Brand	A product name which facilitates product differentiation.
Business Group	A cluster of nominally independent firms linked through either equity or non-equity modes.
Cartel	A group of firms which enter into an agreement to set mutually acceptable prices or a price on the output of a commodity.
Chaebol	A family-controlled, diversified big business group in South Korea.
Commonwealth	Informal grouping of former constituents of British Empire.
Culture	The learned attitudes of a society. It can refer to an organization or to a nation.
Economies of Scale	These arise when expansion of the scale of production causes total production costs to increase less than proportionately with output.
Economies of Scope	These arise when diversification into new product lines permits a reduction of unit costs.
Exchange Controls	The control by governments of dealings in foreign currencies and gold.
Eurodollars	Dollars held by individuals and institutions outside the United States.
European Union	Formed as European Economic Community as a result of Treaty of Rome (1957) and consisting of France, West Germany, Italy, Belgium, Netherlands, and Luxembourg. Subsequently known as the Economic Community and (from 1993) the European Union. Enlarged to include the United Kingdom, Denmark and Ireland in 1973, Greece in 1981, Spain and Portugal in 1986; Sweden, Finland and Austria in 1995; and Cyprus, Czech Republic, Estonia, Hungary, Latvia, Lithuania, Malta, Poland, Slovakia, and Slovenia in 2004.
First Mover Advantages	These are held by the firms which exploit first a new technology, distribution system or organization system. The resulting strong competitive positions represent barriers to entry by 'follower' firms.
Foreign Direct Investment (FDI)	An investment in a foreign firm which involves managerial control.
Franchising	An arrangement whereby one party gives an independent party the use of a trademark that is an essential asset and continued assistance in the operation of the business.
Free-standing Company	A firm that did not grow out of an existing domestic business but was established specifically to operate in a foreign country. This form of company existed in great numbers before 1914.
Gold Standard	The international monetary system prevalent before 1914 (and in the 1920s) whereby the value of national currencies was fixed to gold and their central banks were obliged to give gold in exchange for any of its currency presented to it.
Greenfield Investment	When a multinational opens a new facility in a foreign country as opposed to entering a market by acquiring an existing facility.

Home Economy	The country where a multinational is headquartered.
Host Economy	The recipient country of a multinational investment.
Horizontal Integration	The establishment of plants to make the same or similar goods.
Intangible Asset	Knowledge about technology or market owned and possessed by a firm which yields a rent to the firm.
Inward Investment	FDI by foreign enterprises into a host economy.
Intrafirm Trade	Trade flows across borders but between affiliates of the same company.
Joint Venture	When two or more firms share in the ownership of a direct investment.
Keiretsu	A vertical grouping of companies in Japan. Usually used to describe vertical production *keiretsu* that consist of a core manufacturing company and its numerous subcontractors and affiliates.
Kigyo Shudan	A horizontal grouping of companies in Japan. Six large groups were prominent during the economic miracle decades. Their cohesion and significance declined very sharply in the 1990s.
Lean Production	A production system developed by Toyota in which materials and parts are produced and delivered just before they are needed. Also known as just-in-time or Toyota production system.
Licensing	An agreement whereby one firm gives to another the use of assets such as trademarks and patents.
Managerial Capitalism	A term used to describe a system where the ownership of firms has been separated from the control. Managerial firms are controlled by hierarchies of salaried executives. Developed in the United States and Europe in the last quarter of the nineteenth century.
Mass Production	A production system pioneered by Henry Ford before World War I involving the use of interchangeable parts and assembly line process. Also known as Fordism.
Multidivisional Structure (M-form)	A decentralized form of firm organization under which managerial control over functions such as R & D and sales was located in each corporate division, freeing upper management to make long-term decisions and allocate resources throughout an organization.
Nationalization	Ownership and control by the state.
Oligopoly	A type of market in which there is a relatively high degree of concentration where a small number of firms account for a large proportion of output.
Outsourcing	A situation in which a domestic company uses foreign suppliers for components or finished products.
Outward Investment	FDI by domestic enterprises from their home economy to a foreign country.
Personal Capitalism	A term used to describe family-owned and controlled business in contrast to managerial enterprises. Chandler (1990) uses the term more widely to include a personal 'style' of management not involving the use of complex layers of professional managers.
Portfolio Investment	The acquisition of foreign securities by individual or institutions without any control over the management of the companies concerned.
Privatization	Transfer of assets owned by the state into private ownership.
Sequestration	The forced acquisition and sale of business assets, typically during a war.
Sogo shosha	A Japanese general trading company.

Soviet Union	Socialist and centrally planned economy in existence between 1917 and 1989. Collapsed in 1989 and replaced by a number of independent republics, including Russia.
Strategic Alliance	A collaborative agreement between firms for various reasons, but often concerned with technology or marketing.
Tariff	A government tax usually on imports levied on goods shipped internationally.
Transactions Costs	The costs of transacting in a market arising from bounded rationality, opportunism and asset-specificity.
Vertical Integration	The undertaking by a single firm of successive stages in the process of production of a particular good.
Zaibatsu	The family-owned business conglomerates which were influential elements of the Japanese business system before 1945. Dissolved during the Allied occupation after World War II.

Time line

c.1760–1830	First Industrial Revolution
1776	Declaration of Independence and formation of United States
1792–1815	French Revolutionary and Napoleonic Wars
1833	British government makes slave trade illegal
1852	London and Paris joined by telegraph
1857	British government replaces East India Company as government of India
1859	World's first oil well in Pennsylvania, United States
1861–65	American Civil War
1866	First successful trans-Atlantic cable connection
1868	Meiji Restoration in Japan
1869	Opening of Suez Canal

First global economy

1888	Brazilian government abolishes slavery
1890	McKinlay Act in United States raises tariffs
1908	Oil discovered in Iran
c.1910	Henry Ford develops mass production
1914–18	World War I
1915	Opening of Panama Canal
1917	Communist Revolution in Russia
1925	Invention of television
1927	Oil discovered in Iraq
1927	Bell Telephone and US Department of Commerce conduct first long distance use of television

Disintegration of first global economy

1929–30s	Great Depression
1930	Invention of jet engines
1933–45	Nazi regime in Germany
1939–45	World War II
1941	United States enters war after Japanese attack fleet at Pearl Harbor
1947	Indian independence from British Empire
1947	General Agreement on Tariffs and Trade (GATT) signed
1947	Invention of transistors
1948	Fabrication of first successful transistor at Bell Laboratories
1949	Communist Revolution in China
1950–53	Korean War

Beginning of new global economy

1950s/60s	'Economic Miracles' in Western Europe and Japan
1957	Treaty of Rome and Formation of European Economic Community
1959/60	Origins of Eurodollar market
1960	Organization of Petroleum Exporting Countries (OPEC) founded
1965	Intelsat 1 satellite launched
1965–73	Vietnam War
1971	United States abandons fixed exchange rate
1973	First World Oil Crisis
1975	US Defense Advanced Research Project Agency initiates research to investigate techniques to allow networked computers to communicate which becomes the origins of the internet
1975	Personal computers developed

New or second global economy

1979	Second World Oil Crisis
1979	China begins to liberalize and open its economy
1982	Outbreak of World Debt Crisis
1989	Collapse of Communism in eastern Europe
1990	World Wide Web created
1990	Federal Republic of Germany merges with German Democratic Republic
1991	India begins to liberalize and open its economy
1990s	'New Economy' in the United States based on Internet boom
1990s	Collapse of 'bubble economy' in Japan followed by a decade of economic stagnation
1994	North American Free Trade Agreement (Nafta)
1995	World Trade Organization (WTO) replaces GATT
1997	Asian Financial Crisis begins in Thailand
2001	Terrorist attack on United States on September 11
2002	Euro becomes official currency of twelve members of the European Union
2004	European Union expands by ten new members

■ BIBLIOGRAPHY

Abel, C. and Lewis, C. (eds.) (1985) *Latin America, Economic Imperialism and the State*. London: Athlone.

Abo, T. (1982) 'ITT's International Business Activities, 1920–40: The Remarkable Advance and Setback of a "Pure International Utility Company"', *Annals of the Institute of Social Science*, University of Tokyo, No. 24, 104–28.

—— (ed.) (1994) *Hybrid Factory. The Japanese Production System in the United States*. New York: Oxford University Press.

Abreu, M. P. (1990) 'Brazil as a Creditor: Sterling Balances, 1940–1952', *Economic History Review*, XLIII: 3, 450–69.

Aharoni, Y. (ed.) (1993) *Coalitions and Competition: The Globalization of Professional Business Services*. London: Routledge.

Alfaro, L. and Rodriguez-Clare, A. (2004) 'Multinationals and Linkages: An Empirical Investigation', *Economia*, 4: 2, 113–69.

Almeida, P. and Kogut, B. (1999) 'Localization of Knowledge and the Mobility of Engineers in Regional Networks', *Management Science*, 45: 7, 905–17.

Alvesson, M. and Lindkvist, L. (1993) 'Transaction Costs, Clans and Corporate Culture', *Journal of Management Studies*, 30: 3, 427–52.

Amsden, A. H. (1989) *Asia's Next Giant: South Korea and Late Industrialisation*. Oxford: Oxford University Press.

—— (1997) 'Enterprising Groups and Entrepreneurial Government', in A. D. Chandler, F. Amatori, and T. Hikino (eds) *Big Business and the Wealth of Nations*. Cambridge: Cambridge University Press.

—— (2003) *The Rise of 'the Rest': Challenges to the West from Late-Industrializing Countries*. Oxford: Oxford University Press.

Ando, K. (2004) *Japanese Multinationals in Europe*. Cheltenham: Edward Elgar.

Archibugi, D. and Iammarino, S. (2000) 'Innovation and Globalization', in F. Chesnais, G. Ietto-Gillies, and R. Simonetti (eds) *European Integration and Global Corporate Strategies*. London: Routledge, pp. 95–120.

Armstrong, C. and Nelles, H. V. (1988) *Southern Exposure: Canadian Promoters in Latin America and the Caribbean, 1896–1930*. Toronto: University of Toronto Press.

Arnoldus, D. (2002) *Family, Firm and Strategy. Six Dutch Family Firms in the Food Industry 1880–1970*. Amsterdam: Aksant.

Attman, A. and Olsson, U. (1977) *LM Ericsson 100 Years*, Vol. 2. Orebro: Ericsson.

Bader, M. B. (1980) 'Breast-Feeding: The Role of Multinational Corporations in Latin America', in K. Kumar (ed) *Transnational Enterprises: Their Impact on Third World Societies and Cultures*. Boulder: Westview.

Balasubramanyam, V. N. (1993) 'Entrepreneurship and the growth of the firm: the case of the British food and drink industries in the 1980s', in J. Brown and M. B. Rose (eds) *Entrepreneurship, Networks and Modern Business*. Manchester: Manchester University Press.

—— and Mahambare, V. (2003) 'FDI in India', *Transnational Corporations*. 12: 2, 45–72.

Bamberg, J. H. (1994) *The History of the British Petroleum Company*, Vol. 2. Cambridge: Cambridge University Press.

—— (2000) *British Petroleum and Global Oil 1950–1975*. Cambridge: Cambridge University Press.

—— (2001) 'OLI and OIL: BP in the US in theory and practice', in G. Jones and L. Gálvez-Muñoz (eds) *Foreign Multinationals in the United States*. London: Routledge.

Barjot, D. (1986) 'An Opportunity Seized Early: French Entrepreneurs in the Export Market for Major Public Works (1857–1914),' in W. Fischer, R. M. McInnis, and J. Schneider (eds) *The Emergence of a World Economy 1500–1914, Part II: 1850–1914*. Wiesbaden: Franz Steiner Verlag.

Barker, T. (1986) 'Pilkington, the Reluctant Multinational', in Jones (ed) *British Multinationals: Origins, Management, and Performance*. Aldershot: Gower.

Bartlett, C. A. and Ghoshal, S. (1989) *Managing Across Borders*. Boston: Harvard Business School Press.

Bartlett, C. A. and Ghoshal, S. (1993) 'Beyond the M-form: Toward a Managerial Theory of the Firm', *Strategic Management Journal*, 14: 23–46.

Bayley, C. A. (2004) *The Birth of the Modern World 1780–1914*. Oxford: Blackwell.

Beamish, P. W. and Inkpen, A. C. (2001) 'Japanese Firms and the Decline of the Japanese Expatriate', in P. W. Beamish, A. Delois, and S. Makino (eds) *Japanese Subsidiaries in the New Global Economy*, Cheltenham: Edward Elgar.

Beaton, K. (1957) *Enterprise in Oil: A History of Shell in the United States*. New York: Appelton-Century-Crofts.

Beaud, C. P. (1986) 'Investments and profits of the multinational Schneider group: 1894–1943', in A. Teichova, M. Lévy-Leboyer, and H. Nussbaum (eds) *Multinational Enterprise in Historical Perspective*. Cambridge: Cambridge University Press.

Becker, S. (1998) 'The German Metal Traders before 1914', in Jones (ed) *The Multinational Traders*. London: Routledge.

Behrman, J. N. and Fischer, W. A. (1980) *Overseas R & D Activity of Transnational Companies*. Cambridge, MA: Oelgeschanger, Gunn and Hain.

—— and Grosse, R. E. (1990) *International Business and Governments*. Columbia: University of South Carolina Press.

Bélanger, J. (1999) *Being Local Worldwide: ABB and the Challenge of Global Management*. Ithaca: Cornell University Press.

Belderbos, R. A. (1992) 'Large Multinational Enterprises Based in a Small Economy: Effects on Domestic Investment', *Weltwirtshcaftliches Archiv*, 128: 3, 543–57.

Bell, D. E., Lal, R. and Salmon, W. J. (2004) 'Globalization of Retailing', in J. A. Quelch and R. Deshpandé (eds) *The Global Market: Developing a Strategy to Manage Across Borders*. San Francisco, CA: Jossey-Bass.

Bellak, C. (1997) 'The Measurement of Foreign Direct Investment—A Critical Review,' *The International Trade Journal*, 12: 2, 227–57.

Berger, A. N., Dai, Q., Ongena, S. and Smith, D. C. (2003) 'To What Extent Will the Banking Industry be Globalized? A Study of Bank Nationality and Reach in 20 European Nations', *Journal of Banking & Finance*, 27: 383–415.

Bernard, A. B. and Jensen, J. B. (2003) 'Firm Structure, Multinationals and Manufacturing Plant Deaths', mba.tuck.dartmouth.edu/pages/faculty/Andrew.bernard/deaths.pdf.

—— and Sjoholm, F. (2003) 'Foreign Owners and Plant Survival', *National Bureau of Economc Research Working Paper* No. 10039, 1–24.

Bhalla, A. S. (2002) 'Sino-Indian Growth and Liberalisation', *Asian Survey*, 42: 3, 419–39.

Birkinshaw, J. (2001) 'Strategy and Management in Subsidiaries', in A. Rugman and T. L. Brewer (eds) *Oxford Handbook*.

—— and Hood, N. (eds) (1998) *Multinational Corporate Evolution and Subsidiary Development*. London: Macmillan.

Blaich, F. (1984) *Amerikanische Firmen in Deutschland 1890–1918*. Wiesbaden: Franz Steiner Verlag.

Blomström, M. (1986) 'Multinationals and Market Structure in Mexico', *World Development*, 14: 523–30.

—— (1990) 'The Competitiveness of Firms and Countries', in J. H. Dunning, B. Kogut and M. Blomström (eds) *Globalisation of Firms and the Competitiveness of Nations*. Lund: Lund University Press.

—— and Lipsey, R. E. (1989) 'The Export Performance of US and Swedish Multinationals', *Review of Income and Wealth*, 35: 3, 245–64.

Boje, P. (2000) *Danmark og Multinationale virksomheider før 1950*. Odense: Odense Universitetsforlag.

Bolle, J. (1968) *Solvay*. Brussells: Sodi.

Bonache, J. and Brewster, C. (2001) 'Knowledge Transfer and the Management of Expatriation', *Thunderbird International Business Review*. 43: 1, 145–68.

Bonin, H., Lung, Y., and Tolliday, S. (2003) *Ford The European History 1903–2003*, 2 vols. Paris: Plage.

Borensztein, E., De Gregorio, J., and Lee, J.-W. (1998) 'How does foreign direct investment affect economic growth?', *Journal of International Economics*, 45: 115–35.

Bosson, R. and Varon, B. (1977) *The Mining Industry and the Developing Countries*. Oxford: Oxford University Press.

Bostock, F. and Jones, G.(1994) 'Foreign Multinationals in British Manufacturing, 1850–1962', *Business History*, 36: 1.

Boyce, G. (1995) *Information, Mediation and Institutional Development*. Manchester: Manchester University Press.

—— (2001) *Co-operative Structures in Global Business*. London: Routledge.

Boyer, R., Charron, E., Jürgens, U. and Tolliday, S. (eds) (1998) *Between Imitation and Innovation. The Transfer and Hybridization of Productive Models in the International Automobile Industry*. Oxford: Oxford University Press.

Bowen, H. V., Lincoln, M. and Rigby, N. (eds) (2002) *The Worlds of the East India Company*. Woodbridge: Boydell Press.

Brewer, T. L. and Young, S. (2001) 'Multilateral Institutions and Policies: Their Implications for Multinational Business Strategy', in A. Rugman and T. L. Brewer (eds) *Oxford Handbook of International Business*. Oxford: Oxford University Press.

Broehl, W. G. (1992) *Cargill. Trading the World's Grain*. Hanover, NH: University Press of New England.

—— (1998) *Cargill: Going Global*. Hanover, NH: University Press of New England.

Brown, M. and McKern, B. (1987) *Aluminium, Copper and Steel in Developing Countries*. Paris: OECD.

Brown, R. A. (1994) *Capital and Entrepreneurship in Southeast Asia*. London: Macmillan.

—— (1998) 'Overseas Chinese Investments in China—Patterns of Growth, Diversification and Finance: The Case of Charoen Pokphand', *China Quarterly*, 155: 610–36.

—— (2000) *Chinese Big Business and the Wealth of Asian Nations*. London: Palgrave.

Brown, S. R. (1979) 'The Transfer of Technology to China in the Nineteenth Century: The Role of Foreign Direct Investment', *Journal of Economic History*, XXXIX: (1), 181–97.

Bucheli, M. (2005) *Bananas and Business: The United Fruit Company in Columbia, 1899–2000*. New York: New York University Press.

Buckley, P. J. and Casson, M. (1989) 'Multinational Enterprises in Less-developed Countries: Cultural and Economic Interaction', *University of Reading Discussion Papers in International Investment and Business Studies*. Series B, No. 126.

—— —— (1976) *The Future of the Multinational Enterprise*. London: Macmillan.

—— —— 'Models of the Multinational Enterprise', *Journal of International Business Studies*, 29, 1: 21–44.

Bussière, E. (1983) 'The interests of the Banque de l'Union Parisienne in Czechoslovakia, Hungary and the Balkans 1919–30', in A. Teichova and P. L. Cottrell (eds) *International Business and Central Europe, 1918–1939*. Leicester: Leicester University Press.

Butler, C. and Ghoshal, S. (2002) 'Hindustan Lever Limited: Levers for Change', *Insead Case 302–199–1*.

Cain, P. J. and Hopkins, A. G. (2002) *British Imperialism: 1688–2000*. London: Longman.

Cameron, R. and Bovykin, V. I. (eds) (1991) *International Banking 1870–1914*. New York: Oxford University Press.

Campbell-Kelly, M. (1989) *ICL. A Business and Technical History*. Oxford: Clarendon Press.

Cantwell, J. A. (1989) *Technological Innovation and Multinational Corporations*. Oxford: Basil Blackwell.

—— (1995) 'The Globalisation of Technology: What Remains of the Product Cycle Model?', *Cambridge Journal of Economics*, 19: 155–74.

—— and Piscitello, L. (2002) 'The Location of Technological Activities of MNCs in European Regions: The Role of Spillovers and Local Competences', *Journal of International Management*, 8, 69–96.

Carana Corporation (2004) *Diasporas, Emigres and Development*. Washington, DC: United States Agency for International Development.

Cardoso, F. H. and Faletto, E. (1979) *Dependency and Development in Latin America*. Berkeley: University of California Press.

Carlos, A. and Kruse, J. (1996) 'The Decline of the Royal African Company: Fringe Firms and the Role of the Charter', *Economic History Review*, 49, 291–313.

Carlos, A. and Nicholas, S. (1988) 'Giants of an Earlier Capitalism: The Chartered Trading Companies as Modern Multinationals', *Business History Review*, 62: 3, 398–419.

Caron, F. (1984) 'Foreign Investments and Technology Transfers', in A. Okuchi and T. Inoue (eds) *Overseas Business Activities*. Tokyo: University of Tokyo Press.

Carosso, V. P. and Sylla, R. (1991) 'U.S. banks in international finance', in R. Cameron and V. I. Bovykin (eds) *International Banking 1870–1914*. New York: Oxford University Press.

Carstensen, F. V. (1984) *American Enterprise in Foreign Markets: Singer and International Harvester in Imperial Russia*. Chapel Hill: University of North Carolina Press.

Casson, M. (1982) *The Entrepreneur: An Economic Theory*. Oxford: Martin Robertson.

—— (1983) (ed) *The Growth of International Business*. London: Allen & Unwin.

—— (1985) 'Entrepreneurship and the Dynamics of Foreign Direct Investment', in P. J. Buckley and M. Casson *The Economic Theory of the Multinational Enterprise*. London: Macmillan.

—— (1986) 'Contractual Arrangements for Technology Transfer: New Evidence from Business History', *Business History*, XXVIII: 4, 5–35.

—— (1987) *The Firm and the Market*. Oxford: Basil Blackwell.

—— (1991a) *Economics of Business Culture: Game Theory, Transactions Costs and Economic Performance*. Oxford: Clarendon Press.

—— (ed) (1991b) *Global Research Strategy and International Competitiveness*. Oxford: Basil Blackwell.

—— (1994) 'Institutional Diversity in Overseas Enterprise: Explaining the Free-Standing Company', *Business History*, 36: 4, 95–108.

—— (2000) *Enterprise and Leadership: Studies on Firms, Markets and Networks*. Cheltenham: Edward Elgar.

—— Barry D., and Horner, D. (1986) 'The Shipping Industry', in M. Casson (ed) *Multinationals and World Trade*. London: Allen & Unwin.

Caves, R. E. (1996) *Multinational Enterprise and Economic Analysis*. Cambridge: Cambridge University Press.

Chadeau, E. (1993) 'The Large Family Firm in Twentieth Century France', *Business History*, 35: 4, 184–205.

Chalmin, P. (1985) *Negociants et Chargeurs*. Paris: Economica.

—— (1987) 'The Rise of International Commodity Trading Companies in Europe in the Nineteenth Century', in S. Yonekawa and H. Yoshihara (eds) *Business History of General Trading Companies*. Tokyo: University of Tokyo Press.

—— (1990) *The Making of a Sugar Giant. Tate and Lyle 1859–1989*. Char: Harwood.

Chandler, A. D. (1962) *Strategy and Structure*. Cambridge, MA: Harvard University Press.

—— (1977) *The Visible Hand*. Cambridge, MA: Harvard University Press.

—— (1990) *Scale and Scope*. Cambridge, MA: Harvard University Press.

—— (1994) 'The Competitive Performance of US Industrial Enterprises since the Second World War', *Business History Review*, 68: 1, 1–72.

—— (2001) *Inventing the Electronic Century*. New York: The Free Press.

Channon, D. F. (1973) *The Strategy and Structure of British Enterprise*. London: Macmillan.

Chapman, K. (1991) *The International Petrochemical Industry*. Oxford: Blackwell.

—— (1992) *Merchant Enterprise in Britain*. Cambridge: Cambridge University Press.

Chaudhuri, K. N. (1978) *The Trading World of Asia and the English East India Company, 1660–1760*. Cambridge: Cambridge University Press.

Cheape, C. (1988) 'Not Politicians but Sound Businessmen: Norton Company and the Third Reich', *Business History Review*, 62: 3, 444–66.

Chen, E. K. Y. (ed) (1994) *Technology Transfer to Developing Countries*. London: Routledge.

Chen, S.-F. S. and Hennart, J.-F. (2002) 'Japanese Investors' Choice of Joint Ventures Versus Wholly-Owned Susbidiaries in the US: The Role of Market Barriers and Firm Capabilities', *Journal of International Business Studies*, 33: 1, 1–18.

Child, J. and Faulkner, D. (1998) *Strategies of Cooperation: Managing Alliances, Networks and Joint Ventures*. Oxford: Oxford University Press.

—— —— and Pitkethly, R. (2000) 'National Differences in Acquisition Integration', in D. Faulkner and M. De Rond (eds) *Cooperative Strategies: Economic, Business and Organizational Issues*. Oxford: Oxford University Press.

—— and Kieser, A. (1979) 'Organizational and Managerial Roles in British and West German Companies', in C. J. Lammers and D. J. Hickson (eds) *Organisations Alike and Unlike*. London: Routledge & Kegan Paul.

Chiswick, B. R. and Hatton, T. J. (2003) 'International Migration and the Integration of Labor Markets,' in M. D. Bordo, A. M. Taylor, and J. G. Williamson (eds), *Globalization in Historical Perspective*. Chicago: University of Chicago Press.

Cho, D.-S. (1984) 'The Anatomy of the Korean General Trading Company', *Journal of Business Research*, 12, 241–55.

—— (1987) *The General Trading Company*. Lexington, MA: Lexington Books.

Chomsky, A. (1996) *West Indian Workers and the United Fruit Company in Costa Rica 1870–1940*. Baton Rouge: Louisiana State University Press.

Christensen, C. (1997) *The Innovators Dilemma*. Boston: Harvard Business School Press.

Christian Aid (2004) *Behind the Mask: the Real Face of Corporate Social Responsibility*. London: Christian Aid.

Chung, R., Paddack, K. and Marchand, D. A. (2002) 'Cemex: Global Growth through Superior Information Capabilities', *IMD Case (IMD-3-0953)*.

Church, R. (1986) 'The Effects of American Multinationals in the British Motor Industry, 1911–83', in A. Teichova, M. Lévy-Leboyer, and H. Nussbaum (eds) *Multinational Enterprises in Historical Perspective*. Cambridge: Cambridge University Press.

—— (1993) 'The Family Firm in Industrial Capitalism: International Perspectives on Hypotheses and History', *Business History*, 35: 4, 17–43.

—— (1994) *The Rise and Decline of the British Motor Industry*. London: Macmillan.

Clarence–Smith, W. G. and Topik, S. (eds) (2003) *The Global Coffee Economy in Africa, Asia, and Latin America, 1500–1989*. Cambridge: Cambridge University Press.

Clegg, J. (1987) *Multinational Enterprises and World Competition*. London: Macmillan.

Cleveland, H. B. and Huertas, T. F. (1985) *Citibank 1812–1970*. Cambridge, MA: Harvard University Press.

Coase, R. H. (1937) 'The Nature of the Firm', *Economica*, 4, 386–405.

Cobbe, J. H. (1979) *Governments and Mining Companies in Developing Countries*. Boulder: Westview.

Cochran, S. (1980) *Big Business in China*. Cambridge, MA: Harvard University Press.

—— (2000) *Encountering Chinese Networks*. Berkeley, CA: University of California Press.

Coleman, D. C. (1969) *Courtaulds*, 2 vols. Oxford: Clarendon Press.

Colli, A. (2003) *The History of Family Business 1850–2000*. Cambridge: Cambridge University Press.

Collingsworth, T. (2002) 'The Key Human Rights Challenge: Developing Enforcement Mechanisms', *Harvard Human Rights Journal*, 15, 183–204.

Collins, J. L. (2003). *Threads. Gender, Labor and Power in the Global Apparel Industry*. Chicago: University of Chicago Press.

Contractor, F. J. (1990) 'Ownership Patterns of U. S. Joint Ventures Abroad and the Liberalization of Foreign Government Regulations in the 1980s: Evidence from the Benchmark Surveys', *Journal of International Business Studies*, 21: 1, 55–73.

Corley, T. A. B. (1994) 'Britain's Overseas Investments in 1914 Revisited', *Business History*, 36: 1.

Cortada, J. W. (1993) *Before the Computer*. Princeton: Princeton University Press.

Cox, H. (2000) *The Global Cigarette: Origins and Growth of British American Tobacco 1880–1945*. Oxford: Oxford University Press.

Crafts, N. and Venables, A. J. (2003) 'Globalization in History: A Geographical Perspective', in M. D. Bordo, A. M. Taylor, and J. G. Williamson (eds) *Globalization in Historical Perspective*. Chicago: University of Chicago Press.

Crisp, O. (1976) *Studies in the Russian Economy before 1914*. London: Macmillan.

Crystal, J. (2003) *Unwanted Company: Foreign Investment in American Industries*. Ithaca: Cornell University Press.

Curhan, J. P., Davidson, W. H., and Suri, R. (1977) *Tracing the Multinationals*. Cambridge, MA: Harvard University Press.

Daniels, P. W. (1986) 'Foreign Banks and Metropolitan Development: A Comparison of London and New York', *Tidjschrift voor Economische en Sociale Geografie*, LXXVII: 4, 269–87.

—— and Thrift, N. J., and Leyshon, A. (1989) 'Internationalisation of Professional Producer Services: Accountancy Conglomerates', in P. Enderwick (ed) *Multinational Service Firms*. London: Routledge.

Dassbach, C. H. A. C. (1989) *Global Enterprises and the World Economy*. New York: Garland.

Davenport-Hines, R. P. T. (1986) 'Vickers as a multinational before 1945', in Geoffrey Jones (ed), *British Multinationals: Origins, Management and Performance*. Aldershot: Gower.

—— and Jones, G. (eds) (1989) *British Business in Asia since 1860*. Cambridge: Cambridge University Press.

Davidson, W. H. (1980) 'The Location of Foreign Direct Investment Activities: Country Characteristics and Experience Effects', *Journal of International Business Studies*, 11: 9–22.

Davies, P. N. (1990) *Fyffes and the Banana: Musa Sapientum*. London: Athlone.

Davies, R. B. (1976) *Peacefully Working to Conquer the World: Singer Sewing Machines in Foreign Markets, 1854–1920*. New York: Arno Press.

Daviet, J.-P. (1989) *Une multinationale à la Française*. Paris: Fayard.

Davis, L. and Gallman, R. (2001) *Evolving Financial Markets and International Capital Flows: Britain, the Americas, and Australia, 1865–1914*. Cambridge: Cambridge University Press.

De Geer, H. (1995) *A. Johnson & Co. Inc 1920–1995*. Stockholm: EHF.

—— (1998) 'Trading Companies in twentieth-century Sweden', in G. Jones (ed) *Multinational Traders: Origins, Management, and Performance*. Aldershot: Gower.

Dierikx, M. L. J. (1991) 'Struggle for Prominence: Clashing Dutch and British Interests on the Colonial Air Routes, 1918–42', *Journal of Contemporary History*, 26, 335–51.

Dosi, G. (1988) 'Sources, Procedures, and Microeconomic Effects of Innovation', *Journal of Economic Literature*, XXVI: September, 1120–71.

Dubin, M. (1976) 'Foreign Acquisitions and the Growth of the Multinational Firm', DBA thesis. Boston, MA: Harvard Business School.

Dunning, J. H. (1958) *American Investment in British Manufacturing Industry*. London: Allen & Unwin.

—— (1970) *Studies in International Investment*. London: Allen & Unwin.

—— (1981) 'Explaining the International Direct Investment Position of Countries: Towards a Dynamic or Developmental Approach', *Weltwirtschaftliches Archiv*, 117: 30–64.

—— (1983) 'Changes in the Level and Structure of International Production: The Last One

Hundred Years', in M. Casson (ed.) *The Growth of International Business*. London: Allen & Unwin.

—— (1986) *Japanese Participation in British Industry*. London: Croom Helm.

—— (1988a) *Explaining International Production*. London: Unwin Hyman.

—— (1988b) *Multinationals, Technology and Competitiveness*. London: Unwin Hyman.

—— (1992) *Multinational Enterprises and the Global Economy*. Wokingham: Addison-Wesley.

—— (1993) *The Globalisation of Business*. London: Routledge.

—— and Cantwell, J. and Corley, T. A. B. (1986) 'The Theory of International Production: Some Historical Antecedents', in P. Hertner and G. Jones (eds) *Multinationals: Theory and History*. Aldershot: Gower.

Dyer, D., Dalzell, F. and Olegario, R. (2004) *Rising Tide. Lessons from 165 Years of Brand Building at Procter & Gamble*. Boston: Harvard Business School Press.

Eakin, M. C. (1989) *British Enterprise in Brazil*. Durham: Duke University Press.

Edwards, T. and Ferner, A. (2002) 'The renewed "American challenge": A Review of Employment Practice in US Multinationals', *Industrial Relations Journal*, 33: 2, 94–111.

Encarnation, D. J. (1989) *Dislodging Multinationals. India's Strategy in Comparative Perspective*. Ithaca: Cornell University Press.

—— (1992) *Rivals beyond Trade*. Ithaca: Cornell University Press.

Enderwick, P. (1989) 'Some Economics of Service-Sector Multinational Enterprises', in P. Enderwick (ed.) *Multinational Service Firms*. London: Routledge.

Estape-Triay, S. (2003) 'Ford in Spain: a first stage (1920–1954) — A Multinational Confronts Political Constraints', in H. Bonin, Y. Lung, and S. Tolliday (eds) *Ford: The European History 1903–2003*, 2 vols. Paris: Plage.

Evans, P. B. (1979) *Dependent Development: The Alliance of Multinational, State and Local Capital in Brazil*, Princeton: Princeton University Press.

Evenett, S. J. (2004) 'The Cross-Border Mergers and Acquisitions Wave of the Late 1990's', in R. E. Baldwin and L. A. Winters (eds) *Challenges to Globalization: Analyzing the Economics*. Chicago: University of Chicago Press.

Facio, R. (1972) *Estudio Sobre Economia Costarricense*. San Jose: Editorial Costa Rica.

Fear, J. (2004) *Organizing Control: August Thyssen and the Construction of German Corporate Management*. Cambridge, Mass: Harvard University Press.

Feinstein, C. (1990) 'Britain's Overseas Investments in 1913', *Economic History Review*, XLIII: 2, 280–95.

Feldenkirchen, W. (2000) *Siemens, From Workshop to Global Player*. Munich: Piper Verlag.

Feldman, G. (1989) 'Foreign Penetration of German Enterprises after the First World War: the Problem of *Überfremdung*', in A. Teichova, M. Lévy-Leboyer and H. Nussbaum (eds) *Historical Studies in International Corporate Business*. Cambridge: Cambridge University Press.

Ferguson, N. (1998) *The World's Banker*. London: Weidenfeld and Nicolson.

Ferner, A. and Varul, M. Z. (2000) 'Internationalisation and the Personnel Function in German Multinationals', *Human Resource Management Journal*, 10: 3, 79–96.

Fleming, G., Merrett, D. and Ville, S. (2004) *The Big End of Town. Big Business and Corporate Leadership in Twentieth Century Australia*. Cambridge: Cambridge University Press.

Ferrier, R. W. (1982) *The History of the British Petroleum Company*, Vol 1. Cambridge: Cambridge University Press.

Fieldhouse, D. K. (1978) *Unilever Overseas*. London: Croom Helm.

——(1986) 'The Multinational: A Critique of a Concept', in A. Teichova, M. Lévy-Leboyer and H. Nussbaum (eds) *Multinational Enterprise in Historical Perspective*. Cambridge: Cambridge University Press.

——(1994) *Merchant Capital and Economic Decolonization*. Oxford: Clarendon Press.

Finch, M. H. J. (1985) 'British Imperialism in Uruguay: The Public Utility Companies and the Batllista State, 1900–1930', in C. Abel and C. M. Lewis (eds) *Latin America, Economic Imperialism and the State*. London: Athlone.

Findlay, R. and O'Rourke, K. H. (2003) 'Commodity Market Integration 1500–2000', in M. D. Bordo and J. G. Williamson (eds) *Globalization in Historical Perspective*. Chicago: University of Chicago Press.

Fisman, R. and Khanna, T. (2004) 'Facilitating Development: The Role of Business Groups', *World Development*, 32: 4, 609–28.

Fligstein, N. (2001) *The Architecture of Markets*. Princeton: Princeton University Press.

Foss, N. J. and Pederen, T. (2002) 'Transferring Knowledge in MNCs: The Role of Sources of Subsidiary Knowledge and Organisation Context', *Journal of International Management*, 8: 1–19.

Franko, L. (1976) *The European Multinationals*. London: Harper & Row.

——(1979) *Joint Venture Survival in Multinational Corporations*. New York: Praeger.

——(1989) 'Global Corporate Competition: Who's Winning, Who's Losing, and the R & D Factor as One Reason Why', *Strategic Management Journal*, 10: 451–53.

Freeland, R. F. (2001) *The Struggle for Control of the Modern Corporation: Organizational Design at General Motors, 1924–1970*. Cambridge: Cambridge University Press.

French, M. J. (1987) 'The Emergence of a US Multinational Enterprise: The Goodyear Tire and Rubber Company, 1910–1939', *Economic History Review*, XL: 1, 64–79.

——(1991) *The U.S. Tire Industry: A History*. Boston: Twayne.

Freyssenet, M., Mair, A., Shimizu, K. and Volpato, G. (eds) (1998) *One Best Way? Trajectories and Industrial Models of the World's Automobile Producers*. Oxford: Oxford University Press.

Fridenson, P. (1986) 'The Growth of Multinational Activities in the French Motor Industry, 1890–1979', in P. Hertner and G. Jones (eds) *Multinationals: Theory and History*. Aldershot: Gower.

——(1997) 'France: The Relatively Slow Development of Big Business in the Twentieth Century', in A. D. Chandler, F. Amatori and T. Hikino (eds) *Big Business and the Wealth of Nations*. Cambridge: Cambridge University Press.

Fritsch, W. and Franco, G. (1991) *Foreign Direct Investment in Brazil: Its Impact on Industrial Restructuring*. Paris: OECD.

Frost, T., Birkinshaw, J. and Ensign, S. (2002) 'Centers of Excellence in Multinational Corporations', *Strategic Management Journal*, 23: 2, 997–1015.

Fruin, W. M. (1992) *The Japanese Enterprise System*. Oxford: Clarendon Press.

Fuji Xerox (1994) *Three Decades of Fuji Xerox 1962– 1992*. Tokyo: Fuji Xerox.

Fursenko, A. A. (1991) 'The oil industry', in Rondo Cameron and V. I. Bovykin (eds) *International Banking 1870–1914*. New York: Oxford University Press.

Gales, B. P. A. and Sluyterman, K. E. (1993) 'Outward Bound: The Rise of Dutch Multinationals', in G. Jones and H. Schröter (eds) *The Rise of Multinationals in Continental Europe*. Aldershot: Edward Elgar.

Gereffi, G. (1994) 'The Organization of Buyer-Driven Global Commodity Chains: How U.S. Retailers Shape Overseas Production Networks', in G. Gereffi and M. Korzeniewicz (eds) *Commodity Chains and Global Capitalism*. Westport, Conn.: Greenwood Press.

—— and Evans, P. (1981) 'Transnational Corporations, Dependent Development, and State Policy in the Semiperiphery: A Comparison of Brazil and Mexico', *Latin American Research Review*, 16: 31–64.

Gerretson, F. C. (1958) *History of the Royal Dutch*, 4 vols. Leiden: E. J. Brill.

Ghemawat, P. (2001) 'Distance still matters: The Hard Reality of Global Expansion', *Harvard Business Review*. September.

—— (2003) 'Semiglobalization and International Business Strategy', *Journal of International Business Studies*, 34: 2, 138–52.

Gerlach, M. L. (1992) *Alliance Capitalism: The Social Transformation of Japanese Business*. Berkeley: University of California Press.

Giebelhaus, A. W. (1994) 'The Pause that Refreshed the World: The Evolution of Coca Cola's Global Marketing Strategy', in G. Jones and N. J. Morgan (eds) *Adding Value: Brands and Marketing in Food and Drink*. London: Routledge.

Glover, D. J. (1986) 'Multinational Corporations and Third World Agriculture', in H. Moran (ed) *Investing in Development: New Roles for Private Capital*. Washington, DC: Overseas Development Council.

Godley, A. (1999) 'Pioneering Foreign Direct Investment in British Manufacturing', *Business History Review*, 73, 394–429.

—— (2003) 'Foreign Multinationals and Innovation in British Retailing, 1850–1962', *Business History*, 45: 1, 80–100.

Goffee, R. and Jones, G. (1996) 'What Holds the Modern Company Together', *Harvard Business Review*, 74: 6, 133–48.

Gomes-Casseres, B. (1989) 'Ownership Structures of Foreign Susbidiaries: Theory and Evidence', *Journal of Economic Behavior and Organization*, 11, 1–25.

—— (1990) 'Firm Ownership Preferences and Host Government Restrictions: An Integrated Approach', *Journal of International Business Studies*, 21: 1, 1–22.

—— (2003) 'Competitive Advantage in Alliance Constellations', *Strategic Organization*, 1: 3, 327–35.

Goodman, J. B. (1993) 'Insurance: Domestic Regulation and International Service Competition', in D. B. Yoffie (ed) *Beyond Free Trade: Firms, Governments, and Global Competition*. Boston: Harvard Business School Press.

Graham, B. M. W. and Shuldiner, A. T. (2001) *Corning and the Craft of Innovation*. Oxford: Oxford University Press.

Graham, J. L. (2001) 'Culture and Human Resources Management', in A. M. Rugman and T. L. Brewer (eds) *Oxford Handbook of International Business*. Oxford: Oxford University Press.

Gray, J. M. and Gray, H. P. (1981) 'The Multinational Bank: A Financial MNC?', *Journal of Banking and Finance*, 5, 33–63.

Greenhill, R. G. (1995) 'Investment Groups, Free-Standing Company or Multinational? Brazilian Warrant, 1909–52', *Business History*, 37: 1, 86–111.

Grosse, R. (2001) 'International Business in Latin America', in A. M. Rugman and T. L. Brewer (eds), *Oxford Handbook of International Business*. Oxford: Oxford University Press.

Guex, S. (1998) 'The Development of Swiss Trading Companies in the Twentieth Century', in Jones (ed) *Multinational Traders*.

Guillén, M. F. (2001) 'Is Globalisation Civilizing, Destructive or Feeble? A Critique of Five Key Debates in the Social Science Literature', *Annual Review of Sociology*, 27, 235–60.

Gupta, A. K. and Govindarajan, V. (2000) 'Knowledge flows within multinational corporations', *Strategic Management Journal*, 21, 473–96.

Gupta, B. (1997) 'Collusion in the Indian Tea Industry in the Great Depression: An Analysis of

Panel Data', *Explorations in Economic History*. 34: 2, 155–73.

Guthrie, D. (2001). *Dragon in a Three-Piece Suit: The Emergence of Capitalism in China*. Princeton: Princeton University Press.

Hagen, A. (1997a) *Deutsche Directinvestitionen in Grossbritannien, 1871–1918*. Stuggart: Franz Steiner Verlag.

—— (1997b) 'German FDI in the British Chemical Industry Before 1914', *Business History Review*, 71: 351–80.

Haggard, S. (1989) 'The Political Economy of Foreign Direct Investment in Latin America', *Latin American Research Review*, 24, 184–208.

Häikiö, M. (2002) *Nokia: The Inside Story*. Boston: Financial Times.

Hancock, D. (2002) 'An Undiscovered Ocean of Commerce Laid Open: India, Wine and the Emerging Atlantic Economy, 1703–1813', in H. V. Bowen, M. Lincoln and N. Rigby (eds) *The Worlds of the East India* Company. Woodbridge: Boydell Press.

Hara, T. and Kudo, A. (1992) 'International Cartels in Business History', in A. Kudo and T. Hara (eds) *International Cartels in Business History*. Tokyo: University of Tokyo Press.

Harlfatis, G. (1993) *A History of Greek-Owned Shipping*. London: Routledge.

—— and Theotokas, J. (2004) 'European Family Firms in International Business: British and Greek Tramp-Shipping Firms', *Business History*, 46: 2, 219–55.

Harrison, A. E. and McMillan, M. (2004) 'The Impact of Overseas Investment by US Multinationals on Wages and Employment' (mimeo).

Harvey, C. (1981) *The Rio Tinto Company: An Economic History of a Leading International Mining Concern 1873–1954*. Penzance: Alison Hodge.

—— and J. Press (1990) 'The City and International Mining, 1870–1914', *Business History*, XXXII: 3, 98–119.

Harvey, D. (1989) *The Condition of Postmodernity*. Oxford: Blackwell.

Hatton, T. J. and Williamson, J. G. (1998) *The Age of Mass Migration*. Oxford: Oxford University Press.

Headrick, D. R. (1988) *The Tentacles of Progress: Technology Transfer in the Age of Imperialism, 1850–1940*, Oxford: Oxford University Press.

Healy, P. and Palepu, K. G. (1993) 'International Equity Acquisitions: Who, Where, and Why?' in K. Froot (ed) *Foreign Direct Investment*. Chicago: University of Chicago Press.

Hedlund, G. (1986) 'The Hypermodern MNC: A Heterarchy', *Human Resource Management*, 25: 9–36.

—— and Rolander, D. (1990) 'Action in Heterarchies: New Approaches to Managing the MNC', in C. A. Bartlett, Y. L. Doz, and G. Hedlund (eds) *Managing the Global Firm*. London: Routledge.

Heer, J. (1966) *World Events 1866–1966: The First Hundred Years of Nestlé*. Rivaz: Nestlé.

Hennart, J. F. (1982) *A Theory of Multinational Enterprise*. Ann Arbor: University of Michigan Press.

—— (1986) 'The tin industry', in M. Casson (ed.) *Multinationals and World Trade*. London: Allen & Unwin.

—— (1987) 'Transactions Costs and the Multinational Enterprise: The Case of Tin', *Business and Economic History*, 16, 147–59.

—— (1991a) 'The Transaction Cost Theory of the Multinational Enterprise', in C. N. Pitelis and R. Sugden (eds) *The Nature of the Transnational Firm*. London: Routledge.

—— (1991b) 'The Transaction Costs Theory of Joint Ventures: An Empirical Study of Japanese Subsidiaries in the United States', *Management Science*, 37: 4, 483–97.

—— (1994a) 'International Financial Capital Transfers: A Transaction Cost Framework', *Business History*, 36: 1, 51–70.

—— (1994b) 'Free-Standing Firms and the Internalization of Markets for Financial Capital: A Response to Casson', *Business History*, 36: 4, 118–31.

—— (2001) 'Theories of the Multinational Enterprise', in A. M. Rugman and T. L. Brewer (eds) *Oxford Handbook of International Business*. Oxford: Oxford University Press.

—— and Kryda, G. M. (1998) 'Why do Traders Invest in Manufacturing?', in G. Jones (ed) *The Multinational Traders*. London: Routledge.

Hennart, J. F., Roehl T. and Zeng, M. (2001) 'What Do Affiliate Exits Tell Us About the Challenges Faced by Foreign Affiliates in the United States', in G. Jones and L. Gálvez-Muñoz (eds) *Foreign*

Multinationals in the United States. London: Routledge.

Hennart, J. F., Roehl T. and Zeng, M. (2002) 'Do Exits Proxy a Liability of Foreignness? The Case of Japanese Exits from the US', *Journal of International Management*, 8, 241–64.

——and Zeng, M. (2002) 'Cross-Cultural Differences and Joint Venture Longevity', *Journal of International Business Studies*, 33: 4, 699–716.

Healy, P. and Palepu, K. G. (1993) 'International Corporate Equity Acquisitions: Who, Where and Why,' in K. Froot (ed), *Foreign Direct Investment*. Chicago: University of Chicago Press.

Heras, R. G. (1987) 'Hostage Private Companies Under Restraint: British Railways and Transport Co-ordination in Argentina During the 1930s', *Journal of Latin American Studies*, 19: 41–67.

Hertner, P. (1984) *Il capitale tedesco in Italia dall Unità alla Prima Guerra Mondiale Banche miste e siluppo economico italiano*. Bologna: Il Mulino.

——(1986) 'German Multinational Enterprise Before 1914: Some Case Studies', in P. Hertner and G. Jones (eds) *Multinationals: Theory and History*. Aldershot: Gower.

——(1987) 'Les sociétés financières suisses et le développement de l'industrie électrique jusqu'à la Première Guerre Mondiale', in F. Cardot (ed) *1880–1980: Un siécle d'électricité dans le monde*. Paris: PUF.

——(1990) 'German banks abroad before 1914', in G. Jones (ed) *Banks as Multinationals*. London: Routledge.

——(1993) 'The German electrotechnical industry in the Italian market before the Second World War', in G. Jones and H. G. Schröter (eds) *The Rise of Multinationals in Continental Europe*. Aldershot: Edward Elgar.

Hildebrand, K.-G. (1985) *Expansion, Crisis, Reconstruction: Swedish Match 1917–1939*. Stockholm: Liber Förlag.

Hill, N. K. (1950) 'The History of the Imperial Continental Gas Association 1824–1900', Ph.D. thesis. London: University of London.

Hills, J. C. (2002) *The Struggle for Control of Global Communications: The Formative Century*. Urbana: University of Illinios Press.

Hoch, S. J. and Banerji, S. (1993) 'When Do Private Labels Succeed?' *Sloan Management Review*, 34: 57–67.

Hoesel, R. van (1999) *New Multinational Enetrprises from Korea and Taiwan: beyond export-led growth*. London: Routledge.

——and Narula, R. (eds) (1999) *Multinational enterprises from the Netherlands*. London: Routledge.

Hofstede, G. (1980) *Cultures Consequences*. Beverly Hills, CA: Sage.

——(1996) *Cultures and Organizations*. London: McGraw-Hill.

——and Bond, M. H. (1988) 'The Confucius Connections: From Cultural Roots to Economic Growth', *Organizational Dynamics*, 16: 1, 4–21.

Hollander, S. C. (1970) *Multinational Retailing*. East Lansing: Michigan State University Press.

Hood, N. and Young, S. (1979) *The Economics of Multinational Enterprise*. London: Longman.

Hu, Y. S. (1992) 'Global or stateless corporations are national firms with international operations', *California Management Review*, 34: 2, 107–26.

Huang, Y. (2003) *Selling China: Foreign Direct Investment During the Reform Era*. Cambridge: Cambridge University Press.

Huang, Y. and Khanna, T. (2003) 'Can India Overtake China?', *Foreign Policy*, 137, 74–81.

Huertas, T. F. (1990) 'US Multinational Banking: History and Prospects', in G. Jones (ed.) *Banks as Multinationals*. London: Routledge.

Huff, G. (1997) *The Economic Growth of Singapore: Trade and Development in the Twentieth Century*. Cambridge: Cambridge University Press.

Humes, S. (1993) *Managing the Multinational: Confronting the Global-Local Dilemma*. New York: Prentice-Hall.

Inkpen, A. (2001) 'Strategic Alliances', in A. M. Rugman and T. L. Brewer (eds) *Oxford Handbook of International Business*. Oxford: Oxford University Press.

Jacob-Wendler, Von G. (1982) *Deutsche Elektroindustrie in Lateinamerika. Siemens und AEG (1890–1914)*. Stuggart: Klett-Cotta.

James, H. (2001) *The End of Globalization: Lessons from the Great Depression*. Cambridge, MA: Harvard University Press.

Jardine Matheson (1947) *Jardines and the EWO Interests*. New York: Charles A. Phelps.

Jesudason, J. V. (1990) *Ethnicity and the Economy*. Singapore: Oxford University Press.

Johanson, J. and Vahlne, J.-E. (1977) 'The Internationalisation Process of the Firm—A Model of Market Knowledge and Increasing Commitments', *Journal of International Business Studies*, 8, 23–32.

—— (1990) 'The Mechanism of Internationalization', *International Marketing Review*, 7: 4, 11–24.

Jones, E. (2001) *The Business of Medicine*. London: Profile Books.

Jones, G. (1981) *The State and the Emergence of the British Oil Industry*. London: Macmillan.

—— (1984) 'The Growth and Performance of British Multinational Firms Before 1939: The Case of Dunlop', *Economic History Review*, XXXVI: 1, 35–53.

—— (1985) 'The Gramophone Company: An Anglo-American Multinational, 1898–1931', *Business History Review*, 59: 1, 76–100.

—— (ed) (1986a) *British Multinationals: Origins, Management and Performance*. Aldershot: Gower.

—— (1986b) *Banking and Empire in Iran*. Cambridge: Cambridge University Press.

—— (1987) *Banking and Oil*. Cambridge: Cambridge University Press.

—— (1988) 'Foreign Multinationals and British Industry Before 1945', *Economic History Review*, XLI: 3, 429–53.

—— (1990a) 'The British Government and Foreign Multinationals Before 1970', in M. Chick (ed) *Governments, Industries, and Markets*. Aldershot: Edward Elgar, pp. 194–214.

—— (ed) (1990b) *Banks as Multinationals*. London: Routledge.

—— (1992) 'International Financial Centres in Asia, the Middle East and Australia: A Historical Perspective', in Y. Cassis (ed.) *Finance and Financiers in European History, 1880–1960*. Cambridge: Cambridge University Press.

—— (1993) *British Multinational Banking 1830–1990*. Oxford: Clarendon Press.

—— (1994) 'British Multinationals and British Business Since 1850', in M. W. Kirby and M. B. Rose (eds) *Business Enterprise in Modern Britain from the Eighteenth to the Twentieth Centuries*. London: Routledge.

—— (1997) 'Great Britain: Big Business, Management and Competitiveness in Twentieth Century Britain', in A. D. Chandler, F. Amatori, and T. Hikino (eds) *Big Business and the Wealth of Nations*. Cambridge: Cambridge University Press.

—— (1998a) 'British Overseas Banks as Free-Standing Companies', in M. Wilkins and H. G. Schröter, *The Free-Standing Company in the World Economy, 1830–1996*. Oxford: Oxford University Press.

—— (ed) (1998b) *The Multinational Traders*. London: Routledge.

—— (2000) *Merchants to Multinationals*. Oxford: Oxford University Press.

—— (2002) 'Control, Performance and Knowledge Transfers in Large Multinationals: Unilever in the United States, 1945–1980', *Business History Review*, 76, 435–78.

—— (2005) *Renewing Unilever: Transformation and Tradition*. Oxford: Oxford University Press.

—— and Bostock, F. (1996) 'US Multinationals in British Manufacturing Before 1962', *Business History Review*, 70: 1, 207–56.

—— and Gálvez-Muñoz, L. (eds) (2001) *Foreign Multinationals in the United States*. London: Routledge.

—— and Kraft, A. (2004) 'Corporate Venturing: The Origins of Unilever's Pregnancy Test', *Business History*, 46: 1, 100–22.

—— and Miskell, P. (2005) 'European Integration and Corporate Restructuring: The Strategy of Unilever c.1957–c.1990', *Economic History Review*, 58: 1.

—— and Morgan, N. J. (eds) (1994) *Adding Value: Brands and Marketing in Food and Drink*. London: Routledge.

—— and Schröter, H. (eds) (1993) *The Rise of Multinationals in Continental Europe*. Aldershot: Edward Elgar.

—— and Wale, J. (1999) 'Diversification Strategies of British Trading Companies: Harrisons and Crosfield, c.1900–c.1980', *Business History*, 41: 2, 69–101.

Kawabe, N. (1987) 'Development of Overseas Operations by General Trading Companies 1868–1945', in S. Yonekawa and H. Yoshihara (eds) *Business History of General Trading Companies*. Tokyo: University of Tokyo Press.

—— (1990) 'Overseas Activities and Their Organisation', in S. Yonekawa (ed) *General Trading Companies*. Tokyo: United Nations University Press.

Kelly, J. (1977) *Bankers and Borders*. Cambridge, MA: Ballinger.

Kennedy, C. R. (1992) 'Relations Between Transnational Corporations and Governments in Host Countries: A Look to the Future', *Transnational Corporations*, I, 67–91.

Kennedy, W. P. (1987) *Industrial Structure, Capital Markets, and the Origins of British Economic Decline*. Cambridge: Cambridge University Press.

Kenney, M. and Florida, R. (1993) *Beyond Mass Production*. New York: Oxford University Press.

Kenwood, A. G. and Lougheed, A. L. (1992) *The Growth of the International Economy, 1820–1990*. London: Allen & Unwin.

Khanna, T. (2000) 'Business Groups and Social Welfare in Emerging Markets: Existing Evidence and Unanswered Questions', *European Economic Review*, 44: 748–61.

Khanna, T., Gulati, R., and Nohria, N. (1998) 'The Dynamics of Learning Alliances: Competition, Cooperation and Relative Scope', *Strategic Management Journal*, 19: 3, 193–210.

Khanna, T. and Palepu, K. (1997) 'Why Focused Strategies May Be Wrong for Emerging Markets', *Harvard Business Review*, 75: 4, 41–51.

—— (2000) 'The Future of Business Groups in Emerging Markets: Long-run Evidence from Chile', *Academy of Management Journal*, 43: 3, 268–85.

King, F. H. H. (1991) *The Hongkong Bank in the Period of Development and Nationalism, 1941–1984*. Cambridge: Cambridge University Press.

Kipping, M. (1997) 'Consultancies, Institutions and the Diffusion of Taylorism in Britain, Germany, and France, 1920s to 1950s', *Business History*, 37: 4, 66–82.

—— 'American Management Consulting Companies in Western Europe, 1920–1990: Products, Reputation and Relationships', *Business History Review*, 73: 2, 190–220.

—— and Engwall, L. (eds) (2002) *Management Consulting, Emergence and Dynamics of a Knowledge Industry*. Oxford: Oxford University Press.

Kirzner, I. M. (1973) *Competition and Entrepreneurship*. Chicago: University of Chicago Press.

—— (1979) *Perception, Opportunity and Profit*. Chicago: University of Chicago Press.

Klein, H. S. (1965) 'The Creation of the Patiño Tin Empire', *Inter-American Economic Affairs*, XIX, 3–23.

Kline, B. (1997) *Profit, Principle and Apartheid, 1948–1994*. New York: The Edwin Mellen Press.

Knickerbocker, F. T. (1973) *Oligopolistic Reaction and the Multinational Enterprise*. Cambridge, MA: Harvard University Press.

Knight, F. H. (1921) *Risk, Uncertainty and Profit*. Boston: Houghton Mifflin.

Knox, B. and McKinlay, A. (1999) 'Working for the Yankee Dollar: American Inward Investment and Scottish Labour, 1945–70', *Historical Studies in Industrial Relations*, 7: 1, 1–26.

Kobrin, S. J. (1984) 'Expropriation as an Attempt to Control Foreign Firms in LDCs: Trends from 1969 to 1979', *International Studies Quarterly*, 18, 329–48.

—— (1997) 'The Architecture of Globalization: States Sovereignty in a Networked Global Economy', in J. H. Dunning (ed) *Government, Globalization, and International Business*. Oxford: Oxford University Press.

—— (2001) 'Sovereignty @ Bay: Globalization, Multinational Enterprise, and the International Political System', in A. M. Rugman and T. L. Brewer (eds) *Oxford Handbook of International Business*. Oxford: Oxford University Press.

Kock, C. and Guillen, M. F. (2001) 'Strategy and Structure in Developing Countries: Business Groups as Evolutionary Response to Opportunities for Unrelated Diversification', *Industrial and Corporate Change*, 10: 1, 1–37.

Koehn, N. F. (2001) *Brand New*. Boston: Harvard Business School Press.

Kogut, B. (1989) 'The Stability of Joint Ventures: Reciprocity and Competitive Rivalry', *Journal of Industrial Economics*, 38, 183–98.

—— (1991) 'Country Capabilities and the Permeability of Borders', *Strategic Management Journal*, 12, 33–47.

—— (1997). 'Globalization', in M. Warner (ed) *Concise International Encyclopedia of Business and Management*. London: International Thomson Business Press.

—— and Chang, S. J. (1991) 'Technological Capabilities and Japanese Foreign Direct Investment in the United States', *Reviews of Economics and Statistics*, 73, 401–32.

—— and Parkinson, D. (1993) 'The Diffusion of American Organizing Principles to Europe', in B. Kogut (ed) *Country Competitiveness: Technology and the Organizing of Work*. New York: Oxford University Press.

—— and Singh, A. (1988) 'The Effect of National Culture on the Choice of Entry Mode', *Journal of International Business Studies*, 19, 411–32.

—— and Zander, U. (1992) 'Knowledge of the Firm, Combinative Capabilities, and the Replication of Technology', *Organization Science*, 3, 383–97.

—————(1993) 'Knowledge of the Firm and the Evolutionary Theory of the Multinational Corporation', *Journal of International Business Studies* 24, 625–45.

Kolk, A. and Tulder, R. van (2002) *International Codes of Conduct: Trends, Sectors, Issues and Effectiveness*. Rotterdam: Erasmus University.

Kristensen, P. H. and Zeitlin, J. (2004) *Local Players in Global Games: The Strategic Constitution of a Multinational Corporation*. Oxford: Oxford University Press.

Krug, J. A. and Nigh, D. (1998) 'Top Management Turnover: Comparing Foreign and Domestic Acquisitions of US Firms', in D. Woodward and D. Nigh (eds) *Foreign Ownership and the Consequences of Foreign Direct Investment in the United States*. Westport: Quorum.

Kudo, A. (1994) 'I. G. Farben in Japan: The Transfer of Technology and Management Skills', *Business History*, 36: 1, 159–83.

—— Kipping, M. and Schroter, H. G. (eds) (2004) *German and Japanese Business in the Boom Years*. London: Routledge.

Kuemmerle, W. (1999) 'The Drivers of Foreign Direct Investment into Research and Development: An Empirical Investigation', *Journal of International Business Studies*, 30(1), 1–24.

Kuisel, R. F. (1993) *Seducing the French: The Dilemma of Americanization*. Berkeley, CA: University of California Press.

Kuwahara, T. (1990) 'Trends in Research on Overseas Expansion by Japanese Enterprises Prior to World War II', *Japanese Yearbook on Business History*, 7, 61–81.

Lall, S. (1973) 'Transfer-Pricing by Multinational Manufacturing Firms', *Oxford Bulletin of Economics and Statistics*, 35: 3, 173–95.

—— (1979) 'Multinationals and Market Structure in an Open Developing Economy: The Case of Malaysia', *Weltwirtschaftliches Archiv*, 115, 325–48.

—— (1983) *The New Multinationals: The Spread of Third World Enterprises*. Chichester: John Wiley.

—— (ed.) (1993) *Transnational Corporations and Economic Development*. London: Routledge.

—— and Streeten, P. (1977) *Foreign Investment, Transnationals and Developing Countries*. London: Macmillan.

Langdon, S. W. (1981) *Multinational Corporations in the Political Economy of Kenya*. London: Macmillan.

Langlois, R. N. (ed) (1988) *Micro-Electronics: An Industry in Transition*. Boston: Unwin Hyman.

Lanthier, P. (1989) 'Multinationals and the French Electrical Industry, 1889–1940', in A. Teichova, M. Lévy-Leboyer, and H. Nussbaum (eds) *Historical Studies in International Corporate Business*. Cambridge: Cambridge University Press.

Laster, D. S. and McCauley, R. N. (1994) 'Making Sense of the Profits of Foreign Firms in the United States', *Federal Reserve Bank of New York Quarterly Bulletin*, 19: 2, 44–75.

Laurent, A. (1983) 'The Cultural Diversity of Western Conceptions of Management', *International Studies of Management and Organisation*, 13, 75–96.

Laux, J. M. (1992) *The European Automobile Industry*. New York: Twayne Publishers.

Lehrer, M. and Asakawa, K. (1999) 'Unbundling European Operations: Regional Management and Corporate Flexibility in American and Japanese MNCs', *Journal of World Business*, 34: 3, 267–86.

Levitt, T. (1983) 'The Globalization of Markets', *Harvard Business Review*, May–June, 92–102.

Lewis, C. (1938) *America's Stake in International Investments*. Washington DC: The Brookings Institution.

Lewis, C. M. (1983a) *British Railways in Argentina 1857–1914*. London: Athlone.

—— (1983b) 'The Financing of Railway Development in Latin America, 1850–1914', *Ibero-Amerikanisches Archiv*, 9, 255–78.

Lim, L. Y. C. (1980) 'Women Workers in Multinational Corporations: The Case of the Electronics Industry in Malaysia and Singapore', in K. Kumar (ed) *Transnational Enterprises: Their Impact on Third World Societies and Cultures*. Boulder: Westview Press.

Linder, M. (1994) *Projecting Capitalism*. Westport: Greenwood.

Linder, S. H. (1991) *Das Reichskommissariat für die Behandlung feindlichen Vermögens in Zweiten Weltkrieg*. Stuttgart: Frank Steiner Verlag.

Lindert, P. H. and Williamson, J. G. (2003) 'Does Globalisation Make the World More Unequal?', in M. D. Bordo, A. M. Taylor, and J. G. Williamson (eds) *Globalisation in Historical Perspective*. Chicago: University of Chicago Press.

Lindgren, H. (1979) *Corporate Growth: The Swedish Match Industry in its Global Setting*. Stockholm: Liber.

Lipsey, R. E. (1988) 'Changing Patterns of International Investment in and by the United States', in M. Feldstein (ed), *The United States in the World Economy*. Chicago: University of Chicago Press.

—— (1994) 'Outward Direct Investment and the US Economy', *National Bureau of Economic Research Working Paper*, No. 469.

—— (2004) 'Home and Host Country Effects of Foreign Direct Investment', in R. E. Baldwin and L. A. Winters (ed) *Challenges to Globalization: Analysing the Economics*. Chicago: University of Chicago Press.

—— Ramstetter, E. and Blomström, M. (2000) 'Outward FDI and Parent Exports and Employment: Japan, the United States, and Sweden', *Global Economic Quarterly*, 1: 4, 285–302.

Lipson, C. (1985) *Standing Guard: Protecting Foreign Capital in the Nineteenth and Twentieth Centuries*. Berkeley: University of California Press.

Lopes, T. (2002) 'Brands and the Evolution of Multinationals in Alcoholic Beverages', *Business History*, 44: 3, 1–30.

—— (2005) *Global Brands: The Evolution of Multinationals in Alcoholic Beverages*. Oxford: Oxford University Press.

Lottman, H. (2003) *The Michelin Men: Driving an Empire*. London: I. B. Taurus.

Love, J. F. (1988) *McDonalds, Behind the Arches*. New York: Bantam Books.

Lundan, S. M. (2004) 'Multinationals, Environment and Global Competition: A Conceptual Framework,' in S. M. Lundan (ed) *Multinationals, Environment and Global Competition*. Oxford: Elsevier.

Lundgren, K. (1995) 'Why in Sweden? An Analysis of the Development of the Large Swedish International Firms from a Learning Perspective', *Scandinavian Economic History Review*, XLIII: 2, 204–25.

Lundström, R. (1986a) 'Swedish Multinational Growth before 1930', in P. Hertner and G. Jones

(eds) *Multinationals: Theory and History*. Aldershot: Gower.

—— (1986b) 'Banks and Early Swedish Multinationals', in Alice Teichova, M. Lévy-Leboyer, and H. Nussbaum (eds) *Multinational Enterprise in Historical Perspective*. Cambridge: Cambridge University Press.

—— (1992) 'The Scandinavian Influence on German Business and Enterprises', in H. Pohl (ed) *Der Einfluss ausländischer Unternehmen auf die deutsche Wirtschaft vom Spätmittelalter bis zur Gegenwart*. Stuttgart: Franz Steiner Verlag.

Maeda, K. (1990) 'General Trading Companies in Pre-War Japan; A Sketch', in S. Yonekawa (ed) *General Trading Companies: A Comparative and Historical Study*. Tokyo: United Nations University Press.

Maljers, Floris A. (1992) 'Inside Unilever: The Evolving Transnational Company', *Harvard Business Review*, 70: 5, 46–52.

Marshall, P. J. (2002) 'Afterword: the Legacies of Two Hundred Years of Contract', in H. V. Bowen, M. Lincoln, and N. Rigby (eds) *The Worlds of the East India Company*. Woodbridge: Boydell Press.

Martin, S. M. (2003) *The UP Saga*. Copenhagen: NIAS Press.

Mason, M. (1992) *American Multinationals and Japan*. Cambridge, MA: Harvard University Press.

Mataloni, R. J. and Goldberg, L. (1994) 'Gross Product of US Multinational Companies, 1977–91', *Survey of Current Business*, February, 42–63.

Mathews, J. A. (2002) *Dragon Multinational: A New Model for Global Growth*. Oxford: Oxford University Press.

May, S. and Plaza, G. (1958) *The United Fruit Company in Latin America*. Washington: National Planning Association.

McCabe, I. B., Harlaftis, G. and Minoglou, I. P. (2005) *Diaspora Entrepreneurial Networks: Five Centuries of History*. Oxford: Berg.

McCraw, T. K. (ed) (1995) *Creating Modern Capitalism*. Cambridge, MA: Harvard University Press.

McDougall, R. (2004) 'The People's Phone: The Political Culture of Independent Telephony, 1894–1913', Ph.D. thesis. Harvard University, Cambridge, MA.

McDowall, D. (1988) *The Light: Brazilian Traction, Light and Power Company Limited, 1899–1945*. Toronto: University of Toronto Press.

McKay, J. P. (1970) *Pioneers for Profit. Foreign Entrepreneurship and Russian Industrialization 1885–1913*. Chicago: University of Chicago Press.

——(1990) 'The Rothschilds: Ownership Advantages in Multinational Banking', in G. Jones (ed), *Banks as Multinationals*. London: Routledge.

McKern, R. B. (ed) (1993) *Transnational Corporations and the Exploitation of Natural Resources*. London: Routledge.

McKinlay, A. and Starkey, K. (1994) 'After Henry: Continuity and Change in Ford Motor Company', *Business History*, 36: 1, 184–205.

McKinsey Global Institute (2003) 'Offshoring: Is it a Win-Win game?' San Francisco: McKinsey & Co.

McManus, J. C. (1972) 'The Theory of the Multinational Firm', in G. Paquet (ed) *The Multinational Firm and the National State*. Don Mills, Ont.: Collier-Macmillan.

Melby, E. D. K. (1981) *Oil and the International System: The Case of France, 1918–1969*. New York: Arno.

Mendoza, A. G. (1994) *El 'Gibraltar Economico': Franco y Rio Tinto, 1936–1954*. Madrid: Editorial Civitas.

Meuleau, M. (1990) *Des Pionniers en Extrême-Orient*. Paris: Fayard.

Merret, D. (1985) *ANZ Bank*. Sydney: Allen & Unwin.

Michalet, C. A. and Chevallier, T. (1985) 'France', in J. H. Dunning (ed), *Multinational Enterprises, Economic Structure and International Competitiveness*. Chichester: John Wiley.

Michie, R. C. (1992) *The City of London*. London: Macmillan.

Miller, R. (1993) *Britain and Latin America in the Nineteenth and Twentieth Centuries*. London: Longman.

Miller, S. R. and Parkhe, A. (2002) 'Is There a Liability of Foreignness in Global Banking? An Empirical Test of Banks' Efficiency', *Strategic Management Journal*, 23, 55–75.

Minoglou, I. P. and Louri, H. (1997) 'Diaspora Entrepreneurial Networks in the Black Sea and Greece, 1870–1917', *Journal of European Economic History*, 26: 1, 69–104.

Mirza, H. (1986) *Multinationals and the Growth of the Singapore Economy*. Beckenham: Croom Helm.

Miskell, P. (2004) 'Cavity Protection or Cosmetic Perfection? Innovation and Marketing of Toothpaste Brands in the United States and Western Europe, 1955–1985', *Business History Review*, 78, 29–60.

Modig, H. (1979) *Swedish Match Interests in British India during the Interwar Years*. Stockholm: Liber.

Moon, H. C., Rugman, A. M., and Verbeke, A. (1998) 'A Generalized Double Diamond Approach to International Competitiveness of Korea and Singapore', *International Business Review*, 7, 135–50.

Moore, K. and Lewis, D. (1999) *Birth of the Multinational*. Copenhagen: Copenhagen Business School Press.

Moran, T. H. (ed) (1993) *Governments and Transnational Corporations*. London: Routledge.

Moreno, J. (2003) *Yankee Don't Go Home*. Chapel Hill: University of North Carolina Press.

Morisset, J. (1997) 'Unfair Trade: Empirical Evidence in World Commodity Markets Over the Past 25 Years', Washington, DC: The World Bank.

Morrison, A. J., Ricks, D. A. and Kendall, R. (1991) 'Globalization versus Regionalization: Which Way for the Multinational', *Organization Dynamics*, 19: 3, 17–29.

Muchlinski, P. (1995) *Multinational Enterprises and the Law*. Oxford: Blackwell.

Munro, J. F. (1988) 'Scottish Overseas Enterprise and the Lure of London: The Mackinnon Shipping Group, 1847–1893', *Scottish Economic and Social History*, 8, 73–87.

——(2003) *Maritime Enterprise and Empire*, Woodbridge: Boydell.

——and Slaven, T. (2001) 'Networks and Markets in Clyde Shipping: The Donaldsons and the Hogarths, 1870–1939', *Business History*, 43: 2, 19–50.

Nachum, L., Jones, G. and Dunning, J. H. (2001) 'The International Competitiveness of the UK and its Multinational Enterprises', *Structural Change and Economic Dynamics*, 12: 3, 277–94.

Navin, T. R. (1978) *Copper Mining and Management*. Tucson: University of Arizona Press.

Neebe, R. (1991) *Überseemärkte und Exportstrategien in der westdeutschen Wirtschaft 1945 bis 1966*. Stuttgart: Franz Steiner Verlag.

Nelson, R. R. (1991) 'Why do firms differ, and how does it matter?', *Strategic Management Journal*, 12, 61–74.

—— (ed) (1993) *National Innovation Systems: A Comparative Analysis*. Oxford: Oxford University Press.

—— and Winter, S. (1982) *An Evolutionary Theory of Economic Change*, Cambridge. MA: Harvard University Press.

Nicholas, S. (1982) 'British multinational investment before 1939', *Journal of European Economic History*, II: 3, 605–30.

—— (1983) 'Agency Contracts, Institutional Modes, and the Transition to Foreign Direct Investment by British Manufacturing Multinationals Before 1939', *Journal of Economic History*, 43, 675–86.

—— (1986) 'The Theory of Multinational Enterprise as a Transactional Mode', in P. Hertner and G. Jones (eds.) *Multinationals: Theory and History*. Aldershot: Gower.

Nohria, N. and Ghoshal, S. (1997) *The Differentiated Network: Organizing Multinational Corporations for Value Creation*. San Francisco: Jossey-Bass.

Nonaka, I. and Hirotaka, T. (1995) *The Knowledge-Creating Company*. Oxford: Oxford University Press.

North, D. C. (1990) *Institutions, Institutional Change and Economic Performance*. Cambridge: Cambridge University Press.

Obstfeld, M. and Taylor, A. M. (2003) 'Globalization and Capital Markets', in M. D. Bordo, A. M. Taylor, and J. G. Williamson (eds) *Globalization in Historical Perspective*. Chicago: University of Chicago Press.

Ohmae, K. (1990) *The Borderless World*. New York: Harper Business.

Olegario, R. (1995) 'IBM and the Two Thomas J. Watsons', in T. K. McCraw (ed) *Creating Modern Capitalism*. Cambridge, MA: Harvard University Press.

Olsson, U. (1993) 'Securing the Markets: Swedish Multinationals in a Historical Perspective', in G. Jones and H. Schröter (eds) *The Rise of Multinationals in Continental Europe*. Aldershot: Edward Elgar.

Organisation for Economic Cooperation and Development (1993) *International Direct Investment Statistics Yearbook*. Paris: OECD.

—— (2000) *International Direct Investment Statistics Year book*. Paris: OECD.

O'Rourke, K. H. and Williamson, J. G. (1999) *Globalization and History: The Evolution of a Nineteenth Century Atlantic Economy*. Cambridge, MA: MIT Press.

Osterhammel, J. (1989) 'British Business in China, 1860s–1950s', in R. P. T. Davenport-Hines and G. Jones (eds) *British Business in Asia*. Cambridge: Cambridge University Press.

Ostry, S. (2001) 'The Multilateral Trading System', in A. M. Rugman and T. L. Brewer (eds) *Oxford Handbook of International Business*. Oxford: Oxford University Press.

Ouchi, W. G. (1980) 'Markets, Bureaucracies, and Clans', *Administrative Science Quarterly*, 25, 129–41.

Ozawa, T. (1992) 'Foreign direct investment and economic development', *Transnational Corporations*, 1: 1, 27–54.

Pananond, P. (2001) 'The Making of Thai Multinationals: The Internalisation process of Thai Firms', Ph.D. Thesis: University of Reading.

Panić, M. (1982) 'International Direct Investment in Conditions of Structural Disequilibrium: UK Experience Since the 1960s', in J. Black and J. H. Dunning (eds) *International Capital Movements*. London: Macmillan.

Patel, P. (1995) 'Localized Production of Technology for Global Markets', *Cambridge Journal of Economics* 19, 141–53.

—— and Pavitt, K. (1991) 'Large Firms in the production of the World's technology: An Important Case of Non-Globalisation', *Journal of International Business Studies*, 22, 1–21.

Pavitt, K. and Soete, L. (1982) 'International Dynamics of Innovation', in H. Giersch (ed) *Emerging Technologies*. Tubingen: J. C. B. Mohr.

Pearson, R. and Lonnborg, M. (2003) 'Regulatory Regimes and the Globalisation of Insurance', *Proceedings of the 7th EBHA Conference*. Lowell, MA, June 26–28.

Penrose, E. T. (1959) *The Theory of the Growth of the Firm*. Oxford: Oxford University Press.

—— (1968) *The Large International Firm in Developing Countries. The International Petroleum Industry.* London: George Allen and Unwin.

Phongpaichit, P. (1991) 'Japan's Investment and Local Capital in ASEAN since 1985', in S. Yamashita (ed) *Transfer of Japanese Technology and Management to the ASEAN Countries.* Tokyo: University of Tokyo Press.

Piquet, C. (2004) 'The Suez Company's Concession in Egypt, 1854–1956: Modern Infrastructure and Local Economic Development', *Enterprise and Society*, 5: 1, 107–27.

Platt, D. C. M. (1980) 'British Portfolio Investment Before 1870: Some Doubts', *Economic History Review*, XXXIII: 1, 1–16.

—— (1986) *Britain's Investment Overseas on the eve of the First World War.* London: Macmillan.

Plumpe, G. (1990) *Die I.G. Farbenindustrie AG.* Berlin: Duncker & Humblot.

Pohl, H. (1989) 'The Steaua Romana and the Deutsche Bank (1903–1920)', *Studies on Economic and Monetary Problems and on Banking History*, No 24, Mainz: v. Hase & Koehler Verlag.

Porter, M. (1990) *The Competitive Advantage of Nations.* London: Macmillan.

—— (1998) 'Competing Across Locations', in M. Porter, *On Competition.* Boston: Harvard Business School Press.

—— (2000) 'Locations, Clusters and Company Strategy', in G. L. Clark, M. P. Fedlman, and M. S. Gertler (eds) *The Oxford Handbook of Economic Geography.* Oxford: Oxford University Press.

Priest, T. (2001) 'The "Americanisation" of Shell Oil', in G. Jones and L. Gálvez-Muñoz, (eds) *Foreign Multinationals in the United States.* London: Routledge.

Quigley, N. (1989) 'The Bank of Nova Scotia in the Caribbean, 1889–1940', *Business History Review*, 63: 4, 797–838.

Radetzki, M. (1989) 'The role of state-owned enterprises in the international metal mining industry', *Resources Policy*, 15, 45–57.

Rasiah, R. (2001) 'The Importance of Size in the Growth and Performance of the Electrical Industrial Machinery and Apparatus Industry in Malaysia', in C. Nyland, et al. (eds), *Malaysian Business in the New Era.* Cheltenham: Edward Elgar.

Rauch, J. E. (2001) 'Business and Social Networks in International Trade', *Journal of Economic Literature*, XXVIX, 1177–1203.

Ravenscraft, D. and Sherer, F. (1987) *Mergers, Sell-Offs and Economic Efficiency.* Washington, DC: Brookings Institution.

Raynolds, L. T. (1994) 'Institutionalizing Flexibility: A Comparative Analysis of Fordist and Post-Fordist Models of Third World Agro-Export Production', in G. Gereffi and M. Korzeniewicz (eds) *Commodity Chains and Global Capitalism.* Westport, Conn.: Greenwood Press.

Read, R. (1986) 'The Copper Industry', in M. Casson (ed) *Multinationals and World Trade.* London: Allen & Unwin.

Reed, H. C. (1981) *The Pre-eminence of International Financial Centres.* New York: Praeger.

Reed, P. M. (1958) 'Standard Oil in Indonesia 1898–1928', *Business History Review*, 32, 311–37.

Regalsky, A. M. (1989) 'Foreign Capital, Local Interests and Railway Development in Argentina: French Investments in Railways, 1900–1914', *Journal of Latin American Studies*, 21, 425–52.

Reich, L. S. (1992) 'General Electric and the World Cartelisation of Electric Lamps', in A. Kudo and T. Hara (eds) *International Cartels in Business History*, Tokyo: University of Tokyo Press.

Reich, R. B. (1990) 'Who is Us?' *Harvard Business Review*, January–February, 53–64.

—— and Mankin, E. D. (1986) 'Joint ventures with Japan give away our future', *Harvard Business Review*, 64: 2, 78–86.

Reinders, P. (1999) *Licks, Sticks and Bricks. A World History of Ice Cream.* Rotterdam: Unilever.

Rippy, J. F. (1959) *British Investments in Latin America, 1822–1949.* Hamden, Conn.: Archon Books.

Roberts, R. (1992) *Schroders: Merchants & Bankers.* London: Macmillan.

—— (2001) *Take Your Partner: Orion, The Consortium Banks and the Transformation of the Euromarkets.* London: Palgrave.

Roche, J. (1998) *The International Banana Trade.* Cambridge: Woodhead.

Rodrik, D. (1982) 'Changing patterns of ownership and integration in the international bauxite-aluminium industry', in L. P. Jones (ed) *Public Enterprise in Less-Developed Countries.* Cambridge: Cambridge University Press.

Rodrik, D. (1997) *Has Globalization Gone Too Far?* Washington, D.C.: Institute for International Economics.

Roehl, T. (1983) 'A Transactions Cost Approach to International Trading Structures: The Case of the Japanese General Trading Companies', *Hitotsubashi Journal of Economics*, 24, 119–35.

Rooth, T. and Scott, P. (2002) 'British Public Policy and Multinationals during the "Dollar Gap" Era, 1945–1960', *Enterprise and Society*, 3: 1, 124–61.

Rosenzweig, P. and Nohria, N. (1994) 'Influences on Human Resource Management Practices in Multinational Corporations', *Journal of International Business Studies*, 25: 2, 229–51.

Rubenstein, J. M. (2001) *Making and Selling Cars. Innovation and Change in the U.S. Automotive Industry.* Baltimore: Johns Hopkins University Press.

Rugman, A. M. (2000) *The End of Globalization.* London: Random House.

—— and D'Cruz, J. R. (2000) *Multinationals as Flagship Firms.* Oxford: Oxford University Press.

—— and Verbeke, A. (2001) 'Location, Competitiveness and the Multinational Enterprise', in A. M. Rugman and T. L. Brewer (eds) *Oxford Handbook of International Business*, Oxford: Oxford University Press.

Ruigrok, W. and van Tulder, R. (1995) *The Logic of International Restructuring*, London: Routledge.

Safarian, A. E. (1993) *Multinational Enterprise and Public Policy.* Aldershot: Edward Elgar.

Sahlman, W. A., Stevenson, H. H., Roberts, M. J. and Bhide, A. V. (eds) (1999) *The Entrepreneurial Venture.* Boston: Harvard Business School Press.

Sakamoto, M. (1990) 'Diversification: The Case of Mitsui Bussan', in S. Yonekawa (ed) *General Trading Companies.* Tokyo: United Nations University Press.

Sassen, S. (2000) *Cities in a World Economy.* Thousand Oaks, CA: Pine Forge Press.

—— (2001) *The Global City.* Princeton: Princeton University Press.

Savary, J. (1984) *French Multinationals.* London: Frances Pinter.

Schmitz, C. (1979) *World Non-Ferrous Metal Production and Prices, 1700–1976.* London: Frank Cass.

—— (1986) 'The Rise of Big Business in the World Copper Industry, 1870–1930', *Economic History Review*, XXXIX: 3, 392–410.

—— (ed) (1995) *Big Business in Mining and Petroleum.* Aldershot: Edward Elgar.

Schumpeter, J. A. (1943) *Capitalism, Socialism and Democracy.* London: Unwin University Books.

Schröter, H. G. (1990) 'Cartels as a Form of Concentration in Industry: The Example of the International Dyestuffs Cartel from 1927 to 1939', *German Yearbook on Business History 1988.* Berlin: Springer-Verlag, 113–44.

—— (1993a) 'Continuity and Change: German Multinationals Since 1850', in G. Jones and H. G. Schröter (eds) *The Rise of Multinationals in Continental Europe.* Aldershot: Edward Elgar.

—— (1993b) 'Swiss Multinational Enterprise in Historical Perspective', in G. Jones and H. G. Schröter (eds) *The Rise of Multinationals in Continental Europe.* Aldershot: Edward Elgar.

—— (1993c) *Aufstieg der Kleinen: Multinationale Unternehmen aus Fünf Kleinen Staaten vor 1914.* Berlin: Duncker und Humbolt.

Schröter, V. (1984) *Die Deutsche Industrie auf dem Weltmarkt 1929 bis 1933.* Frankfurt: Peter Lang.

Segreto, L. (1987) 'Le Nuove Strategie Delle Società Finanziarie Svizzere Per L'Industria Elettrica (1919–1939)', *Studi Storici*, 4, 861–907.

—— (1992) 'Du "Made in Germany" au "Made in Switzerland" ', in M. Trédé-Boulmer (ed) *Electricité et Électrification Dans le Monde 1880–1980.* Paris: PUF.

—— (1994) 'Le Rôle des Investissements Suisses dans l'Industrie Électrique Française jusqu'à la Deuxième Guerre Mondiale', in M. Trédé-Boulmer (ed) *Le Financement de l'Industrie Électrique 1880–1980.* Paris: PUF.

Seligson, M. A. (1980) *Peasants of Costa Rica and the Development of Agrarian Capitalism.* Madison: University of Wisconsin Press.

Seth, A., Song, K., and Pettit, R. (2000) 'Synergy, Managerialism or hubris? An Empirical Examination of Motives for Foreign Acquisitions of U.S. Firms', *Journal of International Business Studies*, 31, 387–405.

—— (2002) 'Value Creation and Destruction in Cross-Border Acquisitions: An Empirical Analysis', *Strategic Management Journal*, 23: 10, 921–40.

Shafer, M. (1983) 'Capturing the Mineral Multinationals: Advantage or Disadvantage?', *International Organization*. 37: 1, 93–120.

Shai, A. (1996) *The Fate of British and French Firms in China, 1949–54: Imperialism Imprisoned*. Basingstoke: Macmillan.

Shapiro, H. (1991) 'Determinants of Firm Entry into the Brazilian Automobile Manufacturing Industry, 1956–1968', *Business History Review*, 65, 876–947.

—— (1993) 'Automobiles: From Import Substitution to Export Promotion in Brazil and Mexico', in D. B. Yoffie (ed.) *Beyond Free Trade: Firms, Governments and Global Competition*. Boston: Harvard Business School Press.

—— (1994) *Engines of Growth: The State and Transnational Auto Companies in Brazil*. Cambridge: Cambridge University Press.

Shihata, I. F. I. (1993) *Legal Treatment of Foreign Investment: "The World Bank Guidelines"*. Dordrecht: Martinus Nijhoff.

Sluyterman, K. E. (1992) 'From Licensor to Multinational Enterprise: The Small Dutch Firm Océ-van der Grinten in the International World, 1920–66', *Business History*, 34: 2, 28–49.

—— (1994) 'Dutch Free-Standing Companies Between 1870 and 1940: A Typical Colonial Phenomenon' (mimeo).

—— (1998) 'Dutch Multinational Trading Companies in the Twentieth Century', in G. Jones (ed) *The Multinational Traders*. London: Routledge.

—— (2003) *Kerende Kansen: Het Nederlandse bedrijfsleven in de twintisgte eeuw*. Amsterdam: Boom.

—— and Winkelman, H. (1993) 'The Dutch Family Firm Confronted with Chandler's Dynamics of Industrial Capitalism, 1890–1940', *Business History*, 35: 4, 152–83.

Smith, D. N. and Wells, L. T. (1975) *Negotiating Third World Mineral Agreements*. Cambridge, MA: Ballinger.

Smith, G. D. (1988) *From Monopoly to Competition. The Transformation of Alcoa 1886–1986*. Cambridge: Cambridge University Press.

Solvall, O. and Zander, I. (1998) 'International Diffusion of Knowledge: Isolating Mechanisms and the Rise of the MNE', in A. D. Chandler, P. Hagstrom, and O. Solvell (eds) *The Dynamic Firm*. Oxford: Oxford University Press.

Spar, D. L. (1994) *The Co-operative Edge: The Internal Politics of International Cartels*. Ithaca: Cornell University Press.

Spender, J. A. (1930) *Weetman Pearson: First Viscount Cowdray 1856–1927*. London: Cassel and Co.

Stephan, M. and Pfaffmann, E. (2001/2) 'Detecting the Pitfalls of Data on Foreign Direct Investment: Scope and Limits of FDI Data', *Management International Review*, 41, 189–218.

Stephenson, J. C. (1984) 'Technology Transfer by the Bechtel Organisation', in R. K. Shelp, et al. *Service Industries and Economic Development*. New York: Praeger.

Stevens, G. V. G. and Lipsey, R. E. (1992) 'Interactions between domestic and foreign investment', *Journal of International Money and Finance*, 11, 40–62.

Stocking, G. W. and Watkins, M. W. (1946) *Cartels in Action*. New York: The Twentieth Century Fund.

—— and Dunning J. H. (1983) *Multinationals. Company Performance and Global Trends*. London: Macmillan.

Stopford, J. M. and Wells, L. T. (1972) *Managing the Multinational Enterprise*. London: Longman.

Strange, R. (1993) *Japanese Manufacturing Investment in Europe*. London: Routledge.

Strange, S. (1996) *The Retreat of the State*. Cambridge: Cambridge University Press.

Streeten, P. (2001) *Globalisation: Threat or Opportunity*. Copenhagen: Copenhagen University School Press.

Sullivan, D. (1992) 'Organization in American MNCs:The Perspective of the European Regional Headquarters', *Management International Review*, 32, 237–50.

Tamaki, N. (1990) 'The Yokohama Specie Bank: a Multinational in the Japanese Interest 1879–1931', in G. Jones (ed) *Banks as Multinationals*. London: Routledge.

Taylor, G. D. (1994) 'Negotiating Technology Transfer within Multinational Enterprises: Perspectives from Canadian History', *Business History*, 36: 1, 127–58.

—— and Baskerville, P. A. (1994) *A Concise History of Business in Canada*. Oxford: Oxford University Press.

Taylor, G. D. and Sudnik, P. E. (1984) *Du Pont and the International Chemical Industry.* Boston: Twayne.

Tedlow, R. S. (1993a) 'The Fourth Phase of Marketing; Marketing History and the Business World Today', in R. S. Tedlow and G. Jones (eds) *Rise and Fall of Mass Marketing.* London: Routledge.

—— (2003) *The Watson Dynasty: The Fiery Reign and Troubled Legacy of IBM's Founding Father and Son.* New York: HarperBusiness.

—— and Abdelal, R. (2004) 'Theodore Levitt's "The Globalization of Markets": An Evaluation after Two Decades', in J. Quelch and R. Deshpande (eds) *The Global Market.* San Francisco: Jossey–Bass.

Teece, D. (1998) 'Design Issues for Innovative Firms: Bureaucracy, Incentive and Industrial Structure', in A. D. Chandler, P. Hagström and O. Solvell (eds) *The Dynamic Firm.* Oxford: Oxford University Press.

Terpstra, V. and Yu, C.-M. (1988) 'Determinants of Foreign Investment by U.S. Advertising Agencies', *Journal of International Business Studies,* 19, 34–46.

Thoburn, J. (1977) *Primary Commodity Exports and Economic Development.* Chichester: John Wiley.

—— (1981) *Multinationals, Mining and Development. A Study of the Tin Industry.* Aldershot: Gower.

Tignor, R. L. (1998) *Capitalism and Nationalism at the End of Empire.* Princeton: Princeton University Press.

Tolentino, P. E. E. (1993) *Technological Innovation and Third World Multinationals.* London: Routledge.

Tolliday, S. (1999) 'American multinationals and the impact of the Common Market: cars and integrated markets, 1954–1967', in F. Amatori, A. Colli and N. Crepas (eds) *Deindustrialization and Reindustrialization in 20th Century Europe.* Milan: Franco Angeli.

—— (2000) 'Transplanting the American Model? US Automobile Companies and the Transfer of Technology and Management to Britain, France, and Germany 1928–1962', in J. Zeitlin and G. Herrigal (eds) *Americanization and its Limits.* Oxford: Oxford University Press.

Tomlinson, B. R. (1989) 'British Business in India, 1860–1970', in R. P. T. Davenport-Hines and G. Jones (eds) *British Business in Asia since 1860.* Cambridge: Cambridge University Press.

Toral, P. (2001) *The Reconquest of the New World.* Burlington, VT: Ashgate.

Truitt, N. S. (1984) 'Mass Merchandising and Economic Development: Sears, Roebuck and Co. in Mexico and Peru', in R. K. Shelp, et al. *Service Industries and Economic Development.* New York: Praeger.

Tsang, D. (2002) *Business Strategy and National Culture. US and Asia Pacific Microcomputer Multinationals in Europe.* Cheltenham: Edward Elgar.

Tseng, W. and Zebregs, H. (2003) 'Foreign Direct Investment in China: Some Lessons for Other Countries', in W. Tseng and M. Rodlauer (eds) *China: Competing in the Global Economy.* Washington, DC: International Monetary Fund.

Tweedale, G. (1986) 'Transatlantic Speciality Steels: Sheffield High-Trade Steel Firms and the USA, 1860–1940', in G. Jones (ed) *British Multinationals, Origins, Management and Performance.* Aldershot: Gower.

Uchida, H. (1991) 'The Transfer of Electrical Technologies from the United States and Europe to Japan, 1869–1914', in D. J. Jeremy (ed) *International Technology Transfer: Europe, Japan and the USA 1700–1914.* Aldershot: Edward Elgar.

Unilever Magazine (1984), vol. 53.

United Nations (1980) *Transnational Corporations in the Copper Industry.* UNCTAD: New York.

—— (1992) *World Investment Report: Transnational Corporations as Engines of Growth.* UNCTAD: New York.

—— (1993) *World Investment Report: Transnational Corporations and Integrated International Production.* UNCTAD: New York.

—— (1994) *World Investment Report: Transnational Corporations, Employment and the Workplace.* UNCTAD: New York.

—— (1999) *World Investment Report: Foreign Direct Investment and the Challenge of Development.* UNCTAD: New York.

—— (2000) *World Investment Report: Cross-Border Mergers and Acquisitions and Development.* UNCTAD: New York.

—— (2001) *World Investment Report: Promoting Linkages.* UNCTAD: New York.

—— (2002) *World Investment Report: Transnational Corporations and Export Competitiveness.* UNCTAD: New York.

—— (2003) *World Investment Report: FDI Policies for Development: National and International Perspectives.* UNCTC: New York.

Valdaliso, J. M. (2000) 'The Rise of Specialist Firms in Spanish Shipping and Their Strategies of Growth, 1860–1930', *Business History Review*, 74: 2, 267–300.

Van Helten, J.-J. and Jones, G. (1989) 'British Business in Malaysia and Singapore Since the 1870s', in R. P. T. Davenport-Hines and G. Jones (eds) *British Business in Asia since 1860.* Cambridge: Cambridge University Press.

Vaupel, J. W. and Curhan, J. P. (1969) *The Making of Multinational Enterprise.* Cambridge, MA: Harvard University Press.

—— (1974) *The World's Multinational Enterprise.* Cambridge, MA: Harvard University Press.

Venn, F. (1986) *Oil Diplomacy in the Twentieth Century.* London: Macmillan.

Vernon, R. (1966) 'International Investment and International Trade in the Product Cycle', *Quarterly Journal of Economics*, May, 190–207.

—— (1979) 'The Product Cycle Hypothesis in a New International Environment', *Oxford Bulletin of Economics and Statistics*, 41: 4, 255–67.

—— (1971) *Sovereignty at Bay: The Multinational Spread of US Enterprises.* New York: Basic Books.

—— (1983) *Two Hungry Giants: The United States and Japan in the Quest for Oil and Ores.* Cambridge, MA: Harvard University Press.

von Hippel, E. (1994) ' "Sticky Information" and the Locus of Problem Solving:Implications for Innovation', *Management Science*, 40, 429–39.

Wade, R. (1996) 'Globalization and its Limits: Reports of the Death of the National Economy are Greatly Exaggerated', in, S. Berger and R. Dore (eds) *National Diversity and Global Capitalism.* Ithaca: Cornell University Press.

Wardley, P. (1991) 'The Anatomy of Big Business. Aspects of Corporate Development in the Twentieth Century', *Business History*, 33: 2, 268–96.

Warr, P. G. (1987) 'Malaysia's Industrial Enclaves: Benefits and Costs', *The Developing Economies*, XXV: 1, 30–55.

Wavre, P. A. (1988) 'Swiss investments in Italy from the XVIIIth to the XXth century', *Journal of European Economic History*, 25: 1, 30–55.

Weiher, S. von and Goetzeler, H. (1977) *The Siemens Company.* Berlin: Siemens.

Wells, L. T. (1983) *Third World Multinationals.* Cambridge, MA: MIT Press.

Wernerfelt, B. (1984) 'A Resource-based View of the Firm', *Strategic Management Journal*, 5, 171–80.

West, D. C. (1987) 'From T-square to T-plan: the London Office of the J. Walter Thompson Advertising Agency, 1919–70', *Business History*, 29, 199–217.

—— (1988) 'Multinational Competition in the British Advertising Agency Business, 1936–1987', *Business History Review*, 62: 3, 467–501.

Westall, O. M. (1992) *The Provincial Insurance Company 1903–38.* Manchester: Manchester University Press.

Westney, D. E. (2001) 'Japan', in A. M. Rugman and T. T. Brewer (eds), *Oxford Handbook of International Business.* Oxford: Oxford University Press.

Wilkins, M. (1970) *The Emergence of Multinational Enterprise.* Cambridge, MA: Harvard University Press.

—— (1974a) *The Maturing of Multinational Enterprise.* Cambridge, MA: Harvard University Press.

—— (1974b) 'The role of private business in the international diffusion of technology', *Journal of Economic History*, 34, 166–88.

—— (1986) 'Japanese multinational enterprise before 1914', *Business History Review*, 60, 199–231.

—— (1988a) 'The Free-Standing Company, 1870–1914: An Important Type of British Foreign Direct Investment', *Economic History Review*, XLI: 2, 259–85.

—— (1988b) 'European and North American Multinationals, 1870–1914: Comparisons and Contrasts', *Business History*, XXX: 1, 8–45.

—— (1989) *The History of Foreign Investment in the United States before 1914.* Cambridge, MA: Harvard University Press.

—— (1990) 'Japanese Multinationals in the United States: Continuity and Change, 1879–1990', *Business History Review*, 64, 585–629.

Wilkins, M. (1993a) 'Cosmopolitan Finance in the 1920s' (Paper prepared for Congrès International de Paris, 23–25 Sept. 1993).

—— (1993b) 'French Multinationals in the United States. An Historical Perspective', *Enterprises et Histoire*, 3, 14–29.

—— (1994a) 'Comparative Hosts', *Business History*, 36: 1, 18–50.

—— (1994b) 'When and why brand names in food and drink', in G. Jones and N. J. Morgan (eds), *Adding Value: Brands and Marketing in Food and Drink*. London: Routledge.

—— (2001) 'An Overview of Foreign Companies in the United States', in G. Jones and L. Gálvez-Muñoz (eds) *Foreign Multinationals in the United States*. London: Routledge.

—— (2004) *The History of Foreign Investment in the United States 1914–1945*. Cambridge, MA: Harvard University Press.

Wilkins, M. and F. E. Hill (1964) *American Business Abroad: Ford on Six Continents*. Detroit, MI: Wayne State University Press.

—— and H. Schröter (eds) (1998) *The Free-Standing Company in the World Economy, 1830–1996*. Oxford: Oxford University Press.

Williams, B. (1994) 'Multiple Retailing and brand image', in G. Jones and N. J. Morgan (eds) *Adding Value: Brands and Marketing in Food and Drink*. London: Routledge.

Williamson, O. E. (1975) *Markets and Hierarchies*. New York: Free Press.

—— (1981) 'The modern corporation: origins, evolution, attributes', *Journal of Economic Literature*, 19: 4, 1537–68.

—— (1985) *The Economic Institutions of Capitalism*. New York: Free Press.

Wilson, C. (1954) *The History of Unilever*. Vols 1–2, London: Cassell.

Whittington, R. and Mayer, M. (2000) *The European Corporation*. Oxford: Oxford University Press.

Winter, S. (1987) 'Knowledge and Competence as Strategic Assets', in D. Teece (ed) *The Competitive Challenge*. New York: Harper & Row.

Womack, J. P., Jones, D. T., and Roos, D. (1990) *The Machine that Changed the World*. New York: Rawson Associates.

Wray, W. D. (1984) *Mitsubishi and the N.Y.K. 1870–1914*. Cambridge, MA: Harvard University Press.

Wright, W. R. (1974) *British-Owned Railways in Argentina*. Austin: University of Texas Press.

Wurm, C. (1993) *Business, Politics and International Relations*. Cambridge: Cambridge University Press.

Yamazaki, H. (1987) 'The Logic of the Formation of General Trading Companies in Japan', in S. Yonekawa and H. Yoshihara (eds) *Business History of General Trading Companies*. Tokyo: University of Tokyo Press.

Yasumuro, K. (1984) 'The Contribution of Sogo Shosha to the Multinationalization of Japanese Industrial Enterprises in Historical Perspective', in A. Okochi and T. Inoue (eds) *Overseas Business Activities*. Tokyo: University of Tokyo Press.

Yeung, H. W. (1998) *Transnational Corporations and Business Networks*. London: Routledge.

Yoffie, D. B. (1993) 'Foreign Direct Investment in Semiconductors, in Kenneth A. Froot (ed) *Foreign Direct Investment*. Chicago, IL: University of Chicago Press.

Yonekawa, S. (ed) (1990) *General Trading Companies: A Comparative and Historical Study*. Tokyo: United Nations University Press.

Yoshihara, H. (1987) 'Some Questions on Japan's Sogo Shosha', in S. Yonekawa and H. Yoshihara (eds) *Business History of General Trading Companies*. Tokyo: University of Tokyo Press.

Zaheer, S. (1995) 'Overcoming the liability of foreignness', *Academy of Management Journal*, 38: 2, 341–63.

Zander, I. (1999) 'How do you mean "global"? An Empirical Investigation of Innovation Networks in the Multinational Corporation', *Research Policy*, 2, 195–213.

Zeng, M. and Williamson, P. J. (2003) 'Hidden Dragons', *Harvard Business Review*, 81: 10, 92–9.

■ INDEX

Unilever (*cont.*)
  palm oil production 51–2,65,
    189, 209
  post-acquisition
    management 153–4
  US acquisitions 151, 153–4
United Africa Company
  (UAC) 52, 56, 159–60,
  173–4
United Airlines 161
United Fruit Company 50, 51, 56,
  66, 113, 220, 227, 263, 277,
  280
United Kingdom *see* Great
  Britain
United Nations 213, 222
United States 19, 21, 53, 82, 85
  Alien Tort Claims Act 224,
    225
  antitrust 160, 206
  banking 114, 137, 201–2,
    266–7
  defense contracts 241
  expropriation of German
    assets 203
  foreign direct investment in 21,
    22, 39, 50, 65, 77, 78, 80,
    85, 86, 89, 96–7, 105,
    116, 119, 122, 134,
    151–4, 157, 169, 178,
    183, 188, 255–7, 259,
    274
  foreign direct investment of 21,
    26, 29, 39, 47, 83, 92–3,
    116, 122, 162–3, 172, 176,
    231–2, 234, 236, 238, 274,
    290
  foreign land ownership 202
  Great Depression 27, 28, 29
  immigration 27, 28–9, 37
  lobbying 226
  management of US
    affiliates 178
  mining companies 47
  oil industry 47–8
  outward investment
    policies 219
  postwar manufacturing 92–3
  Prohibition 86
  and protectionism 25, 28
  restrictions on foreign
    firms 204, 206, 208
  retailing 141–2
  utilities 115–19, 121, 123–4,
    133–4

V

Vahlne, J.E. 147, 235
Valdaliso, J.M. 184
Van Helten, J-J. 54
Varon, B. 54
Varul, M.Z. 270
Vaupel, J.W. 150
vegetable oils 51–2, 65
Venables, A.J. 38
Venezuela 49, 63, 64, 67, 69, 187,
  210, 270
Venn, F. 57, 202, 210
Veolia 134
Verbeke, A. 242
Vernon, R. 62, 239, 277
vertical integration 17, 60, 62
Victor Talking Machine
  Company 158
Vietnam 19
Vivendi 134
Vodafone 133, 150, 152
Volkswagen (VW) 96, 97, 103, 279
Voluntary Export Restraint
  (VER) 96
von Hippel, E. 191

W

Wade, R. 4
wages 251
Wal-Mart 104, 141–2
Wale, J. 186
Walt Disney 135
water companies 133–4
Watkins, M.W. 59
Wedgwood 193
Wells, L.T. 56, 157, 177, 180,
  245
Wenerfelt, B. 13
West, D.C. 125, 126
Westall, O.M. 115
Western Electric 192
Westinghouse 79
Westney, D.E. 182
Westphalia, Peace of 16
Whisky 198
Wilemsen 185
Wilkins, M. 22, 25, 29, 30, 32,
  149, 154, 156, 157, 261,
  262, 267, 270, 274, 275
  on home economies 234, 236,
    238, 244
  on management 169, 172, 174,
    188, 191, 195

  on manufacturing 77, 78, 79,
    80, 86, 87, 88, 89, 93
  on natural resources 47, 48, 50,
    54, 57, 63, 64, 66
  on public policy 202, 208,
    209, 210, 211, 219, 220,
    224
  on services 113, 114, 115,
    116, 118, 120, 122, 123,
    124
Williams, B. 196
Williamson, J.G. 19
Williamson, O.E. 10
Wilson, C. 195
Wimpy 142
Winkelman, H. 184
Winter, S. 11, 13
wireless companies 118
Womack, J.P. 96, 97
women and employment
  268–9
Woolworth 139, 140
World Bank 223
World War I 27, 28, 29, 115, 203,
  204, 219, 286
World War II 30, 31, 82, 86, 135,
  175, 205
World Wide Web 36
Wray, W.D. 113
Wright, W.R. 124
WTO (World Trade
  Organization) 223, 227
Wurm, C. 90

X

Xerox 159

Y

Yasumuro, K. 131, 219
Yoffe, D.B. 101
Yonekawa, S. 110
Yoshihara, H. 120
Young, S. 223, 227, 264

Z

Zaheer, S. 5
zaibatsu 111–12, 130
Zambia 62, 66, 67, 69, 72
Zander, I. 13, 164, 191, 193
ZCCM 72
Zeitlin, J. 165, 181, 192
Zimbabwe 66